TEACHING WITH THE INTERNET

STRATEGIES AND MODELS FOR K-12 CURRICULA

BEVERLEY E. CRANE

NEAL-SCHUMAN PUBLISHERS, INC.

NEW YORK
LONDON

Published by Neal-Schuman Publishers, Inc.
100 Varick Street
New York, NY 10013

Printed and bound in the United States of America.

Library of Congress Cataloging-in-Publication Data

Crane, Beverley E.
    Teaching with the internet : Strategies and models for K–12 curricula / Beverley E. Crane.
        p. cm.
    ISBN 1-55570-375-5
    1. Teaching—Computer network resources. 2. Internet (Computer network) in education. 3. Education, Elementary—Curricula. 4. Education, Secondary—Curricula. I. Title

LB1044.87 .C73 2000
371.33'44678—dc21   00-020218

DEDICATION

For the two men in my life, with love—
My father William C. Foust,
who started me on the road to teaching, and
My husband John Kenny Crane,
who encouraged me to achieve my educational goals.

CONTENTS

LIST OF FIGURES

LIST OF TABLES

ACKNOWLEDGMENTS

Sincere thanks go to my research assistant, Lynda Barry Crane, who "surfed the Internet" for new Websites to use in each of the unit plans in the book. It was her diligent efforts, too, that verified all of the URLs in each chapter, identifying defunct sites, and suggesting new ones. Her ideas and enthusiasm led to the creation of the unit on the stock market in Chapter 5. Without her work, this book could not have been completed.

Special thanks go to John Kenny Crane, former dean of the College of Humanities and the Arts at San Jose State University, for his continuing help in reading drafts and editing copy.

I am also indebted to the many teachers whose classrooms I have observed and who shared ideas with me. Many of these teachers are already pioneering the use of the Internet in their classes. The editors of this book at Neal-Schuman—Charles Harmon, Eileen Fitzsimons, and Michael Kelley—also provided valuable suggestions for making this book a practical one for educators.

Beverley E. Crane
Baja, Mexico

PREFACE

Each year teachers and library media specialists search for creative solutions to the growing requests on our limited time. We need to meet the challenges of teaching increasing numbers of non-native English speaking students. We must fulfill the needs of gifted students as well as children with learning disabilities. We have to master and employ a wide range of technology—especially the demands of the Internet.

New books and articles about the "nuts and bolts" of searching the Internet appear regularly. *Teaching with the Internet: Strategies and Models for K-12 Curricula* is designed to go beyond these basics. It attempts to answer critical questions posed by the possibilities of the new technological development. How can the Internet help me teach my students better? It also tries to answer specific questions. How can I make the plight of slaves during the Civil War seem more real to my students? Is there a way that students can visualize the surface of Mars without a trip to a planetarium? In my unit on culture, how can I acquaint my students with customs of people from other countries?

Although often under-utilized by educators, the Internet is truly an exciting and versatile tool in all subject areas. As politicians promote its use by continuing to wire schools, more classroom and library access will become increasingly available. We need models to illustrate how, why, and when to use Internet technology with the daily lessons.

Twenty-five years experience as an educator made me want to create material for colleagues eager to wed technology to practical ideas. I wrote *Teaching with the Internet: Strategies and Models for K-12 Curricula* for teachers and library media specialists at the elementary and secondary levels, as well as those who plan to enter the teaching or library professions. It can also be used by parents who are teaching their children at home or as a text for both library school programs and pre-service teacher education. My goal is to provide librarians, teachers, and administrators with strategies and models they can use as tools integral to instruction, not only as add-ons to the curriculum. The strategies and practical suggestions throughout the book will help educators feel at ease using the Internet as an essential part of lessons and units they teach.

Teaching with the Internet is organized so that a theoretical framework for instruction incorporating the Internet is clear. Each unit plan proposes useful models for creating Internet-based lessons. The suggested activities are intended to encourage original teaching plans that meet the needs of your students and the curriculum. The ideas in unit plans provide vehicles for collaboration between library media specialists and content teachers. They can be used in numerous ways and cover a wide range of subjects.

For example, the Websites and illustrations noted in Chapter 1 could enable a new teacher to view lesson plans created by experienced teachers and visualize the large variety of information available on the Web. The unit on planets in Chapter 4 might serve as a resource for the library media specialist trying to help a fourth grader find facts about Mars. The projects included in Chapter 9 offer educators ideas on how to participate in joint collaborations with classrooms around the globe.

Teaching with the Internet is divided into ten chapters—most contain two parts: "Ideas and Insights" and "Practical Applications." The first part identifies and discusses strategies for teaching: cooperative learning, critical-thinking skill building, employing learning styles to individualize instruction. It explains how these techniques combine with Internet technology through a series of examples in specific content areas—language arts, social studies, science, and elective courses. The second part contains a guide to investigate new ideas for instruction that incorporates the Internet into a variety of curricula.

Examples of practical unit-plan models in different content areas at both the elementary and secondary levels are included. These broad-based examples comprise the core content areas—language arts, social studies and science; elective subjects—the arts, health education, foreign languages, government, and business education and includes interdisciplinary activities. At the end of each chapter, a section called "Teacher Exercises: Now You Try It . . . " offers exercises that give readers an opportunity to practice what they have just learned, become familiar with the Internet, and reflect on the content in the chapter.

The goals and objectives of the instructional tasks of each unit plan are based on national standards and state framework guidelines. The unit plans are designed as models for educators to use as they are presented or to modify to meet the individual needs of their students and their curricula. In addition, I have provided in each chapter a list of Websites that will be useful for the topic under discussion. All were verified in September 1999. Unfortunately, as we all know, Websites can change or disappear.

Each chapter emphasizes one or all of the following suggestions:

1. Incorporate the Internet as a tool into the curriculum for communication, research, collaboration, expert opinions, and connections bringing teachers and library media specialists together;
2. Strive for teachers to create activities that are varied, interesting, and achieve the fullest, most productive involvement of students;
3. Combine instructional techniques with independent, competitive, and cooperative learning; and
4. Involve students in interdisciplinary studies so that they will recognize the connections among subject areas.

Lesson plans are grouped by chapter in three main sections: How the Internet Can Enhance Teaching Effectiveness, How to Integrate the Internet with Different Instructional Styles, and How to Integrate the Internet into Specific Curricular Areas.

Part One focuses on enhancing teaching effectiveness. The first chapter, "The Information Revolution, the School and the Internet," introduces the Internet, indicates the types of information available and why to integrate the Internet into the curriculum. Chapter 2, "Linking Information Literacy, Critical Thinking, and the Internet," focuses on ways searching the Internet can help build critical thinking skills. It also introduces "surfing" techniques necessary to search the Web.

Part Two discusses integrating the Internet and instructional styles. Chapter 3, "Integrating the Internet into Cross-Curricular Units," discusses interdisciplinary learning and planning cross-curricular units that contain Internet components. Chapter 4, "Incorporating the Internet into Individualized Instruction," explains learning modalities and ways the Internet helps individualize instruction and strengthen specific intelligences. Chapter 5, "Using the Internet with Cooperative Learning Approaches," concentrates on small-group learning and illustrates activities using the Internet in a collaborative environment.

The third part covers integrating the Internet into specific curricular areas. Chapter 6, "Using Web Resources in English and Language Arts," contains examples of Web-based language arts projects that incorporate collaborative research, and promote reading, writing, speaking, and listening skills. Chapter 7, "Teaching Second-Language Learners Using the Internet," stresses the importance of understanding language acquisition theory so teachers can create the most appropriate lessons for non-native English speakers. Chapter 8, "Incorporating the Internet into Social Studies Research Assignments," concentrates on resources, such as maps, historical documents, photographs, and interviews and illustrates the use of these documents and techniques with Internet-based instruction. Chapter 9, "Promoting Active Learning in the Sciences Using the Internet," discusses a project approach to studying science and illustrates several collaborative Internet-based projects. Chapter 10, "Bringing the Internet into Other Subject Areas," offers suggestions on how the Internet can help teach content in the arts, foreign languages, health education, and government.

Teaching with the Internet also contains two appendices. Appendix A provides a mini-lesson on how to use search engines. Although this is not intended to be an exhaustive study of search engines, readers can use the lesson to teach students (or themselves) to navigate the Internet. To help readers identify Websites for specific disciplines, Appendix B includes a listing of all Websites found in this book categorized by subject area.

We are fortunate enough to be educators at this fascinating time. We are learning to combine a new world of technological possibilities with innovative approaches to teaching. My purpose throughout has been to introduce and integrate the Internet into the curriculum. I believe *Teaching with the Internet* will help you discover new and exciting ways to explore subject matter, improve communication, and create an interactive learning environment.

Section One

HOW THE INTERNET CAN ENHANCE TEACHING EFFECTIVENESS

Chapter 1

THE INFORMATION REVOLUTION, THE SCHOOL, AND THE INTERNET

PART 1: IDEAS AND INSIGHTS

Thirtieth anniversary of the microcomputer! How surprising that in only thirty years personal computers have become so integral to our daily lives. Computers run our automobiles, help clerks check us out of the grocery store, schedule our air flights—indeed, appear in almost every aspect of our daily lives. Yet in talking to teachers and observing in classrooms, I have realized that computers are not yet an integral part of every classroom.

Many teachers who feel fairly competent with computers use them to record grades, review basic skills, write notes to parents, or devise worksheets. Yet these same teachers experience barriers when asked to integrate the technology into the content they teach and the daily lessons they plan. A study in 1995 indicated technologies in the elementary schools were overwhelmingly used for basic skill exercises but were not connected to the ongoing curriculum (McKinsey and Company, 1995). The same study noted that in middle and high schools, computers were being used primarily to create documents or to teach computer skills.

This study found that only 19 percent of high school English classes, 6–7 percent of secondary math classes, and 3 percent of social studies classes were using computers as part of their disciplines (McKinsey and Company, 1995). In a 1994 survey, less than 10 percent of recent graduates of education schools felt prepared to use multimedia and telecommunications technology in their teaching (Office of Technology Assessment, 1995).

Students attending today's schools will enter the working world in the twenty-first century, by which time several significant changes will have occurred. Unlike the previous century, focused on manufacturing and industrial jobs, in the twenty-first century technology will be integral to job functions. While technology is now a "hook"

---

to draw kids into school work or a job they otherwise might not do, in the twenty-first century technology will be the linchpin around which jobs revolve. In the year 2000 and beyond, it is estimated that 60 percent of jobs will require skills with information technologies. These jobs will pay about 10–15 percent more than jobs not requiring these skills (McKinsey and Company, 1995).

WHY USE TECHNOLOGY?

There is another, compelling reason for increasing the use of technology in education: the Internet. Ten years ago the Internet was a research medium for scientists at universities to use to exchange ideas and data on scientific projects. Now the Internet is available in schools across the country, as well as in many students' homes. Today, there are approximately 110,000 elementary and high schools in the United States (Becker, 1994). About 50 percent of the nation's K–12 schools now connect to the Internet—an increase from 35 percent in 1994. For high schools, the number of connected schools has reached 65 percent, for elementary schools approximately 45 percent. Of some 2.5 million classrooms, 9 percent are directly wired (Office of Technology Assessment, 1995). Web 66, an online registry, states that 1,300 schools in the United States have their own Web pages, out of a total of 2,000 worldwide. Net Day, a collaboration in California between businesses and schools, continues to provide hardware for and connections to the Internet. In fact, thirty-three states now have their own Tech Corp chapters, which are in-state organizations that help schools get wired. Information about Tech Corp chapters is available at Website *www.ustc.org*. With more schools connected every year, the Internet can now provide the vehicle needed to move away from using technology solely for skill development.

This increasing emphasis on online technology and President Clinton's pledge to wire all schools to the Internet point to how important it is that teachers and library media specialists work together to incorporate Internet technology into the current curriculum or to use these new resources to revise the curriculum and make it richer.

There are a number of reasons to encourage us, as educators, to achieve this goal. First, we can make our classrooms into research laboratories, with traditional lessons as beginning points, not ends in themselves. Online resources can help us teach students to recognize bias, propaganda, and commercially driven information; to think both concretely and abstractly; to reason and to question. It is never too early to start preparing our children for new workplace tasks. On the World Wide Web, students can learn about endangered species in Florida, view planets through high-intensity telescopes, or hear immigrants on Ellis Island speak of the hardships of travel to the New World. These resources bring the information to life as students satisfy requirements for a formal class assignment or solve problems in their own lives.

Second, the Web encourages some of the latest trends in learning—for example, the current emphasis toward interactivity in the learning process. Students of all ages learn better when they are actively engaged in a process, whether that process comes in the form of a sophisticated multimedia package or a low-tech classroom debate on current events. For example, students who observe and report temperature changes will understand weather better, and students who "virtually" dissect a frog will gain insight into anatomy.

Third, Internet activities can also heighten motivation. Engaging students using a variety of media and allowing them to feel as if they are a part of the subject matter will often lead to their becoming more interested in the topic under discussion and to their investing more mental energy. When students articulate and share their thoughts, they can grasp the meaning of a subject and thus understand it better.

Fourth, a focus for the twenty-first century will be collaboration and project-based team activities, and cooperative learning is an aspect of teaching that lends itself well to use with technology. Cooperative methods stress interpersonal actions. Jobs in our future economy will require teamwork, problem solving, and the ability to manage diversity successfully. Cooperative learning focuses on these areas.

Technology has given cooperative learning a stronger thrust. Workers need not just work together but also work together using powerful technological tools. Indeed, the growth of the Internet occurred because it provided scientists and researchers in government and higher education with options to share their ideas and their work. Our students will be using technology as a tool for communication, research, and collaboration around the world. Using the Internet provides a way to embrace cooperative learning as an instructional method. We will talk more about cooperative learning in Chapter 5.

Fifth, the world is getting smaller. Being able to communicate with and understand peoples of different cultures will be essential in the twenty-first century. The Internet has the ability to provide communication links for students, to enhance student learning with up-to-date research, and to foster collaboration with peers in other countries, sharing their cultures and bringing the real world into the classroom. Chapter 7 deals with the Internet and second language learners.

Finally, the idea of students "learning how to learn" with teachers as coaches works well with the Internet. Richard L. Measelle of Worldwide Arthur Andersen (1990:78), a nationally recognized consulting firm, said, "Students need to learn actively as children, or they will be ill-equipped to be a part of tomorrow's high-performance teams of knowledge workers. . . . They still learn specifics, but they learn how to learn." Teachers must now look at the curriculum and student needs and then use the Internet and other technologies to devise new approaches to learning.

The World Wide Web has only recently captured the imagination of millions of users. Although the Web has been popular since 1993, it has not become a powerful educational tool even though materials, lesson plans and activities, and resources exist for teachers on the Web. True, some schools are now creating their own Web pages, and businesses that cater to the educational market are increasing the number of "educational documents" on their Websites. But is the Web an integral part of the curriculum? Is it being evaluated by teachers and used appropriately in lesson and unit plans? Are meaningful numbers of students using the Web as they would their textbooks for research and projects? The answer is, no. The purpose of this book and its suggested activities is to provide educators with the tools they need to prepare students for the Information Revolution and to integrate the Internet into their curricula.

OBJECTIVES OF THIS CHAPTER

Chapter 1 provides an introduction to the Internet and the chapters that follow. After reading Chapter 1, educators will be able to:

- identify the importance of the Internet for K–12 students
- enumerate attributes of an information-literate person
- answer critical questions involved in creating an Internet lesson
- evaluate Websites using criteria
- cite Internet sources properly
- identify different types of information available on the Internet
- formulate the framework of an Internet unit

BECOMING AN INFORMATION-LITERATE PERSON

In 1986, Carolyn Markuson (1986:37), a library media specialist, wrote, "In a fluid world, we cannot teach many absolutes about information. It is not the tool that is important; it is the *process*. If we are to produce lifelong learners, then we need to give them the wherewithal to become such—the techniques in addition to the tools, the process, not the product." And in 1987, Roger Summit (1987:61), president of Dialog Information Services and a proponent of online searching for young students, stated, "It is becoming clear that knowing how to determine the existence and location of information is as important as knowing the information itself." Both Markuson and Summit predicted over a decade ago that we should prepare students to understand the process of finding information no matter what the circumstances. We have not heeded their advice. Too often students need only memorize facts from textbooks or lectures to pass exams. We—teachers, library media specialists, and teacher educators—must now take steps to provide students with skills so they can make meaning out of the vast stores of information available to them. Research skills—the ability to obtain, organize, and evaluate information—are basic to a sound education in the twenty-first century and to students' entire lifetimes. The Internet can help them attain these skills—help them become information literate.

In 1987, the American Association of School Librarians (AASL) and the Association for Education Communication and Technology (AECT) answered Summit's and Markuson's challenges and joined together to redesign the role of the library media specialist. The result of this endeavor was *Information Power: Guidelines for School Library Programs*, which provides a philosophical basis for developing library media programs that will meet the needs of students. The premise of *Information Power* is that teachers, principals, and library media specialists form partnerships and "plan together to design and implement a program that best matches the instructional needs of the school" (1988: Chapter 7:1). The mission as stated in *Information Power* emphasizes the following objectives:

- to provide intellectual access to information
- to provide physical access to information
- to provide learning experiences that encourage users to become discriminating consumers and skilled creators of information

- to provide leadership, instruction, and consulting assistance in the use of instructional and information technology
- to provide resources and activities that contribute to lifelong learning
- to provide a facility that functions as the information center of the school
- to provide resources and learning activities

These objectives are aligned with national curriculum standards and state framework goals and form the basis for units in this book.

Christina A. Doyle (1992:3), in the *Final Report to the National Forum on Information Literacy*, defined information literacy as "the ability to access, evaluate, and use information from a variety of sources." She noted that three categories of skills are necessary to become an information-literate person:

1. An information-literate person *accesses information.*
2. An information-literate person *evaluates information.*
3. An information-literate person *uses information.*

The definition of an information-literate person, as stated in Doyle's report, focuses not on knowledge for its own sake but on a process to fulfill a person's need. Doyle's report reinforces the objectives in *Information Power*, and they both have the same goal—to take students beyond the facts and develop the skills to "learn how to learn." Chapter 2 deals further with the concept of information literacy and critical thinking. Throughout this book, the practical models using the Internet have as one of their goals that students know how to access, evaluate, and use information.

APPLICATION OF INTERNET TECHNOLOGY ON INSTRUCTION

When teachers create lessons to help students become information literate, they must understand the differences between instruction with and without technology. Table 1-1 provides a comparison of the characteristics of technology-based instruction and traditional classroom instruction. Note that the characteristics focus on qualities that the national curriculum standards and state frameworks (broad goals for instruction) are emphasizing (we will talk more about the frameworks in Part 2 of this chapter). We will focus on many of the qualities emphasized in technology-enhanced instruction through activities in subsequent chapters of this book.

Specifically, using Internet technology, students have opportunities to converse with experts, research almost any subject, and work with classrooms worldwide on similar projects, in the process learning how to locate, organize, interpret, and present information. These types of projects have the potential to engage and interest all students by providing a differentiated curriculum, in which classroom knowledge and "doing" are powerfully linked. Students in any geographic location, even isolated ones, can find information, see it, and access it on the Internet in a way that makes it real to them. The Internet provides resources that enable students to be in charge of their own learning.

Figure 1-1 provides steps to help you create an Internet-based lesson. By thinking

Table 1-1: Instruction Types	
Traditional Instruction	**Technologically Enhanced Instruction**
Linear progression	Multipath progression
Teacher centered	Student centered
Literal thinking	Critical thinking
Single medium	Multisensory
Isolation	Cooperation
Teacher delivered	Teacher facilitated
Passive learner	Active learner
Structured	Exploratory
Predetermined learning style	Preferred learning style
Classroom interaction	Real-world interaction

of this structure when we are planning an Internet-based lesson or unit, we will have most of the problems identified in advance and a solution for them in mind. However, we must remember that, when using technology, we should always have a back-up plan for the day. The Internet connection may not be working; the computers may have technical difficulties; or the media specialist may be home sick for the day!

CRITICAL ISSUES WHEN USING INTERNET TECHNOLOGY

Internet-based lessons require extensive thought and planning so that students get the most possible from the Internet experience. A chaotic first experience sets the tone for other Internet lessons. As we begin to plan Internet lessons and units, we should keep some key issues in mind.

ATTITUDES

Because teaching and learning will occur in different ways when using the Internet, teachers', students', and administrators' attitudes will need to undergo change.

Teachers

National curriculum standards in social studies, science, and language arts require that learning become more active and less authority dependent. Educational strategies that actively involve students—case studies, cooperative learning, debates, peer projects, collaborative endeavors, to name a few—are being recommended and used to enhance student learning. The goal of using these multidimensional methods is to enable students to function independently and think critically. However, this may require teachers to assume a new role and relinquish more control than they feel comfortable doing. Teachers often teach as they were taught, which may mean lecturing; therefore, becoming a facilitator rather than the "fountain of knowledge" may seem counterproductive. But nothing could be further from the truth.

Figure 1-1: Creating an Internet-Based Lesson

Step 1: Create an overview for the lesson
➢ Determine the theme, lesson, or unit to teach.
➢ Identify the concepts to develop.
➢ Select a topic appropriately connected to student interest and the curriculum.

Step 2: Write the objectives of the lesson
➢ Decide on the purpose of the lesson and the objectives to be met.
➢ Determine when technology is vital to the lesson.

Step 3: Determine the technology connection
➢ Select the part of the lesson in which technology enhances instruction.
➢ Determine what type of technology to use.
➢ Decide how the technology will be used (e.g., research, expert advice, telecommunication).

Step 4: Outline procedures to follow
➢ List the steps necessary to meet the objectives, specifically identifying when and how the technology will be used.
➢ Decide on type of instruction (e.g., whole group, small groups, pairs, individual).
➢ Estimate time elements for each part of the lesson.

Step 5: Develop assessment techniques
➢ Evaluate the learning process and the product.
➢ Create an evaluative method (e.g., checklist, rubric, anecdotal record, journal, presentation).
➢ Develop a tool to assess the effectiveness of using the Internet to provide primary and secondary sources.
➢ Decide upon a way to evaluate the process students used to retrieve the information.

Step 6: Gather materials
➢ Collect equipment or necessary software.
➢ Schedule a time in the computer lab or library.
➢ Make sure the room is arranged as needed.
➢ Identify all relevant URLs needed for the lesson.
➢ Write any needed "tip sheets" for students to follow in the media center.
➢ Make sure the media specialist is available to help.

Technology itself both mandates and assists active learning. We all have certain fears about change; however, we need to overcome the inhibitions that prevent us from using new technology like the Internet:

- fear of change: "I've gotten this far without the Internet." "Why do I need it now?"
- fear of commitment: "I don't have the time to spare to deal with this stuff!"
- fear of appearing incompetent: "The students may know more than I do!"
- fear of the technical aspect (jargon, equipment): "What is html?" "What if I prepare a lesson and the equipment fails me?"
- fear of not knowing where to start: "What do I do first?" "Where can I find good Websites?"
- fear of having to acquire a bulk of knowledge even before being able to start: "I can't even type!"

Students

While technology motivates some students, others may resist methods that require them to assume a more active role in their learning, preferring that teachers give them the "right" answers.

Administrators

For the effort to be successful, administrators must be behind the thrust to integrate these new technologies. Incentives can be made available to teachers to encourage them to adopt technology. Administrators can make sure equipment and access to up-to-date hardware are available. Research demonstrates that staff development is also important and necessary to get enthusiastic staff up to speed. The 1996 report of the National Commission on Teaching & America's Future (1996:6) states, "The school reform movement has ignored one obvious thing: What teachers know and can do makes the crucial difference in what children learn." Although part of school budgets is allocated for staff development, technology changes require even more. The following Websites discuss staff development to help teachers use the Internet: *www.videojournal.com, www.ties.k12.mn.us* and *www.freenet.msp.mn.us.*

Teachers and library media specialists willing to become involved with technology also need an environment that facilitates collaboration. Teachers need time to work together to plan lessons, create materials, accumulate appropriate Websites, and discuss evaluation. Although some preparation may occur on their own time, some school time should be set aside as well. Finally, to gain new ideas and see what works and what does not, educators need opportunities to network with colleagues using technology, such as at national, state, and local conferences. Without changes in attitude among all the shareholders, efforts to incorporate technology into the curriculum may never get off the ground.

STUDENT ABILITIES

Before preparing Internet-based lessons, educators must assess students' abilities. To use the Internet effectively, students must be able to:

- determine whether the Internet is the best tool for the research or whether the information may be found elsewhere, such as in books, magazines, or in the community.
- define the critical attribute or essence of the search topic and phrase requests concisely to target the research topic most effectively. There are millions of bits of information on the Web alone. Neither the teacher nor the student wants to wade through even a fraction of what is available. Formulating search terms to refine and focus a topic will help retrieve the most relevant information.
- limit the search so that it is centered on a focused selection of materials. Selecting sites at the K–12 level or searching sites created by organizations known for accurate information (such as NASA) will narrow the search.
- use a variety of search engines. Search engines such as Yahoo! and AltaVista have search categories designed especially for the K–12 audience. (See Appendix A for a minilesson on search engines.)
- recognize topics that may be too large for searching, or Websites that load too slowly or are error prone. For example, some Web pages containing complex graphics may load slowly and result in students wasting their time online. A minilesson on the pitfalls of Web searching may help before students go online.
- scan through the resources quickly in order to focus on the most valuable information available. Educators may want to teach a short lesson on how to scan information—a useful skill in all subject areas.
- organize and record good findings for further evaluation.

Teachers will need to provide minilessons to teach students the skills necessary to complete each Internet assignment. For example, if the goal of a lesson is for students to identify bias in information, the teacher can provide an activity that illustrates characteristics of bias or that differentiates opinion from fact. Cooperative pairing will also help students acclimate themselves to the technology. Chapter 5 contains more in-depth discussion on cooperative learning.

Process for Surfing

Exploring the Web is unlike the library, where students are trained to use library resources over an extended period of time. There is no librarian on the Internet to guide the way! Therefore, educators must determine what skills about the Internet their students need to possess to accomplish tasks in lesson and unit plans. Often teachers and media specialists collaborate to provide students with the advance organizers for retrieving information. For example, media specialists can conduct an orientation to the Internet, provide step-by-step handouts of procedures for logging on and off or for using browser navigation buttons, and place posters near the computer station(s) to illustrate the procedures for using the Internet. Depending on the research skills of the students, librarians can teach search techniques such as narrow and broad search terms and Boolean connectors like "AND" and "OR." Finally, librarians should determine whether students should look for information on the Internet from Websites only or be involved in news groups, e-mail interaction, or listservs. See Part 2 of this chapter for more on news groups and listservs.

SCHEDULING USE OF THE INTERNET

Educators using the Internet must be well organized. Since Internet access may only be available in the library or computer labs, projects requiring students to use the Internet may need to be scheduled well in advance. That means teachers must allow time in their lessons for preliminary planning and any minilessons. First and foremost, teachers themselves must practice using the Internet—it is important to take time to "surf" some of the sites mentioned throughout this book. In addition, students also need opportunities and time for guided exploration of Websites. Teachers must incorporate time and place into lesson plans and consider the following points when scheduling Internet projects:

- A forty-five-minute class period often comprises too little time for electronic learning.
- Students collaborating on a project may not be able to meet together when Internet access is available.
- Internet-researched projects may take more time than traditional, library-researched projects.
- Internet sites may be busy when students try to connect during class time.
- Students need their own disks to avoid monopolizing the computer.

It is a good idea to schedule Internet activities during a block period if the school uses that type of schedule. If you assign Internet projects, make sure time is available in class and that labs are open during study periods and before and after school. Warn students well in advance when they will be using the computer so they bring their disks to class, or provide disks so students can access and save the information at the computer and return to their own desks to read and evaluate what they have found.

USES OF INFORMATION FOUND

Students should keep track of the information as they retrieve it. Below are some guidelines students will need to refer to as they incorporate Internet resources:

- What is the research question?
- What are the sources and URLs?
- Does the student have enough information, enough sources?
- Is the student's information source(s) biased? Reliable? Why? Why not?
- Is the student's information valid? Current? Give dates and sources.
- Has the student documented the information retrieved from the Web correctly?

Figure 1–2: Internet Resource Sheet

Name:_____ Date: _____

Class:_____

1. Write the research question you are exploring.

2. List the sources you have used for the research project.

3. Write down each URL you have used and a brief description of the site.

4. Check the information you have retrieved.

   Is it reliable (e.g., who were the sources of the Websites)? Is it biased (e.g., does the source have a stated opinion on the topic)?

   Is it valid? Current? Write down dates when Websites were last updated.

5. Write a citation for each Website you visited that you plan to use in your research.

Teachers may want to teach a lesson on documenting information from the Internet and recognizing valid sources. See Figure 1-2 for a sample Internet resource worksheet.

EVALUATION

An important part of any activity is the ability to evaluate what the student has learned. Before beginning an Internet project, teachers must decide how they will do this. Consider the following questions:

- Should evaluation assess individual effort, group effort, or both?
- Should students reflect on their experiences on the Internet as part of the assignment?
- Do students need varied sources, and, if so, how many?

CROSS-CURRICULAR ACTIVITIES

Teachers may want to integrate other curricula content into their own subject areas. Research has shown that students learn best when: (1) new ideas are connected to what they already know and have experienced; (2) they are actively engaged in applying and testing their knowledge using real-world problems; (3) their learning is organized around clear, high goals with lots of practice in reaching them; and (4) they can use their own interests and strengths as springboards for learning (Resnick, 1987).

Teachers who are working in cross-disciplinary teams must ask: Should the lesson be interdisciplinary? If so, how should we plan it? Cross-curricular adaptation using projects is discussed in Chapter 3 and illustrated in the practical models in most of the chapters.

It is important to have guidelines for using the Internet. Each educator must look at his/her own attitudes, determine when to use the Internet, establish a procedure and schedule, and decide how to evaluate the Internet project. Only then can the teacher formulate specific guidelines for integrating the Internet into a subject area.

INTERNET USE POLICIES (IUP)

Anxiety is running high among educators and parents about student safety on the Internet. There is no traffic cop to monitor the credibility of Websites or the appropriateness of the material. Some schools are not allowing any activity; others are requiring students and parents to sign contracts in an effort to limit liability; still others are using software programs to restrict students' ability to "surf" the Web freely.

The Internet should be used in the classroom as a curricular tool. Teachers and media specialists need to decide if Web material will be the best use of student time and school resources. Just as with any activity that is part of a lesson, educators must determine the reasons to incorporate a particular instructional strategy and whether it is the best one to meet the objective(s) for that lesson.

Internet-use policies (IUPs), also known as acceptable-use policies (AUPs), vary. In a conservative model of Internet use, teachers are permitted to provide access to the Internet only on a limited basis; drafts of a district's AUP are reviewed by citizen advisory groups and the school board. Once use policies are approved, the administration distributes information packets to parents and mandates direct instruction for children. At the opposite end of the spectrum is the student manager approach, in which students serve as system operators for the district and are responsible for news groups, bulletin boards, e-mail accounts, and creating acceptable-use forms.

Teachers, media specialists, and administrators are the ones who should determine AUPs at their school. Some questions they should ask are:

- What are the features of the Internet that make responsible use more an issue than has occurred with other media and resources?
- What is the extent and nature of current problems faced by schools who provide student access to the Internet?
- How have schools defined responsible use in traditional media, and how have they formulated policy responses?
- What is the likely extent and nature of the problems as more schools gain access to the Internet?
- How do the issues change with student age, gender, and other demographic factors?

The Bellingham (Washington) Public Schools have created Internet-use policies for students and staff. Consistent policies should make it clear to everyone—parents, staff, and students—when the Internet is a viable tool for an assignment. These policies may be copied or adapted for school use from Bellingham's Website at *www.bham.wednet.edu/policies.htm.*

EVALUATION OF WEBSITES

In looking at policy guidelines implemented by some schools for student Web use, we see that it is important that the sites students explore be appropriate to their age level. In addition, sites must contain meaningful content to help them with their research. Thus, teachers must identify Web addresses, known as URLs (uniform resource locators), that will integrate into our curriculum. One way to do this is for teachers to keep a notebook of Web addresses and annotate each entry, as seen in Figure 1-3, which shows an example from my notebook.

The American Association of School Librarians (AASL) has created criteria for evaluating Websites that are helpful. The AASL at *www.ala.org/ICONN/rating.html* has set up rating criteria in six sections:

1. authority/credentials: Who's in charge of the site?
2. design/style: Is the site well designed and organized?
3. navigation: How easily can the user move around the site?
4. content: Is the information accurate, reliable, up-to-date, unbiased?
5. performance: Can the user download information quickly?
6. curriculum connections: Does the content support and enrich the curriculum? Is the site interactive and useful to students and teachers?

Figure 1-4 provides an example of a Website evaluation form adapted from the one developed by AASL. You may want to develop one similar to this for your own use. By becoming familiar with these criteria, educators will be able to more effectively explore sites that are given in the Practical Models sections of each chapter of this book. A site that obtains a score of 80–100 points based on this criteria may be one worth trying with your class.

Figure 1–3: Sample Notebook Page

Language Arts Internet Page

Types of Sites	URLs	Description	Level	Audience
General	www.bham.wednet.edu/ 2313inet.htm	Policy for student access to info resources	All levels	Teachers
Language Arts	www.ucalgary. ca/~dkbrown/index.html	Guide to children's best books, children's writing, folklore	Elem., middle	Teachers, students
Links	www.napc.syr.edu/textbook/ kidsweb/literature.html	Good for online books, creative-writing sites, other LA links	Elem., middle	Teachers
Content				
Haiku poetry	cc.matsuyama-u.ac.ip/~shiki/	Lesson plan to teach haiku poetry writing	Elem.	Teachers
Of Mice and Men	www.sdcoe.k12.ca.us/ score/mice/micetg.html	Lesson plan and projects	Sec.	Teachers
The Crucible	www.sdcoe.k12.ca.us/score/ cruc/crucstg.html	Info on the play and Web URLs to use in teaching the play	Sec.	Teachers
Citing Online Sources	www.classroom.net/ classroom/ CitingNetResources.htm	Examples of Web, FTP, and Usenet news article citation forms Additional URLs for citing	Sec., middle	Teachers, students
Authors				
Steinbeck	tlc.ai.org/steinidx.htm	Background on his life and novels	Sec.	Teachers, students
Shakespeare	www.shakespeare.uiuc.edu/	Background on life; info about Globe Theater	Middle, sec.	Teachers, students
Mark Twain	www.miningco.com	Info on book banning to use with Huck Finn	Middle, sec.	Teachers, students
Projects	www.gsn.org	Curriculum projects, collaborations, lesson plans	All levels	Teachers, students
Collaboration	www.gsn.org	Collaborative projects	All levels	Students
Listservs	TAWL@listserv.Arizona.edu	Forum for whole language	Elem., middle	Teachers
Newsgroups	www.dejanews.com/news:alt. arts.fine	Search for topics in Newsgroups Newsgroup for fine arts	All levels	Teachers

Figure 1–4: Website Sample Evaluation Form

Criteria for Evaluating Websites

Name of Website: _____

URL: _____

Subject Area: _____ Grade Level:_____

Directions: Assign a point value to each section based on the following criteria.

Authority/Credibility = 10 points
- ✓ Objective, balanced presentation of material
- ✓ Expertise of individual or group who created site identified
- ✓ Bias-free viewpoints expressed
- ✓ Contact information for author/designer available on the site

Content = 30 points
- ✓ Accurate, reliable information
- ✓ Current, recently updated information
- ✓ Links up-to-date, annotated, or evaluated
- ✓ Content correlates to the curriculum
- ✓ Content supports national and state standards
- ✓ Site supports or enhances curriculum
- ✓ Objectives of site stated clearly
- ✓ Instructional support materials available
- ✓ Site content not usually available in school libraries

Design and Technical Features = 20 points
- ✓ Images load within reasonable timeframe
- ✓ Options for printing and/or downloading text and graphics available
- ✓ Site well designed with uncluttered pages and useful subheadings
- ✓ Design consistent throughout the site
- ✓ Intuitive icons, menus, and directional symbols for ease of use

Navigation = 10 points
- ✓ User can move easily around site
- ✓ Site or locator map available
- ✓ Navigational icons consistent throughout site
- ✓ External and internal links work

Learning Environment = 30 points
- ✓ Student input possible at the site
- ✓ Collaboration with other students encouraged at site
- ✓ Sharing of student work possible at the site
- ✓ Interactive opportunities offered at the site

A WEBSITE SAMPLE EVALUATION

The Website for Enchanted Learning, at *www.EnchantedLearning.com,* has been evaluated in Figure 1-5, using the AASL rating criteria above. Enchanted Learning has created a well-organized, aesthetically pleasing Website that is worthwhile to use with students at the elementary level who want to explore science topics. Overall, this Website will aid elementary school teachers, especially those with a limited science background who are preparing science topics for their students. Its clear design and reasonable load time make it easy to obtain information. The awards won by this site suggest that others find this site a "must see" for elementary educators. This is definitely a versatile site to bookmark! Specific comments on the Website follow.

Authority/credibility

This commercial Website was established by Enchanted Learning Software with the sponsorship of Disney Productions. The Website designer relates that she used her own preschoolers as "test cases" when she designed the site. The site is visually pleasing; for example, it employs colorful pictures of dinosaurs, whales, and planets. In addition, her credentials as site designer (available as a link to her home page) are exemplary: she holds a B.S. degree in biology and a master's degree in psychology, which give her the background necessary to work with scientific topics such as dinosaurs, whales, butterflies, and astronomy. She has also had experience designing CD-

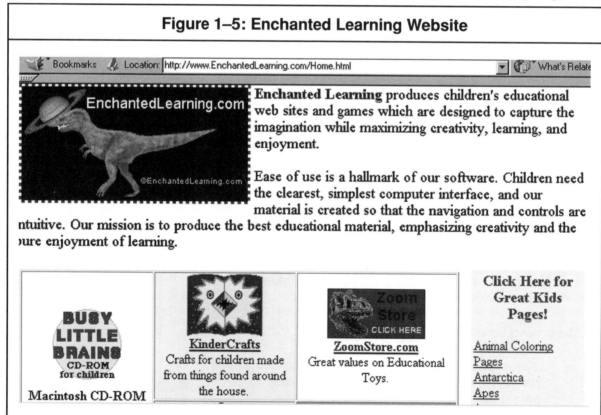

Figure 1–5: Enchanted Learning Website

Reprinted by permission of Enchanted Learning.com at http://EnchantedLearning.com/.

ROMs and other educational software, and teaching computer science. This designer includes an e-mail address so users can contact her with questions or comments about the site. Comments from reviewers of the site state that it has been chosen as one of the "Top 50 Educational Web Sites for Kids" in the magazine *Computing for Kids*, listed as a "USA Today Hot Site," and discussed in other newspapers around the world.

As the Website indicates, this site was created and "designed to capture [a child's] imagination while maximizing creativity, learning, and enjoyment." "Our mission is to produce the best educational material, emphasizing creativity and the pure enjoyment of learning." The purpose suggests that even though this is a commercial site, the company is interested in creating good educational material.

Content

The content on the Website includes different topics related to science. Some of the subjects included are whales, dinosaurs, rain forests, sharks, butterflies, and Zoom School, which contains a variety of geography, language arts, and other science information. A Little Explorers picture dictionary, with over 1,100 entries is available in English, Portuguese, Spanish, French, and German. The right side of the screen has links to safe sites for young children covering other subjects like Antarctica, apes, and animal coloring. Figure 1-6 illustrates the subject page on astronomy.

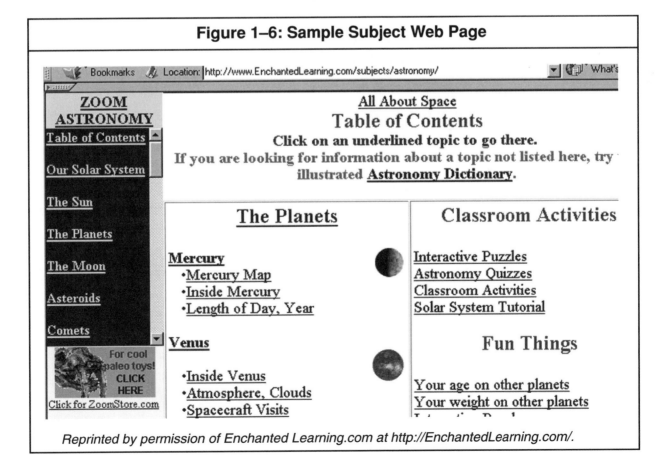

Figure 1–6: Sample Subject Web Page

Reprinted by permission of Enchanted Learning.com at http://EnchantedLearning.com/.

Design and Technical Features

Especially appropriate for young children, topics on this Website are clearly depicted in large type and accompanied by pictures that represent the subject. Despite the number of graphics, the site loads quite quickly. Screens representing different subjects are consistent, so children can easily move from whales to dinosaurs. Although the site uses frames, this feature can be turned off if desired and a text browser used. Each page can be printed from the Web browser. Educators should note that the type of Internet access, equipment (monitor, modem, disk space) and choice of Web browser will affect how a Website appears and is experienced by the user.

Navigation

Users can easily move around the site. Pictures and few words make navigation of the site easy for its intended audience—pre-elementary- and elementary-level students. In addition, the site offers a search engine to locate specific information on the site by the user entering keywords or simple phrases; the search engine corrects spelling and retrieves pictures, too! At the bottom of each Web page, consistent icons allow for navigation around the site and back to the home page. No site locator map is available, nor is one needed. Figure 1-7 illustrates the search form box.

Curriculum Connections

For teachers and students studying dinosaurs or whales, for example, this site provides some valuable information. It also contains games, puzzles, online connect-the-dots, nursery rhymes, and ideas for arts-and-crafts projects that are related to the subject under review; they are appropriate for early elementary children.

Learning Environment

The site offers access to information that might not be available in school libraries. Its goal, however, is not to create an environment for students to share work or collaborate with other students but to provide factual data and activities to reinforce

---

Figure 1–7: Search Form for Enchanted Learning

Enchanted Learning Search

First search engine with spelling correction and pictures!

Search EnchantedLearning.com for all the words:

Enter one or more words, or a short phrase.
You can use an asterisk * as a wild-card.

Search Now!

Reprinted by permission of Enchanted Learning.com at http://EnchantedLearning.com/.

learning. The site does include a way to contribute new information. Enchanted Learning offers different themes each month and maintains an archive of topics already completed, which is helpful for the educator who wants students to use the computer regularly. Each month there are usually links related to geography, history, art, science, crafts, games or sports, animals, literature, and language. Suggestions for new themes are welcome via e-mail at *school@EnchantedLearning.com*.

Educators should keep a few things in mind as they compile URLs and descriptions of Websites. First, it is a good idea to identify the main purpose of the site: for example, links to primary source material, lesson plans, or primary sources. It is also important to note any difficulties experienced at the site, such as slow loading time. The site evaluated here had excellent reviews; however, sites may often receive mixed reactions: there may be compelling reasons to view the content for its learning advantages, but there may be other reasons, such as slow load time or unclear navigation patterns, that prohibit its use.

CITING ONLINE SOURCES

Another issue that surfaces when doing research on the Internet is how to reference the sources that students find. Plagiarism remains a problem, and students should understand that material they retrieve from Web sources must be documented as it would be from books. In addition, they should know how to cite online sources they discover, following their required guidelines. Two common models are those from the Modern Language Association (MLA) at *www.mla.org* and the American Psychological Association (APA) at *www.apa.org/journals/webref.html*.

MLA and APA document Web sources similarly to traditional print sources, using title, author, and date of publication. However, there are some differences. For example, MLA style encloses Internet addresses in angle brackets < >; APA style does not. As a basic guide, the following items should be included in a citation of a Web source:

- the title of a scholarly project, database, periodical, or professional or personal Internet site underlined; if the Internet site has no title, a description, such as "Home Page"
- date of electronic publication and the latest update
- the name of any institution or organization sponsoring or associated with the Website
- date when the researcher accessed the source
- electronic address, or URL, of the source

When typing URLs for electronic sources, it is important to type every letter, number, symbol, and space accurately, because any error makes it impossible to retrieve the source. Figure 1-8 illustrates different ways to cite Internet resources. Teachers may want to give a similar sheet to students before they begin their Internet research. Websites at *www.quinion.com/words/articles/citation.htm* and *www.utexas.edu/depts/uwc/html/citation.html* also provide styles for referencing various types of Web re-

Figure 1–8: Citing Internet Sources

Directions: The following example gives you models of citations from the Modern Language Association (MLA) Style Guidelines and American Psychological Association (APA) Style Guidelines. Write your sources on the appropriate lines below.

Book: Shaw, Bernard. Pygmalion. 1912. Bartleby Archive. 6 Mar. 1998 *<www.columbia.edu/acis/bartleby/shaw>*. [*Note*: The APA would have no angle brackets, nor would a period appear at the end of the URL.]

_____
_____
_____

Article in a Journal: Rehberger, Dea. "The censoring of Project #17: Hypertext Bodies and Censorship." Kairos 2.2 (Fall 1997): 14 secs. 6 Mar. 1998 *<english.ttu.edu/kairos/2.2/index_f.html>*.

_____
_____
_____

Article in a Magazine: Viagas, Robert, and David Lefkowitz. "Capeman Closing Mar. 28." Playbill 5 Mar. 1998. 6 Mar. 1998 *<www1.playbill.com/cgi-bin/plb/news?cmd=show&code=30763>*.

_____
_____
_____

Professional Site: The Nobel Foundation Official Website. The Nobel Foundation. 28 Feb. 1998 *<www.nobel.se>*.

_____
_____
_____

Personal Site: Thiroux, Emily. Home page. 7 Mar. 1998 *<academic.csub.ak.edu/home/acadpro/departments/english/enthrx.html>*.

_____
_____
_____

sources. All of these sites provide cautions and guidelines in a concise format on how to enter URL addresses.

SUMMARY

In Part 1, we have reviewed the importance of technology and the Internet to the information needs of the twenty-first century. We have identified the skills necessary for becoming an information-literate person. We have addressed some critical issues to consider as we plan Internet-based instruction. Finally, we have emphasized the importance of Internet-use policies, evaluating Websites and materials, and citing Web resources properly.

Preplanning is most important to creating a lesson that meets specific objectives, uses the Internet as an integral part of the lesson (not as an add-on), and provides the best experience possible with Internet technology for students. In Part 2, we will look at the kinds of resources available on the Internet and review a step-by-step process for creating Internet-based lessons and units.

PART 2: PRACTICAL APPLICATIONS

As teachers, we know how time consuming it is to create new lessons or unit plans. Thus, we all borrow and adapt good teaching techniques and strategies from each other. Part 2 of each chapter in this book will focus on applications of the theory discussed in Part 1, usually in the form of unit plans. Models will illustrate how the Internet with its diverse resources can be integrated into lessons and units for elementary and secondary classrooms. In this first chapter, however, it is important that we know what resources are available on the Internet so that we can use them to plan effective, challenging lessons for our students. We will take a look at two methods of categorizing these materials. The first method divides the Internet into types of sites based on function. The second method shows different categories of material on the World Wide Web.

TYPES OF WEB SITES

With the World Wide Web as part of the Internet, teachers and students now have vast resources and learning opportunities only a mouse-click away. Because the information is so diverse, it can be used to prepare lessons, expose students to new challenges during a lesson, and provide enrichment as follow-up to the lesson. It also provides the opportunity to use themes that integrate several disciplines—language arts, social studies, math, art, and science.

The Internet performs two main functions for K–12 educators and students: communication and research.

COMMUNICATION

Communication can take several forms on the Internet. Telecollaboration, listservs, and news groups are discussed below.

Telecollaboration

Telecollaboration projects connect classrooms so students can interact on a specific topic. They can be problem-solving projects, information-gathering sessions, interpersonal exchanges of information, or writing. Go to *www.gsn.org* to get information on pen pal or cooperative projects. The sites contained there give examples of collaborative projects, project description guidelines, and more. Project sites are ideal to formulate a "writer's workshop" as part of a language arts unit or to have elementary science classes in Iowa and Ghana compare the weather.

Listservs

A listserv is a group mailing list whose every member receives copies of all mail sent to the list by participants. Therefore, a continuous discussion occurs on topics of common interest to list participants. Some listservs are very narrow in focus, some are highly intellectual, while others are especially useful for teaching. Listservs more often contain information geared to adults than to students. A person must subscribe to a listserv to gain access, usually by typing "SUBSCRIBE firstname lastname" in the body of the message.

Some listservs of interest to teachers include:

- *TAWL@listserv.Arizona.edu,* which provides a forum on whole language
- *listserv@psuvm.psu.edu* for fiction writers
- *listserv@vmd.cso.uiuc.edu* for issues critical to education, especially at the middle school level
- *listserv@nic.umass.edu,* which focuses primarily on educational issues but includes occasional projects aimed at teachers

Newsgroups

These are much like a classroom bulletin board, except that the electronic messages can be viewed by millions, not dozens, of people. Sometimes Newsgroups are sponsored by an online service provider, such as America Online (AOL); a user usually has to have authorization from the Internet service provider to be able to access the newsgroup. Topics of Newsgroups cover virtually anything anyone is interested in and can range from aliens to colleges to snowboarding. Newsgroups can foster debate on a topic, since people who have subscribed to the Newsgroup do not necessarily hold the same views on the subjects at hand. Therefore, a controversial issue like animal rights can generate hot discussion from different viewpoints. These debates bring a world of divergent ideas to the participant and force that person to determine what is true. Above all, it encourages thinking. One caution, however, is that Newsgroups can be the most troublesome regarding censorship. Teachers must make sure to review a Newsgroup's topics before announcing a site to students.

RESEARCH

Websites that students use to gather information related to a topic or issue they are studying can be categorized as research sites. Students could be writing a paper on endangered species, debating the hazards of airbags for small children, looking for background on Shakespeare as they read *Romeo and Juliet*, or researching a topic that is global in nature, such as the Middle East peace talks. There are various ways to obtain the information.

Websites

These are a number of different types of information sites on the World Wide Web that provide diverse information. They include the following types:

- *Commercial sites* are set up by a wide range of companies, such as textbook publishers, manufacturers, television stations, and magazine publishers, to name but a few. These sites, whose URLs end in "**.com**," provide information on their educational products, but they may also include lesson ideas and activities to use in the classroom. Some of the following are examples of commercial sites: *www.scholastic.com, www.cnn.com,* or *www.discovery.com.* Figure 1-9 illustrates a commercial Website emphasizing mathematics.
- *University sites* often have high-level information, because faculty members and/or scientists have placed their research on the Internet to share with colleagues. Of course, some of the research may be too complicated for K–12

Figure 1–9: Sample Commercial Website for Mathematics

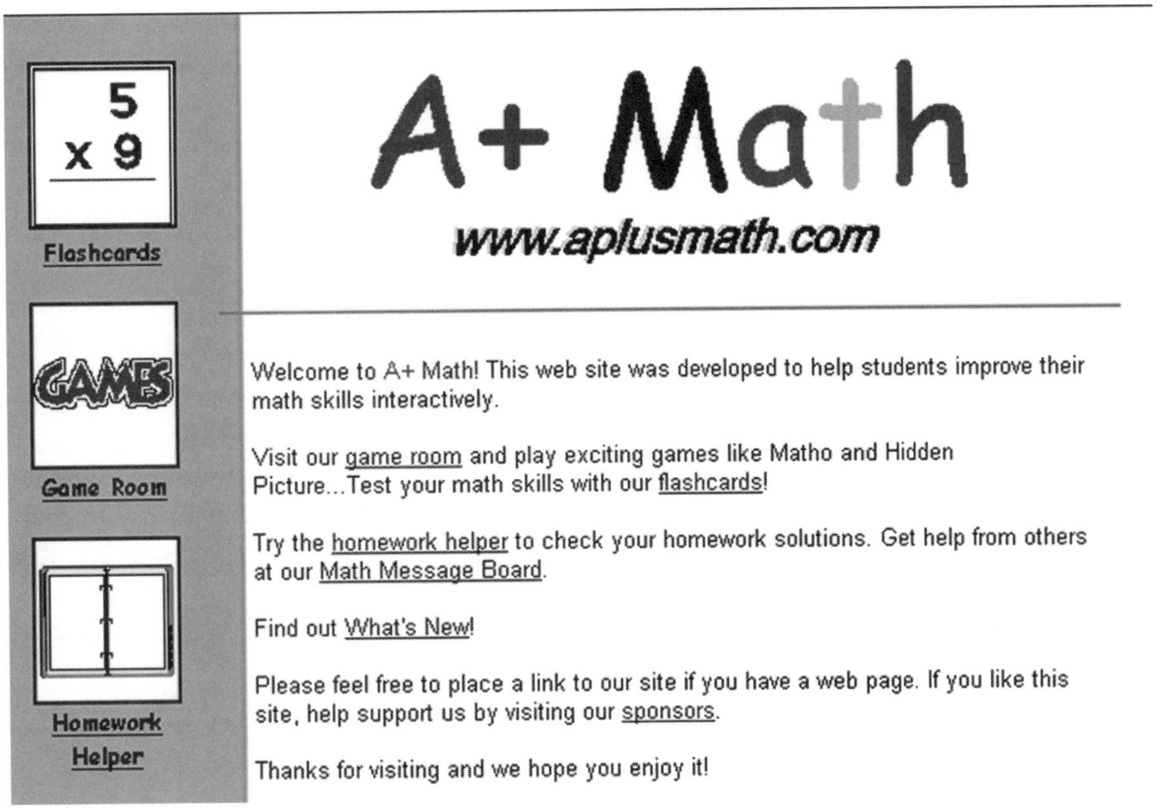

Flashcards

GAMES

Game Room

Homework Helper

A+ Math
www.aplusmath.com

Welcome to A+ Math! This web site was developed to help students improve their math skills interactively.

Visit our game room and play exciting games like Matho and Hidden Picture...Test your math skills with our flashcards!

Try the homework helper to check your homework solutions. Get help from others at our Math Message Board.

Find out What's New!

Please feel free to place a link to our site if you have a web page. If you like this site, help support us by visiting our sponsors.

Thanks for visiting and we hope you enjoy it!

Reprinted by permission of A+ Math at www.aplusmath.com

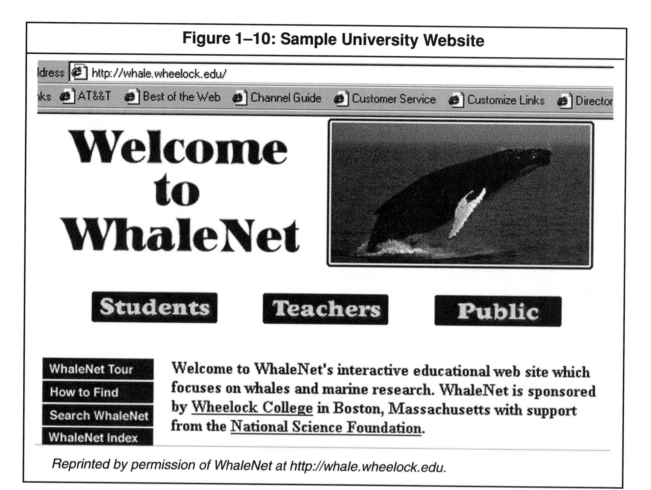

Figure 1–10: Sample University Website

Reprinted by permission of WhaleNet at http://whale.wheelock.edu.

students. However, university departments of education often develop sites specifically for K–12 educators and students. Some have lesson plans; others provide background information on an author or period in history, and many contain links to other resources on the Web. Take a look at WhaleNet, for example, the site on whales illustrated in Figure 1-10, at *http:// whale.wheelock.edu* for a good example.

- *School sites* include K–12 home pages put on the Web by a classroom teacher, a class, or the school. As previously mentioned, the Bellingham Public School site provides its school policies for using the Internet. Sites created by teachers may provide lesson or unit plans that they have used successfully in their own subject areas. Class sites often illustrate a project that the class has just completed, giving students and teachers alike ideas for developing their own projects and home pages. Figure 1-11 illustrates a school Website at *www.zbths.k12.il.us/projects/proj.html.*
- *Organization sites* are usually supplied by professional nonprofit organizations, such as the American Library Association (ALA), the American Association of School Librarians (AASL), or the National Council of Teachers of English (NCTE). Organizations also provide interesting information related to the type of organization. For example, *http://kennedy-center.org* offers ideas

Figure 1–11: Sample School Website

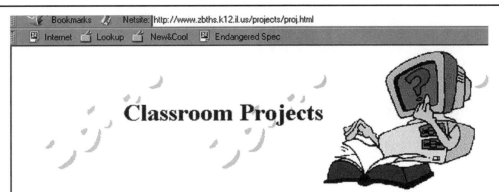

Bookmarks   Netsite: http://www.zbths.k12.il.us/projects/proj.html

Internet   Lookup   New&Cool   Endangered Spec

Classroom Projects

Gomez--Tracing Your Roots

Zolli--College Team Sports

Somers/Bleau/Fishman--Integrated Pathway Human Body Magazine

Budzik/Cavallini/McPherson/Womack--A Snapshot of Contemporary America

Womack--*Crime and Punishment*

Reprinted by permission.

Figure 1–12: Sample Organization Website

A Collaborative Study in

American History

Part of the Great American Cram

20-30% off AP Review Books!

Historical Quote

Click here for another random quotation from a great historical figure...

Try not to have a good time...this is supposed to be educational. - Charles Schulz

study group!

Welcome to *A Collaborative Study in American History*, an online study group that was first utilized extensively by students and teachers across the nation during the 1996-97 school year. Since then, we have added several new *interactive* features including an online quiz, terminology bank, historical document search, and much much more. This site was designed to allow students to interact with teachers and other students in a collaborative effort to understand the various aspects of American history... truly abandoning the "empty-vessel" model of years past. We hope you enjoy the site.

Reprinted by permission from Collaborative Study in American History from ThinkQuest Library of entries, at www.library.advanced.org.

Figure 1–13: Sample General Website

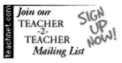 

FREE Computer Manuals For Kids

click here

Free Computer Manuals for Kids

Lesson Ideas

Computer & Internet: General Lesson Ideas

Teachnet.Com
sponsored by

PERSPECTIVE
The Time Line Game
ORDER ONLINE AT A
TEACHNET SPECIAL PRICE

- **Australian Teacher Integrates Book, Support Disks and Website into Comprehensive Teaching Resource**
- **Translate a Poem**
- **What's Your Type?**
- **Quick News**
- **Describing the Internet to Elementary Students**
- **Teaching with the Internet**

▸ Front Page
▸ Search Teachnet.Com
▸ Lesson Ideas
▸ How-To
▸ Teacher-2-Teacher
▸ Take 5 micro activities
▸ Resources & Links
▸ Site Map

Reprinted by permission of Teachnet.Com "Brainstorm of the Day." Copyright 1999 Teachnet.Com. All Rights Reserved.

---

for teaching and learning through the arts; for a history project, *http://library.advanced.org* includes a variety of subjects such as the Collaborative Study of American History depicted in Figure 1-12.

- *General sites* contain information for K–12 educators and students on any topic, unlike some of the sites above that focus more on subject-specific information. Such sites include any of the above types (for example, *www.microsoft.com/education/K–12* or *http://ericir.syr.edu*), and provide lesson plans on a range of subjects. Figure 1-13 (*www.teachnet.com*) illustrates a Website with many different offerings for educators.

WEBSITES CATEGORIZED BY FUNCTION

Many educators have attempted to categorize the information that exists on the Web. Two sites—*http://edweb.sdsu.edu* and *www.kn.pacbell.com/wired/bluewebn/apptypes.html*—provide good distinctions and examples of the following seven categories.

1. *Enrichments.* Enrichments are activities that serve to motivate students when starting or as a follow-up to a unit of instruction. For example, following a unit in which a class has explored the topic of energy, the activity called Studying Wind using Hands-on Science would provide a motivating conclusion (*http://hillside.coled.umn.edu/Wind/Wind.html*).
2. *Lessons/Online tutorials.* These sites provide lesson plans or a tutorial with specific objectives and procedures for completing given activities. Tutorials

---

Figure 1–14: Frog Dissection Tutorial

Whole Frog Project material is from www.itg.lbl.gov/Frog and is Copyright Lawrence Berkeley National Laboratory, University of California. LBNL is a U.S. Department of Energy Laboratory.

---

usually include steps to follow and give feedback to learners as they perform the tasks. Many sites contain lesson plans for the K–12 teacher that include objectives and instructions on how to teach a specific concept (such as writing haiku poetry) or how to introduce a period in history. The Website in Figure 1-14 at *www.itg.lbl.gov/Frog* contains a tutorial for science classes on dissecting a frog.

3. *Tools.* One example of a tool is the search engine. Search engines may be part of a browser, like in Netscape, or a separate entity, like the Yahoo! or AltaVista search engines. E-mail programs like Eudora at *www.eudora.com* are also tools to enable users to send and receive e-mail. Listservs and Newsgroups can be classified as tools. Yahooligans search engine for children at *www.yahooligans.com* is a good example of a tool Website.

4. *References.* References are informational sites that provide complete, in-depth information. These include databases like the CIA Fact Book (at *www.odci.gov/cia/publications/factbook*—see Figure 1-15), an encyclopedia such as Microsoft's Encarta (at *www.microsoft.com*), or terminology used on the Web (at *www.eduplace.com/techcent/staff/glossary.html*).

5. *Resources.* Resources are designed to serve as additional supporting material, with a specific focus. This information is quite prolific on the Web, often in the form of collections, field trips, or other school Web pages. For example, an individual with a hobby or an organization like the Monterey Bay Aquarium may focus on a topic like sea life. Virtual field trips are avail-

Figure 1–15: Sample References Website

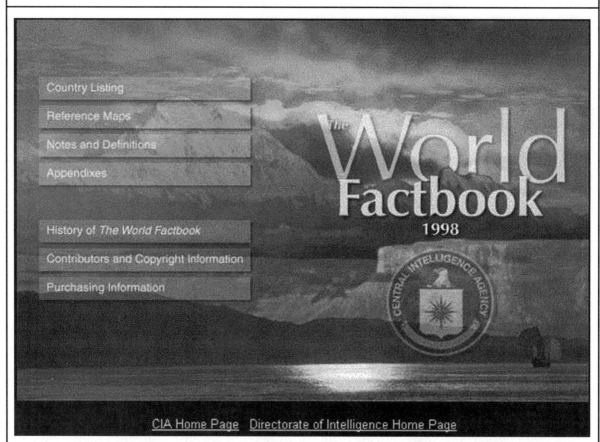

able through museums and Civil War photographs at the Library of Congress Website (see Figure 1-16, which depicts two Civil War generals at *http://memory.loc.gov/ammem/cwphome.html*). If computers are equipped with a sound card, students can hear the Martin Luther King "I Had a Dream" speech at *www.audionet.com/speeches*. Students and school Web pages are also resources. One fifth-grade-class Web page commented on what it might have been like to travel the Oregon Trail; a fourth-grade-class page showed pictures and facts about their study of whales.

6. *Projects.* Long-term projects focus attention on a problem over a period of time. Several projects at the Global SchoolNet Foundation site (at *www.gsn.org*) use e-mail, Web resources, teaching guides, and experts as part of an instructional unit. The site also contains a registry archive of Internet projects. Other projects already completed include Journey North: A Global Study of Wildlife Migration (at *www.learner.org/jnorth*), MayaQuest '97, a journey to the Mayan ruins of South America (at *www.tme.nl/dln/resources.htm*), and International Arctic Project (at *http://ics.soe.umich.edu/ed712/IAPProfile.html*). Organizations and educational institutions like the University of Michigan and others are constantly initiating new projects.

Figure 1–16: Sample Resources Site

7. *Activities.* Activities that take a topic and explore it through various Websites are few in number. However, the teacher who has an idea for a topic can use the activities available on the Web to adapt and incorporate into lessons. This is the true integration of Internet resources into the curriculum. The Blue Web'n Applications site compiles a variety of the above types of materials at *www.kn.pacbell.com/wired/bluewebn/apptypes.html.*

Many different groups create information that fits into the categories we have just discussed. For example, organizations such as NASA (at *www.nasa.org*), commercial sites like the textbook publisher Scholastic (at *www.scholastic.com/EL*), the Discovery Channel (at *www.discovery.com*), software providers like Microsoft (at *www.microsoft.com/education/K-12*), or hardware makers like Apple Computer (at *www.applecomputer.com*) create instructional materials for schools.

As just noted, the current trend on the World Wide Web is to put forth a myriad of information to teachers and students. The number of sites in science, social studies, and the language arts that are suitable for K–12 students continues to proliferate. Thus, for teachers, lesson plans, worksheets, and units in all subject areas can be downloaded with just a few clicks of the mouse. We now want to look at a model for creating Internet-based lesson and unit plans. Similar models will illustrate different subject areas in Part 2 of each chapter in this book.

CREATING THE INTERNET UNIT

The term "unit" is one that is often used rather loosely. An instructional unit can comprise anything from a few days of concentrated study to a whole course. Units range from a five-day writing workshop to a year-long study of China. A teacher may have several units going at the same time. For example, a social studies teacher could be exploring a map-study unit while studying Latin America. In one week, a language arts class may work on a writing unit on Fridays and a drama unit on Monday through Thursday.

In this book, we will illustrate different types of units—some short, others longer—to achieve many objectives. Each model unit contains the teacher's preplanning of the unit, the body of the lessons including a series of activities, sample Websites focused on a theme, evaluation, and follow-up to the unit.

The teaching of any unit depends on the needs, interests, and abilities of the students for whom it has been designed. Building a unit should be based on the teacher's assessment of what a class can and cannot do. Educators will get the most out of the practical models in this book by envisioning their own curriculum and students and how the models in each chapter can be adapted with their own content to fit their particular students. Some of the units in this book focus more on individualized instruction, others on small or whole-group learning. This allows teachers to adapt those plans that fit their own teaching styles or to experiment with another type of unit in their own classrooms.

When creating the Internet unit, we will follow steps similar to building most instructional units. The following steps will serve as a model for the subject-specific units in subsequent chapters.

STEP 1: APPLYING FRAMEWORK STANDARDS—WHAT SHOULD BE TAUGHT?

What areas should we include in our plans in a subject area and at a specific grade level? We begin by looking at national standards and the frameworks for teaching established by content-area curriculum development committees, usually at state levels. Each state has its own guidelines and has outlined content and skills for students to achieve at each grade level. For example, California framework standards require that history and social science courses beginning in kindergarten work toward "improving students' competency in the knowledge of history, geography, and citizenship, as well as their understanding of issues such as diversity, criticism, conflict, and interdependence" (California State Department of Education, 1988). The framework also stresses specific themes and attributes like communication, reasoning, personal development, and civic responsibility. This material helps schools focus on broad goals as they create their own programs of study, and it provides core content and skills to form the basis of teachers' units and lesson plans.

Some concepts and skills cross all subject areas. The example for the model unit lists standards from the California framework to show the connections between these framework standards and the Internet. Units in subsequent chapters will include more content emphasis.

In California, framework standards from language arts, social sciences, and science emphasize achieving the following goals:

- Students will work collaboratively. Studies have shown that learners profit immeasurably from environments that encourage shared learning. Since most businesses today emphasize the team approach to completing projects, working cooperatively is a skill students need to attain before they finish school (see Chapter 5 for more on cooperative learning). The Web presents an especially good environment for collaboration, in which students work together accessing the Internet. Whether students are working in groups on a research project or interacting with a school in another geographic area on a writing activity, they are learning teamwork and shared responsibility.

- Students will become aware that writing is a means of clarifying thinking, and that it is a process which embodies several stages, including prewriting, drafting, receiving responses, revising, editing, and postwriting activities, including evaluation. Using information gathered from a variety of sources, including the Internet, enables students to practice their writing on meaningful, far-reaching topics. The Internet has no geographic boundaries.

- Students will respond both orally and in writing to questions that help them to acquire and use higher-order thinking skills in all subject areas (see Chapter 2 for more on the concept of critical thinking). On the Web, especially, because of the diversity of materials and the combination of fact and opinion that exists on Websites, students (and teachers) must use analysis, evaluation, application, and synthesis to choose what information to use, believe, and refute.

- Teachers and library media specialists will encourage and assist students to use all media and technological resources, such as word processors, computers, library books, films, audio tapes, videotapes, newspapers, magazines, dictionaries, and encyclopedias as learning and communication tools. Although the California frameworks do not yet include references to the Internet (the guidelines were written in 1988), many schools are already using the Internet in classroom lessons. The Internet is one more resource that students should know about. Students must learn how to access the Internet, retrieve information, and evaluate what they find. These will be life skills for jobs in the twenty-first century.

The Web provides a rich variety of media through which to learn, including options like Real Audio at *www.realaudio.com* and video clips, or animations. For example, in language learning, sound and video can immerse the learner in the target culture through authentic materials spoken by native speakers. Students also have access to local and global resources—for example, a class in Sioux City, Iowa, can link to resources in Tokyo, Japan. With the use of varied materials, teachers can adapt their instruction and accommodate different learning styles by providing stimuli for both visual and auditory learners. We need to remember, however, that although the Web is diverse, it is only one of our resources—though admittedly a dynamic one.

As we plan to use the Internet in our instruction, we must look at the topics for units so that we focus on the content and skills sequentially. Units can be built on almost any topic. For example, a second-grade teacher might focus on the family; a high school English teacher, on the other hand, might create a genre unit on the short story or a thematic unit around The Eskimo and His Literature. A physical science teacher who wants to teach the topic of Energy: Its Choices and Their Consequences could create a cross-curricular thematic unit to incorporate a miniunit on persuasive writing. Let the frameworks and your imagination be your guide.

STEP 2: DESIGNING UNIT GOALS AND CREATING SPECIFIC LESSON OBJECTIVES

Because broad content and skills are often described for teachers by national standards, state frameworks, or by local or school curriculum committees, general goals for instruction can be "givens" or fixed parts of the curriculum. These could include goals such as, "Students will work cooperatively together in small groups" or "Students will demonstrate the behavior of civic responsibility." Teachers can create units that incorporate these mandated goals within their own list of unit goals and objectives.

An objective is a statement of what the learner will have attained once the learning experience has been successfully completed. Objectives define where the teacher is going with instruction, and they communicate expectations to the students. They also act as a guide for selecting instructional strategies, learning activities, and evaluation techniques. As teachers write objectives for a unit, they must keep certain principles in mind: objectives should be attainable; there should be ways of evaluating those objectives included as part of the unit; behavioral objectives, commonly taught in teacher preparation programs, should be stated in terms of learner behavior— built around change in the learner and including what the learner will do, under what conditions, and what the criteria of success will be.

An objective for a skill can be easily stated: "I want students to be able to put capital letters at the beginning of each sentence." However, when we want students to learn to appreciate poetry, it is not as easy to write the objective in behavioral terms. The appreciation of poetry can be made up of several behavioral objectives such as: "The student will be able to identify similes and metaphors in a poem" or "The student will be able to write a poem." If students achieve these two objectives, we hope they will "appreciate" the poetry they are reading and writing.

Objectives can be stated in a number of ways:

- as a list of skills or processes the student will master
- as a list of course activities that the student will read, talk about, or write about
- as a description of products—for example, class projects
- as a list of activities that the student will be able to perform at the end of the unit

Finally, it is a good idea to indicate the time allotted for each objective to make sure that it is attainable in the overall timeframe of the unit.

STEP 3: DECIDING ON MATERIALS AND RESOURCES

Good materials enhance and reinforce good instruction. They can help a lesson have a stronger impact and appeal to different learning styles. Thus, teachers need to select the media—whether it is the blackboard, a film, the overhead projector, or the Internet—so that it reinforces the lessons they plan to teach.

The Internet provides multimedia materials to create a multisensory learning environment. However, just as with traditional materials like films, it is important for teachers to preview Websites to which they plan to send students, especially at the elementary level. Selecting a group of sites for a class project focuses the research and allows students to gain the most from the time they spend online. It also decreases the chance they may stumble upon undesirable material on a site.

Search engines like Yahoo! at *www.yahoo.com*, AltaVista at *www.altavista.com*, and Excite at *www.excite.com* enable the searcher to go directly to sites that meet the needs of K–12 teachers and students. For example, a student doing science research on endangered species might use the key words "endangered species" along with "whale" to limit the topic. Many sites have lists of similar topical sites, so finding one good site often leads to others. Remember to keep an Internet notebook and write down URLs in specific categories.

In my own Internet notebook (see Figure 1-3), I have a separate page for each subject—language arts, science, and social studies. I divide each subject category further according to what I will be teaching. I also try to annotate each URL so I remember the content when I plan a lesson.

STEP 4: PLANNING THE INSTRUCTION

We have decided upon and created our objectives and looked at the materials, including Internet resources, we will use in our unit. Now we must plan the instruction. Teachers will want to choose the type of structure(s)—for example, whole class, small groups, individual study, peer learning and tutoring, or activity centers, to name a few. They must also determine a sequence of materials and activities that will meet the unit objectives and provide an interesting mix of activities to accommodate different learning styles. Finally, they will need to include necessary content and transition from one learning activity to another with the ease and fluidity of a conductor moving from one movement of a symphony to the next.

The example that follows from my own teaching emphasizes a student-centered model of a unit plan with the teacher acting as facilitator. At the beginning of a unit, I usually start out in a large group and present *"how" and "why" questions* to orient students to the objectives of the unit: I want to show them what they don't know and kindle an interest in obtaining the knowledge that they lack. Next, I use some *lead-in activities* to motivate my students and at the same time introduce them to the unit. I include details describing each activity, how it is carried out, instructions for the students, and how students will perform the tasks. Further, I try to plan *hands-*

on activities for each concept. Each lesson in the unit covers one significant concept. Often, these hands-on activities occur in small groups. I expect these activities to offer students opportunities to use their imaginations as they explore each concept. To ensure that students understand the concepts, I might have them state the concepts in their own words, list the concepts sequentially so that they build upon each other, identify subordinate concepts under main ones, and describe applications of the concepts in everyday life. Following projects, I use *writing assignments to* reinforce and evaluate what they learned in the hands-on activities. This is also a good opportunity for self-expression and cooperation as students peer-edit other students' papers. Finally, I make sure that I have provided for at least one method of *evaluation* at the end and others throughout the unit. Although I often vary this procedure and adjust it according to the needs of my students, the time I have, and the content I am teaching, nonetheless, I usually encompass all of these components in the units I teach.

STEP 5: PREPARING FOR TEACHER AND STUDENT-BASED ASSESSMENT

No matter what we teach, it is important to evaluate how well students are progressing to make sure that they are learning what we assume they are. Assessment can take many forms.

- monitoring by observation. Process and lab skills or small-group projects can be monitored by observing students as they are engaged in activities.
- monitoring by student evaluations. Students should be given opportunities to review and discuss cooperatively each other's assignments and projects.
- monitoring by examination. A prepared list of questions tests students for understanding and application of the main ideas in the unit.
- monitoring by problem solving. Exercises to test concepts taught in the unit require students to apply concepts they have learned.

Some specific assessment strategies to consider are:

- interviews. Student/teacher dialogues can determine the approaches used in problem solving and students' views of what was learned.
- anecdotal records. Teachers keep anecdotal records of the class and record student questions and behaviors. This can be as simple as recording check marks by students' names each time they demonstrate a behavior, ask a question, or give a statement that indicates understanding.
- model building. Students are asked to construct a physical model of their ideas regarding some topic.
- learning logs. Students record thoughts and ideas about their learning.
- pictures/illustrations. Students draw pictures illustrating their thoughts regarding some concept.
- class notebooks. Students keep records of their daily experiences and activities in notebooks.

- active participation. Teachers rate student involvement in active participation tasks and cooperative exercises.
- role play. Students are asked to role play parts of a process.
- student-taught lessons. Students plan, research, and teach lessons to the class on a topic.
- self-assessment. Students rate their own progress and support their feelings.
- product. Students are asked to create a product or thing that demonstrates their knowledge of a content area.
- peer assessment. Other students in a cooperative group rate the performance of the group's members.

These assessment techniques provide unique ways of evaluating student progress and assessing the lessons teachers create at the same time. Many of these strategies will be used as assessment in the units in subsequent chapters.

SUMMARY

Effective schools literature shows that when teachers work together to build a coherent learning experience for students in all grades and within and across subject areas—one that is guided by common curriculum goals and expectations—they are able to improve student achievement (Lee, Bryk, and Smith, 1993). Effective instruction includes curricular goals and coherent learning experiences. The five steps listed above form the basis for any good unit plan in any subject area. While teachers may emphasize one section more than another in their planning, each area is important to the learning process.

TEACHER EXERCISES: NOW YOU TRY IT...

Before beginning Chapter 2, try out some of the ideas from this chapter. Creating an Internet-based lesson requires some preliminary planning. Try some of the following practice activities.

1. Form a team including a classroom teacher and a library media specialist to work on a lesson/unit plan and its implementation.
2. Choose a lesson in your subject area that you think would benefit from resources available on the Internet. You have already read about some of those resources in this chapter. Don't worry yet about what those resources are, since you will be looking at various Websites during each of the following chapters.
3. Use the Critical Issues section in Part 1 to draft an outline indicating how you would handle each issue at your own school site.
   - Check out the policy guidelines at the Bellingham site at *www.bham.wednet.edu/policies.htm*, listed under "Use."
   - Look at some of the sites offering staff development options listed under "Administration."
4. Look at the Teacher Attitude section in Part 1. Write journal entries describing action plans that indicate how you would eliminate any of the fears that

you might have to teaching Internet-based lessons. (*Note:* Your action plan may include fears listed in the section on Teacher Attitudes, or you may want to discuss other fears that are unique to you.)

5. Explore some of the general Websites listed below. From this list or other URLs in this chapter, identify at least five sites of interest to you and annotate those in your Internet notebooks. These should be useful when you create your own lessons.
   - *www.cnn.com* (CNN TV)
   - *www.tenet.edu/teks/science* (Science Center for Educator Development)
   - *www.ncte.org* (National Association of Teachers of English)
   - *www.nsta.org* (The National Science Teachers Association)
   - *www.nationalgeographic.com* (National Geographic)
   - *www.ncss.org/links* (National Council on Social Studies and links to other sites)
   - *http://thomas.loc.gov* (The Library of Congress and how laws are made)
   - *http://ericir.syr.edu* (lesson plans in a range of subjects)
   - *www.yahooligans.com* (search engine from Yahoo! for kids)
6. Critique a Website using AASL criteria or criteria found at some of the other evaluation sites. Create a lesson plan that has as its purpose showing students how to evaluate a Website.

CONCLUSION

With information exploding into students' lives, we teachers must prepare unit plans that teach children to locate, understand, manipulate, synthesize, and apply information from a variety of sources. In collaboration with library media specialists, we must teach students to be information literate so they can assume the responsibilities of a knowledge-based world. In Chapter 2, we will look at an important aspect of learning—critical thinking and how using the Internet fosters such skills.

REFERENCES

American Association of School Librarians and Association for Educational Communications and Technology. 1988. *Information Power: Guidelines for School Library Media Programs.* Chicago: American Association of School Librarians, and Washington, D.C.: Association for Educational Communications and Technology.

Becker, Henry J. 1994. *Analysis and Trends of School Use of New Information Technologies.* Irvine, CA: Department of Education, University of California, Irvine.

California State Department of Education. 1988. *History–Social Science Framework for California Public Schools, Kindergarten Through Grade Twelve.* Sacramento: California State Department of Education.

Doyle, Christina A. 1992. "Outcome Measures for Information Literacy within the National Educational Goals of 1990." In *Final Report to the National Forum on Information Literacy.* Syracuse, NY: ERIC Clearinghouse on Information Resources.

Lee, Valerie E., Anthony Bryk, and Julia B. Smith. 1993. "The Organization of Effective Secondary Schools." In *Review of Research in Education,* vol. 19, edited by Linda Darling-Hammond. Washington, D.C.: American Educational Research Association.

McKinsey and Company. 1995. *Connecting K–12 Schools to the Information Superhighway.* New York: McKinsey.

Markuson, Carolyn. 1986. "Making It Happen, Taking Charge of the Information Curriculum." *School Library Media Quarterly* 15, No. 1 (fall): 37–40.

Measelle, Richard L. 1990. "Globalization of the Business Environment—Implications for the Accounting Profession and Business Education." *Human Resource Management* 2, No. 1: 77–84.

National Commission on Teaching & America's Future. 1996. *What Matters Most: Teaching for America's Future.* New York: National Commission on Teaching & America's Future.

Office of Technology Assessment. 1995. *Teachers and Technology: Making the Connection.* Washington, D.C.: U.S. Congress.

Resnick, Lauren B. 1987. *Education and Learning to Think.* Washington, D.C.: National Academy Press.

Summit, Roger K. 1987. "Online Information: A Ten Year Perspective and Outlook." *ONLINE* 11, No. 1 (January): 61–64.

Chapter 2

LINKING INFORMATION LITERACY, CRITICAL THINKING, AND THE INTERNET

PART 1: IDEAS AND INSIGHTS

OBJECTIVES OF THIS CHAPTER

Chapter 2 starts educators thinking about connections between critical thinking and information literacy, including techniques that will be used to find information on the Internet. After reading this chapter, readers will be able to:

- identify the connections between information literacy and critical thinking
- explain the value of technology for building critical thinking
- differentiate among three levels of a critical-thinking search model
- create activities to build critical thinking and information literacy by using the Internet

INTRODUCTION

In the 1980s, online searching usually entailed accessing databases containing huge amounts of data through an information service, such as Dialog Information Services, Inc., or Dow Jones. Database searching required electronic equipment, a modem, and a telephone line—which were hard to acquire in many classrooms at the time. Subscribing to a service was also expensive, and searching an online system necessitated that students (and teachers) know a sophisticated set of search parameters. Teachers often had to take in-depth training before they were able to teach the skills to their students. CD-ROM searching, which came into vogue in early 1990, simplified the search process, because no telephone line and modem were required;

thus, the cost and access problems decreased. It was also easier to use. Now, online searching to many people means searching the Internet.

Whether students search banks of databases, CD-ROMs, or the Internet, however, they must be information literate. Alvin Toffler (1984) said in his book, *The Third Wave,* "A powerful tide is now surging across the world. This third wave is the arrival of the super-technological age. The basic raw material of the third wave will be information." John Naisbitt (1982) had already commented in *Megatrends* that the main ingredient for today's jobs will be information. He also predicted that the primary jobs in the 1990s and beyond would be service jobs that would involve working with information. Going forward, information literacy will be required for a majority of jobs in the twenty-first century.

Access to the Internet has increased in the last few years. Because search engines use natural language search terms, it has become easier for teams of library media specialists and teachers to join together in teaching information literacy as part of the curriculum. And because information literacy encompasses critical thinking, this too can be taught at the same time.

We were introduced to the concept of information literacy in Chapter 1. In this chapter, we will look at a model using information searching to improve critical-thinking skills as we strive to enhance information literacy in the classroom. We will discuss answers to questions, such as: What is information literacy, and how does it relate to critical thinking? and, Where does the Internet fit into the teaching model?

DEFINING INFORMATION LITERACY

Information literacy goes beyond the ability to read books and be acquainted with computers. Problem solving, decision making, critical thinking, information gathering, and "sense making" are abilities related to information literacy. These skills must be taught in addition to basic literacy and computer literacy for students to be able to function in an information environment (Demo, 1986).

One definition of information literacy (Breivik, 1985:723) states: "Information literacy is the ability to access effectively and evaluate information for a given need." Christina A. Doyle (1992), in the *Final Report to the National Forum on Information Literacy*, carried this definition a step further. She added the phrase "to use" information as part of her definition of information literacy. She also enumerated certain characteristics in three categories that are necessary to become an information-literate person. First, an information-literate person *accesses information*:

- recognizes the need for information
- recognizes that accurate and complete information is the basis for intelligent decision making
- formulates questions based on information needs
- identifies potential sources of information
- develops successful search strategies
- accesses print and technology-based sources of information
- is a competent reader

Second, an information-literate person *evaluates information*:

- establishes authority
- determines accuracy and relevance
- recognizes point of view and opinion versus factual knowledge
- rejects inaccurate and misleading information
- creates new information to replace inaccurate or missing information as needed

Finally, an information-literate person *uses information*:

- organizes information for practical application
- integrates new information into an existing body of knowledge
- applies information in critical thinking and problem solving. (Doyle, 1992)

Information literacy, then, involves the ability to read and use information that is essential for everyday life. It also necessitates recognizing information needs and seeking information to make informed decisions. It requires the ability to manage complex amounts of information generated by computers and mass media, and to learn throughout life as societal and technical changes demand new skills and knowledge. Schools cannot be expected to supply students with all the facts they will need to know for a lifetime; they will need to "learn how to learn."

As we will see when we look next at some definitions of higher-order thinking, the skills necessary to become information literate and to think critically overlap.

CRITICAL THINKING DEFINED

How does information literacy relate to critical thinking? Bloom (1956) defines learning on a hierarchy or ladder of skills. Memorizing facts or understanding the meaning of material is at the low end of the cognitive ladder, requiring only lower-order skills. Critical or higher-order thinking requires the ability to analyze or separate material into its component parts, to synthesize information or put its parts together to create a new whole, and to evaluate or judge material for a given purpose. These tasks require the learner to go beyond what is written.

From Bloom's chart in Figure 2-1, we notice similarities between the skills identified by Doyle to be information literate and those at the higher end of Bloom's ladder of learning. The logical conclusion, then, is that to be information literate—to be prepared for the information society of the twenty-first century—students need to be able to think critically and creatively.

Studies by the National Assessment of Educational Progress in the late 1980s reported that students were showing little development of higher-level thinking skills, such as problem-solving strategies or critical-thinking skills. According to Smith (1987), the reason for these deficiencies was that many schools did not require students to think, to question, to weigh alternatives, to interpret inferences, or to identify propaganda. Many students today still fall short when asked to apply

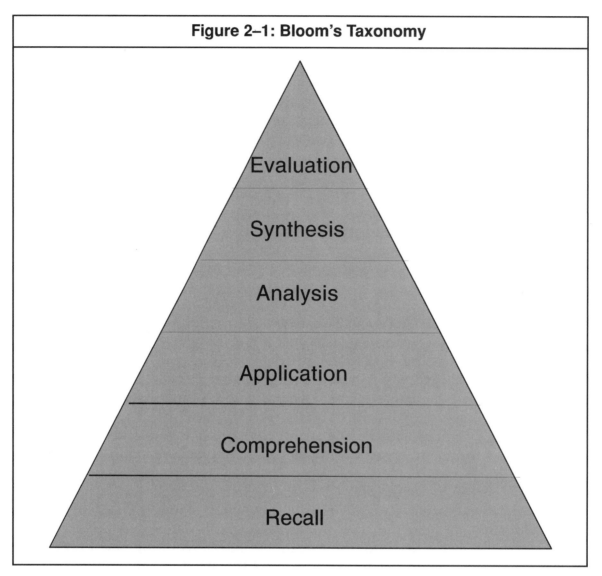

Figure 2–1: Bloom's Taxonomy

Evaluation

Synthesis

Analysis

Application

Comprehension

Recall

critical-thinking skills: A continued criticism by employers of graduating college seniors is their inability to think critically.

Information skills are the tools for inquiry. Smith (1987) also stated that instead of trying to learn facts and concepts that will last throughout their lives, students must learn how to find information, discern what is important in a body of facts, and restructure information relevant to a given situation. In an article in which she discusses inquiry, Sheingold (1987:81) says, "Inquiry is a complex process that includes formulating a problem or question, searching through and/or collecting information to address the problem or question, making sense of that information, and developing an understanding of, point of view about, or 'answer' to the question." As we will see when we look at the critical-thinking models in this chapter, using search technologies has also opened up new possibilities for teaching inquiry.

Library media specialists consistently teach the following critical-thinking skills in their instructional programs:

- distinguishing between verifiable facts and value claims
- determining the reliability of a source
- determining the factual accuracy of a statement
- distinguishing relevant from irrelevant information, claims, or reasons
- detecting bias
- identifying unstated assumptions
- recognizing logical inconsistencies or fallacies in a line of reasoning
- distinguishing between warranted and unwarranted claims
- determining the strength of an argument (Beyer, 1985: 270–276)

These skills can be taught at all levels of schooling. Bellanca (Costa, 1985) suggests that teachers introduce primary students to the following skills at a concrete level and middle- and high-school students at a more abstract level: observing, comparing, naming, sequencing, contrasting, predicting, patterning, grouping, and goal setting.

As proposed by *Information Power* (AASL/AECT, 1988) in its guidelines for school library media programs, now is the ideal time for library media specialists to partner with classroom teachers to design instruction together that merges these competencies with the subject matter. Moreover, since much of a school's technology is now located in media centers, incorporating the Internet into classroom lessons is a logical extension to the current resources in the library.

THE PROCESS
The process of gathering and applying information to an issue or problem has several stages that occur over time. These are conceptual processes in which questions change and evolve as new information is collected and considered. Kuhlthau (1987) proposes a six-stage model of the information search process that identifies strategies and thinking necessary to do a productive search:

1. initiating a research assignment
2. selecting a topic
3. exploring information
4. forming a focus
5. collecting information
6. preparing to present

Teachers must guide students at each step of the search process. Students also need to reflect on the process, in addition to the content, so as to internalize the stages and transfer the skills they learn to other research activities.

CRITICAL-THINKING MODELS
As we prepare lessons, we look for ways to challenge students to think more critically, yet it is not clear how this is best accomplished. Do we use a curriculum package, or integrate critical thinking within the ongoing curriculum? If we choose to integrate, how do we do it?

The Internet with its interactivity and multimedia gives students problem-solving capabilities that are much closer to the kinds of situations they will encounter in the "real" world. Using the Internet and its resources to help develop critical-thinking skills, students are exposed to a rich curriculum that prepares them better for the complexities of the world ahead. Online technology, requiring search and retrieval and communication of ideas and viewpoints to others, motivates students, develops their deductive reasoning and critical thinking, and reinforces concepts and information within a particular discipline (Mendrinos, 1987).

In 1990, Nancy Lourié-Markowitz, a professor of education at San Jose State University, and I began to prepare a guide for teachers to demonstrate how to teach higher-order thinking skills through the use of online database searching. As part of the project, we designed a model incorporating three tiers that teachers could use to build increasingly higher levels of critical thinking (Crane and Lourié-Markowitz, 1994). This model was derived after using database searching with elementary, middle-, and high-school students. We decided to use online search technology for several reasons. First, it provided a catalyst to help redesign the materials used for, and the delivery of, curriculum content. Online searching also familiarized students with strategies for retrieving information, and it involved problem-solving activities that promote higher-order thinking. Last, it supported educational goals of the state frameworks that mandate the teaching of critical-thinking and technology skills as part of the curriculum.

For students to search effectively through online databases, CD-ROMs, the card or online catalog, and the Internet, they must be able to identify keywords that will access subjects of interest. I have adapted the Crane-Lourié-Markowitz model to teach searching on the World Wide Web. The step-by-step process outlined in the model provides activities to help students prepare to search the Web. The three levels are described below, along with the critical thinking that takes place. Part 2 of this chapter will present two sample lessons to illustrate Level 1 for elementary students and Level 3 for a secondary class.

MODEL DESCRIPTIONS

The three levels in the model take students through the steps needed to find answers to a question, to solve a problem, or to resolve an issue. The activities at each level become more complex, requiring higher levels of critical thinking and less help from the teacher. Level 1 focuses on a specific question created by the teacher, Level 2 requires students to make sense of a stated problem, and Level 3 compels students to define their own information need. Included at each level is a brief description of the critical-thinking skills developed. Depending on the skills of their students, teachers may skip one or more levels.

Curriculum Goals

At each level of the model, students practice critical thinking and use of technology, and they also engage in activities that meet goals stated in curriculum guides and state-mandated frameworks. For example, California frameworks identify the following goals:

- *History-Social Sciences Framework* (CSDE, 1988)
  — Define and clarify problems.
  — Judge information related to problems.
  — Recognize the adequacy of data.
  — Draw conclusions.
- *Science Framework* (CSDE, 1987)
  — Reinforce and apply basic skills of organizing, relating, comparing, and inferring in the science classroom.
- *English-Language Arts Framework* (CSDE, 1987):
  — Stimulate the development of higher-level thinking such as analysis, synthesis, and evaluation through activities that extend content and meaning.
  — Extend experiences into research activities in different classes, using source materials.

By creating lessons that meet these goals, teachers and media specialists will be teaching critical-thinking skills and enhancing information literacy. The model that follows helps in this process.

Level 1: Analyzing a Search Question

At Level 1, teachers provide a specific search question for the class to research. Some examples of structured search questions or statements might be: In what state is the panther an endangered species? What methods are used to protect the panther from extinction? How are dogs used to fight against the smuggling of illegal drugs? Find information about the Mir Space Station. What are the pros and cons to animal research? These questions are specific enough to provide students with possible keywords to find information on the topic. This is the easiest level, because the teacher does some of the student's thinking by formulating the search question. Providing a specific question also prevents a common mistake in searching—that of attacking topics that are too broad.

STEP 1: IDENTIFYING KEYWORDS

Although the teacher plays the primary role in the thinking process at Level 1, students still have to use higher-order thinking in their search planning. They must analyze the question and break it down into appropriate keywords. For example, if we analyze the search question, "How are dogs used to fight against the smuggling of illegal drugs?" into possible keywords, we arrive at key terms, such as DOGS, SMUGGLING, and ILLEGAL DRUGS. We can also add synonyms like COCAINE and HEROIN to the major keyword ILLEGAL DRUGS to expand the amount of information we retrieve.

Teachers may also want to have students analyze words to look for the roots and other forms of the words to use in the search. Depending on the search engine used, students may use a wildcard character at the end of the root of a word to locate all variations of a word like SMUGGLING. This helps children see word stems and suffixes.

For example, using the AltaVista search engine, SMUGGL* retrieves SMUG-GLING, SMUGGLED, SMUGGLES, and SMUGGLE. Identifying roots of words and keywords in a sentence is a simple first step, but it requires analysis—Level 3 of Bloom's taxonomy.

STEP 2: UNDERSTANDING BOOLEAN OPERATORS

Because searching the Web may require using more than one keyword, students need to be exposed to the concept of Boolean or logical operators, often called Boolean operators, as part of Level 1. The operators show relationships between search terms. For example, the "OR" operator connects similar words that express the same concept, such as FRUIT OR CHERRIES OR APPLES. The more synonyms used in a search strategy, the broader the search retrieval will be. Using the OR connector is quite useful when searching online databases or even when using a CD-ROM; however, a search on the Internet often retrieves thousands of pages, so it may not be necessary to broaden the Internet search. (*Note:* Different Internet search engines may use special symbols to represent the OR connector. For example, AltaVista uses "+" to connect synonyms. It is wise to familiarize students with the search symbols for one or two search engines and with the HELP screens provided at Websites, such as Yahoo! or AltaVista. Appendix A provides a brief lesson on using search engines and the online course "Using Search Engines Effectively" at Website *www.ala.org/ ICONN* provides a good discussion of the differences among search engines.)

The logical operator "AND" combines different ideas, for example, VIDEO GAMES AND CHILDREN. ANDing together many terms usually retrieves less information, but the data may be more relevant because the search is more focused. Again, the search engine will determine what symbol or word is used to create these relationships.

As students decide upon search terms, they must understand the relationships the concepts have to each other. Perceptually, they will be categorizing and associating similar and different concepts as they determine appropriate terms. Thus, decision making is necessary during the entire search planning process. The search worksheets in Part 2 of this chapter illustrate these concepts.

STEP 3: CHECKING THE WEBSITES

Before students take the next step and logon to the Web, it is always a good idea for teachers to review sites that students will visit. As we learned in Chapter 1, there is no "Internet cop" on the Web to prevent students from visiting inappropriate sites. At Level 1, it is best for teachers to supply specific URLs to Web pages that students will access. For example, in a social studies class I observed in which students were studying current events, they wanted current information on Kosovo to find out if there was going to be a resolution to the conflict. The teacher chose a news Website at *www.cnn.com* to have students see what CNN news had to say about the situation. Since CNN updates its Website frequently, students were able to see the most current news.

Another possibility is to have students pick from several URLs the teacher has previewed. Then, as part of the assignment students can write a journal response reflecting on the factors that made them choose a particular site—again, involving decision-making and reflective skills. Students can also practice inputting search terms and retrieving information using a CD-ROM before accessing information online with the Internet. This process will familiarize students with creating search strategies.

For younger children who have limited typing skills, teachers can even download information from specific sites so that it will appear as if the students are actually seeing the information online. I observed fourth graders who were studying planets in a science class click pictures of the planets on a Web page created by the teacher to see changing images of Mars, Venus, and Saturn.

STEP 4: QUESTIONING THE SEARCH RESULTS

Critical thinking does not stop when students logon to the Web. As their search terms retrieve resulting "hits," or data containing their keywords, they must look at the information to see if it is relevant and whether it is sufficient to answer the search question. Finally, once they logoff, they must evaluate what they have retrieved and question the results. They may also need to synthesize information from several sources to answer the question. For example, in an ESL class, I watched one teacher conduct an effective cooperative learning activity. She asked each student in a group to read one paragraph of the downloaded information about the characteristics of the spotted owl. Next, each student contributed one characteristic to a group drawing of the owl. The group then presented the information and their picture to the rest of the class.

At Level 1, students have begun the journey toward information literacy. They can recognize keywords necessary to retrieve information, and can also use the material to solve problems and apply it to other tasks. Critical thinking has begun.

Level 2: Defining and Clarifying a Problem

When students are able to complete the activities at Level 1, they are ready for tasks to build more complex thinking. Level 2 challenges students to function at a more abstract level of analysis, synthesis, and evaluation—the high end of Bloom's hierarchy. At Level 2, the teacher poses a problem for students in any subject area, be it for a class in economics, advanced biology, health, English, or world history—the need for information is in all. For example, problems could be structured about how a parents' group formed by Tipper Gore is going to control the content of popular music, or how local officials will solve a transportation problem in San Francisco.

STEP 1: ANALYZING THE PROBLEM

The problems can be as complex as the level of critical thinking possessed by the students engaged in the task. Each problem may require that students answer more than one question and perform more than one Web search; it may also involve other information resources. Since no specific question is stated, students have to analyze the information and clarify and define key points to create their own search questions.

In an English composition class I visited in San Francisco, the teacher gave students the following scenario: In the 1989 Loma Prieta earthquake, the Embarcadero Freeway, a major artery for commuters into San Francisco, collapsed. The freeway was closed, causing traffic congestion, as well as making Chinatown less accessible to tourists. Many groups in the city—the City Council, Chinatown merchants, and commuters—had a stake in the outcome. What should have been done?

In groups, they read the scenario and brainstormed key concepts. One group identified EMBARCADERO FREEWAY, ADVANTAGES, and DEMOLITION as its main search terms. Another group agreed on EMBARCADERO FREEWAY, DEMOLITION, and CHINATOWN. Each group then wrote several search questions: What effects will the demolition of the Embarcadero Freeway have on Chinatown? What are the advantages to demolishing the Embarcadero Freeway? How will Chinatown merchants be affected by the demolition of the Embarcadero Freeway? Skills learned at Level 1, such as choosing keywords, root words, and Boolean connectors, were reinforced at Level 2.

STEP 2: GATHERING INFORMATION

At Level 2, students have to find more than a simple fact; they must look at a problem or issue from many perspectives. For the freeway problem, students attended meetings of the City Council and talked to Chinese merchants from Chinatown. They also chose to explore several print sources, such as the opinion pages of the San Francisco *Chronicle* to see if writers expressed different viewpoints; and they searched the Web to see if they could find how other cities had solved similar transportation issues.

STEP 3: USING THE INFORMATION

Each group researched one viewpoint—the City Council, the Chinese merchants, and the commuters to San Francisco. As a culminating activity, they conducted a debate to try to convince the City Transportation Committee to accept the solution that would benefit their individual groups the most.

In this English class, each group of students gathered information from a variety of sources, evaluated all data to determine what best supported their group's goal, and synthesized it to use in the debate. This task required more abstract thinking and the ability to solve a problem by applying the information retrieved.

At Level 2, students start by analyzing a scenario to determine their information needs. They then used evaluation and synthesis to reach a conclusion, the two highest critical-thinking skills from Bloom's taxonomy.

Level 3: Focusing an Information Need

After mastering skills at Levels 1 and 2, students are prepared to explore their own needs for information, with the teacher acting as facilitator rather than director. Their needs may develop from a topic they are studying in a subject area, such as AIDS or biomedical ethics. Such broad subjects, however, result in thousands of Web pages if they search the Web for information. Students must narrow their thinking and focus on the specific information they want to know about the topic. For instance, AIDS might be narrowed to "treatment for AIDS" or biomedical ethics might be refined to "ethics of human cloning," or even further to "pros and cons of cloning a sheep." Unlike activities at Levels 1 and 2, where the teacher formulated all or part of the search questions, at Level 3 students take a broad topic and complete the task of focusing their search questions on their own. To achieve this level of specificity takes much practice.

STEP 1: WRITING INFORMATION QUESTIONS

At Level 3, students first formulate search questions on the general topic they want to research. This may require brainstorming a list of possible ideas about the question, identifying concepts to represent the ideas, and categorizing the words into manageable information questions. For example, a class studying Native Americans may research different ideas about one tribe of Native Americans and refine the search further to their medicine, history, or art. Or a class studying contemporary social issues might want to search several issues, such as abortion, homelessness, and video violence. Creating specific questions is the most time-consuming part of the process and requires teachers to monitor the search questions students write to make sure they are focused narrowly enough. At this stage, students are analyzing a general concept to categorize it into different ideas; then they define each idea in a search question. This process will be described in more detail in Lesson 2 in Part 2 of this chapter.

STEP 2: CHOOSING THE SEARCH TERMINOLOGY

The skills students have mastered at Levels 1 and 2 are once again put into practice to complete their Web searches at Level 3. By the time students reach Level 3, they should be able to choose keywords and Boolean connectors easily.

STEP 3: USING THE INFORMATION

At Level 3, students are likely to have gathered information from many sources. The task of synthesizing it into a coherent product will require that students evaluate the data for bias, determine whether the sources are credible, see how timely the information is, and contrast different viewpoints. They will also have to form their own opinions on an issue based on the information they retrieve.

STEP 4: REFLECTING ON THE PROCESS

At Level 3, students should also be capable of reflecting on the process they have used to obtain their information. Teachers will want to ask questions so students can understand the steps they followed: Which keywords worked; which ones didn't? Why? What Websites provided the best results? Were the most helpful sites of a particular type—organizational, educational, commercial, school sites? What search engine worked best for you and why? What would you do differently in your searching the next time? What advice would you give to students who have not searched the Web?

According to Parker, McDaniel, and Valencia (1991), this metacognitive reflection, where students reflect on their own thinking processes, encourages students to go beyond the search tasks to analyze and evaluate their search decisions. Once they have achieved these aims, students are employing critical-thinking skills at a more abstract level and achieving a higher degree of information literacy.

SUMMARY

In Part 1, we defined the concepts of information literacy and critical thinking, using Bloom's hierarchy. We discussed a three-level model for building critical thinking and enhancing information literacy using the World Wide Web. We identified the critical thinking that occurs at each level in the model. Figure 2-2 compares Bloom's hierarchy with the three-level model for critical thinking. Now, it is time to turn to implementing the theory.

PART 2: PRACTICAL APPLICATIONS

The model lessons in this chapter contain the teacher's preplanning; the body of the lesson, including a series of activities; sample Websites focused on the theme; evaluation; and follow-up. Teachers will get the most out of the models by envisioning their own students and curriculum and how the material can be adapted with their content to fit particular students in their classes. Because it is also important to become familiar with Websites on the Internet, a number of sites for educators to explore are included as part of the plans. Using the bookmark feature on the Web browser to mark sites of interest will help educators identify these sites for future use.

The two lesson plans that follow are constructed to help students prepare for "surfing" the Web, while at the same time building critical thinking. Many of the activities in both lessons can be performed offline to help students understand the process they will go through before they access the Web. Lesson 1 is designed as a Treasure Hunt to be used with students in grades 4–6. The activities are based on Level 1 of the critical-thinking model discussed in Part 1 of this chapter. Lesson 2 on Animal Rights is constructed at a secondary level and requires more complex, abstract thinking. Activities in Lesson 2 are based on Level 3 of the critical-thinking model. The steps for Lessons 1 and 2 follow the curriculum model presented in Chapter 1, Part 2:

1. Look at national standards and state frameworks.
2. Write the lesson goals and objectives.
3. Gather the resources.
4. Create the instruction.
5. Evaluate the results.

Figure 2–2: Bloom's Taxonomy and Levels of Critical Thinking

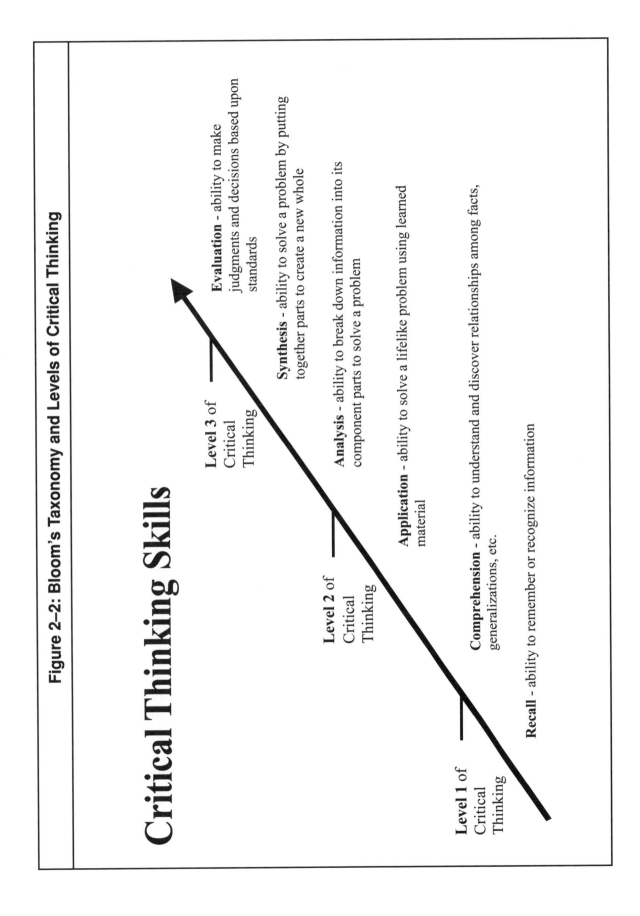

Critical Thinking Skills

Level 3 of Critical Thinking

Evaluation - ability to make judgments and decisions based upon standards

Synthesis - ability to solve a problem by putting together parts to create a new whole

Analysis - ability to break down information into its component parts to solve a problem

Level 2 of Critical Thinking

Application - ability to solve a lifelike problem using learned material

Comprehension - ability to understand and discover relationships among facts, generalizations, etc.

Recall - ability to remember or recognize information

Level 1 of Critical Thinking

LESSON 1 (ELEMENTARY LEVEL): THE TREASURE HUNT

A Treasure Hunt is a good activity to get students familiar with information on the World Wide Web and how to search for it. A Treasure Hunt can also be adapted and refocused with little modification for students in any classroom at any age level. The "hunt" can be for nonrelated topics, it can be used to develop a solid knowledge on one subject, or it can provide enrichment opportunities to enhance a topic that students have been studying. A Treasure Hunt makes use of the myriad of resources on the Web that take students beyond the classroom door and provide information that would take a teacher years to accumulate. A Website at *www.cs.rice.edu/~sboone/ Lessons/Titles/hunt/homebse.html* provides more information on creating a Treasure Hunt.

The Treasure Hunt introduces elementary-age children to a variety of Websites on multiple subjects. Students can then transfer understanding of searching the Web to an in-depth project, such as a unit on native peoples, endangered species, or one that fits other curriculum needs. It is especially important that elementary students have a Web experience that is structured. All sites that students visit should be ones that you have already explored. It is also a good idea, if possible, to have a mechanism in place for monitoring the sites students visit on the Web.

Before you begin to construct the Treasure Hunt, however, consider the best teaching techniques to use with young children—how do they learn best? Research by Edwards and Springate (1995) indicates that:

- Young children are developmentally capable of classroom experiences that call for and practice higher-level thinking skills, including analysis (breaking down material into component parts to understand the structure or seeing similarities and differences); synthesis (putting parts together to form a new whole, rearranging, and reorganizing); and evaluation (judging the value of material based on definite criteria).
- Young children want and need to express ideas and messages through many, different, expressive avenues and symbolic media. They need increasing competence and integration across formats, including words, gestures, drawing, paintings, sculpture, construction, music, dramatic play, movement, and dance. Through sharing and understanding others' perspectives, they move to new levels of awareness. Teachers act as guides.
- Young children learn through meaningful activities in which different subject areas are integrated. Such activities provide opportunities to teach across the curriculum and assist children in seeing the interrelationship of things they are learning.
- Young children benefit from in-depth exploration and long-term, open-ended projects. Adults can act as resource persons, guides, problem posers, and partners to the children in the process of discovery and investigation.

Based on these points, this lesson will (1) include activities to build critical thinking, (2) use varied activities and require different outcomes, and (3) integrate more than one subject area. This lesson provides a concrete foundation for later using the World Wide Web as a research tool with long-term, open-ended projects.

The activities in Lesson 1 are at a beginning level of complexity. Each activity can be completed in about one-half hour. The questions, listed under Step 2: Resources, are intended as examples to generate an information need in the student. They encompass social studies and science topics and have been chosen to stimulate students' interest in research while still relating to classroom content. You can use these or create your own questions.

STEP 1: LOOK AT NATIONAL STANDARDS AND STATE FRAMEWORKS

Goal 3 of the National Education Goals Report (National Education Goals Panel, 1991) stipulated that by the year 2000, American students would leave grades 4, 8, and 12 having demonstrated competency over challenging subject matter in English, mathematics, science, history, and geography. Moreover, every school in America was to ensure that all students learn to use their minds well, so that they may be prepared for responsible citizenship, further learning, and productive employment in our modern economy. This goal formed the basis for students "learning how to learn." Students need to learn how to process information as part of problem solving and critical thinking. To learn these skills requires an active learning environment, and the inquiry approach is basic to active learning.

Likewise, state frameworks indicate a need to build critical-thinking skills and information literacy. For example, the California science framework (CSDE, 1987) states that students in grades 4–6 are expected to master competencies such as organizing data they have gathered, classifying information, analyzing, and synthesizing. A characteristic of the History–Social Sciences Framework in California (CSDE, 1988:7) is to "include critical-thinking skills at every grade level." In other words, students should be able to define and clarify problems, judge information related to a problem, and draw conclusions. The Oklahoma State Department of Education (1986) in its *Suggested Learning Outcomes for Language Arts, Grades 4–6*, states that students will listen critically to interpret, integrate, and evaluate.

It is clear that building critical-thinking skills is considered important at both the national and state levels. Thus, continuing to teach activities that build these skills is crucial to lifelong learning. We have included these skills in the goals and objectives of this lesson where possible.

STEP 2: WRITE THE LESSON GOAL AND OBJECTIVES

Writing goals and objectives for any lesson is important to keep you and your students on track and to relate to the national, state, and district curriculum goals. This lesson enhances and promotes critical-thinking skills, and, at the same time, provides students with opportunities to use Internet technology. It also allows students to learn to work together to accomplish a task with all the inherent decision making that is involved in teamwork. Learning tasks are sequenced so that each task builds on the previous one. Thus, by performing the activities at Level 1, students will be ready to move to more abstract tasks like the ones at Levels 2 and 3, as discussed in Part 1.

Lesson Goals

The goal for this lesson is for students:

- to build critical-thinking skills of analysis, synthesis, and evaluation by planning, performing, and reflecting on Web searches.

Lesson Objectives

More specifically, after completing the activities in this lesson, students will be able to:

- identify keywords based on specific topics
- complete planning worksheets for Web searches
- include Boolean operators when necessary
- search for information from at least one Website
- write journal entries reflecting on the Web searches.

STEP 3: GATHER THE RESOURCES

The Treasure Hunt will help students become familiar with the comprehensiveness of the Web. In the elementary grades, you may first need to develop students' understanding of information and information sources. In a fourth grade class, Dr. Markowitz and I had children work in pairs to list the information they wanted and sources where they might find it. The Internet surfaced as one of the sources they named. This task started students thinking about the concept of information.

You should complete the following tasks to focus the Treasure Hunt and prepare students for less structured searching in the future.

1. Review your curriculum for the year and determine the unit, lesson, or theme that can be enriched by using Web resources.
2. Seek out at least ten sites for students to visit; write down the URLs in your Internet notebook in a category you have named for this activity (see Figure 1-3 for a sample Internet notebook page). Select Websites that are appropriate for your students only. At this level, you should view all sites to which you send students. Don't forget to bookmark them with your Web browser. Use the URLs listed below, which encompass cross-disciplinary topics, or create your own list.
3. Write out one or two questions that can be answered by viewing each Website. Make sure the questions contain at least one keyword relevant to the topic, so students can recognize a general type of information contained at that Website. For example, two keywords in the question, "During the Chicago fire . . . effort? are CHICAGO and FIRE. Students should be able to recognize the appropriate URL for this topic because it contains those keywords. You will notice that some questions are more difficult, requiring children to make connections. In the question about clouds, children will have to decide that clouds relate to the word WEATHER to select the appropriate URL.

- *www.sciam.com/exhibit/033197halebopp/033197/bopp.html*—Who was the first person to spot the Hale-Bopp comet?
- *www.tat.or.th*—How old is the country of Thailand? Describe a Buddhist temple.
- *www.chicagohs.org/fire*—During the Chicago fire, which mayor led the rescue effort?
- *http://sln.fi.edu/franklin/rotten.html*—In what year was Benjamin Franklin born?
- *www.audionet.com/speeches*—When did Martin Luther King deliver his "I Have A Dream" speech?
- *www.itdc.sbcss.k12.ca.us/curriculum/weather.html*—What are the names of clouds? Give one fact about each type of cloud.
- *www.jinjapan.org/kidsweb/japan/q-a.html*—What are the most popular dishes among Japanese children?
- *www.seaworld.org/animal?5Fbytes/tigerab.html*—What are two important facts about Bengal tigers?
- *www.pmel.noaa.gov/toga-tao/el-nino*—What is El Niño?
- *http://seds.lpl.arizona.edu/nineplanets/nineplanets/nineplanets.html*—What are the names of two satellites orbiting Mars? Name the other planets. How many more satellites does Saturn have than the planet Earth?

STEP 4: CREATE THE INSTRUCTION

Activity 1: Planning the Search

Thinking Skills: To complete Activity 1, students will work in pairs. Each pair must select and analyze a search question, breaking it down into its component parts or keywords. The twosome will also use negotiating skills as they decide on the question to research. Finally, they must use deduction to determine which URL will retrieve the information they need to answer the question. Here is the sequence to follow:

1. Depending on the number of students in the class, place students in groups of two or three. Each group will answer one question. Before going online, each pair will create one search worksheet.
2. Have each pair write the question, main keywords, synonyms, and URL on their worksheet. Using an overhead, model the task by filling out a worksheet completely using a sample question before students begin the task.
3. Write the search question on the topic line.
   - Ask students to underline words in the question that might retrieve information on the subject. (Figure 2-3 illustrates planning for a MARS search.) Have students write the word PLANET under Concept 1. This process prepares students for retrieving a topic when the URL is not given to them, as is illustrated in the Level 3 lesson that follows.
   - Have students brainstorm any other synonyms for, or other forms of, the

Figure 2–3: Mars Search Worksheet

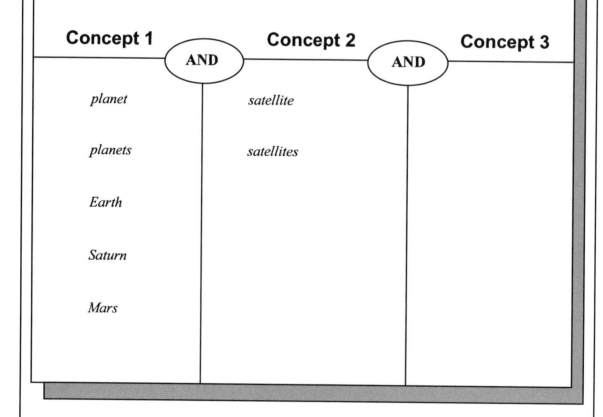

Search Planning Worksheet

Topic: What are the names of two SATELLITES orbiting the planet MARS? Name the other PLANETS. How many more satellites does Saturn have than the planet Earth?

URL: **www.nasm.edu/ceps/**

Concept 1	AND	Concept 2	AND	Concept 3
planet		*satellite*		
planets		*satellites*		
Earth				
Saturn				
Mars				

keyword PLANET and write them on the worksheet. They might choose: PLANETS, SATURN, EARTH, JUPITER, and MARS. When they are actually using keywords at Levels 2 and 3 to search the Internet, having synonyms may produce information when the main keyword is too broad or narrow.

4. Ask pairs to identify a second concept like SATELLITE or SATELLITES.
   - Ask students to draw Venn diagrams showing the relationship of their search terms to each other. Have each pair discuss the following: Is there a broader category that includes the topic (for example, SOLAR SYSTEM)? Is there a narrower aspect to describe the topic (for example, LIFE ON MARS)? Which keywords are synonyms? Which words are different concepts? Discuss the idea of broadening and narrowing a search and which Boolean operator they should use for each. See Figure 2-4 for an example of a Venn Diagram to narrow a search. Emphasize on the worksheet that the Boolean operator "AND" connects different concepts to narrow a search.
   - Have each pair compare the list of URLs to the keywords they have chosen, and choose the URLs that best describe their topics. For this topic, the URL is *http://seds.lpl.arizona/edu/nineplanets/nineplanets/nineplanets.html*

Activity 2: Retrieving the Information

Thinking Skills: Students must comprehend the material they view online to make sure it answers the question. They also need to evaluate what they see for its relevance to the topic. You will:

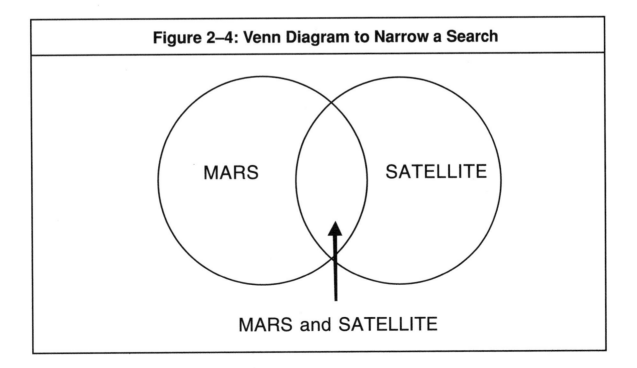

Figure 2–4: Venn Diagram to Narrow a Search

MARS

SATELLITE

MARS and SATELLITE

1. Have students type the specific URLs in the Web browser. If you have the capability, list and link the URLs to the appropriate Websites in advance so students can just click on the appropriate links from a list of URLs. This may be especially helpful for the lower elementary grades.
2. Tell students that they should look for the answers to their questions on the Website they have chosen and write the answers on their worksheets.

Activity 3: Following up on the Search

Thinking Skills: Students will need to evaluate the information they read online to determine if it answers their questions. They should also start reflecting on the Web experience in their journal writing. You will:

1. Have each group share its results with the class, using words and pictures. For instance, for the "planet" question, students can draw a picture of the solar system, labeling each planet, and showing the satellites around Mars, Saturn, and Earth.
2. Have students reflect on their Web experience by writing journal entries. They should include answers to the following questions: What was the hardest part of answering the question? What do you think helped you most to answer the question? What did you learn that will help you work more effectively on the next Web search? What additional fact did you learn from the Website you visited that you did not know before?
3. For a final enrichment activity, write out one question that synthesizes all of the information your class has retrieved. Have students create a collage on butcher paper that represents the most important part of each group's work.

STEP 5: EVALUATE THE RESULTS

An important part of any lesson is for the teacher to evaluate the results. There are three parts involved in evaluating this Web-based lesson: (1) content—did students find the answer to the question(s) they were asked; (2) process—were students able to complete the worksheet, logon, and logoff with Web; and (3) teamwork—could students work together, sharing and equally contributing to complete the tasks.

Evaluation for Lesson 1 involves the following aspects:

- Students must answer their questions and create products of words and pictures to present to the class.
- Students must complete Web search worksheets together, including search questions, URLs, main keywords, and synonyms, if needed.
- You will read and comment on reflective journal entries following the presentations.
- Through your observation, assess the students on how well they worked together and contributed to the end products. You might also want students to do their own self-evaluations on their Web experiences (see Figure 2-5). (Chapter 5 discusses the self-evaluation worksheet in more detail.)

Figure 2–5: Group Self-Evaluation Questionnaire

Group Name: _____   Date: _____

Names of people in the group:

_____   _____

_____   _____

_____   _____

_____

1. List the steps you followed in planning and completing your project.

2. List the contributions made by each member of the group:

    <u>Name</u>   <u>Contribution</u>

    _____   _____

    _____   _____

    _____   _____

3. Identify problems the group had and how the group solved its problems.

    _____

    _____

    _____

4. What changes would you make if you were to do this project again?

    _____

    _____

5. What did you learn from this project?

    _____

After completing this lesson, students in grades 4–6 will have the basis for moving to a more complex Web search requiring more sophisticated thinking skills. Lesson 2 implements a Level 3 model for secondary students in an English composition class.

LESSON 2 (SECONDARY LEVEL): ANIMAL RIGHTS

Once students have completed tasks at Level 1 and/or 2, they should be ready to explore their own needs for information. Students in the elementary grades may be ready to research only simple topics; however, secondary students will certainly need to be able to conduct in-depth projects on their own that will be required of them.

Every day, teachers are confronted by one of the most common problems when students begin conducting research: topics that are too broad. Students do not know just how much information is available on a topic, and they may not have thought about what they want to find out—their information need. A student in one social studies class I observed, for example, wanted to find information about Japan. He went to the library and asked the media specialist if he could go online to find the information. When the student used the search engine and typed in the word JAPAN, he retrieved over 25,000 Website entries, ranging from Japanese food to Japanese poetry. Overwhelmed, the student realized that he needed to narrow his topic. To achieve a high level of specificity requires careful preplanning before beginning the actual Web search.

Lesson 2 provides a plan to take students through the critical thinking necessary to work at Level 3: focusing an information need. At this level, students must decide on problems. The teacher acts more as a facilitator to the learning process, and students must create and focus search questions themselves. This is not an easy task and takes higher levels of critical thinking. I base Lesson 2 on a high-school English class I observed struggling with this process.

STEP 1: LOOK AT THE NATIONAL STANDARDS AND STATE FRAMEWORKS

The California Science Framework (1987) recognizes that science education benefits from repetition of skills at higher cognitive levels. The science curriculum makes use of spiraling, which requires continuous review and progression of knowledge and experiences over different grade levels. Lesson 2 builds on work students would have completed at Levels 1 and 2. The History–Social Sciences Framework (CSDE, 1988) supports the study and discussion of principles embodied in the U.S. Bill of Rights and states that students are expected to master competencies, such as defining and clarifying problems, judging information related to a problem, solving problems, and drawing conclusions. Lesson 2 requires students to understand and form opinions about ideas in the U.S. Bill of Rights and to relate them to other issues. This cross-curricular lesson is also a way for students to see connections between concepts in different subject areas as mandated in all the Frameworks.

STEP 2: WRITE THE LESSON GOALS AND OBJECTIVES

At Level 3 of the critical-thinking model, students must decide on what they want to research. Problems may range from abortion to gangs to violence on television. Our goal in this lesson is the same as in Lesson 1, but it uses different activities, and students must think more abstractly to solve their problems.

Lesson Goal
To build critical-thinking skills of analysis, synthesis, and evaluation by planning, performing, and reflecting on Web searches.

Lesson Objectives
After completing the activities in Lesson 2, students will be able to:

- brainstorm to focus topics
- write manageable search questions
- analyze questions by identifying keywords
- complete planning worksheets for Web searches
- synthesize information from several Web sources
- draw conclusions about their topics based on the information retrieved
- write journal entries reflecting on their Web searches

STEP 3: GATHER THE RESOURCES
When students are looking for their own information, it is often difficult to control the sites they visit and the information they retrieve. Therefore, it is still a good idea to do some preliminary searching on their topics to offer as alternatives. By testing the subjects in advance, you can make sure that no undesirable sources immediately appear. Acting as facilitator during the lesson, you will need to be very alert as you move from one team of searchers to another to monitor students' search processes and the results they retrieve.

To begin the lesson, create a list of potentially controversial topics that coincide with subjects being studied in other curricular areas. The subjects should be broad enough so that students must determine a particular focus to research. The sample list in Table 2-1 suggests possible topics for different subject areas. The topics can also be part of one particular problem or issue being studied in a unit. The sample lesson that follows is based on a collaboration I observed between teachers in English and social studies. Their goal was to create integrated lessons. In social studies the class had just completed a lesson on the Bill of Rights, as part of a unit on Colonial Freedom. The English teacher decided to expand on the concept of freedom and have students do persuasive papers on the topic of animal rights.

STEP 4: CREATE THE INSTRUCTION
The instruction is divided into three activities: (1) focusing the problem, (2) retrieving information to solve the problem, and (3) following up the search. The topic for the class is Animal Rights. Students work in teams to investigate one aspect of this general issue. They must find all relevant information, develop positions supported by evidence, and write persuasive papers supporting their team positions. They should also refer to work that they have completed in social studies on the U.S. Bill of Rights.

Table 2-1: Research Topics	
Subject Areas	**Topics**
Composition	Abortion Drunk driving Violence in video games Gangs
Science	Animal rights Deforestation Global warming AIDS
Social Studies	Homelessness Human rights

Activity 1: Focusing the problem

Thinking Skills: At the beginning of Activity 1, students as a whole class will list and categorize ideas to determine or focus search topics. Then, in small groups, they will analyze their search questions to decide upon search terms. You will:

1. Have students brainstorm a list of all the possibilities for the topic of animal rights while one or two students write the ideas on the board.
2. Ask students to categorize the ideas using a cluster diagram (shown in Figure 2-6).
   - Note to the class that there are many potential topics identified as different strands of the cluster. For example, one topic might focus on rights for different kinds of animals, such as farm animals, lab animals, and animals killed by hunters. Another might explore legislation or court cases on animal rights.
   - Now, have students team up in groups of three or four. Ask each group to choose one of the threads of the subject and further develop it with another cluster. If a group has another choice, it should be cleared with the teacher first. Figure 2-7 illustrates a more narrowed focus to the topic of animal rights. This task also provides them with keywords and synonyms for the next part of the search process.
   - In groups, have students write at least one defined search statement or question on their search worksheets for the strands they have chosen. The following are possible topics for legislative issues: Do court cases prohibit animals from being used in research? What states have adopted animal rights legislation? What are the main components of the legislation? Is there any national legislation? What are the main issues covered? It may take more than one question to resolve the problem or to discuss them fully.

Figure 2–6: Animal Rights Cluster

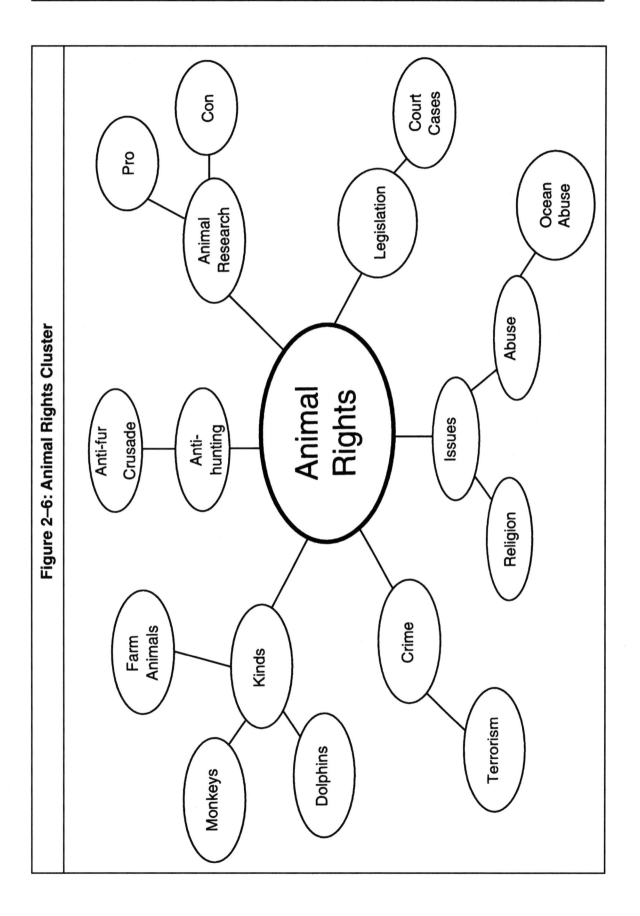

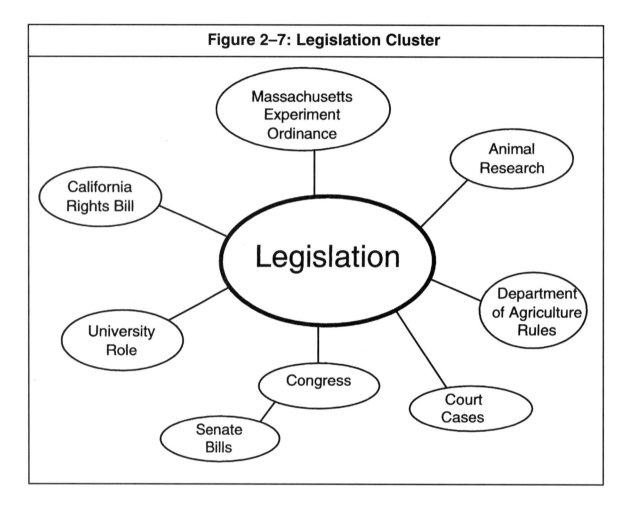

Figure 2–7: Legislation Cluster

- Ask students to talk together to determine what kinds of information they need.

Activity 2: Planning the Web Searches

Thinking Skills: To plan their worksheets, students must analyze the search questions by breaking them down into component parts. While they conduct their searches, they will need to evaluate the information they retrieve. They may also need to synthesize information from several sources.

Students need to determine in their groups who will be responsible for different phases of the research. As a sample, we will illustrate the research on the World Wide Web for the legislation group only.

- Have the legislation group complete the rest of the search worksheet putting keywords in the correct columns, as shown below. They must analyze the search statement and choose two or three terms that best describe the topic. They can also choose synonyms and variant forms of keywords for additional searches. Figure 2-8 illustrates a worksheet created by the group that researched legal implications of animal rights.

Figure 2–8: Legislation Search Worksheet

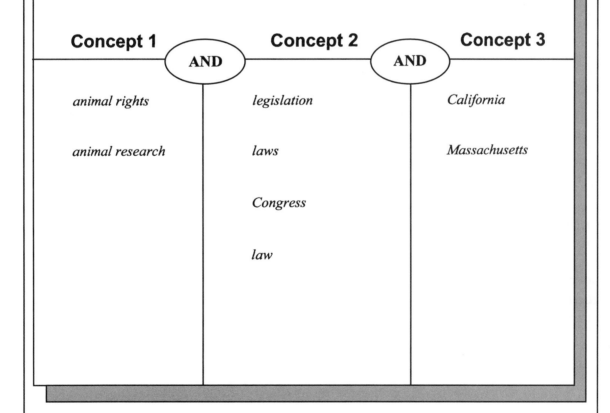

Search Planning Worksheet

Topic: What are some of the laws resulting from the controversy over animal rights?

URL: *www.animal-law.org/huntharass/index.html*

Concept 1		Concept 2		Concept 3
	AND		AND	
animal rights		*legislation*		*California*
animal research		*laws*		*Massachusetts*
		Congress		
		law		

- Give the group a choice of search engines such as *www.yahoo.com*, *www.hotbot.com*, or *www.altavista.com*. Remember the search syntax for wildcard symbols and Boolean connectors is dependent on the search engine.
- Have students review the retrieved information to check for bias, relevance, and currency. They may need to look at several sources and synthesize the information to solve the problems or resolve the issues. Students should use the information to make judgments on the quality of what they have seen, to decide what information to use, and to form their own opinions. During this part of the activity, teachers will need to monitor the Websites students access and make suggestions on search terms where necessary.

Activity 3: Using the Information

Thinking Skills: By writing persuasive papers, students must synthesize their arguments and use evidence to convince groups to commit to a plan of action. Their action plans require them to apply their knowledge and suggest specific steps needed to solve problems. You will:

- Have each group decide on (1) its position for the persuasive paper, (2) the intended audience, (3) the evidence they will use, including reconciling opposing opinions, and (4) a recommended plan of action. For example, the group working on legislation reviewed the following Websites, citing state and federal laws supporting animal rights:
  — *www.api4animals.org/LegislativeUpdates/Legislative Updates.htm*
  — *www.api4animals.org/StateLegMA.htm*, *http://animal-law.org*
  — *http://animalrights.tqn.com*
- For their action plans they wrote a bill requesting Congress to enact tougher laws protecting animals. The Website at *www.justiceforanimals.org* provided help in writing the legislation. Another group that researched the university's role identified why animals were important in university research and cited incidents of major medical breakthroughs as a result of animal research. Each group's goal was to convince opposing parties of the merit of its own position.

Activity 4: Following up for Enrichment

Thinking Skills: By completing any of the follow-up activities, students will use analysis to understand meanings of poems and apply the ideas they gain in writing their own poems. They can also analyze two U.S. Bill of Rights' documents to see similarities and differences, or they can apply their knowledge by helping to protect animal rights. Further enrichment activities for the Animal Rights topic include:

- Have students read from among the poems at Website *http://arrs.envirolink.org/ar-voices/poem.html*. These are poems by famous poets like Shelley, Byron, and Wordsworth. Have them discuss the meaning of the poems and the poets' positions on animal rights. Ask students to create their own poem to represent their points of view.

- Check Website *http://arrs.envirolink.org/Faqs+Ref/bill_of_rights.html* to see the animal bill of rights. Have students compare and contrast the animal bill of rights with the Bill of Rights from the U.S. Constitution.
- Check the site at *http://arrs.envirolink.org/gallery/gallery.html* to find links to photos, slides, and videos that might be useful to show how animals need protection. Make sure to view them first, as some may be too graphic for children.
- Ask students to identify ways they can help animals in their daily lives. Website *http://arrs.envirolink.org/Faqs+Ref* might help with some suggestions.

STEP 5: EVALUATE THE RESULTS

Evaluation for Lesson 2 should be based on:

- content. Papers contained at least three supporting arguments for each group's position. At least three different sources were used. The argument was logical and well supported. A call to action was included.
- process. At least two cluster diagrams and a search worksheet were completed by each group, including focused search statements so that key terms produced relevant searches.
- teamwork. You and each team assessed the work done by group members based on productivity and contribution to the final products (see Figure 2-5).
- reflection. In journal entries, students reflected on their thinking processes to focus topics, create search strategies, and use the results. Some questions you might want students to think about include: Did the clustering activity help you narrow the topic and write search questions? Why or why not? How did you determine which Websites to view? What could you tell from looking at different Websites about the publisher's background, point of view, education, and so on? What perspective did the author bring to the problem? What information was most influential in clarifying your own opinion on the subject? Why?

This lesson requires students to use all of the higher-level thinking skills in Bloom's taxonomy. By completing the activities, students have used the Internet as a tool to practice critical thinking.

TEACHER EXERCISES: NOW YOU TRY IT...

It is always a good idea to test an activity you will model for the class. Before going on to Chapter 3, try out some of the ideas from this chapter. Experiment with some of the activities below before you use the ideas in this chapter to improve critical thinking in your classroom.

1. Review the next unit you will be teaching. Identify keywords that will retrieve information on one or two of the topics. Use one of the search engines: AltaVista (*www.altavista.com*), Hotbot (*www.hotbot.com*), or Yahoo! (*www.yahoo.com*).

2. Write journal entries in your Internet notebooks that follow the process you used to find one of the topics for your unit. Include keywords used, information found, links used. Determine which search engine had the best K–12 information. Write down the subject classifications you used to focus on K–12 material.

3. Bookmark at least five to ten sites that will be useful in your next unit. Create a Treasure Hunt with at least five questions for groups of students in your class. Identify five URLs that will provide answers to the questions you created.

4. At the secondary level, select a general topic for which students will have to focus the subject into two or three search questions. Write a lesson plan that you would use to teach a "focusing" lesson.

5. Check your next unit and write ten questions requiring students to find information using Websites.

CONCLUSION

Progressing through the activities at Levels 1, 2, and 3 of the critical-thinking model required students to think at increasingly higher levels of complexity. At Level 1, as shown in Lesson 1, the teacher created the search questions. Students then analyzed the questions, identifying search terms for their Web searches. They also had to read and comprehend the information to answer the questions. At Level 3, shown in Lesson 2, students took a general subject and focused their thinking so they could formulate several search questions. They then structured the information to win over specific audiences to their points of view.

As students complete this series of activities, they will continue to develop critical-thinking skills necessary to deal with real-life situations, to resolve issues, or to answer questions in the future. Through online searching, students build their critical-thinking skills and become information literate.

Teachers learning how to incorporate this technology into the curriculum have also achieved three important goals: (1) they have built explicit instruction in critical thinking into the ongoing curriculum; (2) they have developed curriculum more relevant to the real world; and (3) they have provided students with the technological expertise critical to succeed in the twenty-first century.

REFERENCES

American Association of School Librarians and Association for Educational Communications and Technology. 1988. *Information Power: Guidelines for School Library Media Programs.* Chicago: American Association of School Librarians, and Washington, D.C.: Association for Educational Communications and Technology.

Beyer, Barry. K. 1985. "Critical Thinking: What Is It?" *Social Education* 49, No. 4 (April) 270–276.

Bloom, Benjamin S., ed. 1956. *Taxonomy of Educational Objectives Handbook 1: Cognitive Domains.* New York: David McKay.

Breivik, Patricia Senn. 1985. "Putting Libraries Back in the Information Society." *American Libraries* 16, No. 10 (November): 723.

California State Department of Education. 1987. *English–Language Arts Framework for California Public Schools: Kindergarten Through Grade Twelve.* Sacramento: California State Department of Education.

California State Department of Education. 1988. *History–Social Science Framework for California Public Schools, Kindergarten Through Grade Twelve.* Sacramento: California State Department of Education.

California State Department of Education. 1987. *Science Framework for California Public Schools, Kindergarten Through Grade Twelve.* Sacramento: California Department of Education.

Costa Arthur L., ed. 1985. *Developing Minds: A Resource Book for Teaching Thinking.* Alexandria, VA: Association for Supervision and Curriculum Development.

Crane, Beverley E., and Nancy Lourié-Markowitz. 1994. "A Model for Teaching Critical Thinking Through Online Searching." In *School Library Reference Services in the 90s,* edited by Carol Truett. Binghamton, NY: Haworth.

Demo, William. 1986. *The Idea of Information Literacy in the Age of High Tech.* Unpublished paper [ED 282 537].

Doyle, Christina A. 1992. *Final Report to the National Forum on Information Literacy.* Syracuse, NY: ERIC Clearinghouse on Information Resources.

Edwards, Carolyn P., and Kay Wright Springate. 1993. "Inviting Children into Project Work." *Dimensions of Early Childhood* 22, No. 1 (Fall): 9–12, 40.

Edwards, Carolyn P., and Kay W. Springate (1995). "The Lion Comes Out of the Stone: Helping Young Children Achieve Their Creative Potential." *Dimensions of Early Childhood* 23, No. 4 (Fall) 24–29.

Kuhlthau, Carol C. 1987. *Information Skills for an Information Society: A Review of Research.* Syracuse, NY: ERIC Clearinghouse of Information Resources.

Mendrinos, Roxanne Baxter. 1987. "The Educational Media Specialist: Training the Trainer." *Library Software Review* 6, No. 5 (Sept.–Oct.): 272–275.

Naisbitt, John. 1984. *Megatrends.* New York: Warner Books.

National Assessment of Education Progress. 1985. *The Reading Report Card: Progress Toward Excellence in Our Schools.* Princeton, NJ: Educational Testing Service.

National Education Goals Panel. 1991. *The National Education Goals Report: Executive Summary.* Washington, D.C.: U.S. Department of Education.

Oklahoma State Department of Education. 1985. *Suggested Learner Outcomes for Language Arts, Grades 9–12,* Oklahoma City: Oklahoma State Department of Education.

Parker, Walter C., J. McDaniel, and S. Valencia. 1991. "Helping Students Think About Public Issues: Instruction vs. Prompting." *Social Education* 41.

Sheingold, Karen. 1987. "Keeping Children's Knowledge Alive through Inquiry." *American Journal of Education* 15, No. 2 (Winter): 81.

Sheingold, Karen, and Martha Hadley. 1990. *Accomplished Teachers: Integrating Computers into Classroom Practice.* New York: Center for Technology in Education, Bank Street College.

Smith, Julia B. 1987. "Higher-Order Thinking Skills and Nonprint Media." *School Library Media Quarterly* 16, No. 1 (Fall): 38–42.

Toffler, Alvin. 1984. *The Third Wave.* New York: Bantam.

Section Two

HOW TO INTEGRATE THE INTERNET WITH DIFFERENT INSTRUCTIONAL STYLES

Chapter 3

INTEGRATING THE INTERNET INTO CROSS-CURRICULAR UNITS

PART 1: IDEAS AND INSIGHTS

OBJECTIVES OF THIS CHAPTER
Interdisciplinary teaching is becoming an increasing part of the curriculum. At the end of this chapter, educators will be able to:

- define integrated curriculum
- understand reasons for using an integrated curriculum
- define what is meant by the "project approach"
- list considerations when setting up project learning activities
- explain how the Internet enhances project learning
- build interdisciplinary units with Internet project components

INTRODUCTION
"Cross-curricular teaching," "interdisciplinary units," "integrated curriculum"—all have similar meanings: integrating subject areas so that concepts and skills are not taught in isolation from each other. For a number of years, educators within disciplines—such as social studies, as an example—have been struggling to integrate history course content with geography. Today, however, the trend is to reach out across the curriculum. From at least the 1980s, language arts educators have urged "writing across the curriculum," designed to practice writing skills in science, social studies, and other subject areas. The middle-school curricula in many schools have embraced an integrated language arts–social studies curriculum, in which social studies and language arts teachers team teach. The content may be focused on historical time periods, like the colonial, and incorporate literature, such as *The Witch of Black-*

bird Pond; or it may be taught using themes, such as "tolerance," the example we will review in Part 2 of this chapter.

Classrooms increasingly contain groups of children with a wide range of abilities—children with different ethnic backgrounds, including those who speak English as their second language; students who learn more easily in one mode than another; students who are gifted and need greater academic challenges than those with perceptual and learning disabilities. These next three chapters will explore some of the instructional methods that support an integrated curriculum: teaching to "learning styles" or "multiple intelligences" and using "cooperative learning." In this chapter, we will look more closely at the definition of integrated curricula, reasons to integrate, and creation of interdisciplinary units. Two units focused on the "project approach" will illustrate how concepts and skills from different subject areas can be combined into meaningful instruction that meets the goals and objectives of national and state frameworks.

WHAT IS CURRICULUM INTEGRATION?

Curriculum integration is a view of knowledge and an approach to curriculum that consciously applies knowledge, skills, and language from more than one discipline to examine a central theme, issue, problem, topic, or experience. For example, one of the units in this chapter looks at the issue of book banning, censorship, and freedom of speech. Although the lesson is focused on the English–language arts curriculum, we could also have explored historical perspectives: why American colonists felt they needed a Bill of Rights and what events were taking place at the time the colonists were framing the Constitution. By combining social studies and language arts knowledge and skills, teachers can emphasize the rich connections between the two disciplines.

WHY USE AN INTEGRATED APPROACH?

Many educators believe that the traditional curriculum fails to meet the needs of students in a complex, technologically advanced, interdependent world. They also suggest that an interdisciplinary curriculum will provide students with the critical-thinking, real-life skills they need when they enter the work force. In addition to providing continuity between students' learning in different subjects, an integrated approach can benefit students in other ways:

- *psychological development.* Individuals learn best when encountering ideas connected to one another or when information is embedded within meaningful contexts or applications. Based on this premise, Jean Piaget (1962) recommended that schooling for young children be organized around interdisciplinary themes, because children at this age experience the world holistically and concretely.
- *sociocultural.* The solutions to the problems that students encounter in the real world—poverty, the environmental crisis, or social unrest—necessitate knowledge and skills from a variety of disciplines and subject matter areas, such as technology, human relations, communications, and the sciences.

- *motivational.* The integrated curriculum with its decreased emphasis on rote learning and isolated content coverage and its increased emphasis on the interconnectedness of curricular concepts may enhance student motivation and interest. Moreover, an integrated curriculum is often organized around student-selected themes, problems, and investigations. As a result, students see how content areas relate, and can increase their perceptions of the relevance of curricular content and its practical or instrumental value. The fact that students have more opportunities for choice can also enhance their interest and motivation.
- *pedagogical.* It is impossible to teach students every fact they will need to know to function in a complex society. Therefore, many educators believe that schools should focus their efforts on encouraging students' capacity for critical reflection and deep understanding.

BUILDING INTERDISCIPLINARY UNITS

At the beginning of each year, teachers analyze what content they plan to teach, identify units of study that they have already created, and determine in what areas additional material is needed. Although science teachers, for example, can create a unit that includes using math skills for graphing and incorporates reading biographies of famous scientists to satisfy language arts advocates, cross-curricular teaching can be much more. It is important for teachers from different subject areas, in collaboration with library media specialists, to work together to create units in which teacher expertise and subject-area goals are woven together to achieve instructional aims.

There are three elements to consider when forming cross-curricular units:

1. *the team.* Subject area teachers representing their disciplines and the library media specialist should create the unit as a team. Team members' responsibilities are to make sure that content and skills from each subject are developed throughout the unit and to provide suggestions on how to accomplish this. In this way, each teacher contributes to the planning and thus develops a sense of ownership for the unit. The team might also solicit student input. Students might brainstorm ideas and discuss them prior to the teaching team's decision on content.

2. *the content.* Focusing the content on a theme, such as a controversial local issue like pollution or gun control or homelessness, can lead to meaningful investigation. The theme must be relevant and thought provoking enough to engage the students as well as others in the school and community who might be interested in hearing what the students have to say about the issue once the research has been completed.

   Teachers must assess potential topics or units of study according to variables within the instructional setting such as:
   - resources available
   - students' interests and concerns

- social, emotional, and cognitive levels and abilities of students
- appropriateness to the ages and developmental levels of learners
- topics that are dynamic respond to current issues and problems, and are worthy of examination.

   Topics should be interdisciplinary, including areas such as geographical, historical, political, economic, legal, aesthetic, scientific, literary, and ethical perspectives. They should require learners and teachers to apply knowledge, skills, and values learned in many content areas.

3. *implementation strategies.* There are several possible strategies for interdisciplinary teaching. They range from adding a random task to a unit that requires students to explore content or knowledge from a different subject area, to totally revamping the curriculum. Teachers should consider the following strategies for placing units of instruction within the school curriculum:

   - Infuse cross-curricular activities into existing courses of study by adding content systematically and pervasively so that it becomes an integral part of the existing curriculum.

   - Extend existing units of study by adding content and activities—usually to the end of units.

   - Create separate courses of study that tend to be multidisciplinary in content.

Of course, developing an interdisciplinary unit will have its share of problems. For example, the administration may not support creation of separate courses. Or you may find that infusing cross-curricular activities into existing courses may suffer from philosophical differences among teachers, scheduling conflicts, and perceptions about who is or is not doing his or her fair share. The end result, nonetheless, should justify the time and effort.

THE PROJECT APPROACH

One way to initiate interdisciplinary units is through the use of projects. Project work is not new to the elementary curriculum; however, there has been renewed interest in this approach based on recent research on children's learning, which has validated the benefits of a hands-on approach to science, integration of the curriculum, cooperative learning, accommodation of different learning styles, and increased emphasis on technology.

A project is an in-depth investigation of a topic that students are interested in and is worth learning more about. The investigation is usually undertaken by a small group of students within a class, although sometimes a whole class or students from different classrooms work on the same project. The key feature of a project is that it is a research effort deliberately focused on finding answers to questions about a topic posed either by the students, the teacher, or the teacher working with the students. The goal of a project is to learn more about the topic rather than to seek right answers to questions posed by the teacher.

The "project approach" complements the formal, systematic parts of the curriculum, especially in the elementary grades. Systematic instruction can:

- help children acquire skills
- address deficiencies in children's learning
- stress extrinsic motivation
- allow teachers to direct children's work, use their expertise, and specify the tasks that the children perform

Projects, however, should be integral to all work included in the curriculum. Project work:

- provides children with opportunities to apply skills
- addresses children's proficiencies
- stresses intrinsic motivation
- encourages children to determine what to work on
- accepts students as experts about their needs

Both types of instruction play important roles in the curriculum.

Why Use Projects?

Projects are an important part of the elementary curriculum because children have the chance to ask questions that guide an investigation and make decisions about the activities to be undertaken. Project work may include drawing, writing, reading, recording observations, and interviewing experts. Results can be summarized and represented in the form of graphs, charts, paintings and drawings, models, and other constructions, as well as in reports to peers and parents. In the early years, dramatic activities can help children express new understanding and new vocabulary. Project work provides a context for applying skills the students have learned in the more formal parts of the curriculum and lends itself to group cooperation. It also supports children's natural impulses to investigate things around them.

For older children at the elementary level who can read and write independently, project work provides a context for taking initiative and assuming responsibility, making decisions and choices, and pursuing interests. Even at the secondary level, project work can be a conduit for students to explore topics, resolve conflicts, share responsibility for carrying out tasks, and make suggestions—all skills necessary for living and working in society.

Phases of a Project

Project-based instruction can be divided into three phases:

1. *Phase 1* is devoted to selecting and refining the topic to be investigated, whether proposed by children or teachers. The topic can be related to students' cultures or everyday experiences. At least some of the children should have knowledge of the topic so they are able to ask or answer questions about it. The topic should also allow for integrating a range of subjects, such as science, social studies, and language arts. The topic should be suitable to

examine in school, and the investigation of the topic should last at least a week. Once the topic is selected, teachers can make a web or concept map by brainstorming with the children to discover their prior knowledge about the topic. [*Note:* We viewed these concept maps in Chapter 2.] Children can also recall any past experiences that relate to the topic. Teachers and students will pose questions to answer during the investigation.

2. *Phase 2* focuses on fieldwork, which is the direct investigation of objects, sites, or events. Sources of information for the investigations can be primary or secondary. Some primary sources might include: firsthand experience of students and teachers, evidence gathered on field trips, or explanations requested from experts in the field. Secondary sources encompass information acquired through research in and out of school, at museums, or through the Internet. For instance, the Franklin Institute Website at *http://sln.fi.edu* offers sources on Benjamin Franklin. The Internet can also provide some primary sources, such as sites where experts answer questions, and collaborative projects where students from different places provide data to each other. For example, to investigate why some animals have become endangered, students could contact an expert on marine biology at *http://whale.wheelock.edu*. As a result of information obtained from these sources, students can make observations from which they draw conclusions. They might construct models, observe phenomena and record findings, predict results, and discuss their new understandings (Chard, 1992).

3. *Phase 3* contains culminating and debriefing events that include preparing and presenting reports of results in the form of displays of findings and artifacts, talks, or dramatic presentations. From working on a project, children learn a new vocabulary, and their knowledge of an object or event deepens and expands.

To learn more about project approach methodology, check the following Website: *www.ualberta.ca/~schard/projects.htm*. This is the Project Approach Home Page and contains extensive information with examples.

SUMMARY

Cross-curricular investigations illustrate to students that different subject areas weave together in real-life situations. Using the Internet allows students to access both primary and secondary sources to help them complete their explorations. These resources often provide information in a more lifelike venue than students would be able to find without field trips, which are not always an option. Projects also allow students to work in groups in a cooperative, social structure. Students become more motivated because they are engaged in the learning.

We must be prepared for the changes that using Internet technology will bring to our classrooms, to the way we teach, and to our students. The units that follow illustrate using the Internet as an integral part of projects in cross-curricular units.

PART 2: PRACTICAL APPLICATIONS

The following three unit plans illustrate using Internet resources in cross-curricular learning. The first unit focuses on the topic of Censorship. This unit can be self-contained or used when studying a work of literature, such as Mark Twain's novel *The Adventures of Huckleberry Finn* or J. D. Salinger's *The Catcher in the Rye*. Increased attention has been trained on book banning as more schools, parent groups, and political factions have demanded a say in determining what literature should be taught in schools at all levels. This unit is designed for high-school students, although some of the activities can be adapted for other grade levels. Although the unit is based on banning books, many of the activities could also be used in the study of the Bill of Rights and the Constitution in a social studies class.

The second unit, on Using Puppets to Explore Culture, employs a project approach to engage students in thinking about different ethnic groups. The unit encompasses language arts and social studies skills and content, but it also encourages the use of drama and art activities. The unit is designed for upper-elementary-school students, although some of the activities can be adapted for the lower elementary grades.

The third interdisciplinary unit, designed for a secondary-school English class, explores the theme of Tolerance as it relates to Harper Lee's novel *To Kill a Mockingbird*. Although the unit is written from a language arts perspective, it does also include activities related to social studies content. Here is a synopsis of the six steps for the following units.

1. Apply framework standards—what should be taught?
2. Identify general goals and specific objectives.
3. Gather materials.
4. Introduce the unit.
5. Create sample activities.
6. Evaluate what was learned.

UNIT 1 (SECONDARY LEVEL): CENSORSHIP

> *"As good almost kill a man as kill a good book; who*
> *kills a man kills a reasonable creature, God's image; but*
> *he who destroys a good book kills reason itself."*
> —John Milton, *Areopagitica*

Censorship has increased in its intensity during the 1990s. A personal example should help to illustrate the problem. During the reading of *The Adventures of Huckleberry Finn* at a local high school where I was supervising student teachers, I noticed an article in the local newspaper that reemphasized the controversial nature of Mark Twain's novel. A parent group from one school district in the area had asked the school board to ban the reading of *Huck Finn* from all schools in the district. Many of us may have had this or a similar experience.

Marie, one of my student teachers, was teaching *Huck Finn* and had been requested by parents to exempt their children from participating in its reading. Marie decided to use the I-Search paper format as a way to have such students address issues that influenced the banning of this book and others at so many school sites. Marie thought that this would be a good alternative assignment to the traditional research papers that other class members were writing on the novel. The assignment and activities that follow are based on the unit that Marie envisioned for this alternative project.

This cross-curricular unit presents a model that can be used either to provide extension activities to follow the reading of a controversial book, such as *The Adventures of Huckleberry Finn*, to propose an alternative to that assignment, or to serve as a stand-alone unit on the topic of censorship. It offers activities that help students learn to listen carefully, speak easily, read efficiently, and write effectively about a controversial issue. It contains learning strategies for all students and employs cooperative group work. It bases the activities and assignments on national standards and state framework goals. Students also practice research skills and critical thinking. As you review the unit, consider what you can use as is, and how you can modify the content for your own grade level and student population.

STEP 1: APPLY FRAMEWORK STANDARDS—WHAT SHOULD BE TAUGHT?

The struggle over whether literary works, such as *Of Mice and Men* by John Steinbeck or *Catcher in the Rye* by J. D. Salinger, should be banned from high school reading lists has long been an issue. Today, many concerned parents and citizen or religious groups base their challenges of a book on its "moral" worth alone. Students, however, may be oblivious to the impact censorship can have on the books they read in school.

The thematic unit on Censorship that follows is designed to make students think about this controversial issue—what the problem is, the pros and cons, and their own positions. Although this unit focuses primarily on censorship as it relates to *The Adventures of Huckleberry Finn*, it could also be used with other books as well.

Outlined below are some of the specific guidelines from the California Framework for English–Language Arts (CSDE, 1987) that form the basis for this unit. These points are included to provide schools with broad goals to focus on as they create their own programs of study, units, and lesson plans. The use of the Internet in student assignments is encompassed in the broad educational goals for English–language arts. The guidelines suggest that:

1. Students work collaboratively. Studies (Johnson et al., 1981) have shown that learners profit immeasurably from environments that encourage shared learning. Most businesses today emphasize the team approach to completing projects; therefore, working cooperatively is a skill vital for students to attain before they finish school. The Internet presents an especially good environment for collaboration. Whether students are working together in groups on a research project or interacting with a school in another geographic area on a writing activity, they are learning teamwork.

2. Students become aware that writing is a means of clarifying thinking and that it is a process that embodies several stages, including prewriting, drafting, receiving responses, revising, editing, and postwriting activities, including evaluation. Using information gathered from a variety of sources, including the Internet, enables students to practice their writing on meaningful, far-reaching topics. As a result, the classroom knows no geographic boundaries.

3. Students respond both orally and in writing to questions that help them to acquire and use higher-order thinking skills in all subject areas. Because of the diversity of materials and the combination of fact and opinion that exists on Websites, students must employ skills of analysis, evaluation, application, and synthesis in choosing what information to use, believe, and refute in class assignments.

4. Teachers and library media specialists work cooperatively to provide ongoing instruction regarding the location and appropriate use of information from varied sources. Although the California English–Language Arts Framework (guidelines written in 1987) does not mention the Internet specifically, Internet resources are one more reference material about which students must be informed.

5. Teachers and library media specialists encourage and assist students to use all media and technological resources, such as word processors, computers, library books, films, audio tapes, videotapes, newspapers, magazines, dictionaries, and encyclopedias as learning and communication tools. Again, providing students with the most up-to-date materials and the means and know-how to access them is important in preparing them for the real world that they will encounter in this technologically advanced information age.

Thus, the English–Language Arts Framework centers on the construction of meaning; focuses on an integrated curriculum of reading, writing, speaking, and listening in meaningful contexts; has an emphasis on a literature base; and encourages the use of technological resources.

STEP 2: IDENTIFY GENERAL GOALS AND SPECIFIC OBJECTIVES

The goals and specific objectives that follow form the basis for the content and skill development of the unit. These goals and objectives reinforce the skills emphasized in the California English–Language Arts Framework.

Goals

Students will:

- work cooperatively in groups to access the Internet
- use technology as an integral tool for instruction
- read from a well-balanced list of literary works that includes different genres (fiction, nonfiction, poetry, drama), chronology, breadth (comedy, tragedy, satire), works authored by both men and women and by writers from other cultures, races, and ethnic groups

- develop effective oral communication skills through both informal and formal speaking activities
- construct meaning from print and apply strategies to learn from text
- promote and enhance their proficiency in writing

Objectives

After completing this unit, students will:

- become familiar with Mark Twain, one of the most celebrated authors in American literature, and issues surrounding his novels
  - — relate freedom of speech to the understanding of works of literature
- access and obtain information from at least five Internet sources
- articulate reasons why books are banned
  - — list the steps to research a controversial topic
  - — persuade an audience orally using evidence to accept a specific point of view
- use a variety of resources, including printed and electronic sources and interviews

To achieve the above goals and objectives, students will participate in the following learning experiences:

- planning and predicting (hypothesizing)
- designing questions to find out what they want to know
- evaluating (deciding which data are most important, relevant, nonbiased)
- synthesizing (combining information from more than one source)
- analyzing and interpreting data
- presenting data for clarity and ease of reading
- documenting material
- gaining social skills (collaboration and responsibility)

These critical-thinking skills were discussed in detail in Chapter 2.

STEP 3: GATHER MATERIALS

When students are doing research, they should obtain information from a diversity of resources to determine their positions and draw conclusions on given subjects. Internet materials, such as listservs, discussion groups, e-mail collaborations, and the myriad of Websites, will provide significant sources, especially for a controversial subject like censorship.

- A discussion group at *www.clairescorner.com/censorship* provides a forum for airing diverse opinions about censorship.
- The Websites in Table 3-1 provide diverse viewpoints on the topic of censorship, including lists of banned books, a historical overview of censorship in the schools, significant court cases, and more.

Table 3-1: Censorship Websites	
Website URLs	**Description of Websites**
www.excite.com/reference/almanac/?id=CE012456	Encyclopedia-like information on the Constitution, Bill of Rights, and amendments
www.excite.com/reference/almanac/?id=A0341699	Dictionary definition of the Bill of Rights
http://lth3.k12.il.us/PET/washington-giftpet/kbrproj.htm	Kids' Bill of Rights project
www.booksatoz.com/censorship/banned.htm	Information on banned books and censorship
www.luc.edu/libraries/banned	Addresses First Amendment, banned books, right to read, intellectual freedom, etc.
www.lib.wmc.edu/lib/staff/suttle/censorship/censors.html	Information on U.S. law and links to government sites with court decisions
www.lsu.edu/guests/poli/public_html/bor.htm	Bill of Rights page and links to other sources on censorship
www.neffzone.com/huckfinn	*Huck Finn* as a banned book on the most challenged book list
http://salwen.com/mtrace.html	Discussion of *Huck Finn* as a racist book
www.excite.com/guide/entertainment/books_and_literature/book_banning?search=censorship+books	Links to sites on censorship, including a chat room
www.libertywon.com/actionlinks.htm	Libertarian Christian site with links to ABC, CBS, *Meet the Press*, *Washington Post*, *The Today Show*, CNN, *N.Y. Times* to write and send opinions on censorship
http://webleyweb.com/lneil/bor_enforcement.html	Talks about online freedom, an up-and-coming topic
http://marktwain.miningco.com/library/weekly/aa092397.htm?pid=2781&cob=home	Arguments for and against banning *Huck Finn*

STEP 4: INTRODUCE THE UNIT

Ken Macrorie (1988) introduced the concept of the I-Search paper, which sees the research paper as "hunting stories" for which students seek answers to questions that interest them. The I-Search paper has four parts:

1. what the author knows or does not know about a specific topic
2. what the author wants to find out about the topic
3. the story of the author's search to find out about the topic
4. what the author learned from the search

The I-Search paper can differ from the traditional research paper in several ways. Often the topic for the paper is chosen by the student, although it must be something the student "needs" to know, not just something that is a casual interest. In essence, the papers are stories of how and what students are discovering about topics. There are three views to the I-Search paper: (1) the student searcher, (2) the authorities consulted, and (3) the person(s) reading the paper. Students in elementary, middle, or high school are able to write this type of paper.

In this unit on Censorship, the I-Search paper format is a natural vehicle to incorporate an Internet component as well as to evaluate students' interactions with the Internet. Censorship is a broad enough topic to give students freedom to choose subtopics they are interested in and conduct research using more than just traditional sources.

Unit Project: The I-Search Paper

Research for a typical I-Search paper includes the usual sources such as books and magazines, but it also encompasses much more. Interviews with experts, visits to agencies or doctors, telephone calls, field trips, and letter writing are all part of the information-gathering process. And now students can add the Internet as another resource.

One reason that the I-Search paper lends itself so well to the Internet is that the process that students go through to conduct their research on the Internet becomes part of the paper. Students identify each step they take to write the paper—for example, evaluating Websites and looking at data for bias. In addition, with an I-Search paper, reflective thinking is part of the project.

Instructions for Student I-Search Papers

The format for an I-Search paper is simple. Students will ask the following four basic questions as they conduct research:

1. What do I want to know (statement of the problem)? In the first section of the paper, they will write what they know, assume they know, or what they imagine about the topic they have chosen. This forms the basis from which their research can progress. For example, students might estimate the scope of the problem and discuss whether book banning has occurred in their community.

2. How did I find the information (procedures followed)? Next, they must test their assumptions and knowledge by researching the topic. They will use all forms of media, from books and magazines to films, authorities, or agencies. They will interview people when possible. They must document all of their sources as they proceed. The search process is written in first-person, narrative form, recording the steps students took to gather data. They will identify highlights of their searches that helped in their understanding of the topics.

3. What did I learn (summary of findings)? When the research is completed, they should compare what they found out with what they assumed they knew before starting the research.

4. What will I do with this information (conclusion)? Students must offer some personal comments and draw conclusions. They must try to persuade their audience to some point of view in the conclusion to the paper.

Figure 3-1 provides a sample questionnaire to use.

STEP 5: CREATE SAMPLE ACTIVITIES

The activities that follow are examples of some that can be included in an Internet-based unit on censorship. The samples are based on *The Adventures of Huckleberry Finn*, one of the most often read books in the curriculum. These tasks will enable students to collect the information they need for the I-Search paper.

Activities to Introduce the Unit

At the beginning of the unit, it is important to draw upon students' prior knowledge and to provide them with the language necessary to understand concepts throughout the unit. To provide background on censorship and assess student information and attitudes, have students:

1. Determine what they believe or know about Mark Twain and his novels by completing the Preassessment Checklist (see Figure 3-2). The Checklist is an informal inventory of students' present understandings of the major concepts they will encounter throughout the unit.

2. Brainstorm all ideas related to censorship in order to come up with words to use to search both printed and electronic sources. Figure 3-3 gives a sample.

3. Do a Quickwrite, in which they list what they know about the topic and why the issue they are going to investigate is important to them at this moment. Have them share their entries with a partner, trying orally to explain why this topic is of importance to them and/or others.

4. Write out their strategies to perform a search of an online catalog and the Internet using the search planning worksheet (see Figures 2-3 and 2-8).

5. Review several Websites for background information on freedom of speech and general ideas about censorship. Try the following:
   - Information on censorship is at the ICONN Website at *www.ala.org/ ICONN/lan_art.html*.

Figure 3–1: I-Search Questionnaire

Student Name: _____

I-Search Topic: _____

1. What do I want to know?

   • What I know _____
   • What I imagine _____
   • What I assume _____
   • Where does the problem take place _____

2. How did I find the information?

   • Books and magazines _____
   • Interviews _____
   • Websites _____
   • Community sources _____
   • Media (films, CD ROM) _____

   3. What steps did I use to find the information?

   a)

   b)

   c)

   d)

4. What did I learn? (Summary) _____

   _____

5. What will I do with the information?

   • Conclusions: _____

   _____

   • Personal comments: _____

   _____

   • Actions to be taken: _____

   _____

Figure 3–2: Preassessment Checklist on Censorship

A. Directions: Read each of the following statements. Place a check on the numbered line next to those statements you would be willing to defend. Think of specific examples you would use to defend the statements you agree with or to refute those you disagree with. These statements represent some of the ideas you will be exploring in preparation for writing your I-Search paper.

_____ 1. Twain could portray nineteenth century life west of the Mississippi River in a realistic manner.

_____ 2. Twain could reproduce the speech patterns of people of all walks of life and provide a portrait of the landscape of the West.

_____ 3. The dialects in Twain's works are faithful reproductions of the speech patterns spoken by the people of the region and era that he chose to represent.

_____ 4. Twain's books should be banned from school reading lists.

_____ 5. Any citizen has the right to tell teachers what books to include in the curriculum.

_____ 6. Mark Twain is a racist.

_____ 7. School boards should have lists of criteria on which to base book banning.

_____ 8. If a book has been banned in more than one school district, it should not be taught in any school.

_____ 9. The Bill of Rights gives schools the right to choose any book for students to read.

_____ 10. Withholding books from students narrows their education.

B. Directions: In small groups discuss those statements with which you disagree. Try to use concrete examples to convince others of your conclusions. Write your notes in the space below.

_____

_____

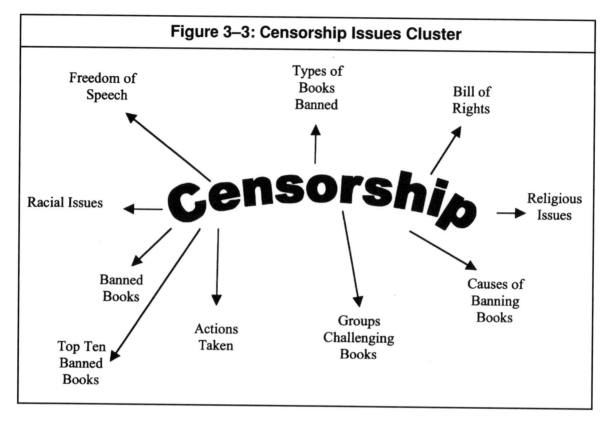

Figure 3–3: Censorship Issues Cluster

- Books that have been frequently banned are listed at Website *www.cs.cmu. edu/People/spok/banned-books.html*
- Links to freedom of speech, censorship, and the First Amendment can be found at Website *www.banned.books.com*.
- Freedom of speech on the Internet is covered at Website *www.vtw.org/ speech/#appeal*.

Activities to Be Used During the Unit

This part of the unit focuses specifically on the question, How and what information did I find? For some of the following activities, students will work in groups; for others, students will work independently. Students must choose activities that provide sufficient information to write the I-Search papers. Each group member is responsible for at least one activity involving Web research. There are two overarching components to this activity, each of which contains multiple facets.

1. Research the topic of censorship based on the novel *The Adventures of Huckleberry Finn*.
   - Check sites, such as the U.S. Constitution and especially the Bill of Rights, to form a benchmark on the freedoms being challenged by censorship.
   - Review the following quotes made by groups who have banned *The Adventures of Huckleberry Finn* (compiled by Humanities-Interactive. Online, at *www.humanities-interactive.org* [August 1999]).

- 1885: Banned in Concord, Mass., as "trash and suitable only for the slums."
- 1905: Barred from the Brooklyn Library Children's Room because "Huck not only itches but scratches, and says sweat when he should say perspiration."
- 1957: Dropped from New York City schools list of readings for frequent use of the "N-word."
- 1969: Removed from Miami-Dade Junior College required reading list because it "creates an emotional block for black students that inhibits learning."

- In small groups discuss the pros and cons of banning the book based on the reasons listed above. State a position for or against the book as required reading in the English curriculum. Check information at Website *http://phnet.esuhsd.org/legend/features/huck.finn.html* for help.
- Read several articles on censorship to get different points of view. Check articles at *www.clairescorner.com/censorship* as a starting point. Also, use some of the Websites listed at *http://marktwain.miningco.com*. This site has points of view by Twain himself, Booker T. Washington, the ACLU, and a member of the Mark Twain Association Governing Board, to name a few. Determine if bias is present. Identify passages, wording, and/or images that substantiate their claims.
- Several sites have articles that cover challenges to the book. Choose from among:
  - *www.seattletimes/com/extra/browse/html/huck_092596.html*
  - *www.kentuckyconnect.com/hearldleader/news/022798/op3lit.shtml*
  - *www.sfgate.com/cgi-bin/chronicle/article.cgi?file=mn42343. DTL& director=/chronicle/archive/1995/10/17*
  - *www.mcall.com/cgibin/slivebsto.cgi?DBLIST=mc85&DOCNUM=7357*
  Compare the newspaper articles with the opinions above for bias.
- Write imaginary dialogues between themselves and Mark Twain about the censorship his book has undergone. The dialogues should include references from the book (as in characters, theme, plot, setting). Students should first list questions to ask Twain, then write the dialogues. Both the questions and the dialogues should sound like casual conversations between Twain and the students. Then choose partners to perform the conversations for the class.
- Interview local school board members, civic groups, and/or parents on whether *The Adventures of Huckleberry Finn* should be banned. If possible, attend a school board meeting to hear a debate on the topic. Review *http://phnet.esuhsd.org/legend/features/huck.finn.html*, a site created by students in a district where a parent group asked that the language in *Huck Finn* be modified if it remained as required reading.
- Investigate possible discussion groups that they can subscribe to on the topic of censorship or freedom of speech. One to check is *www.clairescorner.com/censorship/discuss.htm*.

Figure 3–4: Sample Journal Log	
Events/conversations, facts, opinions	**Personal Reactions**

- During the information-gathering stage, keep logs of their experiences (see Figure 3-4). As part of the logs, students must document sources they have found. They can use examples at *www.mla.org*, *www.apa.org/journals/webref.html*, or Figure 1-8 (Citing Internet Sources). The journal logs will be turned in as part of the final products.

2. Write the I-Search papers. Questions 3 and 4 in the I-Search format—What did I find? And What will I do with the information?—will be answered in this part of the unit. Although this part of the I-Search process does not involve using the Internet, the research students have just completed is integral to this step of writing the paper. Students will:

   - synthesize their I-Search material into written drafts. They must determine audience, purpose, and organization for the paper, as well as supporting details to include. *Note:* The I-Search paper must include the four sections listed at the beginning of the unit.

   - as part of the revision process, pick partners and write several titles for their partner's paper. This will enable the writer to see what the reader thinks is the focus of the paper. Partners will review the titles together to identify the most appropriate ones and determine why certain titles seemed more appropriate than others.

   - read their own rough drafts out loud in their small groups of four, then exchange with partners. With their partners, they will make written comments that will form the basis of the revised drafts, using the checklist in Figure 3-5 as a guide. They should turn in written comments with the final projects

   - in pairs edit their final papers for spelling, typos, and punctuation.

Figure 3–5: Peer Review Checklist

Writer's Name:_____

Reviewers' Names: _____

_____

The purpose of this activity is to help improve writing skills. Please respond thoughtfully and completely to the tasks below.

1. Write the thesis statement, the main idea, that is contained in the introduction to the paper. Is it too narrow? Too broad?

2. What attracts your interest in the introduction to make you want to read further?

3. What is the main idea in paragraph 2? Write down the sentence that tells you the main idea.

4. What are some of the specific details that support the main idea in paragraph 2?

5. What is the main idea of paragraph 3? Write the sentence that states the main idea. List several specific details that show you what the main idea is.

6. List the main ideas for the remaining paragraphs and the sentences that state the ideas.

7. Does the conclusion tie all the ideas together? Does it tell what the writer learned?

8. In your opinion, what is the best part of this paper? What still needs work? Give suggestions.

Activities to Be Used as Follow-up to the Unit

In the English–language arts, Beyond activities that require publishing student work could incorporate the Internet. Having a networked writing environment provides an effective means to get students at all age levels to write more and to learn from one another. As extension activities, have students in groups try one of the following three activities:

1. Design and create their own Website to publish the written results of the I-Search papers.
2. Collaborate with another school to share some of their newly found knowledge about censorship. Try Website *www.inkspot.com* for publication.
3. Censorship exists in other forms beyond literature. Explore other types of censorship, such as censorship of the Internet, comic books, art, or music. Identify issues surrounding censorship and take positions on whether the groups agree or disagree with the need for censorship in this area. Use *www.clairescorner.com/censorship* as a starting point.

STEP 6: EVALUATE WHAT WAS LEARNED

Students will prepare written papers and self-evaluations of the process they went through to complete the I-Search papers. Students will read their I-Search papers out loud while other class members prepare response sheets. Students will receive grades on the written, oral, and self-evaluation reports. In addition, they will be evaluated on how thoughtfully they responded to other students' I-Search reports through their peer evaluations.

SUMMARY

This unit employed an I-Search format to study the topic of censorship as it related to banning the book *The Adventures of Huckleberry Finn*. We required students to use the Internet as a tool for the research of the project. Throughout the unit, we explored Internet sites related to English–language arts.

Before you leave this chapter, explore additional language arts sites and annotate them in your English–language arts notebook. The more practice you have in familiarizing yourself with Internet projects and resources, the more likely that you will include an Internet component in your next unit plan. Remember the Chinese proverb: If you tell someone, they forget; if you show them they understand; but if you involve them, they remember. Involve yourself and your students in English or language arts by actively searching the Internet.

UNIT 2 (ELEMENTARY LEVEL): USING PUPPETS TO TEACH CULTURE

The United States has long been identified as the "melting pot" because it has become the home to so many different cultures. Some states like California have more minority students in its classrooms than Anglos. Therefore, it is important to start early to teach young children about different cultures.

In elementary schools, children should also learn to express themselves in a clear and interesting fashion. One way to achieve this goal is through classroom drama, and puppetry is a good way to introduce dramatic work. For instance, some shy children find it easier to project their language through puppet actors, since puppets can provide masks that allow students to open up. You will often see some students for whom drama is a powerful motivator, but there will be others who shrink from the idea of performing. In this unit, children can choose the roles that best fit their personalities and interests.

Certain dramatic effects can be achieved with puppets that make the productions quite satisfying. The sources for puppet plays are numerous. Children can present improvisations, pantomimes, dramatic readings, debates, interviews, and conversations. They can use poetry, legends, folktales, and historical events as the basis of the drama. When children write plays, they are often more spirited in the performance using puppets. Thus, puppetry presents an ideal vehicle to learn about culture.

Students can also design their own puppets. There are Hand Puppets, Head Puppets, Body Puppets, Shadow Puppets, and Spoon Puppets, to name a few from which to choose. The designs can be kept simple so they are easy for children to make. Puppets can be made from any odds and ends. For example, I have an old cloth bag that contains ribbons, bows, twine, scraps of fabric, pieces of yarn, paper bags, clean, worn-out socks and gloves, paper plates, buttons, and other supplies I find. These materials are ideal for creating a puppet unit.

Keep in mind these guidelines to help make your puppet unit successful:

1. Don't involve too many puppets in one show. About three or four puppets is enough for children to manage easily.
2. Think about audio taping the story on which the puppet show is based; children may have difficulty manipulating the puppets and saying lines at the same time. If children in upper grades are going to speak lines, arrange to have cue cards available so they don't have to memorize them all. You can also use a narrator who reads most of the lines and have the puppeteers just speak the dialogue.
3. Have each child manipulate no more than one puppet. Children should understand what kinds of emotions the puppets display when they nod, shake their heads, or walk. Students should try to express happiness, tiredness, sadness, anger, and friendliness through their puppets.
4. Help children so that they express feelings through their voices. For example, children may need to portray barks, growls, or meows for animal puppets.

STEP 1: APPLY FRAMEWORK STANDARDS—WHAT SHOULD BE TAUGHT?

One of the broad goals of the History–Social Science Framework in California is to understand different cultures, and this theme continues throughout the elementary school curriculum. Students should understand the rich, complex nature of different societies. To meet this end, children need to learn about their history, geography, politics, literature, art, drama, music, dance, education, and more. They must also comprehend the inter-relationships among parts of a nation's culture. They should examine peoples' beliefs as exemplified in their legends, folktales, and myths; however, these beliefs cannot be fully understood without knowledge of poems, plays, dance, and visual art. Above all, students must be taught to respect all peoples through an understanding of their different societies and ways of life. This unit on Using Puppets to Teach Culture starts students thinking about different cultural backgrounds that may exist in their own classrooms and helps them understand other cultures throughout the world.

A goal from the English–language arts framework in California is for elementary school children to learn to express themselves effectively when speaking and writing. Youngsters need opportunities to share a variety of content: for example, stories, poems, and information acquired from research. Oral storytelling is another good way for children to express themselves clearly. According to Strickland (1973), it is important to follow up stories students have heard or read with an oral activity. In her scenario, after hearing a story each day, children began a period of storytelling, puppetry, creative dramatics, role playing, choral speaking, or discussion. These follow-up oral activities improved children's language skills.

Three other researchers also emphasize the importance of telling stories for improving language skills:

- "Reading and telling stories introduces children to the world of written language. They hear new vocabulary and varied language structures from which they learn to model their own language" (Morrow, 1979: 236).
- "There is a humanism inherent in sharing language, sharing stories, dancing and singing. These are approaches to learning about yourself and those around you" (Ramos, 1980:5).
- "Because children participating in drama have to make up the details as they go along, they not only are pressed to produce language, but they capture the vitality and tension of spontaneous human interaction as well" (Wagner, 1979:268).

These educators emphasize language arts standards to improve speaking and promote listening skills. Through the diverse activities in this unit, students should also gain expertise in the use of oral language, enhance their listening abilities, and appreciate others who are different from themselves.

STEP 2: IDENTIFY GENERAL GOALS AND SPECIFIC OBJECTIVES

Several curriculum standards—English–language arts, social studies, and art—serve as guides for this unit. Use the goals and specific objectives that follow as a basis for developing content and improving skills.

Goals

Students will:

- develop cultural literacy by understanding the complex nature of different cultures

- develop respect for the human dignity of all people and understanding of different ways of life
- learn about the mythology, legends, values, and beliefs of different cultures
- develop skills in listening for appreciation and understanding
- develop skills to express ideas in group or individual situations
- develop self-confidence and poise as they work and share together
- use technology for research

Objectives

After completing this unit, students will be able to:

- use their voices and movements to communicate messages
- use visuals and props to add clarity to an oral message
- gather and organize ideas for communicating with others
- participate in the informal give-and-take of small groups
- write or copy and present dialogues

STEP 3: GATHER MATERIALS

Gather materials to represent different subject areas. For example, for art activities, students will be searching for ideas on how to make their own puppets. To incorporate social studies concepts, they will want information about specific cultures. Finally, to build reading skills, they will need to read stories about children in different lands.

The World Wide Web has many resources on the topic of puppets and culture. Websites exist illustrating how to create stick puppets, hand puppets, and many others. They also contain instructions for building a puppet playhouse. Even Jim Henson, creator of the Muppets, and his Muppet characters are represented. Moreover, by exploring specific countries, children can find information on aspects of African, Chinese, or Mexican culture, to name a few. Several Websites provide information on puppetry around the world. Of course, it is a good idea to review any Websites you are planning to use as part of the unit and create a list of URLs so that students can just click the URL links to go to individual sites. Sample URLs are included with specific activities.

In this unit students will look at Internet sites that illustrate different types of puppets. From the sources they research, they will gather ideas to create their own puppets and perform puppet shows for their classmates and parents. Many of the sites in Table 3-2 are used in the puppet activities that follow.

Good books add to a unit on puppetry. Reading some of the literature titles listed here will help children imagine what their puppet characters can look like and provide examples for their puppets' actions and speech. The countries that students choose to depict will determine which titles they read. Within cultures, legends, myths, and folktales are a good starting point, since they appeal to all ages and demonstrate diversity. Some sample titles on the recommended reading list in California may provide some ideas:

Table 3-2: Puppet Web Resources	
Web Site URLs	**Description of Websites**
www.puppet.org/teachers.html	Provides instructions and drawings for making puppets, contains curriculum ideas
www.puppet.org/links.html	Identifies links to puppetry sites around the world
www.muppets.com	Includes all you want to know about the Muppets, including Muppet games for kids
www.henson.com/creatures/ creatures_stage_how.htm	Provides a step-by-step procedure on how to create a creature and bring it to life
www.sagecraft.com/puppetry	Answers questions about puppetry by e-mail
www.sp.uconn.edu/~wwwsfa/bimp	Illustrates construction of different types of puppets, includes links to International Traditions (puppetry in other countries)
http://family.go.com/Categories/ Activities/Features/family_1998_04/ famf/famf48puppetstage/ famf48puppetstage.html	Offers ideas on making a puppet play house, including instructions from Disney

- *Why Mosquitoes Buzz in People's Ears: A West African Tale*, by Verna Azardema
- *The Cow-Tail Switch and Other West African Stories*, by Harold Courlander and George Herzog
- *Tales of a Korean Grandmother*, by Frances Carpenter
- *Magic Listening Cap: More Folk Tales from Japan*, by Yoshiko Uchida
- *Beyond the East Wind: Legends and Folktales of Vietnam*, by Quyen Van Duong and Jewell R. Coburn

Drama is also an excellent way to help students develop reading, writing, speaking, and listening skills in an integrated way. For example, plays provide models for characters' dialogue and actions before students create their own scripts. The following plays are adaptations from folktales and can be used in puppet shows:

- *Plays from African Folktales: With Ideas for Acting, Dance, Costumes, and Music*, by Carole Korty
- *Puppet Plays from Favorite Stories*, by Lewis Mahlmann and David Jones
- *Dramatized Folk Tales of the World*, edited by Sylvia E. Kamerman

STEP 4: INTRODUCE THE UNIT

A culture cannot be fully understood without knowledge of its people, history, literature, dance, music, and art. As students decide upon and complete the activities for this project, they should appreciate that their nation is composed of people whose ethnic backgrounds are diverse. In this unit, groups of students will select a culture that interests them to investigate. As a result of their exploration, each group will become "experts" on that society and its people. Groups will demonstrate their expertise by creating and performing puppet shows illustrating myths or folktales that represent their chosen cultures.

As part of the project, students also make choices about the roles they want to play within their groups. For example, two or three students may like to speak and act in front of their classmates. These children can choose to be performers in the puppet shows. Others may feel more comfortable in the role of creating the playhouse in which to hold the plays. At least one child from each group will need to assume the role of director to help coordinate the activities and act as narrator for the group's show. Whichever roles students assume, they will be involved in language arts, social studies, and art activities. Finally, students will be involved in reading myths and folktales, accessing the Internet to learn more about individual cultures, and participating with other children to achieve common goals.

STEP 5: CREATE SAMPLE ACTIVITIES

The activities that follow will enable students to ask questions about different cultures. Children will use the puppets to make societies come to life through cooperative teamwork (for more on cooperative learning, see also Chapter 5). The presentations will provide the culminating activities for the overall project.

Students should select activities that incorporate content and skills from social studies, language arts, and art. They will also keep project journals in which they include facts and notes about the research on their cultures, write their scripts for the plays, and take notes on performance tips and puppet types.

Activities to Introduce the Unit

In Phase 1, students should establish the parameters of the topics—what they are going to investigate—and explore their prior knowledge about the cultures they have chosen. If students in the classroom belong to different ethnic groups, they should choose cultures different from their own; however, they can still contribute special information and personal experiences about their own countries of origin to their classmates.

Initial tasks ask students to think generally about the concept of "culture" and then to narrow down choices to the specific groups they want to research; African

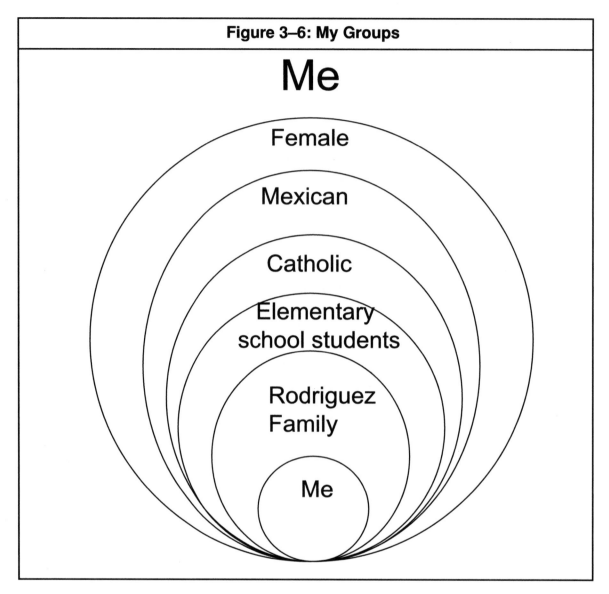

Figure 3–6: My Groups

Me

Female

Mexican

Catholic

Elementary
school students

Rodriguez
Family

Me

culture will be the example used throughout this unit. To draw upon their prior knowledge, students will:

1. Explore the concept of "belonging to a group." Have students list on a sheet of paper all the groups they belong to, then draw a hierarchy similar to the one in Figure 3-6. Teachers should give some examples of how society categorizes people into different groups, such as by age, gender, religion, belief, and nationality. This will help to extend the concept of diversity and to break down stereotypes.
2. Clarify terminology by discussing and writing definitions and examples in their project notebooks for culture, diversity, and stereotype.
3. Create collages with pictures of themselves representing the different groups they belong to.

4. Interview each other or friends and neighbors from different ethnic groups to compile firsthand information about cultures.

Activities to Be Used During the Unit

In student-selected "culture" groups, children will begin research to accumulate information for their puppet shows. The research should include data on the selected countries and myths or folktales created by the people of their countries. There are ten steps involved, though not all need to be performed in the order given:

1. Study maps of countries they plan to research. Draw maps and locate major cities, rivers, mountain ranges, provinces, bordering countries, and bodies of water. See Figure 3-7 for a view of the Website at *www.odci.gov/cia/publications/factbook/figures/802641.jpg*, which contains a map of Africa with surrounding countries.
2. Research Websites to collect information on their ethnic groups. Select five facts and write them in their journals. For example, at *www.afroam.org/children/discover/discover.html*, students can read facts about Africa, such as history, geography, location, size, terrain, land use, and so forth.
3. Consult *www.afroam.org/children/myths/myths.html*, where they will find myths from different countries. For this unit they will choose one of the myths from Africa: myths about the eagle, the rabbit, or wisdom.
4. Read folktales about their cultures in print versions (some titles for different countries are supplied under Step 3: Gathering Materials). These tales will

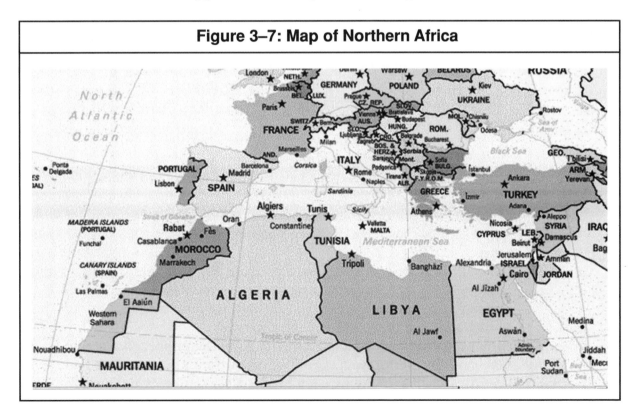

Figure 3–7: Map of Northern Africa

give students ideas and language models to use in their own puppet presentations.

5. As a class, view *www.sp.uconn.edu/~wwwsfa/bimp* to get an overview of how to get started creating a puppet presentation. Examine construction methods and materials and different types of puppets.

6. Send e-mail to *www.sagecraft.com/puppetry* to ask any questions they have about puppetry and creating their own productions.

7. Read the definition of director, playwright, and set designer at *www3.ns. sympatico.ca/onstage/puppets/activity/plays/theatre.html* and select the roles that they will play within their groups.

8. Choose one of the following roles: performers in the play, set designers, or the directors. Each group will now get together to prepare its part of the performance.
   - Actors will:
     — determine the characters and write the scripts to use in their puppet plays. Patterns from folktales they have read and facts gleaned from their research will provide content for the scripts.
     — View puppet patterns that can be downloaded at *www3.ns.sympatico. ca/onstage/puppets/activity/paper.html* or at *http://query.html?qt= puppet&col=family&adtype=default*. These patterns will provide models for students to use as they create their own puppets. Check the African puppets at *www.leyland.com/africana.htm# AFRICAN_ PUPPETS*
     — Check Website *www.henson.com/creatures/creatures_stage_how.htm* or *www3.ns.sympatico.ca/onstage/puppets/activity/index.html* for ideas on how to bring puppet characters to life.
   - All set designers will gather as a group and create a stage or playhouse in which all "culture" groups will perform. Set designers will:
     — consult with the directors regarding the construction of the stage.
     — download step-by-step instructions on making a puppet playhouse at *http://family.go.com/categories/activities/Features/family_1998_04/ famf/famf48puppetstage/famf48puppetstage3.html*.
     — create a poster to advertise their puppet theatre and the shows that will be performed there. The poster should include date, time, and place of the performances and visual images that represent the cultures groups they have chosen to depict.
   - The directors will:
     — consult with all groups on special needs for their performances and supervise the building of the playhouse to meet those specifications.
     — write narratives for the plays including background on their cultures and act as narrators for the performances.
     — organize and direct practice sessions after the puppets are created.

9. Present their puppet performances to the rest of the class and invited guests.

10. Fill in "culture" charts following each group presentation (see Figure 3-8).

Figure 3–8: Culture Chart

My Culture Chart

My name is: _____

Fill in your culture chart after each puppet show.

	Culture Name China	Culture Name Japan	Culture Name Mexico	Culture Name Italy	Culture Name Malaysia
History					
Location					
People					
Traditions					
Dress					
Art					
Music					
Government					
Literature					

Activities to Be Used as Follow-up to the Unit

As a result of completing activities in this unit, students will have had the opportunity to practice speaking, listening, reading, and writing and learned about cultures different from their own. By working in small groups, they will have practiced socialization skills. It is important, too, that they reflect on the tasks that they have just completed:

- Discuss the following questions as a class:
  — Which characters in the plays did they find most appealing/least appealing and why/why not?
  — What are some of the differences and similarities they noticed among the cultures?
- Reflect on the following:
  — Which roles did they assume? Would they choose the same roles again? Why/why not?
  — What difficulties, if any, did they encounter working with their groups? What could they have done to make the performances go more smoothly?
- Write three facts that they now know about their cultures that they did not know before they began their investigations.
- Write letters in which they explain why they would like to visit specific cultures. Include at least three reasons based on their research and the presentations given.

STEP 6: EVALUATE WHAT WAS LEARNED

Evaluation will be based on four aspects: the products they produced in their roles as performers, set designers, and directors; the writing in their project journals; their knowledge of different cultures as exemplified through the "culture" charts and other writing; and their abilities to research using the Internet. Assessment will comprise five elements:

- the products for performers, set designers, and directors. Figure 3-9 provides a handout for teachers to use to assess puppet performances, stage construction, narrative texts, and the scripts.
- review of student journal entries periodically throughout the unit for completeness and to gain insight on students' progress.
- student self-evaluations of the Internet process (see Figure 3-10: Self-Evaluation Checklist of Internet Skills for a model).
- review of culture charts for completeness and content.
- evaluation of letters for clarity, coherence, and command of standard English conventions.

Figure 3–9: Puppet Project Assessment

Name: _____

Directions: As you watch the puppet shows, evaluate each of the roles—performers, set designers, and director in each play—according to the following criteria. Fill in your comments after each puppet show on the following.

The Performers

Criteria	Agree	Disagree	Why/why not
1. The puppets were well made and represented their characters.			
2. The puppets represented the culture through their costumes, dialogue, and performances.			
3. The puppets' dialogues were grammatically correct and expressed the puppets' ideas clearly.			
4. The puppets' dialogues helped me to understand the culture better.			
5. The play represented a folktale and also reflected facts about the culture it illustrated.			
6. The characters expressed emotion in their voices, movements, and dialogue.			

The Set Designers

Criteria	Agree	Disagree	Why/why not
1. The stage was sturdy and accommodated the presentations.			
2. The playhouse incorporated design ideas gleaned from the research.			
3. The poster was visually pleasing, presented a clear message, and was grammatically correct.			

The Director

Criteria	Agree	Disagree	Why/why not
1. The narrative helped the flow of the play, identified the characters, and brought the play to a conclusion.			
2. The narrative presented facts about the culture that helped me to understand the story events, the characters, and the moral of the story.			
3. The director directed the other performers.			

Figure 3–10: Self-Evaluation Checklist of Internet Skills

Specific Skills	The Rating Scale			
	Very Easy	Easy	Difficult	Very Difficult
I can logon to the Internet with my purpose clearly in mind.				
I know how to use a search engine (e.g., Yahoo!) to get information.				
I have kept an Internet notebook containing URLs with a brief description of each.				
I have used Internet resources: a. Websites b. listservs c. collaborative activities d. e-mail				
I can take systematic notes on information I locate.				
I can document Internet sources properly.				
I can incorporate information I find on the Internet into my research.				
I can check Web sources for bias, accuracy, and currency.				
I can select appropriate keywords for my Internet searches.				

Name of Student:

Date of self-evaluation:

Date of teacher-student conference:

Comments by student:

Comments by teacher:

SUMMARY

This unit is designed to enable students to work independently or in groups to explore the concept of culture. As a result, children should have a better understanding of their community and the similarities and differences among the people in it. By allowing students to research cultures of their own choosing, children have had to make decisions about their learning. In addition, they have gained skills in language arts, social studies, and art.

Puppetry provided an excellent vehicle for practicing speaking and listening skills, and it was also an effective way to teach content. Using the project approach for the unit provided students with a wide range of learning opportunities. Students should now understand that people are unique human beings who have varied characteristics not limited by gender, race, class, or ethnic backgrounds.

UNIT 3 (SECONDARY LEVEL): TEACHING TOLERANCE, BASED ON *TO KILL A MOCKINGBIRD*

From the elementary grades forward, students study cultures with the goal of their understanding and appreciating differences among peoples. This cross-curricular, thematic unit on Tolerance has as its central focus the reading of Harper Lee's *To Kill a Mockingbird*, a book frequently read at the secondary school level whose themes include tolerance, prejudice, and misunderstanding. The novel also reveals lessons in courage and facing adversity with dignity. In depicting a small town in the South during the Depression years, it opens up to modern eyes the social problems of blacks versus whites in the South in the 1930s. This complex novel is a good starting point to explore the theme of Tolerance.

Throughout the unit, students will explore these concepts, while at the same time familiarizing themselves with the historical timeframe in which the events of *To Kill a Mockingbird* took place. Students will have opportunities to explore poetry, film, and other media and conduct historical research into the Great Depression and into segregation issues in the South in the 1930s.

This unit offers activities for students to practice language skills, to work in small groups, and to improve research skills. As part of the unit, students will read literature; discuss its themes, plot, characters, and setting; dramatize scenes from the novel; and write about and analyze its messages in essays, scripts, reports, and journal entries. The unit bases its activities on national standards for both English–language arts and social studies. Finally, it presents students with choices on ways to meet the requirements of the unit. The variety of projects enables students to choose those that they are interested in investigating.

STEP 1: APPLY FRAMEWORK STANDARDS—WHAT SHOULD BE TAUGHT?

This unit incorporates standards in English–language arts and history–social sciences. English–language arts standards encourage an integrated curriculum in which students practice language skills in meaningful contexts and strive to promote the acquisition of skills through broad learning experiences. In California, the English framework also has literature as its base. A main goal is for students to become informed, responsible citizens and competent, successful members of the work force through their study and understanding of literature and intensive practice of communication skills, both oral and written.

Reinforcing this is one of the primary goals in history–social sciences, which is to promote democratic understanding and civic values. As a result of their learning experiences in social studies, students should be aware of the history of prejudice and discrimination against minorities, as well as of efforts to establish equality and freedom. They should understand how different minorities were treated historically and consider historical events through a variety of perspectives. They should also recognize how economic and social turmoil can affect ordinary people.

To Kill a Mockingbird is a work of serious social commentary. It illustrates themes of tolerance versus intolerance, courage versus cowardliness, and freedom versus servitude. An in-depth study of the novel and the time period in which it takes place requires students to think about rights and responsibilities of citizens under the Constitution. It also necessitates that students analyze critical issues and speak and write about them. Finally, it provides opportunities for students to link past events of the 1930s with the present. As a result, they should have a better understanding of peoples' and nations' continuing struggles for freedom, survival, and better lives.

STEP 2: IDENTIFY GENERAL GOALS AND SPECIFIC OBJECTIVES

The selection of effective instructional objectives is of utmost importance to any unit of instruction. The following general goals and specific objectives for this unit reflect national standards and California framework goals in the language arts and social studies.

Goals

By the end of this unit, students will be able to:

- discuss the major changes in American society and culture brought about by the Great Depression of the 1930s
- identify connections among past, present, and future historical events
- develop group interaction skills
- understand the struggle to extend constitutional guarantees of equality and freedom to all people
- recognize judgments that are based on reasonable evidence and not on bias and emotion
- understand how literature of and about a period in history helps shed light on the life and times of the people
- respond to literature and write expository essays
- use the Internet for research and communication

Objectives
Students will be able to:

- extract meaning from information about the time period when *To Kill a Mockingbird* was written
- relate their own life experiences to the setting and characters' experiences and attitudes in the novel
- determine characters' traits by what they say about themselves in narration and dialogue
- analyze how the novel is related to the themes and issues of its historical period
- analyze interactions between main and subordinate characters in literary text and how they affect the plot
- use clear questions and coherent research methods to elicit and present evidence
- write clear and focused texts that convey well-defined perspective and tightly reasoned arguments

STEP 3: GATHER MATERIALS
There are three kinds of materials that students might want to gather for this unit: background information on the life and times in which the book took place, data about the author Harper Lee and why she wrote the novel, and analysis of the content of the novel. The Websites in Table 3-3 cover all three topics; some of the URLs are used for the activities in Step 5.

Students should look to other genres for perspectives about tolerance, social injustice, and prejudice, choosing some of the following examples to read:

- *poems.* "Harlem," by Langston Hughes; "Mending Wall," by Robert Frost; "Sympathy," by Paul Laurence Dunbar; "My Guilt," by Maya Angelou.
- *fiction. Black Boy,* by Richard Wright; *Roll of Thunder, Hear My Cry,* by Mildred Taylor; *I Know Why the Caged Bird Sings,* by Maya Angelou.
- *nonfiction. Martin Luther King, Jr.,* by Jacqueline Harris; *Harriet Tubman: Conductor of the Underground Railway,* by Ann Petry; *Malcolm X,* by Arnold Adoff; *To Be a Slave,* by Julius Lester.
- *drama. When the Rattlesnake Sounds: A Play About Harriet Tubman,* by Alice Childress; *The Crucible,* by Arthur Miller; *Romeo and Juliet,* by William Shakespeare.

Teachers might also want to incorporate some of these other works into the unit for the entire class.

STEP 4: INTRODUCE THE UNIT
Writing assignments have often taken the form of an assigned essay, a book, or a history report to be completed by the end of a unit to test students' understanding.

Table 3-3: *To Kill a Mockingbird* Web Resources	
Sample URLs	**Description of Websites**
www.chebucto.ns.ca/Culture/ HarperLee/quizes.html	Quizzes on content of *To Kill a Mockingbird*
www.chebucto.ns.ca/Culture/ HarperLee/index.html	Background on the author Harper Lee
www.chebucto.ns.ca/Culture/ HarperLee/discussion.html	Discussion groups on Harper Lee and the novel
www.lausd.k12.ca.us/Belmont_HS/ tkm/index.html	Annotations, pictures, vocabulary explanations given chapter by chapter for the novel
http://educeth.ethz.ch/english/r eadinglist/lee,harper.html	Biography of the author and her other works
http://educeth.ethz.ch/english/ readinglist/lee,harper.html# mockingbird	Lesson plans, chapter summaries, lists of student activities on the novel
http://library.advanced.org/12111/ novel.html	Close look at the novel with sections on character, point of view, setting, plot, and symbol
www.lausd.k12.ca.us/Belmont_HS/ tkm/background_links.html	Background on life and times when the novel was written
www.tokillamockingbird.com	Picture of the Monroe County Courthouse where the trial of Tom Robinson took place

Writing at the beginning and during the unit, however, can be a way to initiate inquiry or open a discussion. Responses to literature can take the form of essays, journal entries, visual responses, oral interpretations, and discussion. During the reading of *To Kill a Mockingbird*, students will focus on the themes of the novel and the events and issues of the historical period.

This unit offers students choices for their responses and assignments. Once all have read the novel, there are options:

- Discuss *To Kill a Mockingbird*.
- Read at least one other work that deals with tolerance from another genre, such as poetry, drama, the essay, or nonfiction.
- As a group activity, contribute and present research on at least one historical aspect of the life and times in which the novel took place.

- Write one extended essay, and complete journal entries and at least one other writing assignment, such as a script, an advertisement, or short paper.
- In groups or individually, participate in dramatic presentations: for example, role play characters or act out the trial scene.
- Complete two optional tasks from the list of activities, such as an art-based project to design a book jacket.

STEP 5: CREATE SAMPLE ACTIVITIES

Students can choose among the following activities. You may want to have students select activities at the beginning of the unit and list them in the form of a contract for specific grades.

Activities to Introduce the Unit

Research into the period in history in which *To Kill a Mockingbird* took place will help students understand the motivations behind events and attitudes of the characters in the novel. Additionally, some background on the author Harper Lee should give students insight into why she wrote the novel. Activities that follow require students to think about the Depression and segregation issues in the South during the 1930s. The Internet will be particularly useful in completing the research tasks:

- Locate information on the author Harper Lee. Determine what she is trying to say to her readers and why she wrote the book. Check Website *www.chebucto.ns.ca/Culture/HarperLee/index.html*.
- Form groups to conduct Web research on topics that will contribute to an understanding of the events in *To Kill a Mockingbird*. Possible subjects include: the Depression, segregation, the South in the 1930s, the Ku Klux Klan, and Alabama. Pictures at *www.corbis.com/scripts/FDRscript/gallery/pl* illustrate the Depression years. The Website at *www.mindspring.com/~rjones/hpi.html* depicts life in Alabama in the 1930s. Additional sample tasks to research the setting of the novel might include:
  — Interview persons who lived through the Depression. Record answers, stories, or reminiscences from the interviews. Use the template for interviews found in Chapter 8.
  — Listen to Martin Luther King's "I Have a Dream" speech at *www.audionet.com/speeches* to identify some of the issues with which African Americans have had to struggle. This speech was made in 1963. Identify similarities in King's speech to the situation blacks faced during the 1930s in Maycomb, the fictional town in which the novel takes place.
  — Research the life of Martin Luther King at *www.seattletimes.com/mlk/classroom/index.html*. Information about his life and struggles will help students understand some of the issues in the South that African Americans faced.
  — In journals, write about events or experiences in their lives that have caused students to be intolerant or a time when they experienced prejudice. They

must explain the events' impacts on them and how those experiences affected their thinking.

- View the Monroe County Courthouse at *www.tokillamockingbird.com*. This courthouse served as a model for the one in Maycomb where Tom Robinson's trial was held.

Activities to Be Used During the Unit

During the reading of the novel, students will keep journals to write and respond to events, themes, and characters in the book. They will make notes about interesting points or passages in the novel, jot down questions and make predictions as they read, and summarize ideas. Students will:

- Write several guided "freewrites" to help them predict what might happen in the novel at various stages in their reading. Some suggestions for freewrites include:
  — React to the title of the book. Explain what it might mean. What does it make the reader think of? What expectations does the reader have? Website *www.sdcoe.k12.ca.us/score/tokil/mocktg.htm* contains pictures and facts about mockingbirds to help with predictions.
  — Predict what will happen in the rest of the book after reading the first chapter. Support their choices with quotations from the book, if possible.
  — Midway through the book, summarize the problems the characters are facing and suggest possible solutions that might be developed. Explain why these solutions appear logical.
  — At the end of the book, identify reasons they liked or disliked the novel. See Figure 3-11 for guidelines.
- Write extended essays in which they explore an abstract idea like prejudice, intolerance, or courage. They will use personal experiences or events and journal entries already completed to support their definitions.
- Write letters to the jury outlining major points in the trial to convince the jury that Tom Robinson was guilty or not guilty OR write letters to Judge Taylor telling him why Tom Robinson should be set free. Use examples from the book to support their reasons. Website *www.bell.k12.ca.us/BellHS/Fac.Staf/Free/tkamqs.html* discusses the novel chapter by chapter, and experts answer questions about the novel's content.
- Stage a mock trial similar to the trial of Tom Robinson:
  — Choose assignments as reporters, spectators in the upstairs gallery, spectators in the downstairs courtroom, jury members, prosecution attorneys, defense attorneys, witnesses, and the judge.
  — Create dialogue for the characters. For example, each day reporters outside the courthouse summarize the events of the previous day's events in a journalistic style to include what happened, who it happened to, when it happened, where it happened, and why it occurred.
  — Act out the scenes in class in lieu of reading this part of the novel aloud.

Figure 3–11: Reflections on a Reading

Name: _____**Date:** _____

Title of Book: _____

Directions: Think about the novel you just completed. Answer the questions below, reflecting on how it made you feel and how it relates to your life and the times in which you live.

1. How did the author capture your interest as you began to read the book?

2. Are there any similarities between this book and your life and times? Explain.

3. What character would you like to be in the novel? Explain.

4. What character in the book is most like you? How are you alike or different?

5. Do you think the title fits the book? Why or why not?

6. What parts of the book did you like best? Least? Explain.

7. What is the major point the author wants you to remember?

8. Would you recommend this book to a friend? Why or why not?

9. On a scale of 1–10 with 10 the highest score, how would you rate this book? Explain.

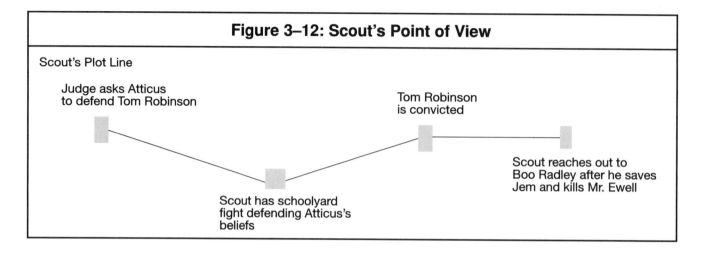

Figure 3–12: Scout's Point of View

Scout's Plot Line

Judge asks Atticus
to defend Tom Robinson

Tom Robinson
is convicted

Scout reaches out to
Boo Radley after he saves
Jem and kills Mr. Ewell

Scout has schoolyard
fight defending Atticus's
beliefs

- Create advertisements for *To Kill a Mockingbird* to entice someone who has not read the book to read it. Some suggestions for the ad include: why they liked or disliked it, quotes that they feel might create interest, and the most interesting thing they learned about the book.
- To use as study guides, generate questions in small groups about chapters of the novel. Vocabulary lists from each chapter at *www.lausd.k12.ca.us/ Belmont_HS/tkm/ index.html* or *http://library.advanced.org/12111/novel.html* may lend some help.
- Create visual representations of the action in *To Kill a Mockingbird* from the points of view of Scout, Atticus, Jem, and Tom Robinson. Create a plot line to indicate the exposition, the complication, the rising action, the reversal, the climax, and the resolution of the climax. See the sample diagram in Figure 3-12, which illustrates the action of the story from Scout's point of view.
- In groups, assume the points of view of Atticus, Tom Robinson, or Sheriff Tate and respond to the mob scene in front of the jail. Solicit reasons from the class as to why characters acted as they did.

Activities to Be Used Following the Unit

To reinforce ideas learned during the unit, students should have the opportunity to relate the themes to their own lives and the society that they live in today. They should also reflect on what they have just read. Students will:

- Create character analyses of major characters in the novel. The directions on the Character Analysis Chart in Figure 3-13 explain what students should analyze about a character.
- Hold a book fair. Create posters and display their original writing, illustrations, book jackets, and collages. In groups, perform different scenes from the novel, such as the trial scene, Atticus at the jail, and Jem attacked by Mr. Ewell.
- Search for information about the history of crimes against people of a cul-

Figure 3–13: Character Analysis Chart

Character Analysis:
Scout Finch

Name: _____

Directions: Scout's character is reflected in her actions, words, and physical characteristics—her "outer" appearance. We also get to know her through her "inner" thoughts, feelings, and reactions to others. Complete the chart giving a brief description of the action, what motivated it, and what you can infer about Scout from the action.

Outer Appearance

	Action	Motivation	Inference
What she does			
What she says			
Physical description			

Inner Character

	Action	Motivation	Inference
What she thinks/feels			
How others react to her (say or do)			
How she reacts to others			

ture, race, or religion, and present trends in America. Hate crimes today reveal that prejudices still exist, as they did in the 1930s. Choose one victimized group—such as people of Asian, African, or Mexican descent; homosexuals; or Jewish people—and identify incidents, such as the burning of synagogues, where intolerance occurred. In expository essays, compare and contrast actions, events, and attitudes toward the victimized group. Document opinions with research. Possible sites include: *http://shamash.org/holocaust* for holocaust information and *www.cnn.com* for hate crimes in the news.

STEP 6: EVALUATE WHAT WAS LEARNED

It is essential when evaluating this unit to perform assessment for both language arts and social studies content and skills. Teachers and library media specialists should collaboratively decide on the evaluation at the time the unit is developed. Strategies for assessment can include:

- periodic review of reading journals and responses to interesting ideas. Correctness and editing problems are not noted, because the journals are intended for exploring language and ideas. Journals will help teachers check on classroom activities and assess student progress in understanding the themes and concepts in the novel.
- student and teacher evaluation of the research process on the Internet. This could include reflecting on the content retrieved from the Internet, as well as the process of conducting the research. Questions that students might ask are: Were sources easy to find? What was the quality of the information retrieved? What barriers to conducting the research did they encounter? How did they use the information?
- review of students' writing portfolios for the unit to be assessed according to standard conventions of English.

SUMMARY

To Kill a Mockingbird has valuable messages for students. Inequality, prejudice, intolerance, and discrimination—themes in the novel—are still with us today. Using a project approach, students had opportunities to investigate issues that concerned and interested them, whether it was the Depression, the Ku Klux Klan, life in a small town, or segregation. As a result, the class was able to conduct in-depth inquiry into the lifestyles and customs of the 1930s in order to understand the characters' attitudes in the novel and what motivated those actions. Internet investigation enabled students to access sources that were not readily available in their classrooms.

It is now time to plan your own cross-curricular units, incorporating the Internet to expand the types and number of resources available to you. On the Internet, students can listen to Martin Luther King's "I Have a Dream" speech, see a replica of a southern courthouse to help them envision the site of Tom Robinson's trial, or compare photos of black slaves taken before the Civil War. Through access to such sources, they can now see the connections between English and social studies and appreciate the role literature plays in bringing history to life.

TEACHER EXERCISES: NOW YOU TRY IT...

It is important to reinforce what you just learned in this chapter by trying some activities yourself. Before going on to Chapter 4, try some of the following:

1. Select one of the two sample units and check the Websites listed in the unit. This will help you identify the kind of information you have available on a specific subject.
2. Choose a country that you plan to explore with your students. Create a Treasure Hunt on the Internet to obtain information about the country. Identify at least ten URLs for Websites that contain appropriate information for the grade level you teach.
3. Choose a novel that you plan to teach this year. Identify at least ten sites that contain information about the novel, the author, the time period in which the novel was written, or themes or issues in the novel. Incorporate these URLs into your unit plan for the novel.
4. Reflect in your journal on the following:
   - How can you use the World Wide Web for primary-level students? Is it appropriate? What must you keep in mind if you have young children go online?
   - In what ways do you see the Web being useful for students in grades four through six?
   - At the secondary level, what precautions would you take when having students do research online? What advantages and disadvantages do you see in using the Internet for interdisciplinary topics?

CONCLUSION

Developments in education have led educators to concentrate more on interdisciplinary curricula. Curriculum integration may be within a subject area, such as in a social studies class, where students read biographies of famous historical figures. It may be more global, as in the thrust to include writing across the curriculum in all subject areas. It may occur in science instruction, where students read and interpret scientific articles and communicate science concepts orally.

Integrated instruction has the responsibility for teaching, reinforcing, and applying basic skills. Content must also lend itself to more than one curriculum area. For instance, reading novels with scientific themes, discussing the ethical implications of social problems like pollution, and studying the mathematical aspects of scientific problems reinforce the idea that all subject areas have value and are interrelated in students' lives. Schools must continue to focus on interdisciplinary teaching, and teachers and library media specialists must work together to create cross-curricular units. The Internet now provides the tools to enable educators to cross curriculum boundaries more easily. In Chapter 4, we look closely at learning modalities as a way to individualize instruction.

REFERENCES

California State Department of Education. 1987. *English–Language Arts Framework for California Public Schools: Kindergarten Through Grade Twelve.* Sacramento: California State Department of Education.

Chard, Sylvia C. 1992. *The Project Approach: A Practical Guide for Teachers.* Edmonton, Alberta: University of Alberta Printing Services.

Johnson, David W., Geoffrey Maruyama, Roger T. Johnson, Deborah Nelson, and Linda Skon. 1981. "Effects of Cooperative, Competitive and Individualistic Goal Structures on Achievement: A Meta-Analysis." *Psychological Bulletin* 89, 47–62.

Macrorie, Ken. 1988. *The I-Search Paper: Revised Edition of Searching Writing.* Portsmouth, NH: Boynton/Cook.

Morrow, Lesley. 1979. "Exciting Children about Literature through Creative Storytelling Techniques." *Language Arts* 56 (March): 236.

Piaget, Jean. 1962. *Language and Thought of the Child.* 3rd ed. New York: Humanities.

Ramos, Ross. 1980. *Storyteller.* 2nd ed. Columbus, OH: Charles E. Merrill.

Strickland, Dorothy. 1973. "A Program for Linguistically Different Black Children." *Research in the Teaching of English* (Spring): 79–86.

Wagner, Betty Jane. 1979. "Using Drama to Create an Environment for Language Development." *Language Arts* 56 (March): 268.

Chapter 4

INCORPORATING THE INTERNET INTO INDIVIDUALIZED INSTRUCTION

PART 1: IDEAS AND INSIGHTS

OBJECTIVES OF THIS CHAPTER

This chapter is designed to focus attention on distinct learning modalities and on activities available over the Internet that emphasize those different intelligences and learning styles. It addresses topics at both the elementary and secondary levels. At the end of this chapter, educators will be able to:

- describe Howard Gardner's seven distinct intelligences
- understand the differences between learning styles and multiple intelligences
- identify components of learning centers
- create learning centers for different intelligences
- build a unit that focuses on different intelligences and includes the Internet

INTRODUCTION

Understanding and teaching to students' learning modalities—or the way individuals learn best—is being emphasized more and more in today's classrooms as a way to meet the needs of all students. There are volumes of research available that speak to the way students learn. Right-brain, left-brain research by Freeley and Perrin (1987), learning-styles studies conducted by Kenneth and Rita Dunn (1987), and the 4MAT concept by McCarthy (1984) all address this issue (see Figure 4-1).

Howard Gardner (1983) in his book *Frames of Mind: The Theory of Multiple Intelligences* denies the definition of general intelligence and offers instead seven dis-

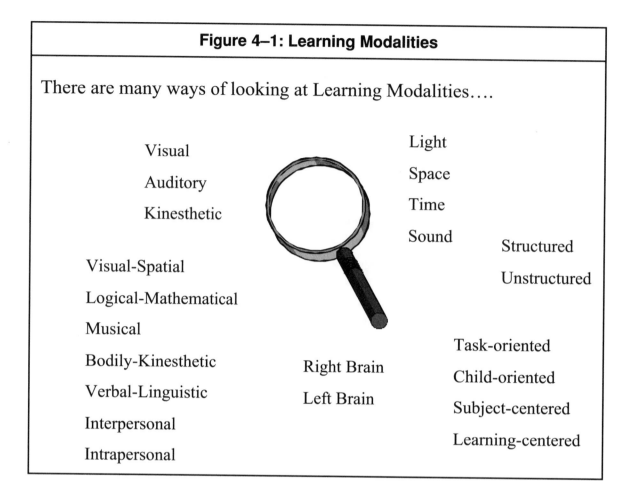

Figure 4–1: Learning Modalities

There are many ways of looking at Learning Modalities....

Visual

Auditory

Kinesthetic

Light

Space

Time

Sound

Visual-Spatial

Logical-Mathematical

Musical

Bodily-Kinesthetic

Verbal-Linguistic

Interpersonal

Intrapersonal

Structured

Unstructured

Right Brain

Left Brain

Task-oriented

Child-oriented

Subject-centered

Learning-centered

tinctive intelligences. It is important here to distinguish between multiple intelligences and learning styles. Dunn and Dunn (1992) suggest that the term "learning style" explains a person's constant way of handling stimuli in the context of learning. Gardner (1983:8) defines "intelligence" as the "capacity to solve problems or to fashion products that are valued in one or more cultural settings." Although it is important for teachers to provide varied learning experiences to deal with students' strengths and weaknesses, we must take a look at both theories in more detail in order to understand them. Then we can try to incorporate activities to accommodate different learning modalities into our unit plans.

FOCUS ON LEARNING STYLES

Research (Dunn and Dunn, 1992) suggests that students develop the ability to learn in different ways as a result of hereditary factors and environmental influences. These different ways of learning are called learning styles. When educators place emphasis on learning styles in their teaching, they pay attention to how students acquire knowledge rather than on teaching styles and student-teacher interaction.

Learning styles are typically categorized into different types: visual, auditory, and kinesthetic-tactile. Research suggests that although most people use all of their senses to learn, there is generally one that is more dominant than the others. According to Walter Barbe and co-authors (1979), about 30 percent of elementary school children have visual modality strength, 25 percent have auditory strength, 15 percent are kinesthetically oriented, and the remaining 30 percent have mixed modality strengths. A visual learner relies on seeing things and internal visualization; an auditory learner depends on hearing and verbalization for learning; and a kinesthetic-tactile learner learns by touching, feeling, and body movement.

Each modality preference has certain characteristics. Visual children learn best by watching, reading, and seeing. They like descriptions because they can imagine the scene; they prefer visual arts; they like to plan and make lists. People who utilize hearing as their primary learning sense can benefit significantly by concentrating on lectures. Auditory children like conversation and dialogue; they prefer music to visual arts; they prefer to hear directions and like to sound out words. A tape recorder can be a very functional tool for an auditory learner. Finally, kinesthetic children learn most effectively through internal and external feelings. They are hands-on learners who find it difficult to sit still while reading. They remember what they do, not what they see or hear.

More than likely, teachers' teaching styles will not match the learning styles of all students in their classes. Therefore, teachers need to adapt their teaching styles when they see students who are not learning. They may also need to modify the curriculum material. It is important to select diverse activities and resources so that material is presented in the styles of the learners. For example, if teachers are giving students directions on how to number papers for a spelling test, they can (a) tell students to number their papers from 1–10, (b) show them how to number by folding a piece of paper in half and writing the numbers 1–10 in the margin, and/or (c) even draw a picture of the numbered paper on the blackboard. By using different methods to identify concepts, teachers can provide for all children's styles of learning: auditory, visual, and tactile-kinesthetic.

FOCUS ON MULTIPLE INTELLIGENCES

In the mid-1980s, Howard Gardner in his *Theory of Multiple Intelligences* proposed a new way of describing intelligence. His research suggested that the human brain seems to have the capacity to process information in seven different ways and that individuals tend to be programmed more strongly in one or several of these intelligences; most learners, however, have some capacity to function in all seven modes. Through his research, Gardner also determined that people who are not especially strong or gifted in one intelligence can improve by focusing on their strengths first and then practicing to improve other abilities. Consequently, it is important for teachers and students to have an understanding of these intelligences and how they affect learning. Gardner's seven intelligences are:

1. *verbal/linguistic intelligence.* Verbal people like to read, write, and listen to stories. They comprehend, they use language fluently and have well-developed vocabularies. They also have good memories for names, places, and

dates. To help improve verbal intelligence, students can read or tell stories, participate in formal and impromptu speaking, and play memory or word games.

2. *logical/mathematical intelligence.* This type focuses on problem solving and reasoning. Students who exhibit logical/mathematical intelligence can recognize patterns; categorize, analyze, and interpret data; and devise experiments to test out things they do not understand. To practice logical intelligence, children can explain a process step-by-step, predict endings to stories or films, and create charts, graphs, and timelines.

3. *visual/spatial intelligence.* Stimulated through the use of pictures, images, and colors, children with this intelligence are usually good with maps, charts, and visual puzzles. They like to draw and see pictures or videos. To improve visual intelligence, children can use art materials, such as clay; illustrate stories; and create maps of the classroom, their own room, or the community.

4. *musical intelligence.* Children whose strength is musical intelligence are aware of rhythm and melody. They may play a musical instrument. To improve musical intelligence, children can listen to sounds and sing in group sing-alongs.

5. *bodily-kinesthetic intelligence.* One's mental abilities coordinate one's own bodily movements. Children who are good at physical activities, and people such as dancers and gymnasts who use their bodies to convey emotions, exhibit kinesthetic intelligence. To improve this intelligence, children should do physical things: exercise, ride a bike, and play charades.

6. *interpersonal intelligence.* This is the ability to communicate well with people, responding to their moods, settling disputes, and sometimes manipulating others. Children with this intelligence are often leaders and like to socialize. To increase interpersonal skills, children can work on cooperative or group problem-solving projects, conduct peer tutoring, and participate in games that require collaboration.

7. *intrapersonal intelligence.* Stimulated by self-reflection and being left to themselves, children strong in this intelligence understand their own emotions and realistically assess their own abilities. These individuals know what they can or cannot accomplish and like to work on individual, self-paced projects. Ways to improve this skill are to write reflectively in a journal or participate in role-play activities that allow these children to express their ideas and opinions.

Gardner would propose that the most effective instruction incorporates all seven intelligences. He indicates that rarely do the intelligences operate independently; rather, they are used concurrently and usually complement each other as individuals develop skills or solve problems. Students tend to be drawn to areas of study that emphasize their strengths. As teachers, however, we should create projects and activities that allow students to develop their less-preferred intelligences. For example, students whose strength is verbal or linguistic should try predictions or brainstorming solutions to problems to develop their logical intelligence more fully. The units in Part 2 of this chapter incorporate activities that address all seven intelligences.

THE INTERNET AND LEARNING MODALITIES

As we plan our teaching activities, we need to think about teaching strategies we can use so students will activate their different learning styles and intelligences. The World Wide Web offers graphics, images, animations, quick-time movies, and real-audio sound. This multimedia approach on the Internet, then, can be used to enhance all learning styles. The variety of Websites that emphasize art, drama, music, reading, and writing provides students with options to reinforce an intelligence strength or improve weaker ones.

In this chapter we will look at two different units, one on Our Solar System, the other using the Website at *www.amazon.com*. In each unit, a myriad of interdisciplinary activities will focus on different intelligences. As we review activities in these two units, we should think about the intelligences and learning styles that are addressed with each task.

LEARNING CENTERS

One teaching technique to individualize instruction in the classroom is through the use of learning centers. A learning center is a collection of materials arranged around stations where students can interact with the materials. At each station, students will find instruction and materials for one particular task. All of the activities at a particular learning center are designed to reinforce a single educational objective. Learning centers provide for expansion and enrichment of concepts and skills that have been introduced by teachers. We often think of learning centers as solely an activity for the elementary school; however, they can also be used at the secondary level.

WHY USE LEARNING CENTERS?

The learning center offers an integrated approach to individualized learning that can be geared to the abilities, interests, and learning modalities of the students in the classroom. They can also motivate children to learn through interaction with a variety of developmentally appropriate materials and equipment. Moreover, the use of centers can help students move from teacher-centered to student-centered learning activities.

Research (Myrow, 1979) on learning indicates that self-determination enhances students' personal development. If students direct the order of the presentation of material, they recall it better. Also, increased involvement in tasks enhances students' long-term retention and heightens their motivation while they are acquiring the content. Finally, freedom to choose has a strong effect on students' attitudes toward instruction, so they are more willing to work longer on tasks. Thus, learning centers are one way to reach individuals by providing opportunities and choices designed to facilitate meaningful student involvement

Learning centers enable students to learn at their own pace and can be designed to address all intelligences. Through center activities, students learn to develop their own goals and work independently, strengthening their intrapersonal intelligence. If they do not understand the first time, they can try again. Students also learn from each other and use different ways of communicating ideas, thus enhancing interpersonal intelligence. Center activities also provide teachers with many opportunities for assessing needs and achievements, and students have chances to evaluate their own progress. An additional benefit of learning centers is that you can change center topics regularly to reflect current events, a new scientific discovery, or changing phenomena in space.

There is no limit to the types of activities that can be incorporated into center learning tasks. Some commonly used centers include: Language Centers, Listening Centers, Science Centers, Art Centers, Music Centers, and Library Centers (Figure 4-2 shows a sample classroom containing several). Centers can be located on a table or a small rug, in a corner of the classroom, and at a computer, to name a few. Centers can be changed according to the interest levels and achievement of goals by students. For example, each learning center might represent the different topics you will teach in science during the year: In the Weather Center, children can investigate weather conditions surrounding the El Niño phenomena; in the Animal Center students can learn about animal habitats, identify similarities and differences among animals, view pictures of animals in their natural surroundings, and hear animal sounds; more specifically, a Genes and Traits Center can focus on DNA or matching parents with children; and a Recycling Center can incorporate activities related to students' daily experiences recycling their own trash.

Using learning centers is an ideal way to teach to multiple intelligences, thereby strengthening students' dominant intelligences and enhancing their weaker ones. Students usually like learning centers because they are fun and provide interesting things to do. Center tasks also provide students with opportunities to learn things that are not in the textbooks. As a result, students develop a multifaceted approach to learning.

LEARNING CENTER COMPONENTS

Learning centers should look enticing, have clear directions for tasks students are to complete, and be designed so that learning opportunities can be extended and expanded. The activities promote students assuming responsibility and experiencing success. Components of a learning center should include:

- objectives
- a variety of materials
- directions for working on tasks
- actual activities to achieve objectives
- a work space that is attractive and colorfully designed
- interests that pertain to individuals and the total class

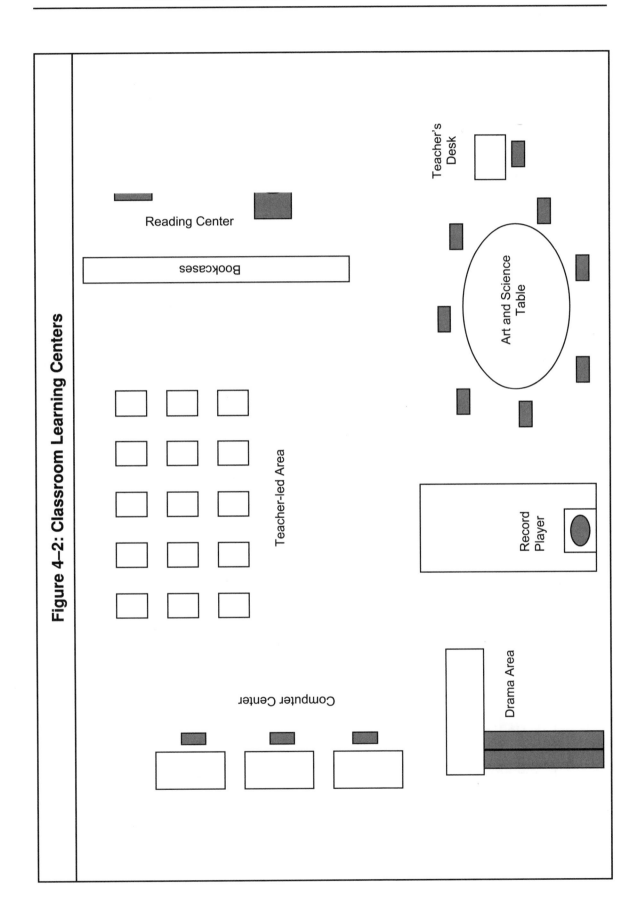

Figure 4–2: Classroom Learning Centers

SETTING UP LEARNING CENTERS

In planning our learning centers, we must determine the following steps:

1. Check the curriculum and separate it into units of study—for example, holiday themes, science concepts, or students' interests.
2. If possible, decide what content objectives will be taught for the selected units in each subject area. Subject areas should include language arts, math, science, art, drama, and music.
3. Design listening activities, role-playing situations, problem-solving tasks, games, and experiments that will reinforce and strengthen skills in the content area, promote interaction among peers, allow students to work independently, and conform to selected unit themes. Activities should range from simple to difficult and concrete to abstract.
4. Create activities that cover different ranges of abilities to meet the needs of all students. For instance, students might self-select some activities; teachers might stipulate others as mandatory. A simple chart or contract stating which activities each student must complete (see Figure 4-3) helps to organize the activities for students and teachers.

Figure 4–3: Learning Center Contracts

Contract for: _____

Date started: _____

I agree to complete:

Activities: _____ | _____ Comments:

_____ _____

_____ _____

_____ _____

Date Completed: _____

Student Signature: _____

Teacher Signature: _____

5. Set up an evaluation mechanism. It could involve self-checking activities with answer keys available at the center, portfolios, or individual conferences with students to discuss their progress.
6. Create a chart, such as the one in Figure 4-4, giving students daily information regarding which centers they should visit, in what order, and with whom to ensure smooth movement from center to center. If the centers are numbered or color coded, students can plan their progress better. For example, the Art Center activities might be coded with blue dots, the Music Center ones with green ones, and the Verbal Center ones with red dots.
7. Set up groups for each center. If there are non-native speakers in the class, pair them with the more fluent English speakers.

Figure 4–4: Scheduling Center Activity

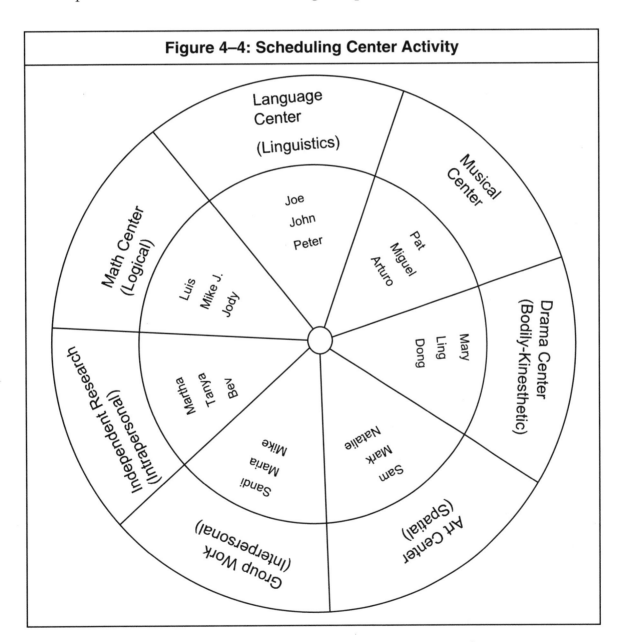

Figure 4–5: Keeping Records

Meteorites & Asteroids Center

Students	Task 1	Task 2	Task 3
Jeff			
Arturo			
Sandi			

8. Design a method that allows students to know when they are to change to the next center. Verbal commands, a flicker of lights, the ringing of a bell—all work well.
9. Keep records of the centers that have been completed by each student. Figure 4-5 gives an example of a simple record-keeping chart.
10. Evaluate the center, the learning that takes place, and student interest in center activities, as illustrated in Figure 4-6.
11. During the center time, function as the facilitator and work with individuals.

LEARNING CENTER ACTIVITIES

Children should be introduced to activities in learning centers either as a total class or in small groups. The introduction of activities should include expected behaviors, outcomes, and choices for activities. Task cards or activity cards comprise a useful and versatile way to present learning activities; directions for completing each activity in the center should be clearly written on the task cards. For example, if students are studying the culture of Japan, one of the activity cards might ask them to identify facts about Japan. Figures 4-7 and 4-8 provide illustrations of activity cards that can be used at the elementary and secondary level grades, respectively.

Figure 4–6: Evaluation

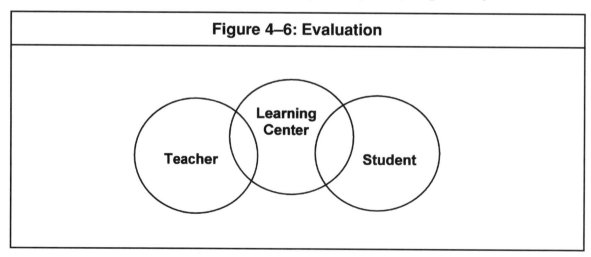

Figure 4–7: Sample Elementary Activity Cards

Physical Features of Planets

Student Objectives

When students complete this
Center, they will be able to:

- Identify physical features of the
  planets in the solar system.
- See patterns to the planet images.
- Use distinct details in their writing.
- Work together with a partner.
- Do a peer review of a partner's
  writing.

Directions to Follow

- Read all of the directions before
  beginning any of the activities.

- Take Activity Card #1 from the
  Learning Center. Complete all
  tasks. Put the card back in the
  Learning Center.

- Do the same with the rest of the
  activity cards. Follow the
  numerical sequence.

- Make sure that all materials are
  replaced before leaving the
  Center.

Sample Activity Card #1

Describing the Planets

1. Type the URL: *www.nasm.edu/GALLERIES/GAL207/
   gal207.html*
2. View the images of the planets and choose one planet to describe.
3. Write a description of one planet using 5–7 sentences.
4. Draw a picture to illustrate the planet.
5. Go to Activity Card #2.

Sample Activity Card #2

Describing the Planets

1. Read the description of your planet to a partner.
2. The partner should guess the name of the planet by hearing the
   description and viewing the picture.
3. If your partner cannot guess the planet, add more details to your
   writing.
4. Have your partner read the description and identify the planet. Then
   reverse the procedure.
5. When both of your planets have been identified, go to Activity Card #3.

Figure 4–8: Sample Secondary Activity Cards

Learning to Use Maps

Student Objectives

When students complete this
Center, they will be able to:
* Read compass directions on maps
  and globes.
* Identify land masses known as
  continents.
* Locate large bodies of water in the
  world.
* Locate various countries within the
  seven continents.
* Identify major rivers in the world.
* Describe and demonstrate the use
  of longitude and latitude.
* Read and interpret various legends,
  scales, and symbols on globes,
  maps, and charts.

Directions to Follow

* Read all of the directions before
  beginning any of the activities.

* Take Activity Card #1 from the
  Learning Center. Complete all
  tasks. Put the card back in the
  Learning Center.

* Do the same with the rest of the
  activity cards. Follow the
  numerical sequence.

* Make sure that all materials are
  replaced before leaving the
  Center.

Sample Activity Card #1

Using the Globe

1. Find the legend on a flat map. Now find the legend on the globe.
   Compare the two legends. Be ready to relate any similarities and
   differences you find to the teacher.
2. Locate the time scale on the globe and discuss why it is necessary.
3. Study the land elevations in the legend. Why is there a need for topography in the legend?
4. Take a sheet entitled "Using the Globe" from the box at the Center and
   complete each question. When this is completed, give it to the teacher.
5. Go on to Activity Card #2.

Activities in each learning center can reflect cross-disciplinary topics; they can focus on distinct learning modalities; or they can emphasize any topic the class is currently studying. Each center should clearly indicate the number of children to work at that center at one time. The two units that follow will illustrate how to use the learning center concept with the Internet. Each incorporates these six steps:

1. Apply framework standards—what should be taught?
2. Identify general goals and specific objectives.
3. Gather materials.
4. Introduce the unit.
5. Create sample activities.
6. Evaluate what was learned.

PART 2: PRACTICAL APPLICATIONS

Two unit plans in Part 2 illustrate using Web resources to address students' distinct learning modalities. The first unit focuses on a science topic: Our Solar System. Internet resources for this topic abound, ranging from startling photographs of planets taken by the Hubble telescope to opportunities to ask questions of astronomers. The unit content centers specifically on the nine planets. It also enables students to use their modality strengths while accomplishing tasks, and it provides activities to strengthen their less-dominant intelligences. The sample unit can be taught at a fifth- or sixth-grade level but could easily be adapted for younger children or a middle school class.

The second unit, designed for secondary-level students, presents activities to involve students in real-life tasks using the Internet. It revolves around the Internet Website *www.amazon.com*, which is engaged in commercial activity. This unit may be taught in a Business Education class, although it is interdisciplinary, incorporating mathematics, language arts, social studies, and art projects in a learning center environment. It also illustrates to high school students the possible future of business in the next millennium.

UNIT 1 (ELEMENTARY LEVEL): OUR SOLAR SYSTEM

Learning centers work for any subject area as well as for interdisciplinary units. For example, each learning center can represent different science topics, such as the solar system, the weather, or sea creatures, to name several. Or they can be set up so that each center focuses on facets of one topic—for example, learning centers on the solar system might have students learn about planets by building models, viewing images of Mars or Jupiter, talking to astronomers, simulating space travel, and more.

To begin Our Solar System unit, choose the specific topics you want to study at your grade level. For our purposes in this unit, we will choose the Earth Science strand from the science curriculum. Subjects included in earth science are astronomy, meteorology, oceanography, and geology. Next, identify Websites that students can explore as part of each center activity.

STEP 1: APPLY FRAMEWORK STANDARDS—WHAT SHOULD BE TAUGHT?

From kindergarten through third grade, students must learn to observe using their senses—seeing, hearing, feeling, tasting, and smelling. They must communicate through speech, pictures, and writing. They should learn to make sensory, relative, and linear comparisons. They must organize by gathering data, sequencing, grouping, and classifying material objects. These tasks correlate with Piaget's (1968) third stage of development: the state of concrete operations that usually develops in children between the ages of seven and eleven years. During this stage children think systematically and logically as long as they are referring to tangible objects. They are not yet ready to deal with abstract thinking.

Based on the National Science Education standards, the following are some of the understandings children between seven and eleven years should develop as a result of activities in grades five and six:

- Students should develop the ability to understand scientific inquiry and conduct research.
- They should be able to make systematic observations, compare ideas, and develop descriptions and explanations using evidence. For example, as a result of investigation, students should realize that the planet Earth is part of the solar system.

In grades three through six, students spend time studying the solar system and its planets. They identify the nine planets, and learn about eclipses of the sun, asteroids, meteorites, and comets. Throughout, children improve their thinking processes by observing, communicating, comparing, organizing, and relating. For example, they might conduct experiments in which they observe the sky at night and describe how planets change positions relative to the stars. They might use a model of the earth, sun, and moon to explain eclipses. They might view some of the valuable photographs of planet surfaces, colors, and other characteristics transmitted by the Hubble telescope. By the sixth grade, students should know that there are nine planets that vary in size and surface features. They should understand that these planets move around the sun. They should also be aware of special features of some planets like rings, moons, and ice particles.

The Internet provides Websites where students can access photos, compare planets using different criteria, identify comets like the Hale-Bopp Comet, and see images from space. In addition, experts can provide answers to students' questions. For this unit we will convert the classroom into the Space Room, which will contain seven learning centers, each emphasizing one of Gardner's intelligences.

STEP 2: IDENTIFYING GENERAL GOALS AND SPECIFIC OBJECTIVES

The National Science Education standards and the California science framework provide guidelines for this unit. Use the goals and specific objectives that follow as a basis for the content and skills developed in the unit.

Goals
By the end of this unit, students will be able to:

- see relationships and make interpretations
- communicate in small group projects
- work individually to complete tasks
- gather information on the solar system from a variety of sources
- use the Internet for research

Objectives
Throughout this unit, students will:

- observe and describe the planets via a telescope
- gain knowledge of how astronomers study the universe
- identify features of all planets in the solar system
- identify contrasts, similarities, and relationships among planets
- construct a model solar system to represent distances between the planets and the sun
- identify differences between living in space and on earth
- recall major events in space exploration

STEP 3: GATHER MATERIALS
The Internet contains such diverse information that it can accommodate all of the intelligences. The multimedia component of the Internet brings sounds, images, music, animation, and text directly to students. Visual learners can view photos of Jupiter; students with logical/mathematical intelligence can predict their weight on Mars; children who learn better by touching and feeling can build models of the solar system. Moreover, hands-on, active learning is required of all students when they use the Internet. The Websites listed in Table 4-1 provide resources to meet all intelligences.

STEP 4: INTRODUCE THE UNIT
For this unit you will set up your classroom into seven centers, each one containing activities about the solar system that require students to use one of Gardner's seven intelligences: musical, interpersonal, intrapersonal, bodily/kinesthetic, logical/mathematical, verbal/linguistic, and visual/spatial. In addition, activities are cross-disciplinary and represent language arts, art, mathematics, and music.

Some of the activities at one center may be extensions of a task at another center. For example, at the visual center children will view photos of different planets, describe the planets, and write facts about them. If they visit the interpersonal center, students will use the information they gathered in the visual center to work with a partner sharing and discussing the facts they learned when viewing the planets.

Students will try at least one of several activities from each center. In this way, they will have to use each of their distinct intelligences and thus strengthen the weaker

Table 4-1: Solar System Web Resources	
Web Site URLs	**Descriptions of Websites**
www.nasm.edu/ceps	View the nine planets
http://tommy.jsc.nasa.gov/~woodfill/ SPACEED/SEHHTML/earlysf.html	View a spacesuit, a walk on the moon, and the first golf shot on the moon
http://quest.arc.nasa.gov/interactive/ index.html	Enter a contest about space, sponsored by NASA
www.seti-inst.edu/sci-det.html	Measure the orbits of planets
http://tqjunior.advanced.org/3521	Graph space routes
http://liftoff.msfc.nasa.gov/kids/ adventure/jigsaw/puzzle.html	Unscramble space pictures
www.EnchantedLearning.com/ subjects/astronomy	Comprehensive site on the solar system for K–4
www.seds.lpl.arizona.edu/nineplanets/ nineplanets/nineplanets.html	View the planets, meteorites, comets, and asteroids

ones. In addition, they will be required to complete all of the activities at one center of their choice—giving them a choice allows students to work at centers where they feel most comfortable. Three to four students may work at one center at a time. Each center contains activity cards that spell out the tasks children can try.

STEP 5: CREATE SAMPLE ACTIVITIES

At each center, activities emphasize one specific intelligence. Most activities involve an Internet resource to help students complete the task. Some activities will require children to work independently; others will mean students work with a partner or in a small group. The tasks are numbered so students progress from one to another in a logical sequence.

Activities to Introduce the Unit

To start, ask students to set aside sections of their notebooks and entitle them "Our Solar System." The following three activities are for the whole class to complete together before students visit the learning centers:

1. They will write in their notebooks observations they have made of the moon and planets at night.
2. Working alone, have students answer yes or no to the following statements in their notebooks and then discuss their answers in small groups. This will provide a baseline of students' understanding of the solar system. Sample statements include:

- The sun is a planet.
- The solar system is a group of planets that revolve around the sun.
- There are eight planets in our solar system.
- Earth is the only planet that has a moon.
- All the planets are very much alike.

3. Students will read excerpts from books about the solar system—the planets, the sun, and Earth's moon. Students will add to this information in their learning center activities. Some nonfiction books about the solar system to consider are:
   — *The Universe of Galileo and Newton,* by W. Bixby
   — *Cosmic View: The Universe in 40 Jumps,* by K. Boeke
   — *Sky Watchers of Ages Past,* by M. E. Weiss
   — *The Nine Planets,* by Franklyn M. Branley
   — *What Is a Solar System?* by Theodore Munch and B. Teidemann
Fiction books might include:
   — *Miss Pickerel Goes to Mars,* by Ellen MacGregor
   — *Matthew Looney and the Space Pirates,* by Jerome Beatty
   — *Dragonfall 5 and the Space Cowboys,* by Brian Earnshaw

Activities to Be Used During the Unit

Any or all of these activities are possible for the learning centers on the solar system. Each center illustrates a different intelligence and uses a resource offered on the Internet. The variety of activities in the seven centers will appeal to all learning styles and intelligences.

VISUAL/SPATIAL INTELLIGENCE CENTER

At the Visual/Spatial Intelligence Center, children will use images, photos, maps, and pictures to discover information about the solar system. Students will:

1. draw a diagram of the solar system, labeling all planets. Figure 4-9 depicts a Website at *http://seds.lpl.arizona.edu/nineplanets/nineplanets/overview.html* that could provide a basis for a model.
2. create a timeline illustrating space travel from Sputnik to the Space Shuttle. Children can obtain the facts they need at Website *http://tqjunior.advanced.org/ 3626*.
3. view images at Website *www.seds.org/pub/images/planets*. They should write a paragraph in their journals comparing two planets.
4. identify facts about the planet Saturn at *www.nasm.edu/ceps/SII/SII.html*. See Figure 4-10 for a sample visual/spatial activity card.
5. find as many faces as they can in the picture of the planet Mars at *www.aspsky. org/html/tnl/25/25.html*.

MUSICAL INTELLIGENCE CENTER

At the Musical Intelligence Center, children will hear music to help them explore their feelings about space. Students will:

Figure 4–9: Solar System Model

Reprinted by permission Bill Arnett www.seds.org/billa

1. take a multimedia tour of the nine planets using sound, movies, images, and text. Check the Website at *www.tesn.net/afiner/intro.htm.*
2. use music to interpret their feelings about space. See Figure 4-11 for a sample musical activity card.

INTERPERSONAL INTELLIGENCE CENTER

At the Interpersonal Intelligence Center, students will work together in pairs, in small groups, or with classrooms across the world on projects that help them understand space phenomena. Students will:

1. answer the question: Is there a man on the moon? Ask an astronomer why or why not at *http://image.gsfc.nasa.gov/poetry/astro/qanda.html* or *http://umbra.nascom.nasa.gov/spartan/ask_astronomers.html.*
2. plan their own flight into space. See Figure 4-12 for a sample interpersonal activity card.

INTRAPERSONAL INTELLIGENCE CENTER

At the Intrapersonal Center, students work independently on tasks that help them delve into space. Activities include:

1. Use Website *http://kids.msfc.nasa.gov/Puzzles/SolarSystem.asp* to put planets in order from closest to furthest from the sun, Mercury to Pluto.

Figure 4–10: Visual/Spatial Intelligence Activity Card

Describing Saturn

1. Look at the planet Saturn at *www.nasm.edu/ceps*
   and answer the following questions.
   • How many satellites does Saturn have?
   • How many moons does Saturn have?
2. View two moons and describe them in your journal. Compare
   the color, lightness and darkness, and diameter.
   • Which is closest to Saturn?
   • How many miles separate the two moons you have chosen?
3. By looking at other information about Saturn, write down two
   additional facts that interest you about the planet.
   Use Web site *www.nasm.edu/ceps.*
4. Go on to Activity Card #2.

Figure 4–11: Musical Intelligence Activity Card

Music and the Planets

1. Listen to a recording of *2001: A Space Odyssey* through the headphones.
2. Draw a picture that illustrates the images that come to your mind
   as you listen to the music.
3. Answer the following questions in your journal.
   What does the music make you think of? A particular planet?
   Comets? Meteorites? The entire solar system?
4. View the photos of the solar system at *www.nasm.edu/ceps.* [visual]
5. Compare your drawing with the images on the Internet. Write
   down the similarities and differences you see. [linguistic]
6. Explain your picture to another classmate. [interpersonal]
7. Go on to Activity Card #2.

Figure 4–12: Interpersonal Intelligence Activity Card

Space Flight to Mars

1. You will be taking a trip into space. You must make a number of decisions before you blast off.
2. With your group answer the following questions in your journals.
   • What food should we take?
   • What activities can we plan to do?
   • What training do we need?
3. Check the Web sites for help at *http://astro-2.msfc.nasa.gov* or *http://spacelink.nasa.gov/NASA.Projects/Human.Exploration.and. Development.of.Space/Living.and.Working.In.Space/index.html*.
4. Write down the essential things that your group will need to survive.
5. Individually, decide on one personal item you would bring if you were limited to only one thing.
6. Explain to the group why you would choose this item.
7. Go on to Activity Card #2.

---

2. Students can create their own planet games using descriptions and drawings of the nine planets (see Figure 4-13).
3. Have students create their own planetary book with photos and text from *http://quest.arc.nasa.gov* and then share the book. Use *www.EnchantedLearning. com/subjects/astronomy* for visuals and descriptions of the planets (Figure 4-14 illustrates the types of information available at the site).

LOGICAL/MATHEMATICAL INTELLIGENCE CENTER

At the Logical/Mathematical Intelligence Center, students will use mathematical concepts to enable them to see relationships and differences among planets. Students will:

1. note the hourly positions of the planets relative to each other on one day. Check Website *http://calweb.com:80/~mcharvey/planet_all.html* for help. Graph the positions of the planets.
2. compare the temperatures on Mars, Jupiter, Saturn, or another planet at Website *http://tqjunior.advanced.org/3521*. Create a bar graph of the different planet temperatures. Which one is the coldest? Hottest? Most similar to Earth?
3. choose one planet, such as Jupiter, and check its weights (see Figure 4-15).

Figure 4–13: Intrapersonal Intelligence Activity Card

Solar System Game

1. Choose nine images to describe by looking at
   www.nasm.edu/GALLERIES/GAL207/gal207.html.
   You will not know which planet the image is depicting.
   • Look for shapes, patterns, and colors (e.g., darkness, light, roughness, smoothness)
2. Enter detailed notes in your journal about what you see when you look at the planets.
3. Try to identify each planet based on its characteristics.
4. Sketch pictures of each planet.
5. Write down scientists' descriptions of each planet. Check the Website
   www.nasm.edu/ceps.
   • Place each drawing with its description.
6. Compare your descriptions with the scientists'. Write down what is similar and different. Use *www.nasm.edu/ceps.*
7. Revise your planet descriptions.
8. Now play a Concentration game. [interpersonal]
   • Turn descriptions and pictures face down, scramble them.
   • Ask students to turn over two cards until they match the correct descriptions with the appropriate pictures and name the planets.
8. Go on to Activity Card #2.

BODILY/KINESTHETIC INTELLIGENCE CENTER

At the Bodily/Kinesthetic Intelligence Center, children will work on building models to demonstrate concepts about the solar system. Students will:

1. build their own clay models or mobiles of the solar system. Check Website *www.windows.umich.edu* for help.
2. unscramble the picture of the astronaut in the spacesuit at Website *http://liftoff.msfc.nasa.gov/kids/adventure/jigsaw/puzzle.html.*
3. use map skills to get home from space at *http://starchild.gsfc.nasa.gov/docs/StarChild/StarChild.html.*
4. make their own model Hubble telescope (see Figure 4-16).
5. construct Mars Pathfinder Landing Models. Get instructions at *www.k12.atmos.washington.edu/k12/projects/landers/index.html.*
6. create edible meteorites. Check *www.soest.hawaii.edu/SPACEGRANT/class_acts/EdibleRocksTe.html* for the recipe.

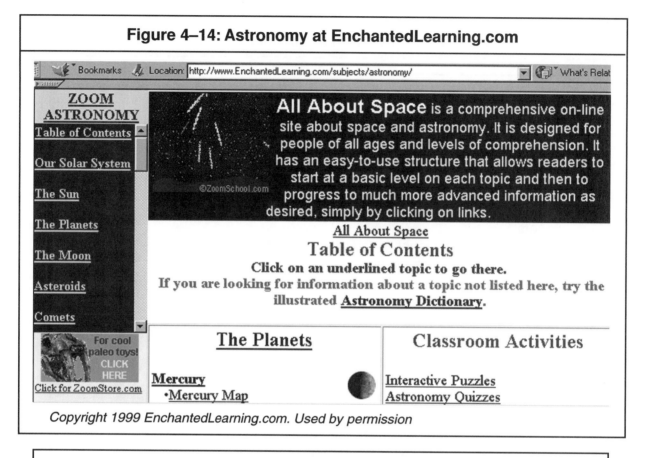

Figure 4–14: Astronomy at EnchantedLearning.com

Copyright 1999 EnchantedLearning.com. Used by permission

Figure 4–15: Logical/Mathematical Intelligence Activity Card for Our Solar System

Calculate Your Weight

1. Choose a planet and write down its name.
2. Write down your weight.
3. At Website *http://liftoff. msfc.nasa.gov/kids/academy/weight.html,* look up the planet you selected in the planet table.
4. Write down its gravity relative to Earth's gravity.
5. Multiply your weight by the gravity factor.
    Example: Gravity x my weight
    This is how much you would weigh on your chosen planet.
6. Calculate your weight on at least three more planets.
    On which planet would you weight the most? The lease?
7. Now, calculate your age on at least one planet.
8. Go on to Activity Card #2.

Figure 4–16: Bodily/Kinesthetic Intelligence Activity Card

Build a Model

1. Find information on the Hubble telescope at *http://heasarc.gsfc.nasa.gov/docs/StarChild.html.*
2. View photographs of the planets taken by the Hubble telescope at *www.seds.org.*
3. Now that you have seen what the Hubble telescope can do, create your own model of the telescope.
4. Find directions to help you construct the telescope at *http://sol.stsci.edu/~mutchier/HSTmodel.html.*
5. Demonstrate the model and explain the process you went through to build it.
6. Go on to Activity Card #2.

[**Note:** This activity could also appear in the Interpersonal Center. This project might be done with a small group of students working together.]

VERBAL/LINGUISTICS INTELLIGENCE CENTER

At the Verbal/Linguistics Intelligence Center, students will read, write, and talk about the solar system. Have students:

1. write three distinguishing facts about each planet using Website *www.nasm.edu/ceps.* Use the T-chart in Figure 4-17 as a model. Then use T-charts to answer the following questions:
   a. How much larger is Venus than Mercury?
   b. Which planet is closest to Earth?
   c. Which are the smallest and the largest planets?
   Refer to the Website above to check results.
2. write a science fiction story that takes place on a planet of their choosing (see Figure 4-18).
3. as a follow-up to the flight to Mars in the Interpersonal Center, write about their new life in a space colony.
4. talk to a partner about the question: What information do scientists have that life exists on Mars? Check the Website at *http://seds.lpl.arizona.edu/nineplanets/nineplanets/nineplanets.html* for help. Present their evidence to the class.

Figure 4–17: Characteristics of Planets

Planets	Features
Mars	Red color Next to Earth but farther from the sun Has solid surface
Jupiter	Largest planet No solid surface Thick, soupy atmosphere

**Figure 4–18: Verbal/Linguistics Intelligence Activity Card
for Our Solar System**

Writing Science Fiction Stories

1. You will write a science fiction story that takes place on the planet that you will choose.
2. First, read other sci-fi stories at *http://sln.fi.edu/planets/planets.html.*
3. Create pictures to illustrate your story. Go to Website *www.nasm.edu/ceps* to see photos of the planets.
4. You can also try some space art drawings to illustrate your story. Look at Website *www.stsci.edu/exined/exined-home.html* to see examples of kid space art.
5. Select a partner to do a peer review of your story. Make revisions based on your partner's suggestions.
6. Publish your story on the bulletin board, along with the illustrations.
7. Go on to Activity Card #2.

Activities to Be Used as Follow-up to the Unit

Students have had opportunities to investigate the solar system through activities at the learning centers that emphasize their dominant intelligences. They have also tried tasks at learning centers that help them improve their less-developed intelligences. As a whole class, groups can now reflect together on what they have learned in their independent studies of the solar system. They can also work with other classes via the Internet on space-related projects. Projects include:

- creating a book on the solar system, with each group choosing a planet to represent on one page of the book.
- joining a project that allows students to compete with other classrooms via the Internet. Check the Website at *http://quest.arc.nasa.gov/interactive/index.html* to see a project that featured space missions and share experiences with other classes.
- sharing their own pictures with other students studying space at *http://spaceplace.jpl.nasa.gov/spacepl.htm*.
- for extra credit, finding information on one of the following:
  - a. Hale-Bopp Comet at *www.yahooligans.com/Science_and_Oddities/Space/Comets/Hale_Bopp* or at *www.sciam.com/exhibit/033197/halebopp/033197bopp.html*
  - b. Shoemaker-Levy Comet at *www.yahooligans.com/Science_and_Oddities/Space/Comets/Shoemaker_Levy-9*

STEP 6: EVALUATE WHAT WAS LEARNED

Evaluation for this unit should involve the teacher, the student, and the learning center (see Figure 4-19). You will want to complete self-assessments to identify your needs, ideas, and feelings about the center approach. Some sample self-reflective questions might include: Am I willing to move to a role of learning facilitator? Do I have the patience to tolerate activity and reasonable noise in the classroom? Do I have the skills to diagnose individual problems and detect progress in students as individuals? Do I believe that students can learn on their own if provided with appropriate materials?

Student evaluation helps to determine the growth students have made based on their interests and abilities and how students feel about their achievements. Some techniques to evaluate work performed in learning centers include: conferences or interviews with students; observations; and review of students' portfolios, which might contain contracts, questionnaires, creative writing and journals, art projects, show-and-tell activities, constructed projects, and records of books read. The process students employ in the learning centers should also be evaluated through student conferences. Finally, students should complete a self-reflection on their experiences with the learning centers. Figure 4-20 provides an example of a student self-assessment questionnaire.

In order for learning centers to be effective, they must be evaluated and renewed

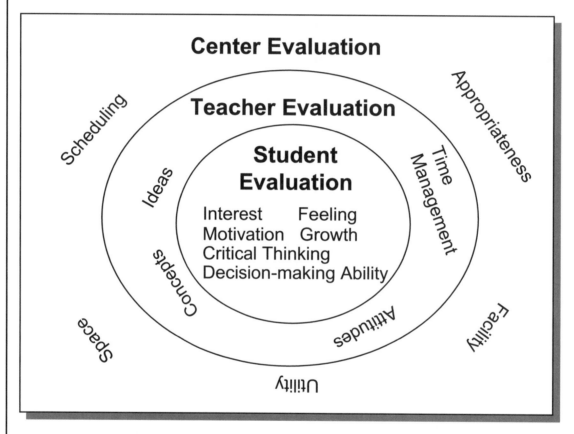

Figure 4–19: Evaluating with Learning Centers

Learning Center Evaluation Components

on a regular basis. Center evaluation should focus on the materials, the space, and the human element (see Figure 4-21 for a sample checklist).

Below are some assessment examples for the unit on the solar system:

- Show students pictures of each planet and have them identify the planets in the pictures.
- Review student portfolios to evaluate their ability to use descriptive words to identify different planets.
- Look at the peer comment sheets to see modifications in descriptions of planets made from peer suggestions.

Figure 4–20: Student Learning Center Evaluation Checklist

Directions: Answer the questions below. Your comments will help me create interesting and instructive learning centers.

1. What did you expect to learn through the center you visited?

2. Were the instructions for activities clear to you?

3. Were the materials appropriate?

4. Could you work well on your own?

5. Could you work well with the group?

6. How did you spend your time?

7. What have you learned?

8. Which center did you enjoy most? Why?

9. Which center did you like least? Why?

10. What would help you to make better use of the learning center?

11. What would you like to bring to add to the center?

- Review records at each center to see what work students completed.
- Have students evaluate the effectiveness of the learning centers using the checklist in Figure 4-21.

Figure 4–21: Center Evaluation Checklist

Use the following as a guide for creating new and modifying existing learning centers.

Questions	Yes/No	Comments
1. Do centers allow for different levels of difficulty?		
2. Do centers have attractive features to entice students to enter?		
3. Are all multiple intelligences or learning styles involved in the centers?		
4. Are some activities open ended to encourage creativity and critical thinking?		
5. Have all of the Internet sites been checked for accuracy of URLs and appropriateness for students?		
6. Do the centers allow students to change physical locations easily?		
7. Is self-checking by students available at the centers?		
8. Do centers offer students choices?		
9. Do the centers encourage positive student attitudes toward activities and other participants?		
10. Do center activities stimulate group cooperation?		
11. Is the time managed so all students are actively involved in the learning process?		
12. Do centers have listings of participants and limits on numbers of students who may participate at centers at one time?		
13. Are objectives of center activities clear to the students and the teacher?		
14. Is there adequate space for center activities?		
15. Do center activities interfere with one another?		

Table 4-2: Weather Web Resources	
Sample URLs	**Description of Websites**
www.cmi.k12.il.us/~fosterbr/WeatherHome.html	Information on weather phenomena for grades 4–6
www.athena.ivv.nasa.gov/curric/weather	Weather charting, predicting weather, and more
www.fema.gov/kids/dizarea.htm	Natural disasters and weather
www.pmel.noaa.gov/toga-tao/el-nino/1997.html	Information on El Niño and other climate information
www.weather.com/education	Provides up-to-date weather information
http://nwlink.com/~wxdude	Provides daily weather, information on El Niño and "stuff" for kids and parents, along with favorite weather books for kids
www.millersv.edu/~edfound/intered/elemplan.html	Provides lesson plans about weather for elementary students
www-kgs.colorado.edu	Contains weather information

OTHER LEARNING CENTERS

The following are examples of two different rooms for science-based topics that can make up your Learning Center arrangement. You can include others that meet the needs of your students, their grade levels, and the curriculum you are teaching.

1. *The Weather Room.* As part of a unit on weather, introduce students to El Niño, a weather phenomenon that affects climatic conditions or how weather influences natural disasters (see Table 4-2).
2. *The Animal Room.* The sites in Table 4-3 could be used in a Learning Center on animals.

Table 4-3: Animal Web Resources	
Sample URLs	**Description of Websites**
http://gopher://informns.k12.mn.us:70/11/mn-k12/mnwr/lessons	Includes lesson plans containing information on habits, animal behavior, ecology and animal adaptation; a learning center could easily be created around this Website
www.si.edu/organiza/museums/zoo/homepage/nzphome.htm	Provides animal photos
www.seaworld.com	Contains whale and marine life information
www.discovery.com	Information on animals of all kinds

SUMMARY

In this unit, we have provided learning activities to teach the solar system through tasks designed to appeal to all children's multiple intelligences and learning styles. We have used the learning center concept to individualize instruction. As you think about creating your own learning centers, remember that their success depends on you—your expertise, your judgment, and, most of all, your planning.

UNIT 2 (SECONDARY LEVEL): BUSINESS EDUCATION

A new way of marketing and selling products has taken the public by storm. Trading on the stock market, buying and selling via auctions, ordering tangible products such as books, videos, and even baby furniture have joined the myriad of free resources already available on the Internet. The rise in the value of Internet-based stocks and changes in business plans of large and small companies suggest that companies today think there is money to be made on the Internet.

A pioneer in the area of Internet-based commerce, known as "e-commerce," is the Amazon Bookseller, located at Website *www.amazon.com*. Amazon does not have bookshops scattered throughout the country; instead it enables its customers easily and quickly to search for and order books, compact disks, videos, and other products online through its Website. Amazon has provided consumers with a cost-effective alternative to visiting the local bookstore. In fact, Amazon has been so successful that major booksellers like Barnes and Noble now offer competing services on the Web.

Thus, e-commerce has become an important business model for many companies, who offer more and more products for sale from Websites on the Internet. High-school students who will soon join the work force must understand how the Internet may affect their lives and perhaps their jobs in the future.

For this unit, cross-curricular activities will be available at different learning centers, each center emphasizing one of Howard Gardner's multiple intelligences. The tasks will require students to view and analyze one commercial Website, *www.amazon.com*. They will engage in some of the activities at *amazon.com* to review the site's features and better understand why it has been successful. (*Note:* A book site was chosen for this unit because it complements the curriculum; however, any commercial site that sells via the Internet could be used.)

STEP 1: APPLY FRAMEWORK STANDARDS: WHAT SHOULD BE TAUGHT?

National standards and framework goals for states such as California provide guidelines for content and skill development in economic literacy. For example, students in twelfth grade in California can sign up for a one-semester course in economics, which teaches fundamental economic concepts. In business education classes, teachers are asking students to understand advertising principles and to question statistics used to sell products. In addition, to promote active learning, teachers create projects that simulate business conditions and ask students to compare marketing programs of two corporations and to write business plans.

In a core subject like English, teachers require students to learn about propaganda and to discuss propaganda techniques in persuasive essays. They ask students to understand how advertising influences the general public to purchase products and the role media plays in consumers' daily lives. In journalism classes, students learn writing techniques that convey messages objectively. Moreover, in mathematics the emphasis is on teaching that goes beyond computation to include problem solving in real-life situations.

This unit integrates many of the framework goals stated above with the use of the Internet so students can discuss business concepts, practice writing, analyze business models, and create a real-life project that allows them to emphasize their distinct learning modalities.

STEP 2: IDENTIFY GENERAL GOALS AND SPECIFIC OBJECTIVES

In this unit, goals for students emphasize observation, evaluation, and discussion to create awareness of how propaganda and persuasion are used to sell products and ideas. Activities also stress how creation of desire and the action of purchasing a product are important to e-commerce on the Internet.

Goals

Students will:

- define terminology associated with e-commerce on the Internet
- demonstrate skills of critiquing and evaluating commercial Websites, pointing out propaganda techniques and persuasive language
- discriminate between writing for print and writing for electronic media, specifically the Internet
- demonstrate a proficiency in basic mathematical skills by solving problems involving income and expenses

Objectives

Through this unit, students will:

- demonstrate an understanding of the current trends in advertising and how the general public is influenced to purchase products
- recognize and identify the devices of propaganda, including glittering generalities, testimonial, bandwagon, and name-calling techniques
- determine and critically analyze content, format, and style of a Website
- recognize the importance of the use of color, modern design, the eye-movement concept, and up-to-date borders and graphics to a Website
- experiment with placement of design elements to create a Website that incorporates dominance to catch the viewer's eye
- write, proofread, and edit copy before and after it is published on the Website
- create an e-commerce Website

STEP 3: GATHER MATERIALS

In Chapter 1, we identified different types of Websites. We noted that some sites are sponsored by organizations, others by educational institutions, and a large number by commercial businesses. The Websites for this unit focus on those which end in the extension *.com*, which are financed and operated by companies or individuals who want to engage in a commercial enterprise. Some of the commercial sites, such as *amazon.com* or *barnesandnoble.com* actually sell products through the Internet; others, such as *microsoft.com*, maintain a Website to advertise their products, provide free software, and assist its customers.

Activities for this unit will revolve around *amazon.com*. Students will, however, view other Websites, such as *www.microsoft.com* or *www.barnesandnoble.com*, in order to analyze and compare different sites as models for creating their own commercial sites.

STEP 4: INTRODUCE THE UNIT

This unit contains two parts. First, students will explore the successful e-commerce Website at *www.amazon.com*. They will have opportunities at different learning centers to choose tasks that emphasize their dominant learning modalities and strengthen their less dominant intelligences. Students will investigate and participate in the many activities that are available at the Amazon site. In this way, they will become familiar with examples of how Amazon entices consumers to its Website. Using the Amazon site as a model, the class will then create a mock-up of its own commercial Website by completing the second activity at each center. The mock-up site can form the basis of a cross-curricular project in which a computer science class creates the actual Website online based on the model.

For the first activity, students should visit centers that emphasize less dominant intelligences and perform at least one task related to learning more about *amazon.com*. After students have familiarized themselves with e-commerce at Amazon, they will form groups and begin to create their own commercial Website. Each center will offer one activity necessary to create the class model Internet site. For this second activity, students can choose a learning center that focuses on their dominant intelligence.

STEP 5: CREATE SAMPLE ACTIVITIES

Here are some ideas for activities that can be used to explore e-commerce on the Web. Some of the activities will help students to familiarize themselves with the meaning of e-commerce. Based on the model Websites viewed, class groups will construct their own Websites. First, they will establish the products they plan to sell online. Then students at each center will complete the activities that will result in a mock-up of the class Website.

Activities to Introduce the Unit

It is important that students understand terminology and see examples of commercial Websites before they begin the activities at the learning centers. The following six tasks will reinforce their prior knowledge about the Internet. The whole class will:

1. identify and define in journals Internet-based terms. There are a number of terms at *www.netlingo.com* from which to choose.
2. discuss advantages and disadvantages of doing business on the Internet.
3. review advertising techniques, such as bandwagon approach, glittering generalities, name-calling, and testimonials, with which they are already familiar. Figure 4-22, an advance organizer that checks for prior knowledge, should help the review.
4. discuss ways to create search strategies and use search engines to find appropriate Websites. (See Chapter 2 for detailed instructions on search strategies, and Appendix A for tips for using search engines).
5. find at least two examples of sites that have the extension *.com*. (Use *www.microsoft.com*, *www.barnesandnoble.com*, or others with which students are familiar.) Make a list of the similarities and differences between the two sites.
6. brainstorm a list of criteria to use in evaluating Websites. Review the criteria for assessing Websites created by the American Association of School Librarians at *www.ala.org/ICONN/rating.html* or read a Website evaluation found in Chapter 1.

Activities to Be Used During the Unit

The activities in the learning centers listed below require the use of distinct intelligences to explore *www.amazon.com*. In doing them, students will investigate all

---

Figure 4–22: Advance Organizer

Directions: In your notebooks, label each statement according to which technique is being used by advertisers. Use G for glittering generalities; B for bandwagon approach; T for testimonials; and N for name-calling. Put a question mark before any statements you are unsure of.

_____ "Our present politicians are criminals and should be put in jail."

_____ "All of my friends use Glow White toothpaste."

_____ "As CEO of TopTel, I know how important it is to use Brand X computer."

_____ "The Fortune 500 companies use the Internet, why don't you?"

_____ "Glow White toothpaste brightens your teeth while it eliminates tartar."

---

aspects and functions of this site. Other activities at the centers will then help them begin to build their own Website.

Logical/Mathematical Intelligence Center.

At the Logical/Mathematical Intelligence Center, students will use basic mathematical concepts to enable them to understand the concepts of budget and expenses and reinforce the process of buying online.

1. Students will spend up to $100 (in play money) at *www.amazon.com* (see Figure 4-23). From the following categories, they must choose books that discuss aspects of the Internet or Web-based commerce:
   - fiction
   - nonfiction
   - history
   - art

   Some possible authors include Bill Gates, Alvin Toffler, and John Naisbett. Students can proceed through the process of selecting books as far as actually placing the order. This will familiarize them with the process of order-

---

Figure 4–23: Logical/Mathematical Intelligence Activity Card for Business Education

Buying and Selling on the Internet

Directions: You have $100 to spend on books on the topic of the Internet or on Web-based commerce. You must stay within your budget.

1. Go to *www.amazon.com* to search for books in each of the following categories: fiction, nonfiction, history, and art. Select the best books for the topic.
2. Determine the total cost of the books, including shipping charges and any sales tax. Reflect on the following in your journal:
   • How easy was the book selection?
   • How much time did it take to collect the books for ordering?
   • How much money remains?
   • Could you have gotten the books faster and more cheaply at the bookstore?
3. With a partner discuss:
   • What search terms did you use?
   • Was the process of ordering efficient?
   • Are there any ways to streamline the procedure?
4. Go on to Activity Card #2.

ing, using credit cards, and shipping. They *do* have the opportunity to abort the order at the end of the process.

2. For the class Website, students will determine prices and procedures to buy or sell via the Website. They should decide how the ordering process will be similar to or different from that of Amazon.

VISUAL/SPATIAL INTELLIGENCE CENTER

At the Visual/Spatial Intelligence Center, students will view images, graphics, and layouts to discover how visual effects influence consumers on the Internet.

1. Students will examine the graphics used on the Amazon site and complete a checklist about the "look and feel" of the site (see Figure 4-24 for a sample checklist).
2. Students should choose a book, video, or music compact disk from Amazon, examine the graphic that represents the book or compact disk, and read any reviews. They then should design a book jacket, video, or compact disk cover.
3. For designing the class Website, students will design graphics, including all visuals, type fonts, and layout of the pages.

MUSICAL INTELLIGENCE CENTER

At the Musical Intelligence Center students will determine how to use music as part of a commercial Website.

1. Students will select two Websites that contain music and answer the following questions: Why do these sites include music? What does the music add to the success or lack of it at the site?
2. Next, have students discuss music at the Amazon site. Amazon does not use music, yet they sell music compact disks. Answer the questions: Why does Amazon not incorporate music? In what ways could Amazon use music effectively?
3. For creating the class site, students will decide whether or not to use music and provide reasons for the choice.

BODILY/KINESTHETIC INTELLIGENCE CENTER

At the Bodily/Kinesthetic Intelligence Center, students will work on actively engaging in construction of a Website.

1. Students will investigate the navigation system used on Amazon's site and answer the following questions:
   - How do users move from one part of the Website to another and back again?
   - Are the links working?
   - In what ways is the navigation system effective for visual, auditory, and/or kinesthetic learners?

Figure 4–24: "Look and Feel" Checklist

Checklist to Evaluate the
Website Visually and Spatially

Directions: Review the Amazon Website at *www.amazon.com.* Consider and answer the following questions to determine whether the site is visually pleasing.

1. Is the screen easy to use? Not cluttered? Well organized?

2. Is the text pleasing to the eye? Easy to read?

3. What is the purpose of the graphics on the Website? Do the graphics slow down the loading time of the site?

4. Is the format consistent? Do you find main headings in the same places on different screens? Is this important or not?

5. Is the use of color consistent? What colors are used and why?

6. How is the screen laid out? Do you see a pattern? Why is that pattern used?

7. Is it easy to identify the different products or services that are offered at the site? How can you identify them?

8. Are all of the different product sites laid out similarly? Why/why not is this important?

9. From a visual and spatial perspective, what would you change if you were designing this site?

10. Do you think that the "look and feel" of the site has anything to do with the Website's success as a business? If so, what?

2. For creating the class Website, students will construct a flowchart of the class's commercial Website, illustrating the navigation system for the site. Other center participants will need to provide suggestions.

INTERPERSONAL INTELLIGENCE CENTER

At the Interpersonal Intelligence Center, students will work together in pairs or small groups to help them understand components for a successful commercial Web-based business.

1. Students will look at the newest components of the Amazon site—its auction house, its drugstore, or its kids' bookstore—and evaluate these products as to how they fit in with Amazon's general theme or business plan. They will also discuss reasons for beginning the new ventures.
2. For creating the class Website, students will create several site titles and review them with students at other centers to gain consensus.
3. The student will decide whether advertising should be included on the class Website and provide reasons pro and con. (This task is a follow-up activity for students who work on advertising at the Intrapersonal Intelligence Center.)

INTRAPERSONAL INTELLIGENCE CENTER

At the Intrapersonal Intelligence Center, students work independently on tasks that help them understand business conducted on the Internet.

1. Students will examine the advertisements on the *Yahoo.com* site (see Figure 4-25).
2. Students will solicit advertising for the class Website. They will first need to determine the criteria for the ads and the characteristics of the audience the class hopes will visit the Website.

VERBAL/LINGUISTIC INTELLIGENCE CENTER

At the Verbal/Linguistics Intelligence Center, students will read, write, and talk about conducting business on the Internet.

1. Students will choose a book to read from the Amazon site that relates to e-commerce and write a book review (see Figure 4-26).
2. For the class Website, students will write the text for individual screens, reviewing language, text size, color, and headings used on other commercial sites—such as *www.barnesandnoble.com*—for models.

ACTIVITIES TO BE USED AS FOLLOW-UP TO THE UNIT

Once students have reviewed examples of Websites on which to model the mock-up of the class commercial site, they will reflect on the process they just completed to create their own site. Students will:

Figure 4–25: Intrapersonal Intelligence Task Card

Advertising on the Internet

1. Go to *www.yahoo.com* to take a look at the advertising. What types of ads are available.
2. Categorize the ads based on the techniques with which you are familiar.
3. Based on the ads, who do you think the audience is for this Website?
4. Look at the ads on the Amazon site at *www.amazon.com*. What are the similarities/differences? Why?
5. Write an audience analysis for the Yahoo! Site, commenting on the following:
    • For whom are the ads intended?
    • What do the ads tell you about the users who visit the Yahoo! site?
    • Identify some of the characteristics of the audience at Yahoo!
6. Support your opinion on whether Amazon should have ads.
7. Go on to Activity Card #2.

Figure 4–26: Verbal/Linguistic Intelligence Task Card

Writing a Book Review

1. Go to *www.amazon.com* and choose a book that interests you.
2. After reading the book, write a book review based on your opinion of the book and one which you want to appear on the Amazon site.
3. Now read at least three reviews by Amazon and comment on the following:
    • What do you find different/similar to your book review?
    • Why do you think Amazon offers book reviews at the site?
    • Why do they allow readers to contribute reviews?
4. Go on to Activity Card #2.

- work together with a computer science class to create an actual Website from the "mock-up" they have made
- reflect in their journals about the process of creating a Website and comment on whether they think e-commerce will survive as a business form
- publicize the class Website to another class in their school

STEP 6: EVALUATE WHAT WAS LEARNED

Evaluation will be based on two components: (1) tasks required to review the Amazon site, and (2) those activities necessary to create the class Website. Your observations will play an important part in the evaluation. Periodically, observe students' participation in the instructional activities at each center, noting in particular their levels of concentration, confidence, and interest. Students' desires to work alone may indicate confidence in their abilities to solve problems or grasp the concepts that are being studied. Also, observe how students approach different types of tasks in order to obtain an understanding of their work habits and learning styles. These observations over the course of the unit should provide you with important general information about students' use of time and materials, perseverance, and ability to organize and plan. While observing, you can also ask students to describe orally their thought processes as they work on different problems. It is important to record these observations in a systematic way, since such records may be the only information available about certain aspects of the students' development. An anecdotal record might look like the one in Figure 4-27.

In addition, assessment of the mock-up of the Website created by each group will be part of the final evaluation. Finally, students will be asked to do a self-evaluation based on activities at the centers. (See Figure 4-20 for a self-evaluation checklist and Figure 4-21 for a center evaluation sheet).

Figure 4–27: Observation Checklist			
Classroom Behaviors for Brian			
Observations	**Week 1**	**Week 2**	**Week 3**
Factual account			
Analysis of the observation			
Recommendations for action			

SUMMARY

Students have had opportunities in this unit to review and evaluate Websites. Through the use of learning centers, they have been able to choose activities that focus on their dominant intelligences. They have then put their learning into action by creating their own commercial Website. This task has required students to think about products, buying and selling, users, purpose, "look and feel," and movement at the site. These activities have involved students in practicing the types of skills that they will need when they enter the work force.

TEACHER EXERCISES: NOW YOU TRY IT...

1. Choose one of the learning center models or a topic from your own curriculum.
   - Determine the objective(s) for the learning center.
   - Select four Websites (or one that has many topics/pages) that are appropriate to the subject and your students' intelligences or learning styles. Write down the URLs in your Internet notebook under the heading Learning Centers and bookmark the best sites on your computer.
   - Write at least five to seven activities for which children should be able to find information at the Websites you have listed. The activities should represent different intelligences.
   - Set up the methods of evaluation for the activities, both individually and as part of a group, if desired. Review Figures 4-6 and 4-20 for samples.
2. Write your reflections about creating these learning centers in your journals. Make sure to include answers to the following questions: How well did your students complete the tasks at the centers? What did the centers students completed tell you about their learning styles? At which centers did students seem to enjoy the activities most? Least? Were any of the task card instructions confusing to students? Which center activities would you omit the next time you taught this unit?

CONCLUSION

This chapter has focused on two ways to individuate instruction: (1) through learning modalities, and (2) through the use of learning centers. Learning modalities research is now shaping the way educators react to students. Knowing about learning styles and distinct intelligences enables teachers to plan more effective instruction that will meet the needs of all students in their classrooms. In addition, it allows teachers to look at their own modes of teaching and reflect on how they can use their own modality strengths to create better learning situations.

Moreover, through the use of learning centers to individualize instruction, educators can provide activities that challenge students and interest them at the same time. The Internet—with its multimedia, its vast stores of information, and its ability to bring classrooms across the world together—has provided educators with a tool that has the potential to meet diverse student needs. In Chapter 5 we will explore ways in which the Internet lends itself to use with cooperative learning.

REFERENCES

Barbe, Walter B., and Raymond Swassing, with Michael N. Milone. 1979. *Teaching Through Modality Strengths: Concepts and Practices.* Columbus, OH: Zaner-Bloser.

Dunn, Kenneth J., and Rita Stafford Dunn. 1987. *Teaching Students Through Their Individual Learning Styles: A Practical Approach.* Reston, VA: Reston Publishing Company.

Dunn, Kenneth J., and Rita Stafford Dunn. 1992. *Teaching Secondary Students Through Their Individual Learning Styles: Practical Approaches for Grades 7–12.* Boston: Allyn and Bacon.

Freeley, Mary, and Janet Perrin. 1987. "Teaching to Both Hemispheres." *Teaching K–8* (Aug/ Sept.): 67–69.

Gardner, Howard. 1983. *Frames of Mind: The Theory of Multiple Intelligences.* New York: Basic Books.

McCarthy Bernice. 1984. *The 4MAT System.* Barrington, IL: Excel.

Myrow, David. 1979. "Learner Choice and Task Engagement." *Journal of Experimental Education* (spring).

Piaget, Jean. 1968. *Six Psychological Studies.* Translated by A. Tenzer and D. Elkind. New York: Vintage.

Chapter 5

USING THE INTERNET WITH COOPERATIVE-LEARNING APPROACHES

PART 1: IDEAS AND INSIGHTS

OBJECTIVES OF THIS CHAPTER

This chapter will focus on cooperative learning and activities on the Internet that provide resources for collaborative tasks. It addresses topics at both the elementary and secondary levels. At the end of this chapter, educators will be able to:

- list important principles of effective cooperative learning
- identify key components of cooperative-learning lessons
- list essential skills for teamwork to take place
- create a Web-based unit using cooperative learning

Now picture this scenario; it took place in a classroom run by Mark, one of my student teachers who planned to use "cooperative learning" in his English lesson. Mark asked the class of thirty-two students to "get into groups" of four each and think about a quote that he had written on the blackboard. After the initial chaos of students deciding on team members and where their groups should locate in the classroom, I observed students talking among themselves and sharing pictures of friends. When Mark announced that five minutes remained to complete the activity, one student in the group closest to me quickly wrote several sentences on a piece of paper. This activity took fifteen minutes of valuable class time but accomplished little learning and engaged few students. When I questioned Mark after class, he remarked, "My education professor told us in our methods class that we should encourage collaborative learning." Mark was a secondary-level student teacher; however, this is not the first time I have been frustrated when viewing classes where "group work" is neither cooperative, collaborative, nor learning-based.

Cooperative learning does not take place just because the teacher tells students to work together in groups. It does not occur when one student on the team does all of the work while other members talk and then put their names on the final product. Cooperative learning *does* occur when the efforts of all team members are necessary to the success of the entire group.

In Chapter 1, the importance of cooperative learning for workers in the twenty-first century was stressed. Likewise, many other chapters of this book have introduced activities that require students to work collaboratively to complete projects, to peer-edit writing, and to discuss ideas. In this chapter, we will dig deeper into how to organize a cooperative-learning experience for maximum learning and the participation of all students. We will determine what the necessary ingredients are for cooperative-learning groups to succeed and how we can assess participants in a cooperative setting. We will also find out how we can combine Internet-based lessons with cooperative learning.

WHY USE COOPERATIVE LEARNING?

Much research has been compiled on cooperative learning, especially at the elementary level, and many educators profess that they are using it. But what does it really mean? Cooperative learning can be defined as any form of educational strategy that involves small, *highly structured* groups of children working together on common problems and learning from and teaching one another (Johnson et al., 1984). Or, to put it another way, collaborative or cooperative learning is a classroom method that relies on structured student interaction to promote intellectual and social achievement.

Research by Johnson et al. (1984), Slavin (1995), and others indicates that lessons structured around cooperative learning result in improvements both in the achievement of students and in the quality of their interpersonal relationships. These studies have also shown that cooperative learning can foster:

- higher intrinsic motivation
- a more positive attitude toward instruction and instructors
- the development of leadership abilities
- a sense of teamwork
- improved self-esteem
- greater acceptance of differences
- decreased dependence on the teacher

In fact, Johnson and his group (1984) noticed superior results in almost every content area when cooperative learning was used, as compared with other techniques.

COMPONENTS OF COOPERATIVE LEARNING

Johnson et al. (1984) set up a systematic structure with specified components for implementing cooperative learning in classrooms. These components include:

- *group heterogeneity.* Educators have used many grouping strategies, ranging from homogeneous to chronological by age and by ability. Researchers like Slavin (1995) believe that heterogeneous grouping results in more critical thinking and greater perspectives when discussing material. Grouping heterogeneously pulls in varied genders, races, cultural and language differences, problematic behaviors, and past academic achievement. Some teachers prefer random assignment to groups—for example, students can count off and the ones form a group, the twos another group, and so forth, or they can choose colored strips of paper, with the same colors forming groups.

  Groups of less mature learners—in this case, those who have only occasionally used cooperative work—should have highly structured tasks to complete, work in smaller groups of three or four students, and have a high level of teacher support. More mature groups of students—those who are used to cooperative work—can have more freedom in selecting products they will create, and they can work in larger groups for extended periods of time. However, all collaborations should still have a high level of teacher support.

- *positive group interdependence.* Positive interdependence is the feeling among group members that no one is successful unless everyone in the group succeeds. Types of interdependence include reward interdependence, in which a reward is given when everyone on the team completes a required task; resource interdependence, in which students share one set of directions for the team project; and task interdependence, in which each student's task is necessary to complete the product. Students have usually had a great deal of practice with competitive and individualistic structures. Positive interdependence will not be as familiar to them and must be communicated concretely in advance of the group work.

- *individual accountability.* Individual accountability usually insures that each student contributes to the group. This key aspect was missing in Mark's classroom and in many others I have observed because the work was not evenly distributed. Students must know in advance what they will be responsible for attaining, and teachers must be able to monitor what each student has contributed and the level of mastery of required skills. This is extremely important to make sure that one or two students do not do all of the work.

- *group processing.* Group processing requires that teachers and students discuss and evaluate the functioning of groups. For example, teachers should observe groups at work, pointing out what they see group members doing well. Students should also take the time to process what they have learned, what went well in working in their groups, and how they might improve.

Some researchers (Kagan, 1990) also believe that team building is an essential component for cooperative learning to take place. According to Kagan, when there is a positive team identity—liking, respect, and trust among team members—there is a context within which maximum learning can occur. A "getting-acquainted" activity designed by the teacher, such as selecting a team name or brainstorming a list of shared interests, may help to develop the team spirit for group work. Although some teachers in the upper-elementary and higher-level grades sometimes feel uncomfortable using team-building activities, creating a team spirit is often a good idea at the beginning of the school year and can alleviate problems later.

Making sure that these components are part of each cooperative-learning project helps insure the success of the activity. In addition, working in cooperative groups provides skills that students then understand are important for their success in school and later in the work force.

COOPERATIVE LEARNING AND THE INTERNET

Using the computer and cooperative learning may seem to some like a contradiction in terms. After all, we often think of one person sitting in front of the computer creating a document, building a database, or working on a spreadsheet. The Internet, however, provides opportunities for students to collaborate in small groups in the classroom, or for connectivity with students in other parts of the world who can work on projects together. A U.S. Department of Labor report for America 2000 (1991) listed collaborative skills, such as negotiating, teaching, and leading projects, as being among the most critical skills necessary for jobs in the twenty-first century. The report also stated that understanding and using technology is an equally important skill. Moreover, research by Male et al. (1994), Anderson (1989), and Johnson et al. (1984) has found that cooperative grouping improves computer-based learning. Studies have shown that students work effectively around computers in small groups. Therefore, it is time for a merging of the two.

COOPERATIVE-LEARNING PROJECTS

There are many major benefits of learning through online collaboration; children acquire social skills, experience different viewpoints, and learn how to work together with people from other countries. In addition, it can instill in students a real excitement for school as well as develop crucial skills that they may use in the future as adult workers.

The projects in Table 5-1 are only some of the interesting educational adventures that originate on the Web each year for students to embark upon with peers worldwide. The activities are challenging for students, and each project has supplementary material for teachers to help them implement the online project into their curricula.

Often past projects are archived on Websites so educators can get ideas to use in their own instruction.

Table 5–1: Cooperative Web-Based Projects		
Project Name	**URL Address**	**Description**
Newsday Project	*www.gsn.org/project/ newsday/index.html*	Students produce their own newspapers based on a theme, incorporating articles they have downloaded and edited and their own original writings.
The Odyssey World Trek	*www.worldtrek.org*	The purpose is to involve students in activities to create positive change in the world and to learn to appreciate nonwestern cultures. Chats with trekkers, information on the region in which the team is traveling, and connecting what they learn to community service are all possible through this project. New projects occur every six months.
Adventure Online	*www.adventureonline.com*	Students can explore the North Pole, Greenland, Africa, and more. Materials include logs of the explorers, photos of the expedition, and a travel map.
Sands of the World	*www.chariho.k12.ri.us/ curriculum/MISmart/oceans /sands.htm*	This school project enables classes to send sand samples for evaluation and posting on their Website. Students can view maps, check related geological sites, view the sand pages, and see data sheets of the sand analyses.
One Sky, Many Voices	*www.onesky.umich.edu/ index.html*	This project focuses on science and provides information on hurricanes and weather. Project activities include planning a virtual field trip, sharing local weather observations, consulting scientists online, and sharing analyses of collected data.
The Mars Millennium Project	*www.mars2030.net*	Students set up a space village on Mars. They interact with experts and design a new community based on what they know about their own regions.

DESIGNING A COOPERATIVE-LEARNING PROJECT

The six key stages of a cooperative lesson are:

1. *warm-up/review.* At this stage, teachers decide on the principle for dividing students into groups and the number of students each group will have. It is also important to create some team-building activities to instill a team spirit. Next, teachers can use graphic organizers, such as a mapping diagram, to reveal what students already know about the lesson objectives and content.

2. *introduction.* During the introduction, teachers must focus student attention on the lesson by prefacing the content for the unit and by establishing the cooperative purpose for the lessons. One way to introduce the content is to brainstorm questions at various levels of thinking (see Figure 5-1 for some sample question types, which are based on Bloom's taxonomy, discussed in Chapter 2).

3. *presentation.* At this point teachers should clarify goals for the lessons and plan the final product for a specific audience. For example, students may be creating a student newspaper to give their parents to inform them about a unit they have been studying. Teachers should also provide new information and activities for the students to work with. As students work on these tasks, teachers must check students' levels of understanding of the new information, as well as making sure all students are on task.

4. *practice.* Now is the time to provide practice activities that are structured for positive interdependence and individual accountability. The work must be divided among group members, and decisions must be made on how students will find the information necessary to complete their portions of the product. It is also necessary that the teacher identify how to monitor student practice and provide feedback to students.

5. *evaluation.* Although evaluation may take place at the end of the unit, teachers should determine and clarify how they will structure individual and group accountability on the content objective. They should also determine how they will process the cooperative-learning objective at the beginning of the unit.

6. *application.* Finally, to reinforce the learning, students should have opportunities to apply what they learned. They might present to the class and parents, create a Website illustrating what they have achieved, or interact with other classrooms online by communicating the results of their research. In all cases each student must have some responsibility for the final product.

The Teacher's Role

In a cooperative-learning activity, the teacher will assume many different roles, providing direction, guiding students through tasks and activities, and helping groups work to achieve their goals. The teacher is also responsible for producing resources through which students can learn new information. During practice, the teacher's role is to facilitate learning, to give students opportunities to discover information on their own, to share their knowledge with other children, to evaluate their new knowledge, and to draw conclusions.

Figure 5–1: Question Types for Brainstorming

1. **Recall** (recalling facts, observations, or definitions)
   - Who?
   - What?
   - Where?
   - When?
   - Why?
   - Define [the word symbol].

2. **Comprehension** (giving descriptions, stating main ideas, comparing)
   - Describe [what happened when Jack stole the money].
   - What is the main idea [in this story]?
   - How are [two countries] alike?

3. **Application** (applying techniques and rules to solve problems that have a single correct answer)
   - If [Susan has 60 cents], how many [8-cent balls] can she buy?
   - What is [the capital of Pennsylvania]?
   - Classify [these poems as ballads, sonnets, or odes].

4. **Analysis** (identifying motives or causes, making inferences, finding evidence to support generalizations)
   - Why [did the United States enter World War II]?
   - Now that we've studied this, what can we conclude about [life on Mars]?
   - What does this tell us about [the author's attitude toward war]?
   - What evidence can you find to support [the principle that air expands when heated]?

5. **Synthesis** (solving problems, making predictions, producing original communications)
   - Can you think up [a title for this story]?
   - How can we solve [this problem]?
   - How can we improve [our project]?
   - What will happen [now that we've discovered that there is water on the moon]?
   - What do you predict would happen [if the killing of whales was not regulated]?

6. **Evaluation** (giving opinions about issues, judging the validity of ideas or the merit of problem solutions or the quality of products)
   - Do you agree [with Ralph]?
   - Do you believe [that this is the best solution to the problem]?
   - Do you think [that it is right to have stronger gun laws]?
   - What is your opinion [on abortion]?
   - Why did you choose [this novel]?
   - Would it be better [to do it this way]?

The teacher also monitors group work and collects information on group interactions, perhaps interacting with a group to guide them in the activity—asking questions of the group, praising them, or reinforcing their skills. Observations and interactions within the group help the teacher to diagnose group strengths and weaknesses and plan future lessons.

Essential Skills for Teamwork

Several skills are essential for real teamwork to take place, and teachers should not assume that students automatically have them. Teachers will need to monitor the skills listed below to make sure that students are working cooperatively in their groups by:

- *listening* to each other's ideas and comments. They should be building on the responses and ideas of their teammates.
- *asking questions* of each other. They should interact by discussing and posing questions to all members of the group.
- *using persuasion*. Students will often need to defend or rethink their own ideas and influence others to their points of view.
- *respecting* the opinions of others. Students should encourage and support each other's ideas and efforts.
- *helping each other*. Students must offer advice, suggestions, or assistance to one another.
- *sharing* ideas and thinking. Because the result is a team effort, students must report their findings and synthesize each other's results into the final group product.
- *participating* as part of the group. Each student's contribution is important to the outcome of the project.

In Part 2 of this chapter, we will employ the concept of cooperative learning in two Web-based units, one at the elementary level and the other at the secondary level. These units will give practical suggestions for using the Internet as part of the curriculum in a cooperative environment.

PART 2: PRACTICAL APPLICATIONS

Cooperative learning allows students in their small groups to interact with one another, learn from each other, solve problems together, and use one another as resources. The two units in Part 2 join collaborative learning with the power and versatility of the Internet. In the first unit, designed for students at the elementary level, students will go on a "virtual" archeological dig to uncover information about dinosaurs. In the second unit, students at the secondary level will perform tasks necessary to learn about the stock market and conduct a "real-life" experiment by preparing and monitoring their own stock portfolios. Many of the activities in each unit can be adapted for different grade levels.

UNIT 1 (ELEMENTARY LEVEL): DINOSAURS

Team learning is an effective method for developing and strengthening content area abilities. Producing newspapers can be used with any subject area and is a good cooperative activity in that it provides a variety of jobs and meets the needs of students of different backgrounds, interests, and learning styles. Completing this team task requires students with diverse talents to make contributions; thus, a cooperative effort enables every member of the group to share ideas. Newspapers are also good public relations pieces to give to parents, libraries, and community centers. Indeed, class newspapers can serve many purposes, both educational and communicative—and the children have fun producing them.

In this unit students will learn about dinosaurs and apply practical skills by publishing a paper: organizing, prioritizing, meeting deadlines, and solving problems creatively. The theme approach provides students with opportunities to undertake meaningful, satisfying visual, literary, and performance activities. The methods help develop and enhance self-esteem, personal pride, flexibility, and critical thinking. Students will also gain improved problem-solving, social, and communication skills as they collaborate with their peers.

As part of this interdisciplinary unit, students will also work with students in classrooms around the world through the Global Schoolhouse newspaper project at *www.gsn.org/project/newsday/index.html.* Participation in this project enables students to pursue their own special interests and see their work published. Students will research their news stories, ask experts questions when needed, draft their articles, and then revise them after discussions with their groups.

STEP 1: APPLY FRAMEWORK STANDARDS—WHAT SHOULD BE TAUGHT?

In both national science standards and state science frameworks, earth science is an important area for investigation. Students must develop knowledge of the geological history of the earth, including historical implications revealed by fossils. They will also examine and identify various types of fossils. In addition to study of the subject matter, science frameworks also emphasize cross-curricular learning, as we saw in Chapter 3. The California Science Model Curriculum Guide (1987), for example, states that experiencing, reading and writing about science content is important to the study of science. In this unit science and language arts are intertwined.

National science standards also encourage experiences that foster group interaction, such as experiments and research. The California science framework (CSDE, 1987b), for example, states that students should work together in collaborative groups, searching for solutions to given or selected problems with little outside help. A final recommendation by the science framework is that technology be integrated into the curriculum, especially to exemplify science phenomena.

The unit on dinosaurs carries through these goals when children use the Internet and its multimedia capabilities as a tool for research, to communicate in writing and through discussion, and to create a product—their newspapers—that requires them to work together to make decisions and solve problems.

STEP 2: IDENTIFYING GENERAL GOALS AND SPECIFIC OBJECTIVES

As part of their growth and development throughout their school careers, students will work independently, competitively, and cooperatively on tasks and projects. During this unit, the primary focus will be students working collaboratively.

Goals

Throughout the unit, students will:

- develop cooperative skills and attitudes as a part of social growth
- practice research skills to pursue knowledge
- become familiar with the computer as a tool for solving problems
- improve their writing and critical thinking

Objectives

By the end of the unit, students will:

- understand the definition of fossils and identify various types of fossils
- identify geologic periods of time when dinosaurs lived
- name, categorize, and describe well-known dinosaurs
- see relationships between prehistoric dinosaurs and animals in the world to-day
- create newspapers containing their writing and artwork about dinosaurs

STEP 3: GATHER MATERIALS

The subject of dinosaurs is a popular one on the Internet, and many Websites provide information on dinosaurs ranging from eras in which they lived to similarities and differences among these types of prehistoric creatures. We will use several of the sites listed in Table 5-2 in the activities section of the unit plan.

STEP 4: INTRODUCE THE UNIT

In this unit students will work cooperatively in small groups to research information about dinosaurs. Using information they obtain in their research, each group will create its own newspaper to illustrate to parents what they have learned about these prehistoric beasts and to demonstrate their writing, artistic, and creative abilities.

The Product

Newspapers will contain the following:

- feature articles
- news stories
- legends with section contents and pages listed

Table 5–2: Web Resources on Dinosaurs	
Web Site URLs	**Description of Websites**
www.libsci.sc.edu/miller/dinosaurs.htm	Thematic unit on dinosaurs at primary level
www.eagle.ca/~matink/dinosaur.htm	Dinosaur resources
http://viking.stark.k12.oh.us/~greentown/dinosaur.htm	Resources and links for a dinosaur unit
www.k12.nf.ca/stgeorges/dinosaur/dino01.html	Dinosaur resources
www.sedl.org/scimath/pasopartners/dinosaurs/focus.html	Lesson plans and activities for teachers to use in the classroom
www.mov.vic.gov.au/dinosaurs/dinosintro.htm	Global Classroom on dinosaurs
http://dinodon.com/index.html	Dinosaur dictionary, art, and news
www.nationalgeographic.com/dinorama/frame.html	Info about dinosaurs and methods to learn about them
www.EnchantedLearning.com/subjects/dinosaurs	Dinosaur facts, myths, activities, and more
http://sciam.com/explorations/121597dinosaur	Sounds of dinosaurs and simulations
www.yahooligans.com/Science_and_Nature/Living_Things/Paleontology/Dinosaurs/Dinosaur_Extinction	Theories on how dinosaurs became extinct

- enjoyable activities, such as crossword puzzles, contests, jokes, limericks, and more
- letters to the editors

Groups will be responsible for designing the masthead, determining page layout, writing and editing articles, drawing maps and pictures, and creating activities. Each team member must produce at least one story, game, or article for the newspaper. Students are not limited to the contents above—for example, they may want to add a sports section containing a Dinosaur Olympics or a travel section that takes visitors on a safari through Jurassic Park.

The Process
Within their teams, students will have responsibilities for research and for some aspect of creating the newspapers. They will assume roles that might include editors for each page, reporters, artists, game persons, and researchers. Roles can be deter-

mined based on students' learning styles, interests, or teacher selection. Once roles are assigned, each group will discuss and decide who will write feature articles, produce puzzles, and create contests. The assigned group recorder will give team lists of assignments to the teacher. Delineating tasks at the beginning of the project helps insure individual accountability.

For research on the Internet and for peer revision of their writing, students will work together with partners. Numerous team activities—such as determining the names of their newspapers, deciding on articles to submit to the Global Schoolhouse project, and making decisions on contents of the newspapers—will require students to work together as a whole group.

STEP 5: CREATE SAMPLE ACTIVITIES

The activities that follow will enable students to research a specific topic using the Internet, create a product for a specific audience based on that research, and emphasize cooperative skills necessary when students work together on the Internet and produce newspapers.

Activities to Introduce the Unit

Before introducing the unit, you must determine how much students already know about dinosaurs and begin to prepare students to work together in their cooperative teams. Because students often have little experience collaborating on projects, it might be necessary to acquaint students with one another, as well as to help them begin building a group identity. Finally, you will need to familiarize students with newspaper contents.

As an introduction to this unit, students will:

1. define vocabulary that will be used during the unit—for example, "dinos" in dinosaur means terrifying, and "sauros" means lizard. Some other terms that will be critical are: "era," "paleontology," "fossil," "prehistoric," to name a few. The Websites at *www.zoomdinosaurs.com/allabout* and *www.Enchanted Learning.com/subjects/dinosaurs/dinofossils/index.html* have good dictionaries of terms.
2. read or have the teacher read to them some books on dinosaurs. *Dinosaurs: An Illustrated History* by E. H. Colbert contains superb illustrations and an historical approach to dinosaurs' beginnings that might peak students' interests about the topic before they conduct their own research.
3. examine and discuss the different sections of a newspaper, such as feature articles, news stories, the editorial page, letters to the editor, sports, advertisements, comic strips, and travel. Students might even view an online newspaper at *www.cnn.com* as a model.
4. divide into groups and do at least one team-building activity, discussed in Part 1 of this chapter, to foster team spirit.
5. gather together in their groups to determine the name for their newspaper, establish deadlines, and outline a team plan for researching, writing, and creating their newspapers.

6. based on newspapers they have reviewed, brainstorm on a large sheet of paper a list of contents they want to include in their own newspapers.

Activities to Be Used During the Unit

Each team will thoroughly research specific types of dinosaurs so they have the information they need for at least one feature article and other news stories for their newspapers. They will also need material for activities, such as dinosaur crossword puzzles or "word finds," poems, and contests (perhaps to build the "best" dinosaur); these tasks may be done in pairs. As a group, each team will also be responsible for preparing their own newspaper.

During the unit, check on social skills of team members and for individual accountability. For example, as teams complete their work, call on individual members to explain how their group reached a conclusion or made a decision. These spot checks and assurances help keep all members working cooperatively and effectively together. You may want teams to divide the following tasks among their members so each student is responsible for specific learning outcomes. Student progress reports are also a good idea to encourage individual accountability (see Figure 5-2).

During this unit, students will:

1. learn how fossils form. Each group member will research one aspect about fossils, such as how they form, how they are dated, what types there are. As experts, they will teach other members of their teams about fossils. Figure 5-3 illustrates the Website at *www.EnchantedLearning.com/subjects/dinosaurs /dinofossils/index.html*, which provides useful information on fossils.
2. create a timeline of the different eras in the prehistoric period when dinosaurs lived (see Figure 5-4). Groups will identify different types of dinosaurs and give an example of one type of dinosaur that inhabited the Earth during each era. They should also write a brief description of each era. Website *www.EnchantedLearning.com/subject/dinosaurs* can help.
3. draw diagrams classifying dinosaurs according to kingdom, phylum, class, and order. Check Website *www.zoomdinosaur.com*.
4. research some dinosaur myths at *www.zoom.dinosaur.com/allabout/din Myths.html* to answer questions about dinosaurs, such as whether all dinosaurs were huge, whether man lived at the same time as dinosaurs, or whether dinosaurs flew. Figure 5-5 illustrates some possible myths.
5. within their groups, in pairs choose one dinosaur to research thoroughly. They can use the information sheets on dinosaurs from A to Z at Website *www.zoomdinosaur.com* to obtain information. Students should take notes on what they looked like, what they ate, how large they were, what distinguishing characteristics like horns or claws they had, where they lived, how they moved, and any other interesting facts.
6. draw pictures or obtain photos of the dinosaurs they researched to include in the newspapers. Use Figure 5-6 at *www.zoomdinosaur.com* for examples to

Figure 5–2: Student Progress Report

Name: _____ Date: _____

Progress Report Number: _____

Tasks accomplished this week:

A. Dinosaur Research
    1. _____
    2. _____
    3. _____
    4. _____
    5. _____

B. Newspaper Tasks
    1. _____
    2. _____
    3. _____
    4. _____
    5. _____

Problems encountered this week and ways I resolved them:

1. _____
2. _____

Successes I had this week:

1. _____
2. _____

The most exciting thing I learned/did this week:

_____
_____

Questions I have for my teacher this week:

_____
_____
_____

Status of my progress:

☐ My group is progressing on schedule, and we will be ready to turn our assignments in on time.

☐ My group needs more time because _____

☐ I am having trouble completing my part of the assignment because _____
_____

Figure 5–3: Dinosaur Website

Dinosaur Dictionary.

All About Dinosaurs:

- What is a Dinosaur?
- 98 Dinosaur Information Sheets, including Apatosaurus, T. rex, Triceratops, Velociraptor, and more!
- 30 Simple Dinosaur Print-outs
- How Dinosaurs are Named
- Dinosaurs and Birds
- Record Breakers
- Dinosaur Myths

Dino News:

- News Index

Anatomy and Behavior:

Extinction:
Why did the dinosaurs go extinct?

- What is Extinction?
- The Alvarez Asteroid Theory
- Other K-T Extinction Theories
- Studying Extinctions

Fossils:

- First Dinosaur Fossil Discoveries
- What are Fossils?
- How Fossils Form
- Types of Fossils
- Finding Fossils
- Excavating Fossils
- Dating Fossils
- Bony Jigsaw Puzzles

use as models. Students can send their dinosaur art work to *www.dinodon. com/dinosaurs/kidsart.html* (illustrated in Figure 5-7).

7. write stories entitled a "Day in the Life of a Dinosaur." For their stories, students should know about characteristics of their dinosaurs, the eras in which they lived, other dinosaurs that lived at the same time, how their dinosaurs got food, and so on. They can obtain all of these facts from their earlier research, or ask Dino Russ any questions they have about dinosaurs at *www.isgs.uiuc.edu/dinos*. The writing process will require that students:

- write rough drafts, exchange them with partners, and provide suggestions to their partners on the drafts. (See Figures 3-5 and 3-11 for sample peer review guides.)
- revise rough drafts, obtain a second peer edit, and write final copies.

Figure 5–4: Dinosaur Timeline

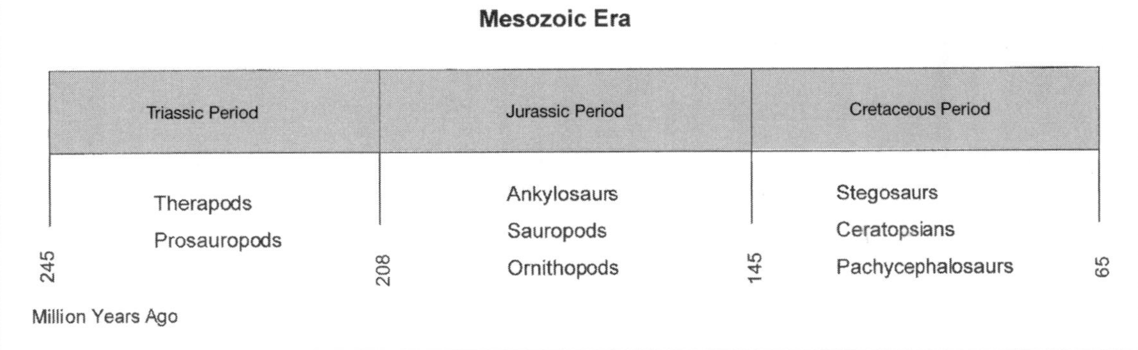

Mesozoic Era

Triassic Period	Jurassic Period	Cretaceous Period
Therapods	Ankylosaurs	Stegosaurs
Prosauropods	Sauropods	Ceratopsians
	Ornithopods	Pachycephalosaurs

245   208   145   65

Million Years Ago

Figure 5–5: Dinosaur Myths

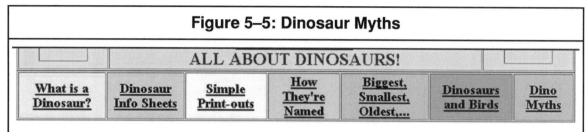

ALL ABOUT DINOSAURS!

| What is a Dinosaur? | Dinosaur Info Sheets | Simple Print-outs | How They're Named | Biggest, Smallest, Oldest,... | Dinosaurs and Birds | Dino Myths |

Dinosaur Myths

Do you know the answers to these dinosaur questions? Don't rely on popular images from dinosaur movies or cartoons! They're frequently wrong.

1. Were all huge, prehistoric animals dinosaurs?
2. Did any dinosaurs swim or fly?
3. Were all the dinosaurs huge?
4. Did cavemen live alongside the dinosaurs?
5. Did all the dinosaurs live at the same time?
6. Did all the dinosaurs die out?
7. Why were the dinosaurs a failure?

Copyright 1999 EnchantedLearning.com. Used by permission.

Figure 5–6: Types of Dinosaurs

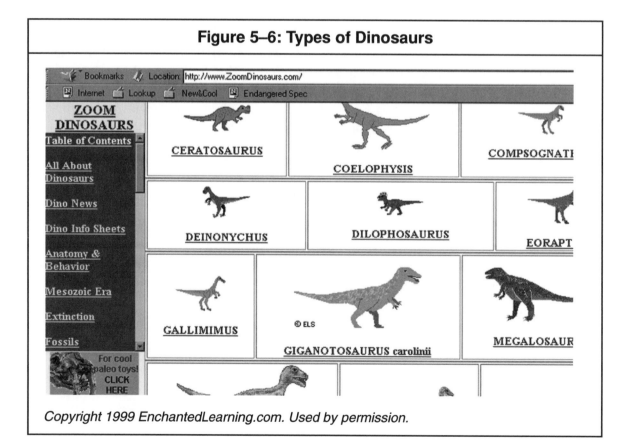

Copyright 1999 EnchantedLearning.com. Used by permission.

Figure 5–7: Kids' Dinosaur Art Site

KIDS' DINOSAUR ART

Send Us Your Dinosaurs!
Have your art posted on
the Dino Don site!

The latest! <u>Kids' dinosaur art from Ashburn, VA!</u>

Each month we'll post a gallery of your dinosaur images. Kids up to age 15 can send us their dinosaur art. Since Dino Don is color blind, a bad artist and has no taste, don't be offended if your drawing isn't chosen.

Art posted on the site will be listed by First name, Last Initial, City and State.

Send your art to:

Kid's Art
c/o Dinosaur Productions
PO Box 461
Newton, MA 02159

Be sure to include:

Your first name and last initial
Your city and state (or country)

Reprinted by permission of Dinodon.com, Dinosaur Productions, Inc., design by Charley Parker.

---

8. Find out about archeological sites where dinosaur fossils and remains have been found. Use the Website at *www.isgs.uiuc.edu/dinos* for information.
9. Trace the dinosaur discoveries of archeologists. On a world map identify sites of dinosaur discoveries. Use Website *http://dinosaurs.eb.com* for help.
10. Based on the research they have gathered, create newspapers as outlined under Step 4.

Activities to Be Used as Follow-up to the Unit

It is important that students apply the knowledge gained from researching dinosaurs to life in the twenty-first century. For example, students should be able to compare animals in their world, such as crocodiles, ostriches, lizards, and turtles, to those from the dinosaur eras. They might look at endangered animals today and why they are becoming extinct. They might also simulate an actual hunt for fossils. As follow-up, each team will:

1. choose an article to submit to the Global Schoolhouse project at *www.gsn.org/project/newsday/index.html* (see Figure 5-8) site.
2. build its own "super" dinosaurs using specific parts of different dinosaurs researched. For example, the head of the "super" dinosaur might be from the Tyrannosaurus Rex, the legs for rapid running from Struthiomimus, and protective armor from the Stegosaurus. The Website *www.dinodon.com/gallery* shows two dinosaurs from the dinosaur gallery.
3. go on an archeological dig using information at *www.yahooligans.com/Science_and_Nature/Living_Things/Paleontology/Dinosaurs/Museums_and_Exhibits* or *www.EnchantedLearning.com/subjects/dinosaurs/dinofossils/index.html*. Students will:
   - decide what equipment to take
   - determine where they will go
   - list the steps they will go through to uncover the "finds," get them ready to be transported to the lab and exhibited in a museum.

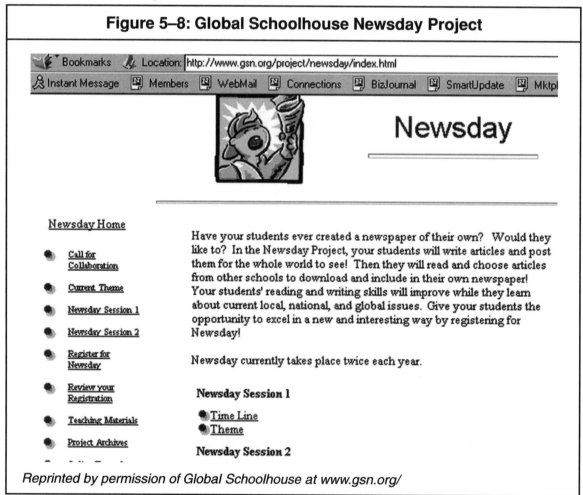

Figure 5–8: Global Schoolhouse Newsday Project

Reprinted by permission of Global Schoolhouse at www.gsn.org/

STEP 6: EVALUATE WHAT WAS LEARNED

Evaluation for the unit should be based on two basic elements: (1) the product, and (2) the cooperative-learning process. The articles and games students have written to demonstrate their writing and creative expertise can be assessed based on a scoring rubric such as the one in Figure 5-9. You will also evaluate students' knowledge of dinosaurs by their newspapers, which will show how much they have learned about dinosaurs.

You will be evaluating the cooperative-learning process through your observations during the activities. It is also a good idea to have students do a self-evaluation on group dynamics. Have them write answers to the following questions in their journals:

- What did they do well as a group, and what do they need to do better?
- What problem(s) did the group encounter, and how did the group solve the problem?
- What one thing did each member of the team do that was helpful to the group?
- What could each member do to make the group function better?

In addition, it is useful to discuss the questions and responses as a whole class so that more skillful participation occurs in subsequent cooperative activities. The evaluation checklist in Figure 2-5 is a good model to use.

Figure 5–9: Evaluation Rubric

Student Name:_____   **Date:** _____

Assignment: Dinosaur Articles

1. The writing includes at least five specific facts about a dinosaur.   **1 2 3 4 5**

2. Each fact is explained in a separate paragraph containing at least three sentences.   **1 2 3 4 5**

3. The writing uses descriptive language to "show" specific details about the dinosaur.   **1 2 3 4 5**

4. Paragraphs are indented.   **1 2 3 4 5**

5. Stories have titles.   **1 2 3 4 5**

Additional Comments:

SUMMARY

In this unit, students had opportunities to explore content in geological science when they learned about fossils and dinosaurs. They also enhanced their social skills because they worked in a cooperative learning environment conducting research, producing newspapers, and communicating with peers on a worldwide project on the Internet. Finally, by creating their newspapers, students practiced language skills—reading and writing. This unit has integrated language arts, science, and art and used the Internet as a tool for research, cooperation, and communication.

Although all students should work independently and competitively, today's workplace also values cooperation and "being a good team player." Employees in the "real world" also use technology as a means to attain job goals. Students in all of our classrooms will benefit by learning, using, and practicing cooperative skills and by understanding the role technology plays in research and communication.

UNIT 2 (SECONDARY LEVEL): THE STOCK MARKET

We began a discussion of e-commerce in the business education unit in Part 2 of Chapter 4. In fact, e-commerce is exploding on the Web, with sales more than doubling from the end of 1997 to 1998. The Internet has also made life easier for the do-it-yourself investor in the stock market. In the past, stock was usually bought and sold through a stock broker, who was paid a commission for completing stock transactions. On the Internet, individuals can now access company financial statements and reports filed with the Securities and Exchange Commission, which monitors stock trading in the United States. These and other stock-related documents make stock trading on the Internet possible for the small investor.

This unit on the stock market employs skills and concepts from mathematics, economics, and language arts and teaches students how they can invest their money wisely and how international events influence the stock markets worldwide. The incredible rise in stock market value during the 1990s provides a powerful and exciting example of economic principles for students.

This unit on the stock market introduces students to vocabulary such as IPOs, e-trade, stocks, NASDAQ, Dow Jones, and New York Stock Exchange, to name a few. Students will observe how daily events around the world can change the values of stocks, how money is made and lost, and how real stocks are bought and sold. They will also learn to balance accounts. Throughout the unit, students will operate in real-life situations as they would in the workplace, creating stock portfolios, analyzing individual components of their portfolios, and learning to work within a budget.

STEP 1: APPLY FRAMEWORK STANDARDS—WHAT SHOULD BE TAUGHT?

One of the major strands comprising the California History-Social Sciences Framework is that students achieve economic literacy. Students will examine influences on economic order, such as inflationary and deflationary pressures, worker productivity, and national and international political events—all factors that impact the banking industry and the stock markets of the world. Although this is a course primarily in social sciences, students will also be using mathematical concepts when they create graphs, tables, and charts. This unit introduces activities so students can gain a conceptual understanding of the stock market as well as a practical knowledge of its workings and relation to current events.

Finally, national standards in all subject areas encourage increased emphasis on students working cooperatively together. For example, a major goal emphasized in the California History-Social Sciences Framework (CSDE, 1988) from kindergarten to grade 12 is to foster group interaction skills, such as the ability to listen to differing views of others, participate in making decisions, and to plan and take action in a collaborative setting. These skills are especially important for high-school students, who will soon be joining the work force where teamwork is a quality most businesses seek. In this unit, students will explore the stock market through cooperative activities requiring them to set team goals and make decisions that will affect group products.

STEP 2: IDENTIFYING GENERAL GOALS AND SPECIFIC OBJECTIVES

The goals and objectives for this unit are based on national standards in social sciences and economics. Students will deepen their understanding of economic problems and institutions of the nation and the world in which they live. They should learn to make reasoned decisions on economic issues and build on the economic understandings they have acquired in previous grades. They will also increase their skills in working with others to accomplish common goals.

Goals

Students will:

- retrieve and analyze information by using computers and other electronic media
- read and interpret charts, tables, and graphs
- demonstrate proficiency in basic mathematical skills

Objectives

Students will:

- define vocabulary related to the stock market and trading online
- create an in-depth company profile of at least five companies
- track the stock market to determine the financial health of different companies
- create graphs and charts and/or spreadsheets to illustrate companies' stock histories
- using visuals present concise oral reports on their stock portfolios

STEP 3: GATHER MATERIALS

Because of the increase in e-trading, Websites that offer help to prospective traders have proliferated recently. Websites offering free information that ranges from tracking the current value of a stock portfolio to reading comments by financial analysts have enabled more consumers to trade in the stock market. With these resources, students can now simulate real-life stock trading without investing the dollars. Table 5-3 lists some Internet sites that may be useful for the activities in this unit. Some sites like *http://quote.yahoo.com* provide stock quotes, news on the market, information on Initial Public Offerings (IPOs)—new companies offering stock to the public—and company financial statements. Others are more specialized, like Website *www.stocksheet.com*, which provides profiles of companies.

STEP 4: INTRODUCE THE UNIT

This unit is an ideal one for cooperative-learning activities. Just keep in mind that cooperative activities must be designed so there is individual accountability, positive interdependence, and group processing.

Each group will be allotted $10,000 to invest the way it chooses, with the following stipulations. Students must:

- buy a minimum of ten shares of each stock
- list stocks they have chosen and keep weekly journals of the market prices of the stocks
- at the end of a specified time (six weeks to three months), sell their stocks and determine the profit/loss margin
- provide an oral assessment of their stock portfolios at the end of three months
- track at least one company and report results to the class

STEP 5: CREATE SAMPLE ACTIVITIES

The sample activities that follow offer a range of suggestions for tasks students might engage in while exploring the stock market. At the beginning of the unit, you may want to make specific assignments from the list of activities to help insure individual accountability. A contract (as shown in Figure 4-3) will provide a model and help in the evaluation process.

Activities to Introduce the Unit

The stock market is only one aspect of teaching economics. Before starting this unit, check out Website *http://ecedweb.unomaha.edu/teachsug.htm*, where there are some suggestions that teachers might want to use with students as an overview or review of economic concepts. To prepare themselves for the stock market, students will:

1. list and define terms in their journals related to the stock market and economics in general. They will use this terminology throughout the unit. Some terms might include: stock market, stock exchange, ticker symbol, stock certificate, e-trading, market analyst, stock listings, and so forth. Use Websites *www.crews.org/media_tech/compsci/8thgrade/stkmkt/glossary.htm* and *www.excite.com/reference/almanac/?id=A0672446* for help.

Table 5–3: Stock Market Websites	
Sample URLs	**Description of Websites**
http://quote.yahoo.com	Provides basic stock quotes, ability to set u a free portfolio, research, and recent news
http://investor.msn.com	Illustrates comparative stock performances through charts
http://dailystocks.com	Compiles stock resources throughout the Web on a stock symbol
www.insidewallstreet.com	Provides stock quotes and other information
www.internetstocks.com/launch.html	Includes news on Internet stocks
www.stocksheet.com	Provides company profiles
http://askmerrill.com/mlol/main/ index.asp	Contains research reports from Merrill Lynch
www.freeedgar.com	Includes company financial statements
www.youngmoney.com	Articles for teens on finances and stock market
www.crews.org/media_tech/compsci/ 8thgrade/stkmkt/glossary.htm	Contains basic terminology on the stock market

2. review how the stock market relates to economic concepts. Use Website *http://ecedweb.unomaha.edu/ec-cncps.htm* for an overview.
3. trace the history of the stock market. Use Website *http://library.advanced.org/ 10326*.
4. form their teams based on grouping principles discussed in Part 1 of this chapter. Each cooperative group should contain four to six students. As a team-building exercise, have students:
   - discuss what they know about money management and investing. Websites *www.investorguide.com/Kids.htm* and *www.iionline.com/investor_ university* have information on different aspects of investing, such as risks involved and basic money management for beginners.
   - participate in a real-time stock market simulation at Website *http://library. advanced.org/10326/simulation/simulation.html* to become familiar with how the stock market works. See Figure 5-10 for information about the simulation.
   - create a list of companies that the group members have heard about. Students might think of companies for which their parents work or others that have been in the news and on television. Possible choices might be IBM, General Motors, Xerox, McDonalds, Dow Chemical, U.S. Steel,

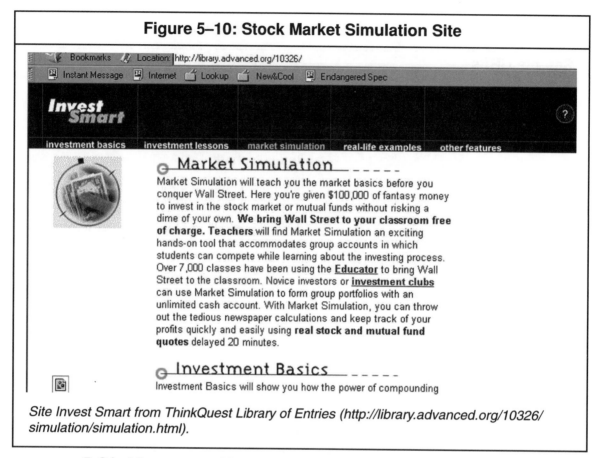

Figure 5–10: Stock Market Simulation Site

Bookmarks   Location: http://library.advanced.org/10326/

Instant Message   Internet   Lookup   New&Cool   Endangered Spec

InvestSmart   (?)

investment basics   investment lessons   market simulation   real-life examples   other features

Market Simulation

Market Simulation will teach you the market basics before you conquer Wall Street. Here you're given $100,000 of fantasy money to invest in the stock market or mutual funds without risking a dime of your own. **We bring Wall Street to your classroom free of charge. Teachers** will find Market Simulation an exciting hands-on tool that accommodates group accounts in which students can compete while learning about the investing process. Over 7,000 classes have been using the **Educator** to bring Wall Street to the classroom. Novice investors or **investment clubs** can use Market Simulation to form group portfolios with an unlimited cash account. With Market Simulation, you can throw out the tedious newspaper calculations and keep track of your profits quickly and easily using **real stock and mutual fund quotes** delayed 20 minutes.

Investment Basics

Investment Basics will show you how the power of compounding

Site Invest Smart from ThinkQuest Library of Entries (http://library.advanced.org/10326/ simulation/simulation.html).

RCA, Netscape, or Home Depot. Based on the simulation, they will discuss the pros and cons to investing in companies on their lists, looking at Website *http://library.advanced.org/10326/investment_lessons/index.html* to understand different types of stocks. Label their stocks by types.

- brainstorm criteria that the group might consider as they decide on their stock portfolios (see Figure 5-11).
- with a partner from the group check the Website at *www.secapl.com/secapl/ quoteserver/search.html* to identify ticker symbols for the list of companies they have just generated. This task will enable them to become familiar with locating stock information on the Internet.

Activities to Be Used During the Unit

Now students must think about which stocks they will invest in, what their stock portfolios will include, and how they will manage their portfolios. Tracking the stocks and the companies in which they have invested is very important. Groups will:

1. create their portfolios. Some of the activities below will be completed as a whole group; much of the research will be done in pairs.
   - At Website *http://library.advanced.org/10326*, students will review the introduction to the stock market to help them select stocks (see Figure 5-12).

Figure 5–11: Stock Market Issues

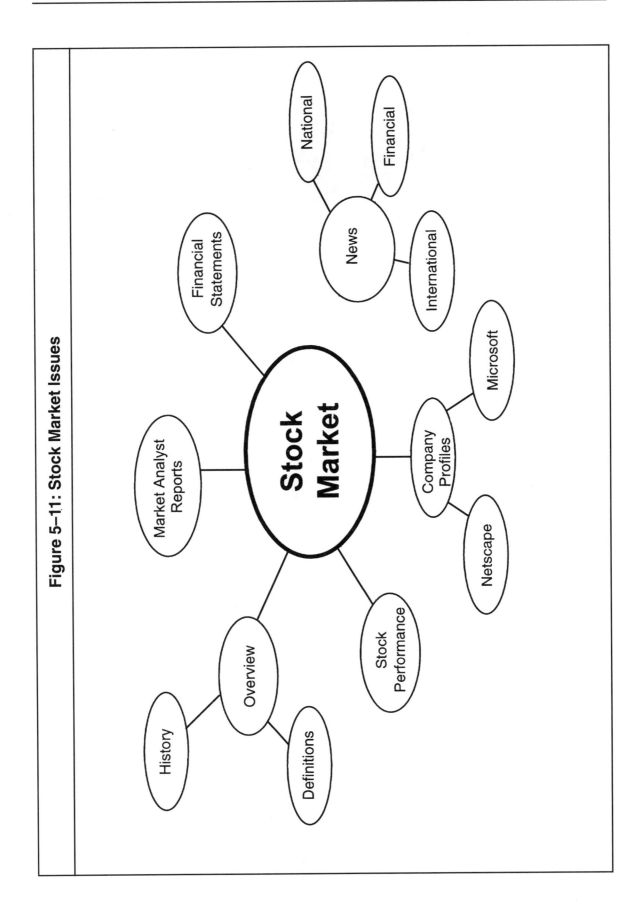

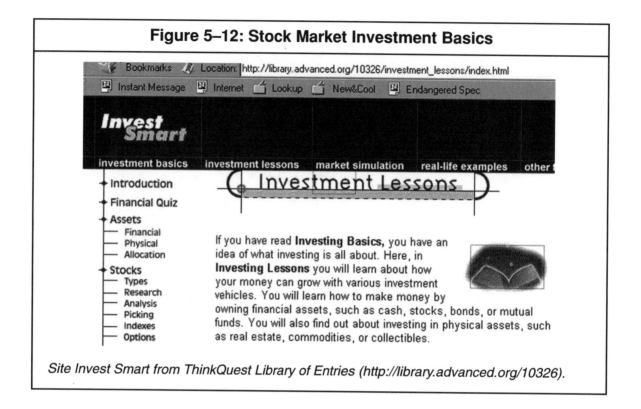

Figure 5–12: Stock Market Investment Basics

Site Invest Smart from ThinkQuest Library of Entries (http://library.advanced.org/10326).

- The group will determine at least ten stocks they want to buy. In pairs, they should identify at least three companies in which they want to invest to discuss with the group, using a Website offering company profiles such as the one at *www.freeedgar.com*.
- Students will identify ticker symbols for each company using Website *www.secapl.com/secapl/quoteserver/search.html*.
- Partners will select one of the proposed companies to research and look at profiles of that company. Based on the company information, they will explain in journal entries reasons for selecting each company. Website *www.freeedgar.com* provides profiles for a large group of companies. Each pair will share their entries with the rest of its group.
- Pairs will check market analyst reports at *http://quote.yahoo.com* to determine what expectations the industry has for each company in the proposed portfolios. Each pair will write a summary on two companies to share with its group.
- Students will create ledgers that indicate the cost of each company's stock, number of shares they will buy, commissions, if any, that need to be paid, and balance based on their $10,000 initial account balances. They will obtain stock quotes for each company at *http://quote.yahoo.com*.
- After selecting at least five out of the companies they have just researched for their final portfolios, they will start spreadsheets listing all company names.

- A group portfolio at *http://quote.yahoo.com* will enable them to track their companies online automatically.

2. track the companies in their portfolios. This activity will extend over a three-month period. Groups should assign tasks so that some students are tracking companies, others are reading news reports, and some are maintaining spreadsheets.

   - Each group will create written profiles of each company, describing the companies, their financial status, any stock changes, and anything else affecting the companies' stock prices. Use Website *http://investor.msn.com* to obtain charts with comparative stock performances.
   - Students' spreadsheets will contain important information on their stock performance: company names; ticker symbols; stocks' fifty-two-week highs and lows; the high, low, and close stock prices; and the net changes. Viewing *http://library.advanced.org/10326* will help them understand terms they will see on stock listings either in the newspaper or online. This site will explain the parts of the spreadsheets.
   - Students will add data to spreadsheets once a week for a three-month time span. See Figure 5-13 for a sample spreadsheet of portfolio performance.
   - Each group will create a ledger that tracks money spent on stock, commissions (if any must be paid), and balances in the group accounts.
   - Partners will read national and international news stories each week about one company, summarizing in their journals news that might affect the groups' stocks. Some possible issues might be increase in inflation, world crises, natural disasters, and changes in country leadership. Check Website *http://cbs.marketwatch.com* for news related to the financial world; visit *www.cnnfs.com* or *www.cnn.com* for the latest national and international news. Discuss as a group how current events have affected the stock market.
   - Using *http:www.freeedgar.com* for complete financial reports on all publicly traded companies, students will check the financial status of all companies in the portfolios.
   - Students will read market analyst reports on the five companies in their portfolios, referring to Website *http://askmerrill.com/mlol/main/index.asp*.
   - Each week, students will provide oral summaries on the progress of their portfolios to the class.

3. present their portfolios to the class. Groups will play the roles of financial planners discussing the merits of their portfolios before the class. To insure individual accountability, each team member will take part in the analysis. The presentations will include:
   - complete analyses of each of the companies in their portfolios
   - charts or graphs to indicate each stock's progress over the three-month period (Website *http://investor.msn.com* provides models of charts).
   - predictions about their portfolios for the future and recommendations for changes they would make in their current company choices.

Figure 5-13: Stock Portfolio Spreadsheet							
Name	**Tick. Sym**	**52wk. High**	**52wk. Low**	**Wk's High**	**Wk's Low**	**Wk's Last**	**Net Chg.**
Abbott Lab	ABT	53 5/16	34 7/8	53 1/8	47	52 15/16	3 7/8
Allstate	ALL	52 3/8	34 3/4	39 3/8	36 13/16	38 13/16	2 3/16
Home Depot	HD	67 1/3	31 5/8	64 1/3	58	62 7/16	− 7/8
Exxon	XON	83 1/2	62	83 1/2	76 5/8	78 5/16	−1 5/8
Frontr CP	FRO	57 1/4	24	54 4/5	49 4/9	54 1/4	1 1/5
GenMills	GIS	84 2/3	59 3/16	80 1/2	77 3/4	79 1/2	1/3
Knight Ridder	KRI	59 5/8	40 1/2	56 1/5	53 3/8	55 3/16	1
Lucent Tch	LU	67	23 23/32	62 7/16	51 7/8	61 1/16	4 1/8
Microsoft	MSFT	95 5/8	40 15/16	88 1/2	80	86	−0.625

Activities to Be Used as Follow-up to the Unit

Once students have a basic knowledge of the stock market, how it works, and how trading takes place, they can apply what they have learned. Activities on the Web enable students to collaborate online about the stock market with other economics classes or school investment clubs. They can participate in competitive stock market games or start their own competition. Groups will:

- choose one Website, such as *www.virtualstockexchange.com, www.crews.org/ media_tech/compsci/8thgrade/stkmkt/index.htm,* or *www.agedwards.com/ bma/index.shtml,* and sign up for a student stock tournament.
- set up their own stock portfolio at *www.quicken.com* to see how much they have learned, creating charts that track their investments weekly for six months.
- check their financial savvy against other students' investments at *www.younginvestor.com/pick.shtml.*

STEP 6: EVALUATE WHAT WAS LEARNED

For this unit students should be evaluated on (1) what they learn about the stock market and (2) their participation in their groups and with partners. Establishing a point system for completing each of the activities, such as creating a company profile or reading and writing summaries of news articles about their companies, will provide quantitative assessment and individual accountability. In addition, students should have opportunities for self-evaluation. During the unit you should observe students as they participate in instructional activities. Through anecdotal observations, you can gain insights about the learning and development of your students as they complete each activity. By playing several financial-based games at Website *www.younginvestor.com/dnldfile/yig.dcr,* students can reinforce the concepts they have learned about the stock market and determine if review is necessary.

You can assess student progress during the unit in several ways. Students will write summaries of current events that affect their portfolios, create charts and graphs to illustrate the progress of their stocks, write entries in their journals that define terminology, and reflect on the successes of their investments and their group work. Students will also provide brief oral reports to the class on the progress of their stocks at the end of each week. For their culminating projects students will assume the roles of financial planners who present reports to the class indicating the success or failure of their portfolios and recommendations for future investments. Thus, students are individually accountable for their own learning, and they are assessed on their contributions to the success of the group achievement.

SUMMARY

Through this cooperative unit, students have had opportunities to work collaboratively in deciding which stocks to include in their portfolios. They have used mathematical concepts to create charts, graphs, and spreadsheets to track their stocks. In addition, they have had the chance to compete online against other students working on similar stock-market-related projects.

This unit's combination of independent, cooperative, and competitive tasks teaches students how to accomplish real-life goals. Moreover, it teaches them about investments and money management and about the factors that influence markets throughout the world. The Internet offers a wide range of resources and cooperative activities to help students learn about the importance of the stock market and its effects on the world economy.

TEACHER EXERCISES: NOW YOU TRY IT...

The following exercises will help you practice what you have learned in this chapter. It is important to follow up immediately to reinforce the skills and concepts presented.

1. Choose one of the cooperative-learning units as a model and try some of the activities suggested as a student would. For example, try setting up your own investment portfolio or researching one type of dinosaur.
2. Write journal entries about your experiences exploring the above Websites. Ask yourself: Will students enjoy these Internet activities? Was the Internet a useful resource for the unit? If so, how? How can the Internet help me in a lesson I want to create?
3. Look for at least five Internet sites that will be useful to an upcoming lesson.
4. Identify and bookmark Websites that you might use in units that have a cooperative-learning component.
5. Create a Web-based lesson that includes cooperative-learning activities. Then, (a) determine how you will group students; (b) decide how individuals will be held accountable; and (c) determine how you will assess group participation and individual achievement.

CONCLUSION

Major focuses for the work force of the twenty-first century will be collaboration, project-based team activities, and the use of technology. In addition, our work force will continue to be very diverse. As we have seen in this chapter, cooperative learning is a teaching strategy that lends itself well to the use of technology. Cooperative methods stress interpersonal interactions and help teachers to manage classroom diversity successfully.

The Internet provides a way to embrace cooperative learning as an instructional method, aiding students in collaborating with other students around the world; it is also a means through which to retrieve and share information in a cooperative setting with all participants working together toward common goals. Students who know how to work in teams and use the Internet will have the advantage in the workplace of the twenty-first century.

REFERENCES

Anderson, Mary. 1989. *Partnerships: Teambuilding at the Computer.* Arlington, VA: Ma-Jo Press.

California State Department of Education. 1988. *History–Social Science Framework for California Public Schools, Kindergarten Through Grade Twelve.* Sacramento: California State Department of Education.

California State Department of Education. 1987. *California Science Model Curriculum Guide.* Sacramento: California State Department of Education.

California State Department of Education. 1987. *Science Framework for California Public Schools: Kindergarten Through Grade Twelve.* Sacramento: California State Department of Education.

Johnson, David W., Roger T. Johnson, Edythe J. Holubec, and Patricia A. Roy. 1984. *Circles of Learning: Cooperation in the Classroom.* Alexandria, VA: Association for Supervision and Curriculum Development.

Kagan, Spencer, 1990. *Cooperative Learning Resources for Teachers.* San Juan Capistrano, CA: Resources for Teachers.

Male, Mary, David Johnson, Roger T. Johnson, and Mary Anderson. 1994. *Cooperative Learning and Computers: An Activity Guide for Teachers.* Santa Cruz, CA: Educational Apple-cations.

Slavin, Robert. 1995. *Cooperative Learning: Theory, Research, and Practice.* Needham Heights, MA: Allyn and Bacon.

U.S. Department of Labor, Secretary's Commission on Achieving Necessary Skills. 1991. *What Work Requires of Schools: A SCANS Report for America 2000.* Washington, D.C.: U.S. Department of Labor.

Section Three

HOW TO INTEGRATE THE INTERNET INTO SPECIFIC CURRICULAR AREAS

Chapter 6

USING WEB RESOURCES IN ENGLISH AND LANGUAGE ARTS

PART 1: IDEAS AND INSIGHTS

OBJECTIVES OF THIS CHAPTER

This chapter is designed for use by English–language arts educators at both the elementary and secondary levels. By the end of this chapter, educators will be able to:

- state advantages of using the Internet in language arts education
- build a language arts unit that includes the Internet
- identify at least ten language arts–related Websites

An English–language arts curriculum has the responsibility to teach students to listen well, speak effectively, read and think critically, and write clearly. To accomplish these tasks, we, as English–language arts educators, expose students to literature in the form of fiction, nonfiction, poetry, and drama. We require students to discuss and create meaning from texts they read. We provide opportunities for students to speak in small groups and to the whole class about their experiences with literature. We create assignments that require students to write about their thoughts and experiences, and analyze ways that literature provides meaning for their own lives.

Many of us have also been using technology in our English–language arts classrooms. For example, we have students write and revise their essays on computers or use desktop publishing to create newsletters or the school newspaper. We may even be communicating with other classrooms in other countries to learn and write about different cultures and share experiences. A few of us may even have our students access online databases as sources for their research papers.

We are, however, in the minority in terms of using technology in the language arts. A recent survey—"National Survey of Internet Usage: Teachers, Computer Co-ordinators, and School Librarians, Grades 3–12" (printed in The Heller Report, March 1997)—indicated that the number of educators using the Internet to support English studies was not even included in the top ten curriculum areas. There are, however, an increasing number of English and language arts resources on the Internet that comply with national standards and achieve state framework goals.

This chapter explores ways to integrate the Internet into English and the language arts content instruction. In Part 2, the structure of the model unit presented in Chapter 1 illustrates two sample unit plans.

USING WEB RESOURCES IN ENGLISH–LANGUAGE ARTS

With the Internet almost a household word in many homes and schools, we as educators must figure out how to incorporate this new technology in the English–language arts curriculum. The Internet can provide students and teachers with resources for each part of a language arts unit: "Into," "Through," and "Beyond." In the "Into" part of the unit, we see how to take advantage of students' prior knowledge to establish a foundation for the concepts we will be teaching in the unit. This part may also provide background for the subject. For example, before studying Shakespeare's play, *Romeo and Juliet*, students can look at the Globe Theatre in which Shakespearean plays were performed or compile facts about his life. Or, if teachers need background on topics—such as: What was life like during Shakespeare's time? What did people wear in the sixteenth and seventeenth centuries?—there are many sites, especially university sites, where this type of information is readily available (*http://the-tech.mit.edu/Shakespeare/works.html*) and can help teachers in the planning stage of a unit. Additionally, teachers may want to search the Internet for lesson plans created by teachers who have taught the same topic, such as at *http://falcon.jmu.edu/~ramseyil/shakless.htm*.

For the "Through" part of each unit, we provide activities and assignments to convey our subject content. For example, teachers may be looking for unique or interesting activities or strategies to aid them in teaching the material. Again, other teacher sites are one source of different methodologies, as are textbook or magazine publisher sites, such as Scholastic's at *www.scholastic.com*, which display lessons, ideas, pictures, and other resources. If we want students to do a major research project—an essay, an oral presentation, a research paper, or a debate—the Internet can provide a wealth of information for students to use as support for their ideas. Resources from the Internet—video clips, audio, government documents, answers from experts, a listserv where discussion on an issue is ongoing, or a news group where students can ask and receive answers to their questions—make this "virtual library" a dynamic medium for assisting students.

Once we complete the objectives for the unit, we will want to expand students' thinking—perhaps by discussing how themes in a work of literature relate to students' own lives or alternative situations. Going "Beyond" provides enrichment activities to reinforce the lesson and to extend to the teacher an alternative to the unit test as a means to assess students' learning. For example, when studying *Romeo and Juliet*, students can act out scenes using simple puppets made from paper bags and masks. Often students are more comfortable during classroom performances because the student actor has something to hide behind, something to use to become someone else. Publishing on a Website can also provide culmination and an authentic audience for student writing completed during the unit. Several Websites, such as *http://longwood.cs.ucf.edu/~MidLink* or Kids' Space at *www.kids-space.org/frame/KS_R.html* are locales where student stories and artwork can be published.

"Into," "Through," and "Beyond" activities will be illustrated as part of the sample unit plans in Part 2 of this chapter.

EXAMPLES OF ENGLISH–LANGUAGE ARTS PROJECTS

The Internet currently offers a wide range of resources for the language arts, ranging from complete works of literature online to lesson plans and activities for K–12 teachers. For example, the Gutenberg Project from the Massachusetts Institute of Technology at *www.promo.net/pg* lets learners search the text of a literary work using keywords. Teacher-developed unit plans at *www.sdcoe.k12.ca.us/score/cyberguide.html* contain units of instruction that incorporate Internet resources on core works of literature.

There are also many projects that classrooms can join. These projects range from telecollaboration among classes to publication sites. For example, a third-grade class in California published their researched work about African Americans on their own Website at *http://marin.k12.ca.us/LLMC%20Bookmarks/heroes.html*. Students wrote biographies of men and women whom they felt performed as heroes during the fight against slavery and for civil rights. They also included modern-day African American heroes, such as artists, entertainers, and sports stars. The Internet provides an authentic audience for these students' written work.

In another example, the Global Schoolhouse at *www.gsn.org/project/newsday/index.html* (see Figure 6-1) involves students in producing their own newspapers based on news articles submitted by student correspondents to the *Newsday* newswire service. In this project, students become news reporters, editors, layout and graphic artists, and publishers. Because students around the world may participate, issues discussed in the newspapers lead to an understanding of broad problems, not just local concerns. Classes can join the Global Schoolhouse for free at *www.globalschoolhouse.com/join*.

My Hero at *www.myhero.com/home.asp*, shown in Figure 6-2, is an interactive writing project produced by the Fund for Innovative TV. Students can submit writing about their heroes, be they family members, friends, teachers, scientists, poets, artists, athletes, or writers. Some of the heroes students have written about include Nelson Mandela, Eleanor Roosevelt, Langston Hughes, Maya Angelou, and Mother Teresa. Using text, images, and audio, the writings provide biographical information and students' perceptions and feelings about the heroes. In addition, a listing of Web resources offers information on these heroes for further research.

Several projects promote writing for a "real" audience and communicating for a

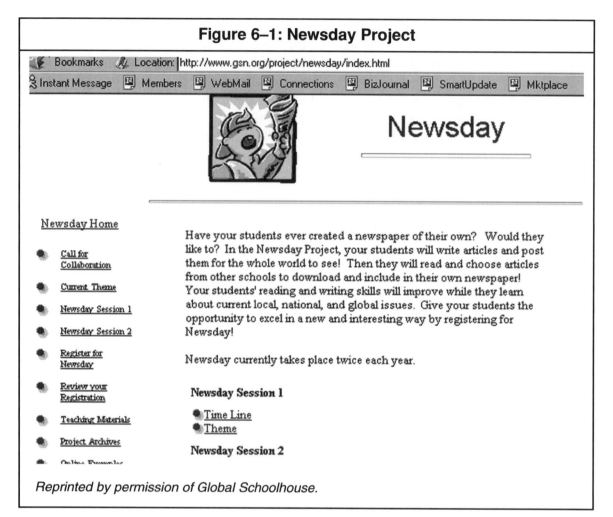

Figure 6–1: Newsday Project

Have your students ever created a newspaper of their own? Would they like to? In the Newsday Project, your students will write articles and post them for the whole world to see! Then they will read and choose articles from other schools to download and include in their own newspaper! Your students' reading and writing skills will improve while they learn about current local, national, and global issues. Give your students the opportunity to excel in a new and interesting way by registering for Newsday!

Newsday currently takes place twice each year.

Reprinted by permission of Global Schoolhouse.

purpose. One, devoted to improving student writing—the Laws of Life Essay Project, located at *www.iearn.org/iearn/projects/laws*—is an international essay venture. To participate, students reflect on and write about values that have helped shape their lives. Essays are chosen to be published, and selected students are invited to read their essays at an annual international conference. At *www.realkids.com* students are prompted to write about dangers they have faced where they have had to use their wits to save themselves or others. At this site, students can also interact with children from all over the world by joining the Young Writer's Clubhouse or receive critiques of their writing through the Young Writer's Critique Group. A teacher resource lounge, a chat forum, and writing tips make this site one that may help students become better writers. And at Website *www.diaryproject.com*, students are encouraged to communicate with teens of all cultures to share their thoughts, aspirations, questions, and ideas with other young people. This project is designed to open up a worldwide dialogue about issues teens confront growing up in today's world—topics such as relationships, tolerance, friends, family, violence, and stress, to name a few. Submitting their own writing and reading the writing of other young people can enhance journal writing, which is usually part of all language arts classes.

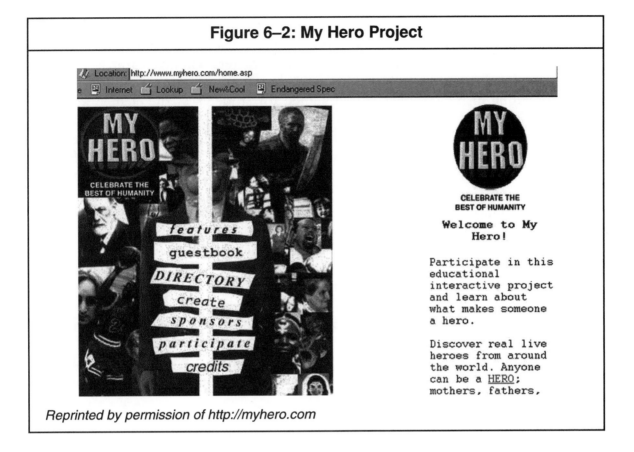

Figure 6–2: My Hero Project

Reprinted by permission of http://myhero.com

The two units that follow illustrate other ways to use Internet resources as part of the English–language arts curriculum. The steps for the following units involve:

1. Apply framework standards—what should be taught?
2. Identify general goals and specific objectives.
3. Gather materials.
4. Introduce the unit.
5. Create sample activities.
6. Evaluate what was learned.

PART 2: PRACTICAL APPLICATIONS

Two unit plans will illustrate using Web resources in English and language arts. According to a Gallup survey (1989), Shakespeare's writings, especially *Romeo and Juliet*, comprise the most widely read works in high schools across the country. The first unit, for secondary level, emphasizes the material on Shakespeare, his plays, and his background that can be obtained from the Internet. The unit is designed to introduce Shakespeare and place his writings into a historical context, to highlight

Shakespeare as a man of the theater. For example, if students understand details about the Globe Theatre—such as the audience that viewed Shakespeare's plays from the Globe pit—then the language, themes, and characters will be clearer.

The second unit is entitled "Heroes" and is based on a nonfiction genre, specifically the reading of biographies. It is designed for students at the elementary level when they first begin their study of famous people. Starting in the third grade, students write biographies about famous people. In fifth grade students continue reading and writing biographies. Since "heroes" can be found in all walks of life, this topic dovetails well with studies in other curricular areas. For example, heroes such as Daniel Boone, Sacagawea, or Sam Houston appear in social studies when students learn about the westward movement. Studying the American Revolution, students discuss the accomplishments of Ben Franklin and George Washington. In science, Madame Curie and George Washington Carver appear.

In each unit, students will work with partners, individually, and in small groups. They will experience a variety of speaking and listening activities that integrate with reading and writing and are designed to build critical thinking. These topics are just two examples of many language arts topics that can be enriched using Internet resources.

Before beginning the unit plans, think about issues discussed in detail in Chapter 1 you may encounter when incorporating the Internet and make sure you address the following questions:

- Have you determined which lesson/unit you will teach?
- Will it incorporate Internet resources?
- Have you established student policies for Internet use and made sure the administration supports you?
- Have you explored enough Websites to suggest material for the unit?
- Do you have the URLs written down?
- Have you thought about the process—how much time in the unit is devoted to Internet usage?
- Can students access the Internet from school? When can they access it?
- Have you determined how to group students to access the Internet?
- How are you going to evaluate the Internet component of the project?

Figure 6-3 provides a checklist to use as you begin your first Internet-based unit in English–language arts.

UNIT 1 (SECONDARY LEVEL): SHAKESPEARE

By high school, students should be exposed to literature that helps promote a striving for values. Novels, drama, poetry, and nonfiction should be read and interpreted so students can benefit from the literature's subtle and morally demanding themes. Teachers of English structure their literature programs in different ways to meet these goals. There are four common teaching approaches:

Figure 6–3: Checklist for Web-Based ELA Lesson

Directions: Make sure you keep in mind the following questions as you create your ELA Web-based lessons.

Objectives

1. List objectives you will achieve in your lesson by using the Internet.

   _____
   _____
   _____

2. Identify new vocabulary, grammar, and content for the lesson.

   Vocabulary: _____
   Grammar: _____
   Content: _____

3. Discuss how you will use cooperative learning in your lesson. Will students work in pairs or small groups? Heterogeneous grouping?

   _____
   _____

Materials:

1. List URLs on the Internet that you will use in your lesson.

   _____
   _____
   _____

Procedures:

1. List opportunities students have for speaking, listening, reading, and writing.

   Speaking: _____
   Listening: _____
   Reading: _____
   Writing: _____

2. What is the reading level of the Internet materials? Identify any new vocabulary that students will encounter at the sites you have chosen.

   _____
   _____

Evaluation:

1. Explain how you will evaluate the four skills. Decide how to assess grammar forms.

   _____
   _____

2. Assessment: ☐ Peer evaluation   ☐ Teacher evaluation   ☐ Self-evaluation

1. teaching brief but important periods of literary history
2. studying the works of a single major writer
3. looking at the literature associated with a single literary movement or major literary idea
4. linking literature that deals with a single theme to students' lives.

Whichever approach teachers select, the works of literature should promote student interest in literature—and include long works, such as novels and plays, that are complex enough for intensive study as well as works of cultural significance. Above all, literature selected for the curriculum should be suitable for students' levels of emotional and intellectual maturity and contain compelling intellectual, social, or moral content so it is appealing for widespread study.

Because studying Shakespeare and his plays is an important part of the English curriculum at the high-school level, school boards encourage at least one complete unit on Shakespeare. Often students read more. For example, they may have their initial exposure to Shakespeare with *Romeo and Juliet* in ninth grade, and then go on to read *Othello, Hamlet, Julius Caesar,* and/or *Macbeth*. By the end of twelfth grade, students have usually read two or three of Shakespeare's plays.

Often, background information at the beginning of a unit on Shakespeare is dispensed through lecture; though worthwhile, this format sets the tone: the teacher talks and students listen. This unit provides a model for using the Internet to introduce students to the life and historical times in which Shakespeare lived so that they become the "experts" on Shakespeare and transmit their knowledge to others in the class. Thus, throughout the unit they are speaking and listening to partners as they conduct Internet searches, reading information from Websites, and synthesizing the information through their writing into a format that they can present.

Although the unit can be modified to precede the reading of any Shakespeare play, some of the activities and the Websites used here focus specifically on *Romeo and Juliet*. Students will practice their research skills—the ability to find and use information—as they work in cooperative groups. These skills will be indispensable for lifelong learning and self-direction in the workplace. Moreover, students will use increasingly more difficult levels of the critical-thinking model outlined in Chapter 2 when they create their keyword searches. Finally, the unit emphasizes national standards and state framework goals for the ninth-grade English curriculum.

STEP 1: APPLY FRAMEWORK GOALS—WHAT SHOULD BE TAUGHT?
This unit supports the California framework goal of providing a challenging curriculum for all students in the following ways:

- The research will illustrate interdisciplinary connections between English literature, history, and the performing arts.
- Students will use analysis—a critical-thinking skill from Bloom's taxonomy discussed in Chapter 2—as they prepare Boolean searches.

- The activities using the Internet will develop students' research skills as emphasized in *Information Power* (see Chapter 1).
- Students will become acquainted with Internet technology and understand how it can be used to find answers to curriculum-related questions.
- Performance-based assessment will be used to measure whether students can use the computer to find specific required information.

As a result of engaging in the activities in this unit and working together using technology, students will become information literate, a goal as stated in *Information Power*.

STEP 2: IDENTIFY GENERAL GOALS AND SPECIFIC OBJECTIVES

The goals and objectives for this unit are based on the national standards for English and the California English–Language Arts Framework. Following this unit, students should be prepared to read *Romeo and Juliet* with greater understanding. They should also be able to use the Internet to do topical research.

Goals

When searching for background information on Shakespeare, students will:

- use Internet technology to find information
- read for understanding
- build critical thinking skills
- increase their knowledge of Shakespeare's life and historical times

Objectives

More specifically, as part of each goal, students will:

- formulate search queries using precise language and correct spelling
- choose appropriate Websites and link to related sites
- scan for specific information to answer search questions
- interpret content and make inferences
- compile information about Shakespeare's life, the Globe Theatre, the City of Verona as the setting for the play, Elizabethan criminal justice, and the social and historical context for the play

STEP 3: GATHER MATERIALS

There are numerous Websites that relate to Shakespeare, the man and his plays. In addition, sites offer lesson plans to help in teaching the language and themes of his dramas. Some of the resources listed in Table 6-1 will be used in the activities that follow.

STEP 4: INTRODUCE THE UNIT

This research unit on Shakespeare introduces students to background information on him and the historical time period in which he lived and wrote. Each of the searches

Table 6–1: Shakespeare Web Resources	
Sample URLs	**Description of Websites**
www.viterbo.edu/academic/ug/education/ edu250/ajdepaolo.htm	Hamlet and other Shakespeare plays
http://the-tech.mit.edu/Shakespeare	Complete works of Shakespeare
www.edu/academics/courses/shakespeare/ othersites.htm www.rdg.ac.uk/AcaDepts/ln/Globe/ home.html	Information about the Globe Theatre
www.jetlink.net/~massij/shakes	The Shakespeare Classroom
www.zbths.k12.il.us/projects/burd-strauss/ shakespeare.html	Romeo and Juliet lesson plan for ESL students called The Shakespearean Era: Connections to Our Lives and Times
www.qesn.meq.gouv.qc.ca/schools/ bchs/rjshunt.htm	Romeo and Juliet scavenger hunt
www.tech.mit.edu/Shakespeare/works.html	Searchable works of Shakespeare

students must complete will require them to employ increasingly higher levels of critical thinking as they create search strategies and synthesize information from a Website. Students will work together in pairs to complete their Web research. In their first searches, they will look for information about Shakespeare; then they will search for material related to the setting of the play, including the city of Verona and social issues of the times. It is important for students to be familiar with Elizabethan England in order to understand the actions taking place in *Romeo and Juliet*.

CREATE SAMPLE ACTIVITIES

The activities that follow can be used to develop background material about Shakespeare, his birthplace, and his plays. The tasks implement the critical-thinking model discussed in Chapter 2. All searches are based on using the Yahoo! search engine at *www.yahoo.com*.

Activity 1

In this first activity, you will give students the URL of the Website you want them to visit to search for biographical information about Shakespeare (use *www.stratford-upon-avon.com.uk*). Ask each pair of students to find answers to two or three questions that you assign and to retrieve at least one additional fact not already requested. This activity will require students to focus on comprehension, a critical-thinking skill at the lower end of Bloom's cognitive ladder.

Figure 6-4 presents a sample worksheet for this activity.

Figure 6–4: Worksheet about Shakespeare's LIfe

The Life and Times of William Shakespeare

Directions: Using the Yahoo! search engine, enter the following Internet address (URL)--*www.stratford-upon-avon.com.uk*--in the search box. Browse the site to find information to answer the questions listed below.

1. When was William Shakespeare born?   _____

2. Where was he born?   _____

3. Who were his parents?   _____

4. What was his father's profession?   _____

5. What civic position did his father hold in Stratford?   _____

6. Whom did Shakespeare marry?   _____

7. How old was he when he married?   _____

8. How old was his wife?   _____

9. Where did Shakespeare receive his education?   _____

10. What was the school's schedule during the summer?   _____

    In the winter?   _____

11. What subject did the school emphasize?   _____

12. How many plays did Shakespeare write?   _____

13. How old was he when he died?   _____

Activity 2

In this activity, students will use Websites as resources. Throughout, they will be required to analyze what they have read and select specific information from the reading. Direct students to go to the Website at *www.geocities.com/Broadway/1796/ shakespeare.html* and to read the selection. Each student should then write a well-organized paragraph containing at least five facts learned about Shakespeare's plays and language. The Website at *www.shakespeare.uiuc.edu* may also help.

Figure 6–5: Worksheet about Stratford-upon-Avon

A Visit to Stratford-Upon-Avon, England

Directions: In this exercise, you do not have a specific URL. Using the Yahoo! search engine, enter the following keywords: STRATFORD-UPON-AVON and MAYOR—in the search box. Browse the site to find a link to a site that reflects these terms. Click the link (blue text) to find information to answer the questions listed below.

1. List the URL for the Website you are using to answer the following questions.

_____

2. Why is the town called Stratford-upon-Avon? _____

3. Where is William Shakespeare buried in Stratford? _____

4. What buildings once owned or lived in by William Shakespeare and members of his family still survive in Stratford today? _____

_____

5. What organization maintains these buildings today? _____

6. Find a photograph/picture of the Avon. What is the Internet address (URL)?

_____

7. Where is Stratford-upon-Avon located in England? _____

Activity 3

In this activity, students will need to use search terms to identify a Website that discusses Stratford-upon-Avon, England, birthplace of Shakespeare. Provide students with search terms, such as STRATFORD-UPON-AVON and MAYOR. Have students use the Boolean connector "AND" to connect their search terms (see Chapter 2 for more information about Boolean connectors). Ask students to identify and check links to Websites that offer information about Shakespeare's birthplace. Students should be able to answer the sample questions after reading the information at these Websites. Figure 6-5 provides a sample worksheet for this activity.

Activity 4

Now it's time for students to decide on their own search terms. After entering them in the search engine, they will then need to review the resulting sites and determine which one(s) seem to provide answers to the sample questions listed in Figure 6-6. They should talk together with their partners to determine keywords and why they

---

Figure 6–6: Worksheet about Verona

A Visit to Verona

Directions: In this exercise, you do not have a specific URL, nor are you given search terms. Using the Yahoo! search engine, enter keywords of your choice that you think will provide sites to answer the questions below. Scan the site(s) you have located to find possible matches for this topic and choose those you think are best suited to provide information about Verona.

1. What search terms did you use to find this site(s)?_____

2. List the URL(s) you used to answer the questions. _____

_____

3. What governments have controlled Verona over the centuries?_____

_____

4. During what centuries was Verona a city-state? _____

5. What building in Verona is known as "Romeo's House"? _____

6. Where is "Juliet's House" in Verona? _____

7. When was the story of Romeo and Juliet first written down? _____

8. Who recorded the story? _____

9. What period of Verona's history does the story come from? _____

_____

10. Describe Verona (its climate, the countryside around the town). _____

_____

---

chose specific sites to review. Ask them to include, along with their answers, the search terms they used and the URLs where they retrieved the best information.

Activity 5

In this activity, have students write a paragraph in which they compare and contrast the Old Globe Theatre and the New Globe Theatre. Naming specific landmarks should help students select keywords. Ask them to include the URLs where they retrieved the best information along with their answers.

Activity 6

For the last search, students, working in groups of three, will use the search techniques they have been practicing—selecting keywords, identifying Websites based on a list of titles, and analyzing and synthesizing data from several sites. By reviewing the questions below, students should be able to choose keywords to retrieve information on their topic. If they seem to be struggling with the task, you might provide a hint: the topic is about the Tyburn Tree and executions in Elizabethan England. Along with their answers, they should include the search terms they used and the URLs where they retrieved the best information. The task for students is, using the skills that they have learned, to find a Website(s) that provides information to answer the following questions. Once they have gathered the data, each group will give an oral presentation to teach the class about this custom in Elizabethan history.

- What was Tyburn Tree?
- How many people could be executed at one time on Tyburn Tree?
- What type of criminal was executed at Tyburn Tree?
- What was a dying speech?
- Whose dying speeches are included at this Website?
- Describe the typical procedure for an execution at Tyburn Tree.

EVALUATE WHAT WAS LEARNED

Evaluation for this unit takes several forms. First, students should think about what they have learned. It is a good idea to have them reflect in their journals on the searches they conducted and the information they retrieved. For example, they should ask themselves the following questions: How did I choose my search terms? Which ones worked best? Why? What cautions would I list for other students who are searching the Internet? Did the Internet provide information that improved my knowledge and understanding of William Shakespeare's life and the world in which he lived?

Second, observation can help assess performance of the research tasks. Some students may be able to conduct searches easily when the URL is provided; however, they may have more difficulty when deciding upon their own search terms. By watching students while they are conducting their research at the computers, you can quickly identify those who are struggling and give appropriate assistance. Students who are not learning the skills necessary to complete the searches will not be able to respond to the questions included with each activity.

Third, a performance-based evaluation is needed. Students' work includes search worksheets, fact sheets, writing samples, and their oral presentations. A rubric similar to the one in Figure 6-7 will help you assess students' progress.

SUMMARY

Shakespeare has been one of the main constants in the American high-school English curriculum. Our main goal in teaching Shakespeare is to teach him in a way that makes our students want to continue to approach him through reading or performances. The Internet provides valuable, extensive information on Shakespeare's

Figure 6–7: Rubric for Evaluation		
Evaluation for an Internet-based Unit on Shakespeare		
To What Extent Has the Student Shown Ability	**Points Possible**	**Points Awarded**
The Internet	20	
✓ Enters URLs and connects to appropriate Websites		
✓ Chooses keywords effectively		
✓ Chooses appropriate information from Websites		
Fact Sheets	25	
✓ Uses Internet material effectively to complete fact sheets		
✓ Well-written and complete fact sheets		
Writing Samples	30	
✓ Organizes ideas		
✓ Supports ideas with specific details		
✓ Revises and edits final writing		
Oral Presentations	25	
✓ Content complete		
✓ Presentation (enunciation, volume, gestures, posture)		
Other Comments		

world and his works. Whether the classroom is comprised of honors English students, at-risk students, or second-language learners, the Internet provides a tool to help them become part of the Shakespearean experience.

UNIT 2 (ELEMENTARY LEVEL): HEROES

Reading, writing, speaking, and listening are communication skills without content of their own; thus, they can be acquired when children obtain content from the real world and the world of books. Literature, in which authors have skillfully crafted sentences to tell stories and paint pictures, forms a natural core from which oral and written language can emerge. It provides content to stimulate language production—for example, in talking about stories or poems after reading selections aloud. It stimulates writing, which should evolve naturally out of discussion about literature. For instance, children can start with structured writing, as when children model their own haiku poems on ones they have just heard, and expand to open writing where the writer has free choice over topic, style, and word usage.

Children learn language sequentially, moving from listening and speaking to reading and writing. Thus, the language arts are inter-related and should not be taught in isolation. This unit on Heroes includes extensive reading on which to build oral and written language, integrating new information with past knowledge as students speak and write. The unit also includes a Web-based component.

The unit on Heroes combines reading biographies and researching famous people to include the more abstract concept of what constitutes a "hero." Activities will allow children to explore heroes as famous people, unsung heroes, and modern-day heroes in students' daily lives. Heroes for this unit could include men and women worldwide from all ethnic groups and from all walks of life; however, to provide focus for the activities, our "hero" will be Benjamin Franklin—author, statesman, scientist, and inventor. The unit involves tasks to practice reading, writing, speaking, and listening skills. Activities and projects are based on state frameworks for the language arts. While the unit is designed for upper-elementary students, it can be tailored to other grade levels. For example, during Black History Month the focus could be on a hero like Martin Luther King, or students could identify African American heroes from the Civil War, during the Civil Rights Movement, and in modern day. On *Cinco de Mayo* students could learn more about a Chicano hero such as Cesar Chávez.

STEP 1: APPLY FRAMEWORK GOALS—WHAT SHOULD BE TAUGHT?

At the elementary level, students should experience literature of a number of types and genres. They should be reading and hearing fiction and nonfiction, poetry and prose, and drama. As students read and respond to literature, their abilities to think critically, interpret, and explain what is written will improve. As students participate in writing tasks, their interest in reading and writing will also be enhanced.

By the time children reach fourth grade, they have usually acquired the basics of reading and can now use this skill to learn. At the upper-elementary level (from the fourth to sixth grades), students enjoy adventure stories, such as Scott O'Dell's *Island of the Blue Dolphin*; "tall tales" featuring folk heroes like Paul Bunyan; myths and legends, such as *D'Aulaires' Book of Greek Myths*; and biographies and autobiographies that portray models of individuals who have made significant cultural, political, religious, literary, or scientific contributions. At this level, we want reading literature to be an enjoyable part of each school day; however, we want students to read to acquire knowledge.

Nonfiction, which includes biographies, essays, and general informational material, is important to students who will spend increasing amounts of time in all subjects reading for information. It is important that they not be "turned off" to this material by feeling that it is uninteresting. Through reading biography, students learn about the lives of others who may have overcome adversities. They may also find solutions to personal questions or situations they might confront in the future.

California's English–Language Arts Framework (CSDE, 1987) also emphasizes the use of technology. The Internet is a strong resource for studies of famous people throughout the world.

STEP 2: IDENTIFY GENERAL GOALS AND SPECIFIC OBJECTIVES

The English–Language Arts Framework in California serves as a guide for goals and objectives for the unit.

Goals

When teaching about heroes, students will work toward these goals:

- thinking, speaking, and writing about what they have read on a wide range of subjects
- reading, publishing, and displaying individual and class projects
- employing the writing process, including prewriting, writing, revising, and editing, while writing on self-selected and teacher-assigned topics
- using appropriate tone, style, and voice when preparing oral and written presentations for intended audiences
- developing an interest in and lifelong enjoyment of reading
- reading in different ways for different purposes
- analyzing literature of and about a period to understand better historic times, places, and people
- using technology, specifically the Internet, for research

Objectives

The unit will provide content and strategies so that by the end of the unit students will be able to:

- articulate the definition and attributes of heroes
- recognize the contributions of heroes to the political, economic, social, and cultural development of the United States or other countries in the world
- role-play their heroes for the class
- practice describing people orally and in writing
- create reports and posters representing characteristics of their heroes, their contributions, and the time periods in which they lived
- access Websites for information on specific heroes.

STEP 3: GATHER MATERIALS

In gathering materials for this unit, students have many resources at their disposal. They can ask parents, relatives, and neighbors; use printed or electronic encyclopedias, biographies, almanacs, their social studies textbooks, and biographical dictio-

Table 6-2: Biographical Web Resources	
Sample URLs	**Description of Websites**
www.biography.com	Over 15,000 names from A&E TV's Homework Central
www.ties.k12.mn.us/ugrr/lessons/week7	Heroes and heroines of the Underground Railroad
http://isd.ingham.k12.mi.us/~99mich/bios.html	Student-written biographies on historical figures, athletes, entertainers, scientists, and community servers from Michigan
http://206.183.164.3/cmslmc/Grade6/heroes.htm	Heroes of the Civil Rights Movement
http://marin.k12.ca.us/~parkweb/african_american/HeroContents.html	A Website of biographies on African American heroes written by third graders
www.smsu.edu/contrib/library/gandhi.html	The legacy of Gandhi
www.bangalorenet.com/system1/pooch/index.html	Gandhi facts and accomplishments
www.gale.com/gale/cwh/teresa.html www.ewtn.com/motherteresa	Biography of Mother Teresa, including her early years, quotes, accomplishments
www.kn.pacbell.com/wired/fil/pages/huntharriettu.html	Info on Harriet Tubman created by middle school students
www.camalott.com/~rssmith/Moses.html	Tubman as the Moses of her time
http://lcweb2.loc.gov/ammem/jr.html	Info on Jackie Robinson, baseball, and breaking the color line
www.seattletimes.com/mlk/classroom/index.html	About Martin Luther King, created as a school resource

naries; and, of course, access the Internet. Because "heroes" encompasses all subject areas, there is a great amount of data on the Internet. Table 6-2 contains sites that supply resources for different heroes whom students might choose. (Websites specifically pertinent to Ben Franklin are listed with the activities in Step 5.)

STEP 4: INTRODUCE THE UNIT

Unit Project

Often when we teach students about literary characters and historical people and events that have made a difference in our world, we sometimes sense that they are learning only names and dates and that the greater significance is lost. Our aim in this unit is to communicate to students the full impact of these lives and events on history, on today's world, and on themselves.

Students will assume the roles of famous persons. These can be explorers, scientists, medical experts, athletes, political figures, to name a few. Benjamin Franklin will be the example "hero" for the unit.

As part of the project, students will:

- select persons whose contributions to the world resulted in either biographies or autobiographies being written about them.
- read books about the famous persons, keeping note cards with principal facts about them. Data should include personal information, important events in their lives, their attitudes, reasons they are famous, their effects on society, and issues important to them. Students should know how their characters would think, what their values and beliefs would be, what they would wear, about whom they cared, and any other information that will give the class complete portraits of the famous people.
- research at least two additional sources, besides the biography, about their heroes, keeping bibliography cards on these sources.
- create "Picture My Life" posters to represent their heroes visually.
- write reports that include information from print biographies and electronic sources.
- use information from the reports to role-play their famous persons and the times in which they lived. In the process, they will be teaching each other about their heroes.

STEP 5: CREATE SAMPLE ACTIVITIES

The activities that follow are examples of some that can be included in a language arts unit on Heroes with an Internet-based component. The tasks will enable students to collect the information to role-play their characters, in this case Benjamin Franklin, and provide adequate information to teach class members about them, their accomplishments, and the time periods in which they lived.

Activities to Introduce the Unit

Initial tasks require students to think generally about the concept of "hero" and then narrow their focuses to specific heroes, based on criteria they will determine. The activities that are starred are mandatory for all students. To draw upon their prior knowledge and understanding of the concept "hero," students will:

- name some heroes and then answer questions in groups about them. Questions might include: What makes a person admirable? Why does a person become a national hero? What are the best qualities a person can have? Figure 6-8 illustrates Ben Franklin as hero.
- think about characteristics that constitute a hero. Students will create a cluster diagram on the blackboard with the teacher's help similar to that in Figure 6-9.

Figure 6–8: Ben Franklin as Hero

Site Benjamin Franklin from ThinkQuest Library of Entries (http://library.advanced.org/22254/home.htm).

- *write and explain their own definitions of a hero and identify three standards or criteria upon which they can judge heroes.
- do "quickwrites" on the characters they have chosen—five to ten minutes of writing without stopping about what they know or have started to realize about their heroes. Turn the comments from the quickwrites into questions that they will explore in their research.
- *brainstorm and cluster ideas for their own heroes. See Figure 6-10 for a cluster on Ben Franklin.

Activities to Be Used During the Unit

Students must complete a number of tasks to compile sufficient information about their heroes to be able to teach other students about them. Students will:

- *read biographies about their heroes. Some questions they might consider: What were the heroes trying to do with their lives? Were their goals accomplished? What influence did their lives and work have on others at the time? What effects are these persons' lives still having on us today? Biographies of Ben Franklin include *What's the Big Idea, Ben Franklin?* by Jean Fritz; *Ben Franklin of Old Philadelphia* by Margaret Cousins; *Benjamin Franklin: Founding Father and Inventor* by Leila Merrell Foster; or Franklin's own *Autobiography* at *http://earlyamerica.com/lives/franklin/index.html.* Another

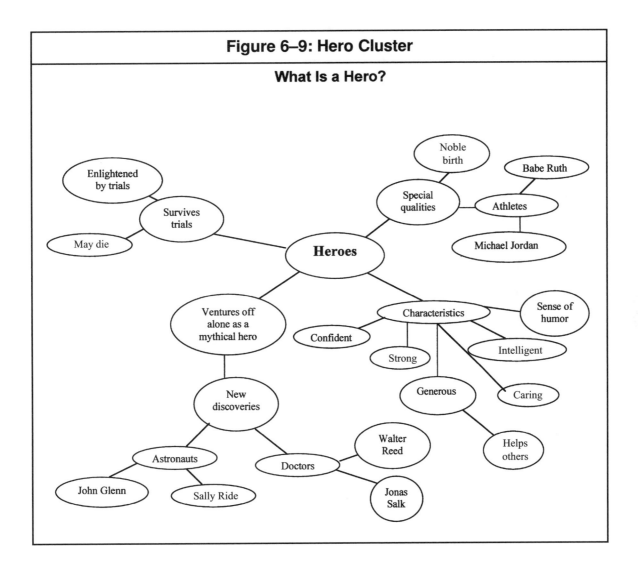

Figure 6–9: Hero Cluster

possible source of information about Benjamin Franklin is his *Poor Richard's Almanac.*

- *write each day in their journals on selected topics so they feel as if they are "stepping into the shoes" of their heroes. Some sample topics might include: "Picture yourself in the home of Ben Franklin. Describe his/her living room." "How does Ben Franklin celebrate his birthday?"
- *keep track in their journals of all ideas about their heroes, noting all sources, sketches of costumes worn during a specific historical period—if different from today's dress—and quotations made by or about their heroes. Check Websites *http://library.advanced.org/22254/home.htm* or *www.rsa.org.uk/franklin/toc.html* for information about Franklin, the times he lived in, the clothes he wore, and the inventions he created.
- draw pictures using symbols to represent their heroes and quotations to support their choices of symbols that represent their heroes. The symbols should encompass as many character traits of their heroes as possible. Since Ben

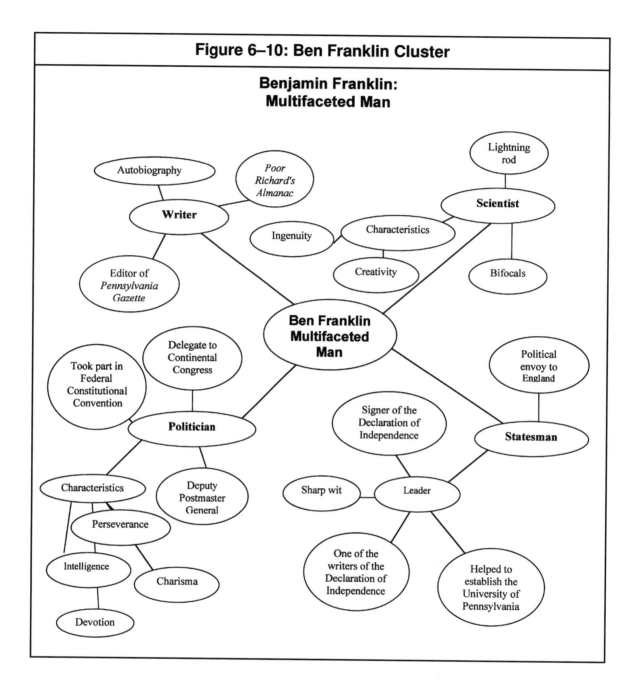

Figure 6–10: Ben Franklin Cluster

Benjamin Franklin:
Multifaceted Man

Figure 6–11: Ben Franklin Timeline

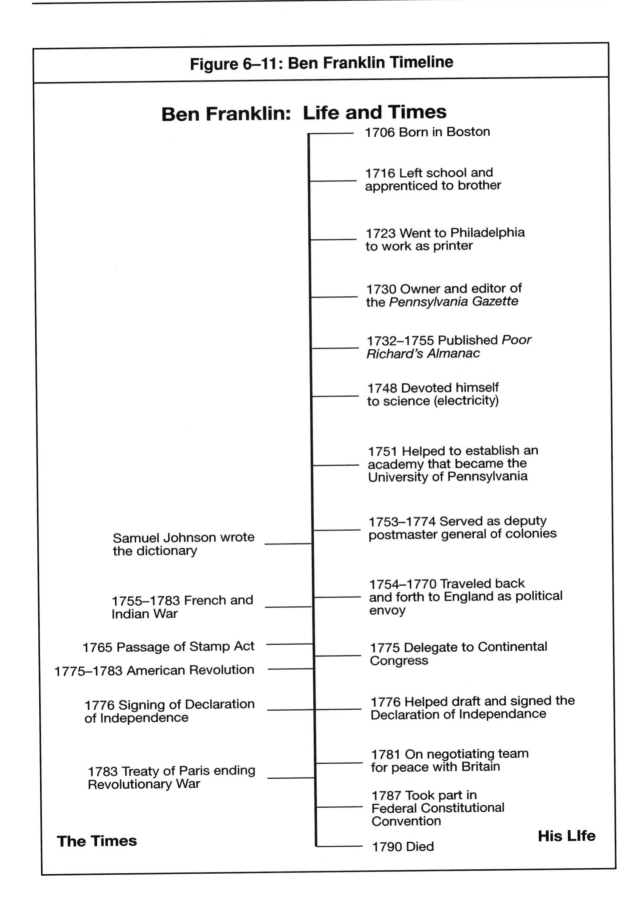

Ben Franklin: Life and Times

His Life

- 1706 Born in Boston
- 1716 Left school and apprenticed to brother
- 1723 Went to Philadelphia to work as printer
- 1730 Owner and editor of the *Pennsylvania Gazette*
- 1732–1755 Published *Poor Richard's Almanac*
- 1748 Devoted himself to science (electricity)
- 1751 Helped to establish an academy that became the University of Pennsylvania
- 1753–1774 Served as deputy postmaster general of colonies
- 1754–1770 Traveled back and forth to England as political envoy
- 1775 Delegate to Continental Congress
- 1776 Helped draft and signed the Declaration of Independance
- 1781 On negotiating team for peace with Britain
- 1787 Took part in Federal Constitutional Convention
- 1790 Died

The Times

- Samuel Johnson wrote the dictionary
- 1755–1783 French and Indian War
- 1765 Passage of Stamp Act
- 1775–1783 American Revolution
- 1776 Signing of Declaration of Independence
- 1783 Treaty of Paris ending Revolutionary War

Franklin was a multifaceted individual, we could use the symbol of a lightning bolt with Franklin's eyeglasses on it to symbolize him as a "man of ideas" or a "man of enlightenment." Check Website *http://library.advanced.org/22254/home.htm* or *http://sln.fi.edu/tfi/exhibits/franklin.html* for quotations to use and information about his life.

- create timelines of major events in their heroes' lives and historical events at the times their heroes lived. Figure 6-11 provides a sample timeline of the life and times of Ben Franklin. Use Website *www.english.udel.edu/lemay/franklin*, which provides a documentary history of Ben Franklin and his times to discover what events were taking place.

- compile pictures, drawings, and quotations to use in creating "Picture My Life" posters about the lives of their heroes. Website *http://library.advanced.org/22254/home.htm* will provide some quotations for Ben Franklin. The Franklin Institute site at *http://sln.si.edu/franklin/rotten.html* has images of his inventions.

- for more modern-day heroes, interview parents, relatives, and community members to find out their impressions of the individuals' lives and accomplishments. For example, since Ben Franklin is not a modern-day hero, questions to ask might be: "In what ways has Ben Franklin touched your life?" "What do you feel was Franklin's most significant contribution to society?" "Do any of Franklin's inventions impact your life today?"

- using the timelines as guides, create a series of original illustrations of incidents in the lives of their heroes. These will be used when students act out the characters for the class.

- create rough drafts that will be read and responded to by two other students. Students must turn in their rough draft peer reviews with the final reports. Points for the peer reviews might include:
  — The most important thing about this hero is _____ .
  — Characteristics of the hero are _____, _____, _____, and _____.
  — The main contributions of the hero are _____ .
  — I want to learn more about _____ .
  — The best thing about this report is _____ .
  — I need to improve _____ .

- using the timelines, symbol pictures, posters, and any other information, assume the roles of their heroes to teach the class about them. Students will act out their characters using costumes where possible. The class will take notes on each hero presented to incorporate later in their own writing.

Activities to Be Used as Follow-up to the Unit

As extension activities, have groups of students try some of the following:

- Select one of the following activities and prepare writings to send for publication to Website *http://myhero.com/home.asp* (see Figure 6-2 that illustrates the "My Hero" Website).

— Identify and write about modern heroes using the criteria they have established for heroes.

— Select persons they know personally whom they think are heroes and write essays on what makes them heroes.

— Explain how heroes they just learned about affect society even after they have died.

- Do "quickwrites" in their journals comparing the definitions of hero they now have after hearing other students' reports with the ideas they held about heroes at the beginning of the unit.

- Using their notes from the student presentations, choose two heroes and write paragraphs showing how they are similar and different. Heroes might be compared on their contributions, their characteristics, or the times in which they lived.

STEP 6: EVALUATE WHAT WAS LEARNED

It is important to evaluate both student work (the product) and students' working (the process). For this unit evaluation will be based on:

1. assessment of the reports and posters students create, as well as their presentations on heroes. Evaluation will take into account creativity (the character demonstration was interesting, informative, and clearly presented), content (the information was thorough and accurate), and process (students were able to use the Internet).

2. review of student journal entries periodically throughout the unit to determine students' progress in their research.

3. thoroughness with which students respond as peer evaluators.

4. student self-evaluation of Internet skills (refer to Figure 3-10 for the Self-Evaluation Checklist of Internet Skills).

SUMMARY

This unit considered the theme "heroes" and required that students become familiar with the genre of nonfiction, specifically biographies. They used listening, speaking, reading, writing, and thinking critically to accomplish the tasks for the unit. They studied the topic of "heroes" through literature and by researching their heroes on the Internet. Note that this topic provides a bridge to social studies educators who might be studying specific periods in history at the same time as you are teaching this unit.

TEACHER EXERCISES: NOW YOU TRY IT...

To prepare to create your integrated plans using the Internet, complete the following exercises:

1. Go through one of the sample units as if you were a student in the class. Search the sites listed. This will allow you to experience the same activities,

frustrations, and skill-building as your students. You will also be able to identify places where you might need to teach a specific skill or offer additional help to students before you actually teach an Internet-based unit.

2. Sign up for one listserv of interest to you. Keep a journal with two columns: messages you receive that pique your interest, and your personal reactions to messages: Are they interesting? Are they appropriate for students, and at what age level? Are they biased?

3. With the above units as models, create your own unit that will include writing assignments. The unit must also include an Internet component—researching Websites for information on the subject, publishing data on a Web page, connecting with another classroom to provide live audience interaction, to name just a few.

4. Do one of the following:
   - Check the Website at *www.qesn.meq.gouv.qc.ca/schools/bchs/rjshunt.htm* to serve as a model and write your own treasure hunt for another of Shakespeare's plays.
   - Select a "hero" and find at least five Websites with information useful to your students' level of experience and maturity.

CONCLUSION

Skills learned in English–language arts form the basis for all work students will do in other curricular areas. Students must be able to analyze what they read in a history or science textbook; they must listen for understanding of content-specific vocabulary; and they must be able to express their ideas clearly both orally and in writing to their peers and teachers. Literature study allows students to appreciate excellence in the writing and illustrations they find in books, and it helps children interpret and evaluate stories. At the same time it expands their perceptions beyond traditional stereotyped views. With the added resources on the Internet, educators can offer students a world vision that encompasses many diverse viewpoints and understandings of different cultures.

In subsequent chapters we will explore how the Internet may be incorporated into social studies and science instruction.

REFERENCES

California State Department of Education. 1987. *English–Language Arts Framework for California Public Schools: Kindergarten Through Grade Twelve.* Sacramento: California State Department of Education.

Gallup Organization. 1989. *A Survey of College Seniors.* A poll conducted for the National Endowment for the Humanities.

"National Survey of Internet Usage: Teachers, Computer Coordinators, and School Librarians, Grades 3–12." 1997. *The Heller Report* 2, No. 9 (March).

Chapter 7

TEACHING SECOND-LANGUAGE LEARNERS USING THE INTERNET

Imagine this classroom. Maria speaks fluent Spanish and some English but was finding a mainstream history class difficult. Chang can speak to his classmates in English, reads and writes Chinese characters, and has learned the English alphabet, but has a hard time understanding textbook material in subject areas. Arturo, a recent immigrant from Mexico, can communicate somewhat in English but is motivated only to get a job, not to improve his reading and writing skills. And then there's Natasha, who has had a number of years of formal education in Russia and communicates easily in English but continues to make extensive errors in syntax when writing. These students have all been placed in the same intermediate ESL classroom. Their goal is to get their English-language skills—speaking, listening, reading, and writing—to a level that will enable them to succeed in mainstream science, social studies, and language arts classes with native English-speaking students.

Today, students like the four above fill classrooms throughout the United States. In the twenty-first century, students with different ethnic backgrounds, language skills, and motivation will comprise a typical classroom in even greater numbers. How can a teacher be expected to teach literacy and communication skills to this broad range of students while still teaching science, social studies, and literature content? How are educators going to motivate and instill in all of their students the desire to learn English? These are some of the challenges facing many classroom teachers. As exemplified in the classroom above, there are often enough limited-English proficient (LEP) students to warrant special classes to focus specifically on building English skills. In some locales, however, there may be only a few LEP students, so they are placed in mainstream classes with their more proficient English-speaking peers. These students do not comprehend, speak, read, or write English well, yet they are expected to keep up with their peers. This situation definitely affects teachers and how they conduct their lessons.

Whatever the situation, teachers may or may not have been trained to teach students with special linguistic needs. What is a teacher entering such a multiethnic, multilevel, multigoal class going to do? How will the teacher accommodate all of these different needs? What materials will be most useful?

This chapter focuses on using the Internet with LEP students; however, it is structured somewhat differently from the other chapters in this book. Part 1 in Chapters 1 through 6 discusses theoretical underpinnings of each topic and then applies the theory in lesson and unit plans in Part 2. In contrast, Parts 1 and 2 in Chapter 7 focus on the needs of LEP students at two different language levels. Part 1 discusses insights and strategies for students practicing English language skills, and Part 2 helps students apply their language skills to content areas, such as social studies and science.

More specifically, Part 1 looks at students who are trying to master language skills—speaking, listening, reading, and writing. It provides some theoretical basis for how students learn a second language so teachers are better prepared to create lessons that practice language-building skills. This section also emphasizes how the Internet can play an integral role in providing materials for language learning. Finally, language activities using the Internet are presented to serve as models for teachers who will be creating their own language-based Internet lessons. After reading Part 1 of this chapter, educators will be able to:

- evaluate teaching materials for LEP students
- understand how learners obtain competence in a second language
- identify teaching strategies for LEP students
- identify types of Websites for English as a Second Language (ESL) teaching
- develop Internet-based lessons that provide practice in the four skills
- create an Internet-based unit for LEP students

Part 2 goes beyond the language classroom and focuses on LEP students who have achieved adequate English-language skills to undertake mastery of content-based material such as history and science. This section discusses content-based language instruction and use of the Internet in subject area classes. It also presents a model unit for content-based language instruction. Finally, a step-by-step plan illustrates the use of the Internet in a science-based series of activities on energy conservation. By the end of Part 2, educators will be able to:

- understand the differences between BICS and CALP
- identify parts of the CALLA lesson model for LEP students
- integrate the Internet into content-based instruction for LEP students
- create a content-based Internet unit for LEP students

PART 1: TAKING THE INTERNET TO THE SECOND-LANGUAGE CLASSROOM

THE PROBLEM

Language is a common problem for Arturo, Chang, Maria, and Natasha. Like most newcomers to the United States, Arturo requires intensive training to improve his speaking and listening skills. Chang and Maria, who have been in the United States for two years and can converse with their peers, have what Cummins and Swain (1986) call basic interpersonal communication skills (BICS). However, neither has enough academic English skills to read and discuss *Romeo and Juliet* in a literature class or the causes of the Civil War in social studies. According to Cummins and Swain, it takes non-native speakers from five to seven years to attain this level of academic competence. Natasha is the most proficient in English, but she still has trouble writing research papers. Natasha is typical of non-native speakers who usually acquire competence in writing last in their mastery of the English language.

These students also have another dilemma. While they attempt to master English, they are also trying to assimilate a new culture and do it in the few hours a day they spend in an English as a Second Language classroom. These tasks are often as overwhelming to the newcomers who are isolated through lack of English skills and understanding of their surroundings as they are to the teachers who are trying to teach such a diverse group of students.

ATTAINING COMPETENCE IN A SECOND LANGUAGE

Anyone who has tried to learn a second language knows the difficulties involved in mastering it. Linguists and psychologists have conducted extensive research to try to understand how a learner develops competence in a second language. This chapter is not intended as a treatise on second-language acquisition and learning; nonetheless, some knowledge of the theory is necessary to help teachers who must create lessons for LEP students.

When teaching LEP students, educators must keep several principles in mind. Taylor (1974) in his research on language learning and teaching suggests that, for most learners, acquisition of a second language will only take place as learners are exposed to and engaged in contextually rich, meaningful communication. Other research findings (Krashan, 1978) indicate that most adult learners are not successful when they learn grammar rules and then try to use those rules in communication. Rather, communicative competence is achieved for most learners by subconsciously acquiring the language through active participation in real communication, such as conversation that is interesting to learners. This is similar to the way children acquire their first language. In other words, according to Taylor, language is best acquired when it is not studied in a direct way. It is acquired most effectively when it is used as a vehicle for doing something else—when learners are directly involved in accomplishing something via the language and thus have a personal interest in the outcome of what they are using the language to do. Therefore, when there is an immediate need and when the motivation is high, acquisition of a second language seems to coalesce. Johnson (1979) has indicated that one of the major purposes of communication is to bridge an "information gap." Thus, a methodology that emphasizes communication needs to create situations in which learners share information not previously known by all participants involved in the task.

As teachers, then, we must maximize opportunities for language acquisition to take place by including a strong communication component in our lessons. This means that we need to create opportunities for students to be exposed to, and engage in, real communication. Our activities must be meaningful to students and motivate them to use communication to accomplish a specific goal, such as solving a problem or completing a task.

Another important element in language learning is the setting where students engage with the second language. The environment must be structured yet provide a supportive, nonjudgmental atmosphere so that students feel free to take risks in communicating in the second language. For example, students in a classroom where they feel relaxed about answering questions in the second language, reading aloud, and talking together in groups experience better language success (Stevick, 1980).

Finally, true communication only takes place if the content is interesting and involves the learners. Teachers must create task-oriented activities that require students to use the second language and focus on issues that are relevant and meaningful to them. If these activities are undertaken in an atmosphere conducive to active participation, they will engage students directly and students will find them intrinsically motivating. Grammatical skills will be naturally addressed in the course of their communication, and performance can be evaluated in terms of success or failure in completing a task.

TEACHING STRATEGIES FOR LEP STUDENTS

What are the implications of these theories for second-language teaching? How can we, as teachers, help to acclimate LEP students both linguistically and culturally? Below are seven suggestions for the classroom based on the second-language theory we just reviewed.

1. Try to set students at ease. If they are relaxed about the idea of learning English and if they are willing to risk making mistakes as they practice English skills, they will be more likely to succeed.
2. Provide a meaningful context for the introduction of new items and engage students' interest in this context. The Internet can provide an interesting context for students through its multimedia presentation of information and by acting as a vehicle for communication in the activities that follow.
3. Bring the focus of the class to the level of students' experiences. Allow them to feel that their experiences are valid, important, and relevant to the learning of English. The unit plan in this chapter incorporates concepts that most students know about and feel are important.

4. Encourage students to use English for social reasons. Having students work in groups and talk with one another as part of completing a task provides a vehicle for real communication for a specific purpose. According to Johnson and Johnson (1975), much of what is learned grows out of peer interaction rather than the adult-child relationship of the traditional class.

5. Provide opportunities to practice the four skills—speaking, listening, reading, and writing—while encouraging vocabulary building and grammatical competence.

6. Show respect for students' native cultures by illustrating the importance of contributions by members of their ethnic groups. At the same time, continue to familiarize students with the culture in which they are living.

7. Teach to the needs of different learning styles. It is especially important with non-native speakers, who are struggling with language and cultural differences to learn in the style that best suits them. (Chapter 4 discusses learning styles in more detail.)

TEACHING MATERIALS

We need to find those "ideal" textbooks or materials that are accurate and imaginative, offer flexibility, and provide variety, yet respond to defined instructional goals. Because of the range of abilities and backgrounds in an ESL class, teachers usually find that one textbook does not contain exactly what all students need. Supplementary material is required.

The LEP student needs materials that:

1. facilitate communicative abilities of interpretation, expression, and negotiation

2. focus on understandable and relevant communication, not grammatical forms

3. promote learners' interests and involve them intellectually and creatively

4. include different types of text and media that participants can use to develop their competence through a variety of activities and tasks.

In addition, instructional aids that allow students to progress at their own pace cater to different learning styles and provide opportunities for independent study.

AN ANSWER: THE INTERNET

The Internet has the resources and multimedia capabilities to teach language and instruct about the learners' environment (see Chapter 1 for its resources—many meet the goals for materials for LEP students). However, materials are only a starting point. Teachers make materials work for students by adapting them to the context in which they teach—for example, by presenting content, facilitating communication among learners, and practicing the application of language concepts.

Using a variety of resources can help promote interest in learning for LEP students and provide a change of pace in the language classroom. One resource, the Internet can also serve as a strong motivator to learn English. Many students are eager to learn this new technology, and since much of the information on the Web is in English, students are forced to improve their English skills to understand the content of the Web or communicate with a keypal through e-mail. Students interested in "surfing" the Web who have computers at home or can use the Internet in the library will have a tool outside of the ESL class to practice English skills.

In addition, many of the projects on the Internet are interactive. For example, searching for information involves students in identifying English keywords; writing to a keypal requires students to write and read English.

Evaluation of Internet Materials for LEP students

A context-rich environment for instruction helps LEP students understand new vocabulary and concepts, and diverse materials play an integral role. Below are some qualities teachers should look for when "surfing" the Internet for materials appropriate for LEP students:

- content that is relevant, interesting, and linguistically rich. If the subject matter is interesting, students are more likely to be curious and try to decipher new vocabulary and difficult concepts.
- materials that provide language practice. For example, Websites with audio capabilities reinforce the visual images on the site.
- materials that teach students useful content.
- Websites that require students to carry out communicative tasks, for example, projects and e-mail with other classes throughout the world.
- Websites that contain culturally appropriate material. If students do not have background on a subject, it will be hard for them to make predictions about their reading, and the text will be difficult to read.
- sites that are visually inviting. Pictures help to clarify the meaning of new concepts and vocabulary. Headings help isolate main ideas. Text in short sentences with vocabulary that can be deciphered from context helps provide language that is comprehensible to LEP learners. A Web page with too much print is especially difficult for the struggling LEP reader.
- information presented clearly and in a logical order. If words and phrases are repeated or if supporting details and examples are given, LEP students will be better able to decipher meaning.

PRACTICAL APPLICATIONS

When you plan instruction for your ESL classes for the year, think about using the Internet as a tool in your units. There are many ways to structure classes to provide opportunities for students to be actively engaged in communicating. Students are provided opportunities to cope with receiving information that is new and unexpected, to exercise both linguistic and informational choices in forming their responses, and to do so at a natural pace. Thus, students practice authentic communication rather than solely language forms. As they plan and execute their projects or discuss their tasks, they are engaging in purposeful communication that focuses on content and real issues. A Website like Kids Space at *www.kids-space.org/frame/KS_R.html* is an ideal spot for practicing language skills. Students can publish their artwork, stories, and original musical pieces, or they can write to keypals.

The theoretical base of language acquisition and language-learning theory, appropriate teaching strategies, and selectively chosen materials form the theoretical base for the practical applications that follow. The next section presents types of sites that should be useful to ESL teachers. Following that, a model unit on culture illustrates how the Internet can provide meaningful, interesting materials for improving speaking, listening, reading, and writing skills. The unit also emphasizes specific grammar structures as part of each activity.

TYPES OF WEB SITES

Several types of Websites can help ESL students acquire English-language skills and understand cultural similarities and differences.

Teacher Aids

Numerous Websites exist to support teachers in creating lessons for ESL classes or in using the Internet as an integral part of current units of study in mainstream classes that contain LEP students. You should explore some of these sites to evaluate activities and ideas other teachers are using with their LEP students.

- The Internet TESL Journal, a companion to the print journal published by the National Association of Teachers of English to Speakers of Other Languages (TESOL), provides lesson plans, teaching ideas, and activities based on current research in ESL methodology. ESL teachers should bookmark the site: *www.ai.tech.ac.jp/~iteslj*.
- Companies that produce materials for the ESL market also provide lesson plans to help with ESL instruction. The Website at *www.teachnet.com/index.html* contains ESL lesson plans and a teacher forum, and Houghton-Mifflin at *www.eduplace.com/ss/index.html* has lesson plans.
- Colleges and universities maintain Websites—such as the one at *www.csun.edu/~hcedu013/eslindex.html*—that include information for teaching ESL and many links to other ESL-related sites.
- There are also many sites on the Web that are not designed specifically for LEP students but that creative teachers can incorporate into their own ESL lessons.

Keypal Sites

What better way to promote reading and writing competence in authentic situations than by communicating with a class in another part of the world? This is especially important for ESL classes, where there are many diverse cultural backgrounds.

- The Website at *www.iecc.org* lists classes willing to participate in cross-cultural communication via e-mail (see Figure 7-1).

Figure 7–1: Intercultural Connections Website

Bookmarks ⚓ Location: http://www.iecc.org/ ▾ 🔍 Wh
🧍Instant Message 🖂 WebMail 🖂 Contact 🖂 People 🖂 Yellow Pages 🖂 Download 🖂 Find Sites 📑 Channels

Intercultural E-Mail Classroom Connections

http://www.iecc.org

IECC (Intercultural E-Mail Classroom Connections) is a free service to help teachers link with partners in other countries and cultures for e-mail classroom pen-pal and project exchanges. Since its creation in 1992, IECC has distributed over 28,000 requests for e-mail partnerships. At last count, more than 7650 teachers in 82 countries were participating in one or more of the IECC lists: how many are participating today?

• Announcement: *Intergenerational IECC*

• **General information about IECC**
• **About using this page**

• **Books of Interest**
• **Related Resources**

• How to Subscribe to IECC

Reprinted by permission of www.iecc.org.

- The Website at *www.pacificnet.net/~sperling/student.html* provides a forum for communicating with other ESL classes via e-mail. The same general site (but at *www.pacificnet.net/~sperling/guestbook.html*) also has a place for you to interact with your peers about ESL instruction.

Classroom Websites

Websites created by school classes use multimedia and simple-to-read language to present a class project, showcase student work, or provide background about the students or the school. These can be valuable models for teaching, all the while highlighting the skills of LEP students.

Chat Sites

Some Websites maintain chat rooms that discuss issues of interest to ESL teachers. Two such ESL sites are *www.teachnet.com/ttforum.html* and *www.eslcafe.com/chat/chatpro.cgi*. Figure 7-2 illustrates Dave's ESL Cafe, a versatile site that offers a chat room as well as many activities and suggestions for ESL teachers.

GETTING STARTED: A MODEL ESL INTERNET-BASED UNIT

It is a good idea to start slowly when integrating the Internet into the ESL curriculum. Students must continue to learn new vocabulary, use specific grammatical struc-

Figure 7–2: Dave's ESL Cafe Website

Where English is Fun!

For ESL/EFL Students and Teachers from Around the World

Reprinted by permission www.eslcafe.com

tures, and practice their four essential skills. It is also important to keep in mind that you must create an optimal environment for mastery of the second language. The following steps offer a framework for building a unit that will acclimate students to the Internet. These are only sample activities; others will present themselves as you share ideas and see the materials the Web contains.

Step 1: Plan the Internet-based Lesson

As you plan each part of your Internet lesson for diverse populations, review how well it will serve each of the areas below (refer also to the checklist in Figure 6-3):

- *objectives.* Can you meet objectives using the Internet that would be difficult to achieve otherwise? Have you considered content, vocabulary, and grammar? Have you provided cooperative-learning experiences and the chance to learn about the new culture?
- *materials.* Can you find materials on the Internet that might otherwise be difficult to find at your school, for example, information about other countries, pictures of native costumes, and country maps?
- *procedures.* Can you provide opportunities for speaking, listening, reading, and writing? How will you deal with grammar and culture as part of the lesson? Are different ethnic groups working cooperatively together? Is the

Internet activity motivating and interesting? Is the information at the reading level of the ESL class?

- *evaluation*. Have you evaluated the four skills? Have you tested the grammar forms? Have you included peer, teacher, and self-evaluation?

Step 2: Create Sample Activities

To start an ESL class on its Internet adventure, begin with simple activities to familiarize students with the Internet and its content. The levels can range from finding answers to factual questions to improving literacy skills. For each activity that follows, LEP students will view Websites by typing in URLs supplied by the teacher, use Web navigation buttons to move between Web screens, and complete tasks that require them to view and comprehend language and create correct grammatical forms.

1. Have students learn facts about Ben Franklin, a famous American statesman and scientist, at the Franklin Institute Website at *http://sln.fi.edu/franklin/rotten.html*. See a short movie on Franklin's life, hear sound effects, and try experiments based on some that Franklin performed more than 200 years ago.
   - Direct students to locate information so they can answer the following in complete sentences using past tense verbs: What is one invention created by Ben Franklin? When was Ben Franklin born?
     — *Model Grammar Form*: Ben Franklin created . . .
2. Appeal to different learning styles using *www.i-channel.com/ellis*. Take a tour of Ellis Island through audio clips narrated by people who immigrated to the United States.
   - Each student should choose one person on Ellis Island and, after viewing pictures and hearing him/her speak, write a brief description of the person. In this activity, students will use concrete adjectives and prepositions of space, such as "at the top," "above," "below."
     — *Model Grammar Form*: Joseph had a long, jagged scar below his right eye.
3. Teach students how to use a search engine, like the one at Website *www.yahooligans.com*.
   - Have each student write a step-by-step procedure that includes identifying keywords to locate specific information from this Website. Then each should ask another student to use the instruction to try the process to find the information. This is also a good activity to teach sequencing vocabulary, such as "first," "next," "second," "then," "finally." In addition, it provides a model for a lesson in which students create their own process—how to cook Chinese noodles, how to use chopsticks, how to make a piñata, or how to teach a partner to find a site on the Web.
     — *Model Grammar Form*: First, logon to *www.yahooligans.com*. Next, type in the keywords . . .

4. To improve reading, writing, and summarizing skills, try using *www.cnn.com* for up-to-the-minute national and international news.

   • Students should choose one news story of interest and write down five words that are unfamiliar in their vocabulary notebooks. They can look up and write down the definition and a sentence containing each word. In partners, they can take turns reading the story; then assume the role of reporter and write a brief summary of the article to read to the class. Use past tense verbs, and make sure they include the five W's—who, what, when, where, and why.
     — *Model Grammar Form*: NATO bombed Kosovo yesterday. One Stealth bomber was shot down . . .

Step 3: Integrate the Web into Your ESL Curriculum

Now, choose a unit you plan to teach and determine where the Internet offers unique material—for example, students in an ESL class can learn about the cultures of their classmates by studying individual countries. The Internet has Websites for most major countries and even some less well-known ones. Using the Web, each student or groups of students can take a "virtual tour" of a specific country to help understand different cultures within one ESL class and to emphasize the value of those cultures. The virtual tour can also be used for a single country chosen by each small group of students who each explore one aspect of the country, such as education, weather, food, and famous places.

SAMPLE UNIT: "VIRTUAL TOUR" OF JAPAN

Before we begin, there is one cautionary note: Make sure that vocabulary is at an appropriate level for LEP students in your classes. Review unfamiliar vocabulary with your students before starting any activity.

Task. For this task, divide the class into two groups. Group A will be "tour guides" whose native country is Japan. Group B will comprise three classmates who have never been to Japan and want to visit it. The tour guides (Group A) will introduce their peers (Group B) to various aspects of Japan. Guides must choose five things they think their friends would like to know about this country—Japanese food, customs, famous places, heroes, government, education, anything they think is interesting. The tour guides will plan a "virtual trip" to their country via the Internet. They must precede the Internet trip with any material that will help their classmates prepare for the trip. For example, knowledge of climate will help the tourists decide on clothes to bring.

As part of planning the virtual tour, Group A must complete the following to give to their friends:

1. a hand-drawn map of Japan showing cities and physical features
2. a step-by-step process that both groups will follow together on the "virtual tour," including a list of URLs to visit.

After the tour, both groups will present to the class:

1. a collage in the form of a poster that represents the main features of Japan so the rest of the class will be interested in the country and want to visit it
2. a letter to convince other students to visit Japan

Unit Objectives. By the end of this unit on cultures, the tour guides and visitors will be able to:

- write facts about Japan's culture using correct language forms
- locate Japan on a world map
- identify regions and cities in Japan
- read and write paragraphs about Japanese customs
- orally present information to the class about Japan using correct language forms in writing and speech

Create the Instruction. Have the tour guides try all or some of the following activities to prepare them to take their visitors on the virtual tour. Tour guides should keep all of the information they find out about Japan in their journals.

1. Guides should prepare answers to the following questions from Website *www.jinjapan.org/kidsweb/japan/q-a.html*. They can draw or cut out pictures to illustrate the answers and write captions using sample language forms.
   - What are the most popular foods among Japanese children?
     — *Language Form*: We like . . .
   - When Japanese children eat in a restaurant, where do they go and what do they like to eat?
     — *Language Form*: We go to . . . and we like . . .
   - Why do Japanese take off their shoes when they enter the house?
     — *Language Form*: Japanese take off their shoes because . . .
   - How many earthquakes does Japan have yearly? Look at Website *http://lcweb2.loc.gov/frd/cs/jptoc.html* for help.
     — *Language Form*: Japan has _____ earthquakes.
2. Have guides go to *http://lcweb2.loc.gov/frd/cs/jptoc.html* to find answers to questions visitors might want to know about Japan. They should show similarities and differences using grammatical structures that show likeness, such as "same as," "similar to," "alike," and differences, such as "different from," "unlike," "opposite."
   - What kind of climate does Japan have?
     — *Language Form*: Japan has . . . It is different from . . .
   - Read about elementary schools in Japan. What are two ways elementary education in Japan is the same as education in the United States? Write the similarities in journals.
     — *Language Form*: Children in Japan have three hours of homework each night, similar to children in the United States.

3. Guides can view a map of Japan by going to *www.jinjapan.org/kidsweb/japan/map/j_regi.html*.
   - Point out the hometowns of group members on the map.
   - Draw their own map of Japan and label their hometowns and other major cities near them.
   - Write five sentences in their journals locating their hometowns using prepositions of space, such as "near" and "between," and directions like "north" "south," "east," and "west."
   — *Language Form*: Tokyo is near the sea. It is north of Osaka.
4. Establish a keypal connection with students in Japan. At KidsWeb Plaza at *www.jinjapan.org/kidsweb*, send e-mail to a class in Japan with questions the tour guides are curious about and think will interest their visitors. With keypals, students can practice reading and writing skills in a communicative situation.

Follow-up Activities. You may want to follow up the "virtual tour" with other culture-related activities.

- Haiku is a form of Japanese poetry. Have students read about haiku at Website *www.cc.matsuyama-u.ac.jp/~shiki/English-Haiku.html*. Students will:
  — explain in their own words what haiku is by checking *www.cc.matsuyama-u.ac.jp/~shiki/intro.html*
  — write their own haikus. This will emphasize the value of Japanese literature. The Website at *www.cc.matsuyama-u.ac.jp/~shiki/Start-Writing.html* will provide some ideas.
- After finishing the "virtual tour," the visitor group will write persuasive letters to other friends to convince them to go to Japan.

Evaluation. One assessment will be of the comprehension levels demonstrated by the tour guides and visitors when explaining to the class what they learned about Japan as they show the collage as part of their presentation. You will also assess the persuasive letter according to written standards of English.

Additional Material. There are various sites with information on other countries for students to explore. Start at Website *www.yahooligans.com/Around_ the_World/ Countries*, which lists different countries to investigate such as Mexico, China, and more. Other possible sites are illustrated in Table 7-1.

Step 4: Explore Other ESL Sites
Many resources exist on the Web to help both a novice and experienced teachers create lessons and activities for ESL students. It takes time to accumulate a list of Websites that will be useful and to integrate them into the curriculum, so try to set aside a brief period each week to explore the Web for new resources and to make

Table 7-1: Cultural Resources	
Sample URLs	**Description of Websites**
www.afroam.org/children/discover/ discover.html	Information on African nations and their people
www.sas.upenn.edu/African_Studies/ Home_page/AFR-GIDE.html	A K–12 guide to African resources
http://pharos.bu.edu/Egypt/Cairo	Information on Egyptian culture

sure your favorite Websites still exist. The following steps will help you organize your Web resources so you can access the appropriate URLs as you plan lessons.

Start a notebook of Websites divided into sections for each unit planned for the year (see Figure 1-3 for a sample).

- Write down URLs and annotate each with enough information so that you can determine where it will be used in a lesson or unit.
- As part of each annotation, identify which of the four skills students will practice and note the grammar structure that you will teach based on the content of the Website.
- Bookmark Websites that you might use in several units.
- Don't forget to add some sites that are just for fun.
- Periodically, check URLs to determine if they have changed or disappeared, and correct your notebook entries accordingly.

There are so many Websites available that, without an organized plan to keep track of them, you will be awash in a sea of URLs. If you don't use a specific method, you are in danger that some URLs will be incomplete, others will not provide the information needed to plan a lesson, and still others will get lost. Once you have compiled a good set of URLs, much of the time-consuming effort of looking for materials has been satisfied.

TEACHER EXERCISES: NOW YOU TRY IT . . .
Force yourself to take the time to complete the following activities. It will save valuable time in the long term.

1. Start your Internet notebook. Begin by visiting the following sites, annotating them, and bookmarking the most useful:
   - *www.ai.tech.ac.jp/~teslj*
   - *www.stolaf.edu/network/iecc/index.html*
   - *http://eslgames.com*
   - *www.links2go.com/topic/English_As_a_Second_Language*

Figure 7–3: ABCs at Dave's ESL Cafe

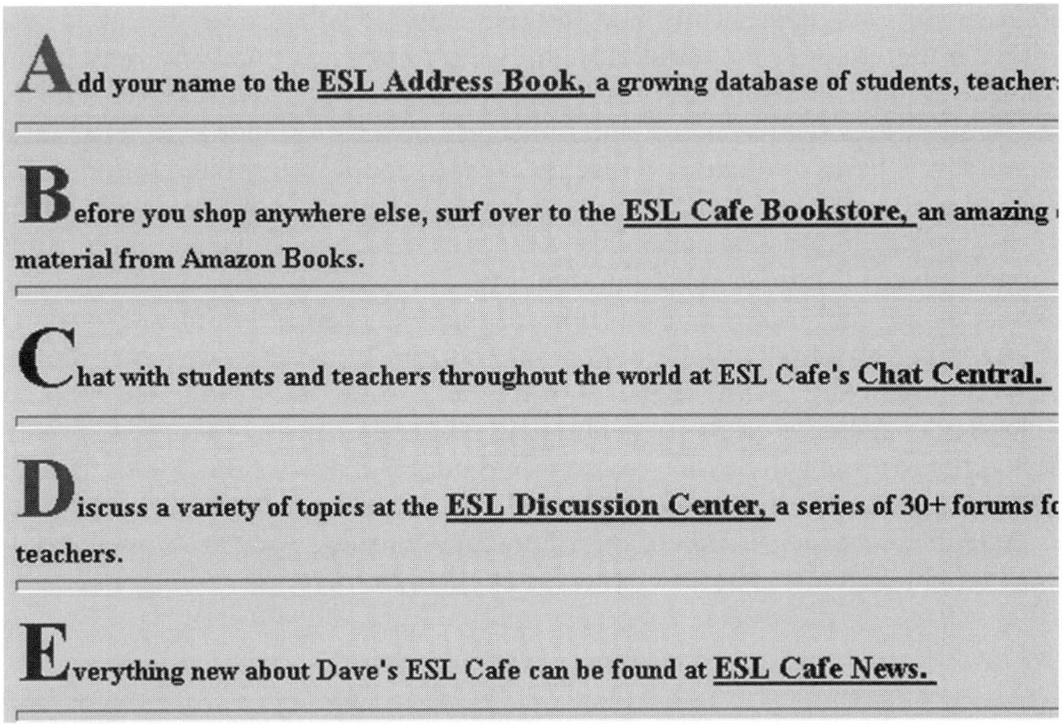

Add your name to the **ESL Address Book,** a growing database of students, teacher:

Before you shop anywhere else, surf over to the **ESL Cafe Bookstore,** an amazing material from Amazon Books.

Chat with students and teachers throughout the world at ESL Cafe's **Chat Central.**

Discuss a variety of topics at the **ESL Discussion Center,** a series of 30+ forums f teachers.

Everything new about Dave's ESL Cafe can be found at **ESL Cafe News.**

Reprinted by permission of www.eslcafe.com.

---

2. Take time to join an ESL e-mail, discussion, or chat session. Try the URLs below to see which one best suits your needs:
   - *www.eslcafe.com/chat/chatpro.cgi*—a chat room for ESL teachers
   - *www.eslcafe.com/discussion*—a discussion among ESL teachers
   - *www.eslcafe.com/mx*—a place for a message exchange for ESL teachers
   - *www.pacificnet.net/~sperling/student.html*—a site to communicate via e-mail with other ESL teachers
   - *www.teachnet.com/ttforum.html*—a forum to discuss issues related to ESL with other teachers

See Figure 7-3 at Dave's ESL Cafe for other possible choices.

3. Choose one unit that you plan to teach in the next quarter and incorporate an Internet component into it. Determine how you will manage the tasks with the computers available, what skills students will learn, and what grammar structures students will practice.

4. In your Internet notebooks, keep a separate section as your journal. Write two journal entries: complete entry 1 *before* teaching the Internet lesson and discuss what concerns you have about the upcoming lesson; write entry 2 *after* the lesson and comment on successes and areas to improve. What went well? What should you have done differently? Use your reflections as you begin your next Internet-based lesson.

SUMMARY

There are times when the ESL teacher requires new ideas and ways to instill some excitement into language study. The Internet now provides a wealth of ideas and multimedia materials so that students can listen to or watch a story, view phenomena, and communicate with peers in another country. These activities often lend themselves to situations in which students must use authentic language. With Internet activities as the basis, students can discuss the information they have found, practice new vocabulary, and review grammatical forms. In small groups or with partners, they can write their conclusions and read them to the class. Thus, activities using the Internet reinforce listening, speaking, reading, and writing skills. And since the information is not tied to any one culture or language group, the Internet provides a nonthreatening atmosphere where students can work at their own pace doing research, communicating with keypals worldwide, or practicing language skills. Even if a classroom includes the varied language skills of Maria, Arturo, Chang, and Natasha, the teacher will be able to prepare them for mainstream classes using multimedia and authentic materials from the Internet. In Part 2 of this chapter, these four students take the next step in their language journey. They are now ready for a content-based language classroom and the challenges there.

PART 2: USING THE INTERNET IN ESL CONTENT-BASED INSTRUCTION

Maria, Chang, Arturo, and Natasha, students enrolled in an intermediate-level ESL class, have progressed well. They can now communicate with their classmates in a social setting, and they have developed basic skills in speaking, listening, reading, and writing. In other words, they are ready to move from the ESL classroom to a mainstreamed class or to an ESL "sheltered" environment that teaches subject matter in science, social studies, and literature. These students must now become proficient in "academic English" to succeed in school. Content-based language instruction provides that academic framework. A bit of theory about content-based language instruction and second-language learners will enable teachers to understand better the model plan that follows. Part 2 will define "content-based language instruction," illustrate how the Internet can aid in teaching content to LEP students, and provide a model and sample plan for integrating the Internet into a content-based language classroom.

WHAT IS CONTENT-BASED LANGUAGE INSTRUCTION?

Many labels are given to the concept of content-based instruction for LEP students, such as "integrated language and content instruction," "sheltered subject matter teaching," or "sheltered English," to name a few. In the content-based language instruction approach, ESL language teachers use instructional materials, learning tasks, and classroom techniques from academic content areas as the vehicles for continued development in language, content, cognitive and study skills. English is the medium of instruction for academic subjects. Instruction is usually given by a language teacher or by language and content teachers working together.

Content-based language instruction synthesizes several components of quality teaching and second-language acquisition research, allowing students to progress through content areas while continuing to acquire English-language skills. As content mastery and language proficiency are of equal importance, content-based language instruction is a valuable solution for schools that have the problem of a number of language groups and limited staff to serve them.

Content-based instruction is designed for students who have received intensive language training and have some proficiency in the English language. At this point in their education, Maria, Chang, Arturo, and Natasha have all acquired basic interpersonal communication skills (BICS)—they are linguistically able to express most of their immediate needs in school and in the community. The material learned is not very cognitively demanding, and learning situations are usually face-to-face interactions where teachers can clarify any misunderstandings students might have. Ordering food in a restaurant, depositing money in a checking account, or writing a personal letter illustrate interpersonal communicative competence. Cummins and Swain (1986) suggest that it takes about two years to acquire these basic interpersonal communications skills. After most students complete an intermediate-level ESL class, they should be competent in BICS.

COGNITIVE-ACADEMIC LANGUAGE PROFICIENCY

Cognitive-academic language proficiency (CALP) is much more cognitively demanding than BICS. Cummins and Swain (1986) suggest that academic proficiency or CALP is necessary for learning concepts, such as comparing the governments of China and Taiwan or writing a research paper. CALP often refers to abstract ideas or concepts. For example, in a social studies class, academic proficiency might require students to answer a question like: "What is the sequence of events that led to the Civil War?" Yet, the terms "sequence," "events," and "Civil War" may not be concepts LEP students understand. These concepts are more abstract than the more concrete ones they use to communicate with their peers and require higher-level thinking skills. Acquiring cognitive-academic competence may take from four to seven years.

The teacher's job, then, is to bridge the gap between students' interpersonal communication skills and academic-language proficiency. To achieve this goal, teachers must:

- provide "comprehensible input" or information that is understandable to LEP students (Krashan, 1992). Teachers must deliver instruction in such a way that they make sure students comprehend the vocabulary, concepts, and learning strategies necessary to understand the content.
- create active learning situations. Heterogeneous grouping and encouraging group solutions in which students must talk together requires students to engage in their learning.

- include the following elements in the lessons: *see, tell, try, do* (Cummins and Swain, 1986). Students should have the opportunity to see the concept through demonstrations, models, exhibits, diagrams, or charts. They should also be told about the concept through lectures, reading, films, or other multimedia. They should be able to try the concept through clustering, discussions, role playing, experiments, and recitations, to name a few. And, finally, they should be given the chance to work with the concept and experience the learning.

THE INTERNET AND CONTENT-BASED INSTRUCTION

Internet resources add to the bag of tricks of content-based and ESL teachers. The Internet can set up teachers with "comprehensible input" and an active learning environment in which students can work together in groups. It can also introduce students to a subject, reinforce their learning, and provide them with material to "try" and "do," as recommended by Cummins and Swain.

Chamot and O'Malley (1987) have created a model lesson format for content instruction of LEP students that works well with the *see, tell, try, do* model. The Cognitive Academic Language Learning Approach (CALLA) continues academic English-language development through content-area instruction in science, social studies, and language arts. As part of the instruction, students are also taught to use learning strategies to assist their comprehension and retention of both language skills and concepts in the content areas. By incorporating the Internet into this lesson format, teachers have ready-made experiences, pictures, concrete objects, simulations, and activities to help students understand content and clarify academic concepts. The Internet also provides methods for communication and enrichment.

The CALLA model has three components:

1. a curriculum correlated with mainstream content areas
2. English-language development integrated with content subjects
3. instruction in the use of learning strategies.

CALLA is based on two types of knowledge: declarative knowledge, or facts, rules, and definitions—what we know about a given subject; and procedural or language development and learning strategies—what we know how to do. The model includes three types of learning strategies:

1. *Metacognitive* strategies (such as advance organization or previewing the main ideas and concepts of material to be learned) help students prepare for new concepts.
2. *Cognitive* strategies (such as note taking, summarizing, and inferencing) help students understand new concepts.
3. *Social-affective* strategies (such as questioning for clarification and cooperation) help students clarify new material and work together to solve problems.

These strategies provide students with techniques they need as they study academic content. We will see some of these strategies implemented in the sample unit on energy conservation.

PRACTICAL APPLICATIONS

A MODEL UNIT PLAN

By analyzing each component of a CALLA lesson plan, you will come across some of the many resources on the Internet that meet the needs of LEP students studying content-based subjects. Use the sample template in Figure 7-4 to design your own lesson plan.

Step 1: Create the Objectives

When teaching subject content to LEP students, teachers must focus on both content and language; therefore, each lesson in this model has two sets of objectives.

1. *Content objectives*: Each subject area—science, social studies, and language arts—has its own set of concepts and skills that must be introduced, practiced, and/or applied to solve a problem.
2. *Language objectives*: As students learn the content, they must also practice specific language skills, such as vocabulary development, listening comprehension, oral-language proficiency, reading comprehension, and writing.

Step 2: Gather Materials

Materials appropriate for LEP students and for teachers using content-based language instruction abound on the Internet. Some of the following sites provide useful materials for students:

- *http://seds.lpl.arizona.edu/nineplanets/nineplanets/nineplanets.html* contains pictures such as a lifelike view of the solar system
- *http://curry.edschool.Virginia.edu/go/frog* and *http://george.lbl.gov/ITG.hmpg.docs/Whole.Frog/Whole.Frog.html* will make science concepts more real to children using simulations, such as dissecting a frog
- *www.city.net/countries* has maps of Japan, China, and Africa that will help children visualize geographic concepts more easily in social studies
- *www.i-channel.com/features/Ellis* lets students studying immigrants practice listening skills as they view and hear immigrants on Ellis Island speak about some of the hardships they encountered arriving in the United States
- *www.pacificnet.net/~sperling/student.html* is a keypal site where students can find a content-based science class to communicate with on measuring rainfall—this type of project engages LEP students in an authentic dialogue to help them improve writing skills
- *www.pacificnet.net/~sperling/student.html* has an "Ask an Expert" site that not only provides an audience to answer questions that are important to stu-

Figure 7–4: Content-Based Lesson Plan Template

Design the Lesson

Class: _____ **Date:** _____

Unit: _____ **Lesson:**
_____

1. **Objectives:**
   _____
   _____

2. **Materials:** List the URLs you will use.
   _____
   _____

3. **Learning Strategies:**
   _____
   _____

4. **Procedures:**
   _____
   _____

5. **Practice:**
   _____
   _____

6. **Evaluation of students:**
   _____
   _____

7. **Evaluation of Internet process:**
   _____
   _____

8. **Follow-up activities**
   _____
   _____

dents, but also requires them to practice grammar as they write questions for the experts, who are readily available to answer queries in science, social studies, and language arts

There are also materials for teachers:

- *www.ncte.org/notesplus/Owen-March1994.html* offers lesson plans, such as for teaching Shakespeare to LEP students
- *www.eslcafe.com/chat/chatpro.cgi* has chat rooms for teachers and/or students who are interested in specific ESL topics
- *www.ai.tech.ac.jp/~teslj*, dealing with the teaching of non-native speakers, presents research findings that can improve the quality of lessons you create

Some of these materials are included in the sample unit that follows.

Step 3: Determine the Learning Strategies

Each activity in the lesson should specify the learning strategies that will be practiced during an activity. For example, using a metacognitive learning strategy such as advance organization will familiarize students with the Globe Theatre at Website *www.shakespeare.uiuc.edu* and set the stage for LEP students to begin acting out the play *Romeo and Juliet*. In determining keywords to perform a Web search, students have to classify words or concepts according to their attributes. They also use the learning strategy of grouping for this activity. Students can practice the cognitive strategy of summarizing, either in writing or verbally, when they read or listen to information on a Website, receive responses from keypals, or participate in a chat session or discussion between teachers and/or students. Working together with fellow students to solve a problem, share information, model a language activity, or get responses on oral or written performance requires cooperation, a social-affective learning strategy. By incorporating these strategies and others into lessons, you provide LEP students with skills necessary to assimilate information in academic courses.

Step 4: Establish Procedures for the Lesson

PREPARATION

In preparing for the lesson, you must find out what students already know about the concepts to be presented and practiced, what gaps in prior knowledge must be addressed, and what students have been taught about approaching a particular science process or social studies concept. During this phase, students should have the opportunity to activate their schema or recall their prior knowledge and start to link it to the lesson topic, to develop labels in English for concepts they already know, and to share ways to discuss and solve problems.

Use some of the following Internet materials and activities as you prepare lessons:

- For a lesson on planets, students can view a Web screen at *http://seds.lpl. arizona.edu/nineplanets/nineplanets/nineplanets.html* showing a view of the solar system. This colorful image (see Figure 4-9) allows ESL students to visualize the size of different planets, their relationship to each other, and other distinguishing features, such as the rings around Saturn or Jupiter's moons.

- A class studying energy might brainstorm a list of ways they are conserving energy in their homes. Before doing the brainstorming, they can view the URL *http://solstice.crest.org/renewables/wlord/index/html* to see a solar house and the different ways one family is saving energy.
- A map of China at *www.lib.utexas.edu/Libs/PCL/Map_Collection* or *http://nationalgeographic.com/xpeditions/main.html?main=atlas* illustrates the size of China and indicates the mountain ranges, rivers, and major cities. This will help a student from Mexico visualize a country so far away yet similar geographically to his or her own. Asking the student to list three similarities and three differences by looking at the maps of China and Mexico and reporting to the class strengthens new vocabulary, develops critical thinking, and improves speaking skills.
- Finally, before beginning a language-arts writing workshop, students in, for example, a fourth-grade sheltered class in San Jose, California, might write e-mail messages to their keypals in Bethlehem, Pennsylvania, describing themselves and their hobbies. This is a good way for students to get to know their writing partners and practice using descriptive words. This activity lowers the anxiety level for the academic writing to follow.

PRESENTATION

At this stage of the lesson, introduce and explain new information to students. It is important that LEP students comprehend the new material so they can practice it accurately later in the lesson. Materials used in this phase must be at a level that students will understand; therefore, you should preview Websites and choose those that contain standard vocabulary. Slang and idioms are difficult for LEP students to comprehend, so stick to short, simple sentences, free from cultural assumptions. Visual images and concrete objects help to clarify meaning. Be sure to present the information in a variety of modes. For example, in a biology class, listening to a description and watching a simulation on the Internet on the dissection of a frog helps to impress the process on LEP students and introduces new vocabulary in context.

Above all, make sure the anxiety level in the classroom is low. For example, focus on the meaning students are trying to express, rather than on the language errors. Accepting differences in language abilities and unsophisticated explanations of scientific concepts, modeling question types, encouraging students to ask questions, and empathizing with students help to create an atmosphere in the content-based language classroom where students are not afraid to make mistakes and contribute to the group.

Step 5: Provide Practice

Give students a variety of types of practice so students can assimilate the new information and use it in different ways. Cooperative grouping in heterogeneous teams is a good technique to use. (*Note:* For a more in-depth discussion of cooperative learning techniques, see Chapter 5.) For example, students can work in groups of three on drawing the map of China viewed on the Web page cited above; a team of biology students can dissect their own frog based on the model at *http://curry. edschool.virginia.edu/go/frog*; and a group gathering climate statistics can create a graph showing rainfall changes and present a report to the class and/or write a summary of their findings to send to their keypal class. In all of these activities, the Internet has become an integral tool in their learning.

Step 6: Evaluate the Learning

Evaluation can take several forms—by teacher, by student, and by oneself. Check the level of your students' performance to gain an understanding of what they have learned and any areas they need to review. Reviewing journal writing and Internet notebooks with new vocabulary or having students write out the processes they went through to make something are just some of the ways to evaluate content mastery and language competency of your LEP students.

Employ cooperative activities for student evaluation. For example, teams can discuss how useful the sites they visited on the Web were or how they might get better results the next time they logon. Finally, have students engage in individual self-evaluation by asking them to determine the effectiveness of the keywords they used in their search strategies.

Step 7: Follow Up with Expansion Activities

To follow up, give students a variety of opportunities to think about their new concepts and skills—about how to integrate them into their existing knowledge framework, to make real world applications, and to continue to develop academic language. There are many types of follow-up activities for which the Internet is an integral tool: a social studies class posts its findings on China on its own Web page; a language-arts class creates a book of stories with pictures and sends it to a sister class via e-mail; or an English debate class argues issues surrounding animal rights from information they obtained from a Web search at *http://arrs.envirolink.org/Faqs+Ref*. Once again, the Internet has provided the research material, the vehicle to publish student results, and a method to communicate with peers. LEP students struggling to attain academic-language competence need these kinds of successes and opportunities to practice their language skills in authentic situations.

SAMPLE CONTENT-BASED LANGUAGE UNIT: ENERGY CONSERVATION

This model unit on energy conservation will illustrate how you can use the Internet in content-based language classes. Science frameworks begin the study of energy in elementary school. Energy study can assume many forms, from looking at alternative energy sources to understanding how the nuclear reactor at Chernobyl operates.

In Chapter 9 we will explore a unit on alternative energy sources at a secondary level, but this unit focuses on conserving energy and is designed for students who have transitioned from an intermediate ESL class to a content-based language class. The material is at approximately a seventh-grade level. Incorporated into the unit are activities to emphasize Cummins and Swain's model—see, tell, try, and do. The unit also follows the CALLA lesson format you just reviewed.

Step 1: Create Objectives

This unit builds on earlier science study about energy. Students will now focus on practical applications for conserving energy.

CONTENT OBJECTIVES

By the end of the unit, LEP students will be able to:

- write a list of five ways to conserve energy
- define technical vocabulary in sentences
- conduct energy audits in their own homes and at school
- compare and contrast wattage figures of appliances, based on figures at a Website

LANGUAGE OBJECTIVES

By the end of the unit, LEP students will be able to:

- spell and provide definitions of vocabulary related to energy conservation
- read and comprehend energy facts from a Website
- listen for specific information
- orally summarize the results of their home energy audits
- write questions to an energy expert
- write letters outlining how their school can conserve energy

LEARNING STRATEGIES

By the end of the unit, students will be able to:

- work cooperatively in groups. (social-affective)
- take notes (cognitive)
- summarize in writing facts from Websites (cognitive)

Step 2: Gather Materials

The following Websites will provide background material for you as you prepare for your unit on energy conservation. If your expertise is not in science, you will find these sites particularly useful. They provide resource material beyond the textbook, including hands-on projects, facts, and communication practice.

- *www.energyed.ecw.org* (Energy Education Online). This site provides class-

Figure 7–5: Energy Quest Website

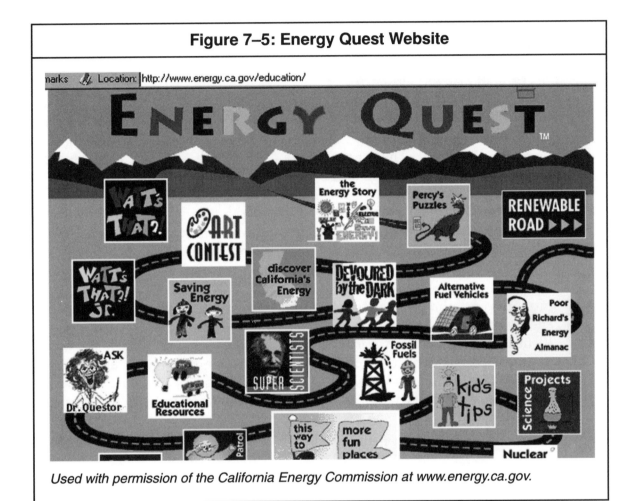

Used with permission of the California Energy Commission at www.energy.ca.gov.

room ideas, teacher resources, Internet links, "field trips," an energy listserv, and an energy slide show presented by the energy center of Wisconsin.

- *www.energy.ca.gov/education* (Energy Quest). This site has many activities, projects, and games for children. The Energy Story provides complete background for understanding the concept of energy. Ten chapters include information on all aspects of energy, such as wind and solar energy and energy safety. Material can be used as is or adapted for students, depending on students' language proficiency. Figure 7-5 illustrates the numbers of activities possible at this site.

- *http://ecep1.us1.edu/ecep/ecep.htm* (Energy Conservation Enhancement Project). The project at this site will help you instruct students on how to save energy and conduct energy audits at their schools. Students acting as "energy detectives" can patrol their schools looking for energy problems.

Step 3: Determine Learning Strategies

During the unit students will practice metacognitive, cognitive, and social-affective learning strategies. Some of the specific learning strategies include advance organization and self-evaluation (metacognitive); note-taking, grouping, summarizing, imagery, elaboration (cognitive); and cooperation (social-affective).

Step 4: Establish Lesson Procedures

Procedures for the unit focus on show, tell, try, and do. First, you will show students, with the help of visual aids, a broad overview of the topic to help them form a mental picture of the material they will learn. You will tell them the vocabulary and new information they need. Then they will try out what they have learned. Finally, after students can use the language and execute the skills successfully, you will give them an activity to do, given little or no context.

To begin, determine what students know about the topic of energy and review vocabulary necessary to obtain new information about energy conservation. Several Websites will prove useful as you prepare students for the new content.

1. During the "show" stage on the blackboard, have students brainstorm a list of words and phrases that come to mind when they think about energy and energy conservation.

2. Identify new vocabulary words that will be used in the unit, such as "watt," "energy conservation," "energy audit," to name a few; use Website *www.leeric.lsu.edu/educat/what's_a_watt.htm* for help. In their energy notebooks, have students write definitions of the words and use the words in sentences.

3. Have students prepare a list of questions related to energy conservation. During the "show" stage, review question word order and question words, such as who, what, where, when, why, and how. Have them contact an energy expert at *www.eren.doe.gov* to get answers to their questions, and have them articulate the answers in their own words.

4. Also at *www.eren.doe.gov*, in groups of three, have students look at the frequently asked questions about energy (FAQs) for more information. Each group should choose at least three questions of interest from the site, write down the questions, summarize the answers in their journals, and report their answers to the class. In this activity, students will practice listening, speaking, reading, and writing.

5. Explain what is meant by an energy audit. For example, students will list all of the ways energy is used in the home and determine places where they can conserve energy. Have students view the examples of saving energy in the home at *www.sprint.com/epatrol/ep-energy.html* to provide a model for their own energy audits.

6. To "show" students energy conservation, have them view a Website depicting energy uses created by a New York elementary school class at Website *http://k12.cnidr.org/gsh/schools/ny/che.html* to understand how this class researched energy conservation in their homes.

Figure 7–6: Wattage for Household Appliances

Energy Consumption of Household Appliances

appliance	average wattage	appliance	average wattage
Blender	290-385	Electric water heater	5000
Dishwasher	1190-1250	Radio	70-80
Freezer(15cu ft.)	341-600	Television, colo	175-450
Refrigerator(12cu ft	330	Curling iron	40-50
Frying pan	1100-1250	Television, B&W 12"	60-10
Iron	1000	Stereo tape player	60-250
Microwave oven	300-1450	Hair dryer	500-150
Sewing machine	100	Saw, circular	800-1200
Toaster	1100-1250	Saw, table	800-950
Popcorn popper	1000	Drill, 318' variable	240
Washing machine	375-550	Belt sander	600
Coffee maker	850-1500	Area Lighting	60-100
Vacuum cleaner	1260	1/3 HP well pump	350-600
Air conditioner	3000-5000	1/2 HP well pump	400-800
Ceiling fan	25	Circulation pump	80

$$W = V \times A$$

Watts = Volts x Amps

renewable energy education::: solar energy education::: environmentaleducation

Courtesy of solarsteve@aol.com.

Step 5: Provide Practice

Students have considered factual data about energy conservation. They have seen how others have conserved energy in their homes. Now, they must put energy conservation into practice. Using the Websites they have studied and the answers to questions from the energy expert, students will assess energy use in their own homes.

1. Have students conduct energy audits in their own homes. In their energy notebooks, have them list the rooms in their houses (e.g., kitchen, bedroom, bathroom, laundry).

2. For each room, have them write down equipment or appliances that consume energy. Then refer to the Website at *http://solardome.com/SolarDome72.html* to determine how much energy these appliances use up. Have students, working in groups of three, evaluate appliances in their own homes and the wattage for each appliance. Have them discuss together, comparing and contrasting wattage for different appliances, and record three ways they can save energy in their homes by understanding wattage. This activity incorporates math skills into language and science. See Figure 7-6 for help.

3. In journal entries, have students write down two energy-saving measures they initiated in their homes. Have students read entries to the class while you or another student writes the ideas on the board.

Step 6: Evaluate the Lesson

Evaluation will take the form of student, teacher, and self evaluation, as illustrated in the following activities:

- Have each group of students create an energy collage, depicting the ways in which energy is used in their homes. The collages should include labels for each energy user and a sentence indicating how the students are saving energy.
- Students will share their collages with the class. Have students take notes in their energy notebooks on the ways that classmates have discussed to save energy.
- Have each group create T-Lists (see Figure 7-7). On the left side, enumerate the energy-saving measures; on the right side, include examples of how energy will be saved.

Step 7: Follow Up with Expansion Projects

Several follow-up activities will help students reinforce and apply what they have learned about energy conservation.

1. Have students write letters to their parents asking them to try one form of energy conservation in their own homes.

2. Have students share their data about energy with another school. Projects are available at *www.energynet.net*, a site for community involvement.

3. Have students compose letters to the school board persuading the board to implement three energy-saving ideas at their school.

4. To continue reinforcing the concept of energy conservation, have students join the E-Patrol at Website *www.sprint.com/epatrol/ep-energy.html*. As members of the E-Patrol, students will monitor energy usage in their homes.

TEACHER EXERCISES: NOW YOU TRY IT . . .

It is important to reinforce what you have just learned. Try the following exercises before going on to Chapter 8.

Figure 7–7: Energy Savers T-List

Energy-Saving Measures	How Energy Will be Saved
1. Completely load dishwasher	Saves electricity and water because dishwasher runs less times/week.
2. Turn off lights whenever I leave my bedroom.	Saves electricity; decreases electric bill.
3. Take shorter showers	Saves water.
4. Use energy-saving toilets	Employs less water usage.

1. You have just reviewed a unit on energy conservation. Use the same sites listed in the text and assume the role of the students in your class. Check sample Websites and adapt the activities to students in your class. Add, delete, and modify the unit so it accommodates the learning environment at your school.

2. Choose another subject area and create your own unit for ESL students. The following URLs for *Romeo and Juliet* will help you get started.

   - *www.ncte.org/notesplus/Owen-March1994.html*—Teaching Shakespeare to ESL Students
   - *www.zbths.k12.il.us/projects/burd-strauss/engproject.html*—Shakespearean Era: Connections to Our Lives and Times
   - *www.zesn.meq.gouv.qc.ca/schools/bchs/rjshunt.htm*—A *Romeo and Juliet* Scavenger Hunt

3. Write journal entries focused on your experiences exploring Websites for content-based ESL lessons. Ask yourself these questions: Is the content at a level appropriate for your ESL students? Will the pictures/graphics at the site help your students to understand the concepts expressed by the text of the site? For what part(s) of the lessons will you use the Internet—to introduce the lesson, to teach concepts, to provide an extension activity?

4. Test at least four content-based Websites with your students. Note the results in your journals: advantages and disadvantages, language levels, visual aids.

CONCLUSION

Increasing numbers of limited-English proficient students are entering classrooms throughout the United States. In California alone, more than 1 million LEP students attended public schools during the 1997–1998 school year. It is important that the needs of this large population be addressed in order that these students learn as efficiently and effectively as possible. Combining second-language acquisition principles with content instruction and using the Internet as a tool for teaching and learning provides educators with a way to motivate LEP students to learn content while improving their language abilities at the same time. We cannot neglect the needs of this population in the twenty-first century.

REFERENCES

Chamot, Anna U., and Michael J. O'Malley. 1987. *The Cognitive Academic Language Learning Approach (CALLA) for Limited English Proficient Students.* Rosslyn, VA: InterAmerica Research Associates.

Chamot, Anna U., and Michael J. O'Malley. 1987. *The Cognitive Academic Language Learning Approach: A Bridge to the Mainstream.* TESOL *Quarterly*, 2: 217–249.

Cummins, James, and Michael Swain. 1986. *Bilingualism in Education: Aspects of Theory, Research and Practice.* New York: Longman.

Johnson, David, and Roger Johnson. 1975. *Learning Together and Alone: Cooperation, Competition, and Individualization.* Englewood Cliffs, NJ: Prentice-Hall.

Johnson, Keith. 1979. "Communicative Approaches and Communicative Processes." In *The Communicative Approach to Language Teaching*, edited by C. J Brumfit and Keith Johnson. Oxford: Oxford University Press.

Krashen, Stephen D. 1978. "The Monitor Model for Adult Second Language Performance." In *Viewpoints on English as a Second Language*, edited by Marina Burt, Heidi Dulay, and Mary Finocchiaro. New York: Regents Publishing.

Krashen, Stephen D. 1992. *Fundamentals of Language Education.* Torrance, CA: Laredo.

Stevick, Earl W. 1980. *Teaching Languages: A Way and Ways.* Rowley, MA: Newbury House.

Taylor, Barry P. 1974. "Toward a Theory of Language Acquisition." *Language Learning* 24: 23–25.

Widdowson, Henry G. 1978. *Teaching Language as Communication.* Oxford: Oxford University Press.

Chapter 8

INCORPORATING THE INTERNET INTO SOCIAL STUDIES RESEARCH ASSIGNMENTS

PART 1: IDEAS AND INSIGHTS

OBJECTIVES OF THIS CHAPTER

This chapter is designed for use by social studies educators at both the elementary and secondary levels. After reading Chapter 8, they will be able to:

- understand the differences between traditional textbooks and multimedia resources
- identify problems created by using multimedia
- analyze and evaluate photographs, historical documents, and maps
- prepare students to conduct oral interviews
- identify steps to create a Web-based social studies unit at the elementary and secondary levels
- create a Web-based unit in social studies

Technology, specifically the Internet, has opened the social studies classroom to an array of data, artifacts, and perspectives. For example, technology has allowed the teacher to go beyond the traditional textbook view of history to explore varying perspectives about the heroes, explorers, military commanders, and events of the past and present. Searches on the Internet can provide information on historical events and personages ranging from the Revolutionary War era to the time of Abraham Lincoln to the Vietnam War. Information from different sites reveals many different viewpoints on the same historical event or hero—for example, both British and American points of view on the Revolutionary War.

Although being exposed to differing opinions allows students to evaluate the information to gain their own meaning, it also creates problems. Using these new resources requires students to analyze bias, not previously present in the one-textbook version of history used in today's schools. These changes in the study of social studies add value to learning a lot of facts, forcing students to think critically about the validity, the personal or organizational bias, and the political nature of the information they retrieve.

This chapter examines the types of resources typically used in social studies research. It provides a checklist of questions teachers can use to implement multimedia into unit plans, and it employs two sample unit plans—native peoples for elementary-school students, and immigration for secondary-level students—to model the creation of Web-based research examples in the social studies.

TEXTBOOKS VERSUS MULTIMEDIA

Teachers reviewing a map of Eastern Europe in their social studies textbook may find that countries such as Macedonia, Bosnia, and Croatia are not represented, that the Soviet Union is, or that maps may not have been updated to provide accurate information regarding the soviet states comprising the Commonwealth of Independent States. Recent changes taking place in the world outpace the development of maps and texts used by social studies students in our classrooms. Current social studies textbooks cover past events, but do little to bring discussion of current world changes into the classroom. This paucity of materials is a serious obstacle for social studies educators.

The solution is the Internet. The Internet, and especially its multimedia resources—sound, images, animation, text—connect you to primary sources and topical information in the social studies to help make history immediate and realistic. However, incorporating these new materials can present problems for the educator, since there are significant differences between relying on a textbook and using multimedia. Textbooks are valuable in:

- presenting vocabulary and concepts at a specific grade level
- providing morally and ethically appropriate materials in a screened text.
- eliminating offensive language and undemocratic sentiments
- depicting one single, coherent story of social, political, and economic transformation over time

Textbooks enable the teacher to control the content being studied and the manner in which it is presented to students. They teach students basic information; however, an important task for social sciences educators is providing students with the tools that will help them go beyond the textbook.

Web resources let them do just that. For example, material on the Internet may present different viewpoints on an event; it may contain bias; and it may possibly include ideas that teachers do not want to present to their students. Why use Web sources, then? Why take chances with new technologies in the classroom? Because teachers must show students how to ask questions, to look for the information they need, and to formulate and present their findings to their peers—in other words, to become independent learners. These skills will help students attain success in an increasingly complex world in which issues do not fit into discrete categories and problems cannot be solved by individuals working alone. In this mode, the teacher sets the stage, makes sure that all students are involved in working groups, and then serves as a coach while students make the discoveries. The student is an active learner, exploring topics of interest.

CHALLENGES AND ADVANTAGES

Teachers face several challenges when using Web resources. The first lies in the very nature of primary sources, which are supposed to depict faithfully language, behavior, and thinking. Thus, slave narratives, an example of a primary source on the Web, may use language that is offensive or different from contemporary values because words of the slaves are authentically depicting their lives as slaves on a southern plantation in 1860. The second challenge is that information on the Internet is not controlled—students can observe many different sites with varying points of view in a variety of mediums. For example, students may form different opinions about human rights issues in China depending on whether they look at news articles from the *Washington Post* or the *China News Digest*, both available on the Web. The Asia Watch Website may present a third opinion, as contributors to the site discuss alleged human rights abuses on mainland China. These differing perspectives can present problems in the classroom because there is no one source that represents the right answer. Therefore, students are forced to think critically to identify bias, weigh diverse opinions, and formulate their own views.

One particular advantage of using the Internet, however, is its multimedia capabilities. Websites often contain materials such as photographs, films, video, maps and graphs, and audio recordings. Hearing a speech by Winston Churchill or viewing a battle scene from the Civil War is a powerful motivator to help students understand history. Check out the Library of Congress American Memory collection of oral histories, pamphlets, photos, films, and political cartoons at Website *http://memory.loc.gov/ammem*, which provides rich primary sources to interest students and provokes questions about the study of history (see Figure 8-1). Or, if students are studying a unit on immigrants, they can go to *www.i-channel.com/ellis* to hear audio clips from people on Ellis Island who were waiting to enter the United States

Some notes on sound: To hear some of these audio clips, you can download the Real Audio Player free from Progressive Networks at Website *www.realaudio.com/products/player/index.html#download*. Students can also play video clips with the free player at *www.vdonet.com*. However, the computer must have sound and video capabilities. It also takes more computer memory and time to download sound and pictures. If students want to use them, they should try retrieving these early or late in the day to save time.

Figure 8–1: Civil War Photographs at American Memory Website

ASPECTS OF SOCIAL STUDIES RESEARCH

Expanding beyond the text requires students to learn many new skills, such as analyzing photographs and pictures or making meaning from a recording or an oral history. Teachers must prepare students for these tasks before introducing them to an array of multimedia sources. The checklists that follow will guide students in their investigation of nontext sources, such as photographs, oral histories, historical documents, and maps.

CRITIQUING PHOTOGRAPHS

Visual history provides compelling information for students. To receive the most from this medium, students must know what to look for and how to analyze what they see in a photograph or picture. For instance, when students view a photograph from the Civil War Archive and see the face of a soldier right after battle, what does this tell them about conditions during war? What distinguishing elements in the photo make that clear to them? What inferences can they make? Whether students are viewing photographs on the Web or in hand, the following four steps will help them become familiar with this new methodology.

1. Identify general information: the five Ws.
   - Who took the photo? Professional? Friend? Family?
   - Why was it taken? Historical record? Propaganda? Keepsake?
   - What audience was the photo taken for? Family? General public?
   - When was the photo taken?
2. Examine the photo critically.
   - What is the subject of the photo? Describe the action, if any.
   - Analyze and describe the background, individuals, or objects in the photo.
   - What is the age of the photo? How do the details help determine the photo's age?
3. Evaluate the photo.
   - Is the photo a valid historical representation?
   - What other sources will confirm the accuracy of information that you have discovered in the photo?
4. Determine the photo's usefulness.
   - What information from the photo is useful to develop the topic?
   - What other questions about the topic does the photograph suggest?

Figure 8-2 provides a model worksheet for analyzing photographs.

PREPARING FOR AND USING AN ORAL INTERVIEW

Students can also perform research for social studies by capturing oral history, either conducting live interviews or listening to interviews through Websites to obtain eyewitness accounts, to validate other data, to collect opinions reflecting different points of view, to acquire background and perspective, and to collect memories that are not written down in books. Website *http://memory.loc.gov/ammen/cwphome.html* in Figure 8-3 includes interviews recorded with slaves who lived during the Civil War. The following five steps will help students as they prepare to use live interview material; in fact students should think about these questions when deciding whether to pursue interview material on the Web.

1. Prepare for the live interview.
   - Decide if an interview is appropriate and then whom to interview.
   - Learn as much as possible about the topic of the interview—the individual and/or event—before interacting with the person.
2. Conduct or listen to the interview.
3. Examine the material recorded or noted.
   - Write a summary of the interview to include only the most appropriate material.
   - Note what the interviewee said about the topic.
   - Note what the interviewee stated about lifestyle, culture, government, economy, education, and the like.
4. Evaluate the information and the source.
   - Is the interviewee a dependable source of information?
   - Can dates and places mentioned in the interview be verified?

Figure 8–2: Analyzing Photographs Worksheet

Directions: Look carefully at your photograph and fill in all of the information you can.

❶ Identify general   The photo was taken:
    information: 5Ws   ➤ By whom?   _____
                         ➤ When?   _____
                         ➤ Why?   _____
                         ➤ Where?   _____
                         ➤ For what purpose?   _____

❷ Describe the photo   ➤ The action or subject_____
                         ➤ Background,
                            individuals, objects _____
                         ➤ Details   _____
                         ➤ Age based on details_____

❸ Evaluate the photo   ➤ Validity as historical
                            representation   _____
                         ➤ Verification of data
                            obtained from photo_____

❹ Determine   ➤ Useful for topic   _____
    usefulness   ➤ Other questions
                            suggested from
                            the photo   _____

- Is the factual information valid? Compare this information with other primary and secondary sources.
5. Determine the usefulness of the information.
    - What information from this interviewee is useful for the development of the topic?
    - What does this information add to the development or analysis of the topic? How can incorrect information or biased viewpoints be used?
    - In what form will this information be most effective?

See the sample worksheet in Figure 8-4 for conducting an oral interview.

Figure 8–3: Slave Interviews Website

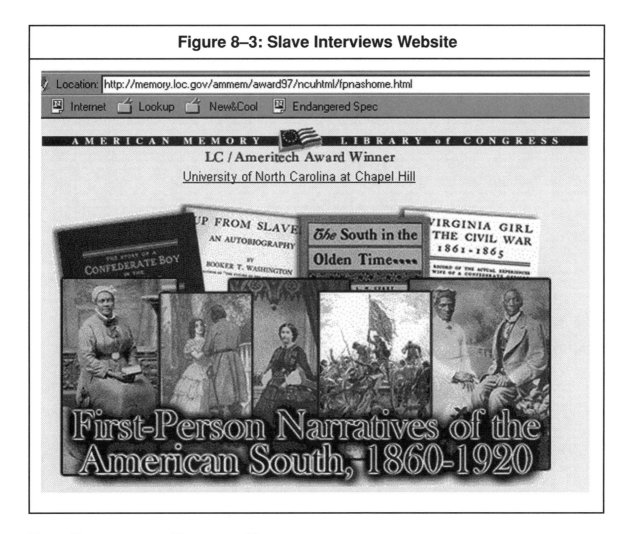

USING DOCUMENTS IN HISTORICAL RESEARCH

Written documents, such as letters and diaries, can provide valuable information about people and events. For example, at the National Archives and Records Administration Website at *www.nara.gov*, students can view posters from World War II; or they can obtain presidential speeches and biographies at Website *www.ipl.org/ref/POTUS*.

It is quite important, however, to evaluate the information to decide how useful it will be to the development of the topic. If students review each of the four steps of the process and ask themselves the following questions about the documents they are using for their social studies research, they should be able to assess the material's validity, any bias, and its relevance.

1. Identify the basics about the document.
   - What type of document is it (newspaper, government record, historical society document)?
   - What was the origin of the document?
   - Can the author be identified?

Figure 8–4: Worksheet for Oral Interviews

Conducting Interviews

Directions: Plan carefully for your interview and fill in all of the information you can.

1. Prepare for the interview.
   - ➢ Why should I do the interview? _____
   - ➢ What do I already know about the interviewee? _____
     _____
     _____
   - ➢ What URLs will I use for my Web interview? _____
     _____
   - ➢ For my live interview, what questions will I ask? _____
     _____
     _____

2. Conduct the live interview or listen to the interview several times on the Website.

3. Examine the material gathered.
   - ➢ Write a summary of the interview. _____
     _____
     _____
   - ➢ What did you learn about the times in which the interviewee lived?
     _____
     _____
     _____

4. Evaluate the information and the sources.
   - ➢ How will you judge the dependability of the source of information? _____
     _____
   - ➢ Verify the dates and places mentioned in the interview, if possible.
   - ➢ Compare the information from the interview with other primary and secondary sources. Is it valid?
     _____

5. Determine the usefulness of the interview for the topic under investigation.
   - ➢ What information is useful for developing your topic? _____
     _____
   - ➢ Is any information biased or incorrect? _____
     _____
   - ➢ How will you use the information in your research? _____
     _____

- When was the document created?
- For what audience was the document created?
- Why was the document created?

2. Examine the document carefully.
- Read the document through to get a general idea of the content. Find meanings for unknown words.
- Read the document a second time, breaking it into smaller parts. What does the document state about lifestyle, governmental affairs, historical events, laws, and beliefs?
- If the document is not dated, can an approximate date be determined from the information in the document?

3. Evaluate the information.
- Is the information given in the document reliable? How is that determined? What other sources can be used to verify the document's accuracy?
- Did the author take part in the event, or was he/she reporting what others had said?
- Does the author have a positive or negative interest in the events?

4. Determine how the document will be used in the project.
- What information from this document is useful for the topic?
- What does this information add to the development or analysis of the topic? How can incorrect information or a biased viewpoint be used in the analysis of the topic?
- What other questions or lines of inquiry does this document suggest?
- Is the document a good visual for a project or media presentation?

Figure 8-5 provides a model to use when viewing historical documents.

USING MAPS FOR SOCIAL STUDIES RESEARCH

Another important area in social studies is map research. Websites for map study range from maps of different countries—as at Websites *www.yahooligans.com/ Around_the_World/Countries*, *www.odci.gov/cia/publications/factbook*, and *www.nationalgeographic.com/xpeditions/main.html?main=atlas*—to maps that focus on specific locales—such as those at *www.lib.utexas.edu/Libs/PCL/Map_ collection.html* or *www.city.net*. The map of Africa in Figure 8-6 from the government Website above illustrates just one example.

The following four steps can guide students in incorporating map study into Internet-based research projects (see also Figure 8-7).

1. Identify specifics about the map.
- Who made the map? Amateur? Professional?
- When was it drawn?

2. Examine the map's content.
- What is the subject of the map?
- What topography, such as bodies of water, elevations, geology, and vegetation, can be identified?

Figure 8–5: Sample Historical Document Worksheet

Analyzing Historical Documents

Directions: Look carefully at the historical document and fill in all of the information you can.

❶ Identify parts of the document

Basics of the document:
- ➢ Type? _____
- ➢ Origin? _____
- ➢ Author? _____
- ➢ Date created? _____
- ➢ For what purpose? _____
- ➢ For whom? _____

❷ Examine the document

- ➢ Identify unknown _____
  words _____
- ➢ List details _____

  _____

❸ Evaluate the information

- ➢ Age, based on _____
  details _____
- ➢ Verify document's _____
  accuracy _____
- ➢ Author bias? _____

❹ Determine its usefulness

- ➢ Fit with topic _____
- ➢ Other questions _____
  suggested from _____
  the document _____

Figure 8–6: Map of Northern Africa

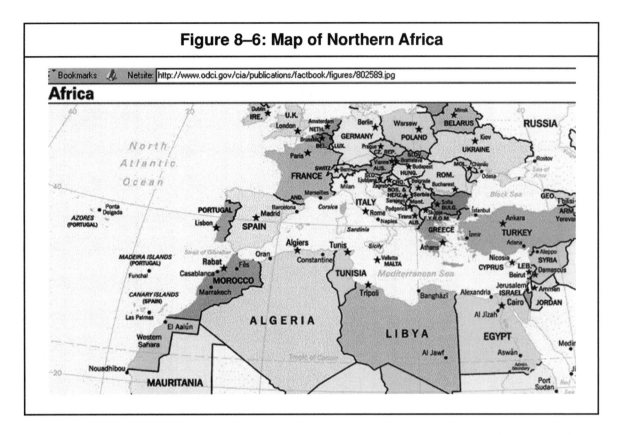

- How and where have cities/towns grown? What patterns do you find?
- What relationships are there? Are transportation routes affected by geology? Are cities/towns located on waterways? Why?
3. Evaluate the map.
   - Is there a way to check the accuracy of information suggested by the map?
   - How does the map compare with others of the same area or time?
   - What changes have occurred to the space depicted on the map since the map was made?
4. Determine the map's usefulness.
   - What information from this map is useful for the topic?
   - Is the map a good visual addition for the project?

Before students use multimedia Web resources, teachers should create some short minilessons to make sure they are adept at understanding and critically analyzing these new tools.

Figure 8–7: Sample Map Worksheet

Analyzing Maps

Directions: Look carefully at the map and fill in all of the information you can.

❶   Identify specifics about the map

Basics of the map:
- ➤   Mapmaker   _____
- ➤   Date created   _____

❷   Examine the map's contents

- ➤   Subject of map   _____
- ➤   List topographic features   _____
     _____
- ➤   Patterns you see
- ➤   Relationships   _____

❸   Evaluate the map

- ➤   Age, based on details   _____
     _____
- ➤   Verify map's accuracy   _____
     _____
- ➤   Changes since map created   _____
     _____
- ➤   Compare to other maps   _____
     _____

❹   Determine the map's usefulness

- ➤   Fit with topic   _____
- ➤   Good visual addition?   _____
     _____
     _____

PART 2: PRACTICAL APPLICATIONS

Two unit plans in Part 2 will illustrate using Web resources in social studies. These units are designed to help you transition from a textbook, skill-based classroom to a multisource, hands-on approach to learning. The first unit focuses on Native Peoples, an important part of study from the third grade forward. For example, in the fourth grade when students study their home state, they discover how Native Peoples played an important role in the history of each state; in the grade 5 social studies curriculum, westward expansion is an integral part of a course in U.S. history. The unit presented could be taught at either a fourth- or fifth-grade level, but many of the activities can be adapted for other grade levels as well.

Immigrants have been an important part of the composition of the U.S., from its inception to the twenty-first century. The second unit on Immigration fits in well to the framework competencies in a course of study on U.S. history and geography at grade 11. Activities from the unit could also be adapted for use in an eighth-grade class in which students might be studying contributions of their ancestors.

As part of each unit, students will have to use higher-level thinking skills, as in analyzing historical documents and maps, understanding data collected in interviews, and evaluating photographs.

UNIT 1 (ELEMENTARY LEVEL): NATIVE PEOPLES

In the United States, the indigenous peoples are known by many terms: Native Americans, Indians, American Indians, Native Peoples. For the sake of continuity, we shall use Native Peoples to identify these people.

Stereotypes and myths about "Indians" exist and are often perpetuated in classrooms. For example, one common myth is that "American Indians" comprise a similar group of people who share a common language and culture and live together in similar places. This unit will attempt to use some of the numerous resources created by and about Native Peoples to eliminate some of the bias and myths that currently exist in teaching about cultures, lifestyles, differences among Native Peoples, and their contributions to American life.

The activities and projects contained in the unit can be accomplished at different grade levels, and the identified Websites may be useful as you develop your own units with objectives for your specific grade levels. Throughout, students will have opportunities to investigate the tribal identity of Native Peoples who lived in a region: their customs; the locations of their villages and why they were situated there; buildings they constructed; methods they used to get food; clothing they wore; and tools and utensils they used—to name a few.

The unit that follows provides a sample for you to build on. It contains learning strategies for all students and offers activities so students learn how to listen carefully, speak easily, read efficiently, and write effectively. It bases activities and tasks on national standards and state framework goals and objectives, and makes use of cooperative group work. As you review the unit, you should consider what you can use and how you will modify the content for your own grade level and student population. Here is a synopsis of the steps for this unit:.

1. Apply framework standards—what should be taught?
2. Consider levels of student development.
3. Identify general goals and specific objectives.
4. Gather materials.
5. Introduce the unit.
6. Create sample activities.
7. Evaluate what was learned.

STEP 1: APPLY FRAMEWORK STANDARDS—WHAT SHOULD BE TAUGHT?

From the mid-1980s forward, there has been a battle among educators to teach a more inclusive history curriculum that includes not only traditional American heroes but also African American and other ethnic groups. For example, New York's new social studies curriculum stresses more multicultural themes and encourages critical perspectives. America 2000 initiated the establishment of national standards to guide history instruction. From their work a detailed plan emerged for teaching historical thinking skills and essential content understandings. Many states have adopted their own standards, based on national guidelines. For example, the California History–Social Sciences Framework (CSDE, 1988) stated that history should be treated as a skill to be developed rather than as knowledge to be acquired. In other words, students should be taught to understand past and present connections in history so they can make meaning out of the future.

Using the standards as the basis for curriculum development helps elementary school students achieve important goals of history instruction. Beginning in kindergarten, standards require that history and social science courses work toward improving students' competency in their knowledge of history, geography, and citizenship, as well as their understanding of issues such as diversity, criticism, conflict, and interdependence. New state frameworks focus on specific themes and attributes like communication, reasoning, personal development, and civic responsibility. The California History–Social Sciences Framework (1988), for example, contains three broad goals: (1) knowledge and cultural understanding, (2) democratic understanding and civic values, and (3) skills attainment and social participation. These goals are further divided into strands that teachers and curriculum developers believed were necessary to achieve the goals. These strands serve as unifying forces from kindergarten through the twelfth grade. The specific objectives excerpted from this same Framework are outlined below and are incorporated into the unit on Native Peoples:

- incorporating primary-source documents and helping students understand what people are saying and why they are saying it
- integrating the teaching of history with other fields, such as language arts, science, and the visual and performing arts
- enriching the study of history with the use of literature of the period and about the period

- incorporating a multicultural perspective that reflects experiences of men and women of different races, religions, and ethnic groups
- engaging students actively in the learning process through local and oral history projects, writing projects, debates, role-playing, dramatizations, and cooperative learning
- including critical-thinking skills at every grade level to include learning to detect bias in print and visual media, to recognize illogical thinking, and to reach conclusions based on solid evidence

STEP 2: CONSIDER LEVELS OF STUDENT DEVELOPMENT

When creating a unit for the elementary grades, you should first consider the level of development of the students—what they can effectively achieve in a particular grade. For example, in kindergarten through the third grade, curricular activities are based on the learning children have developed during their preschool years. Activities in the primary grades, then, need to be connected to the young child's immediate world and link back in time and space to people, places, and events that allow appreciation of times past. Throughout these early grades, students will learn about and understand how Native Peoples lived in their natural environment, developed an economy, and expressed their cultures in art, music, and dance.

They will also be introduced to the mythology and literature of Native cultures. For instance, an objective in first grade is for students to develop a cultural awareness of both now and long ago; listening to Native folktales from California, the Great Plains, Alaska, and the Southwest can help acheive that awareness. In third grade, children have an idea of the landscape and topography of the region in which they live; they can now consider the Native Peoples who first lived there and the resources of the region that they used. They can also compare and contrast these Native Peoples with those in other regions of the United States.

According to Piaget (1962), students in fourth through sixth grades have now entered intellectually into a stage of development in which learning activities become increasingly abstract and multidimensional. Children can be asked to compare and contrast among source material and test their hypotheses through analysis. For example, students might contrast the lifestyles of Native Peoples residing in the Southwest, those of the Pacific Northwest, nomadic tribes of the Great Plains, the Aleut population in Alaska, and the woodland peoples east of the Mississippi.

STEP 3: IDENTIFY GENERAL GOALS AND SPECIFIC OBJECTIVES

The California History–Social Science Framework acts as a guide for standards in the unit. The goals and specific objectives that follow form the basis for the content and skills of the unit.

Goals

Students will:

- identify Native Peoples as they really are by being historically accurate and fair

- be cognizant of the negative effects of stereotypes and the prejudice and discrimination in treaties and government practices in the treatment of native peoples
- understand continuity, change, and chronology in history
- make connections between the language arts and social studies curricula
- gain insights into their own lives and contemporary events
- develop cooperative skills
- use the Internet for research

Objectives
The unit will provide content and strategies so students will be able to:

- list facts about Native Peoples in their own regions
- recognize the contributions of Native Peoples
- compare and contrast Native Peoples, including their art, food, work, and play
- provide historical information on Native cultures and lifestyles throughout the Americas
- develop an appreciation of Native Peoples and their accomplishments

In addition, by the end of this unit you will have achieved important goals in history instruction. You want children to realize Native Peoples are still a real part of today's society, that they have problems and make contributions. The activities and materials in this unit will contribute to a greater understanding of Native Peoples.

STEP 4: GATHER MATERIALS
In states like California and Oklahoma where Native Peoples culture is prevalent, museums that specialize in Indian cultures provide publications, pictures, and artifacts that help children understand the daily lives of these Natives and how their cultures adapted to the environments in which they thrived. However, often it is not possible to organize trips to bring children to these rich sources of history. The World Wide Web offers a comprehensive collection of primary sources that go beyond the materials available in an elementary school library. Children can explore the history and culture of Native tribes throughout the Americas on the Web and compare and contrast similarities and differences among tribes.

One of the difficulties in providing an unbiased curriculum when teaching a unit on Native Peoples has often been the reliability of the information in textbooks, movies, and television programs. In response, Native People themselves have insisted upon accurate and unbiased accounts of their own history (National Education Association, 1983) and have recently created materials to provide detailed information about all aspects of Native Peoples on the Internet. The World Wide Web also enables children to examine different points of view so they are aware of individual differences. Thus the myth that all Native Peoples are the same can be exploded.

Instruction about the past is aided by sounds—speeches and narratives—and images of history, such as photos of tribal chieftains and events like the Trail of Tears journey. These authentic pieces provide a total historical picture of Native tribes and Alaskan Natives. "Virtual field trips" on the Web can contribute to a depth of understanding of individual tribes, like the Seminoles, Sioux, and Cherokee.

In this unit students will look at Websites that provide examples of different tribes. These rich resources create some exciting challenges. The material on the Web may be at different reading levels; it may be scattered throughout many different Websites; and there is the possibility of offensive language. This means that you must assure that materials are reviewed prior to the start of a unit and that you monitor students carefully as they conduct their research on the Web.

Web Sites about Native Peoples

Some of the Websites in Table 8-1 will provide information for activities in this unit, but not all of the work for this unit will be completed using the Internet. You should also enhance history instruction through children's literature. Elementary-level historical fiction, biographies, and reference materials related to history can be incorporated. Teachers and library media specialists must work together to identify appropriate titles from the library for a study of Native Peoples. Some sample titles are:

- *Folklore of the North American Indians*, compiled by Judith Ullom
- *Squanto, Friend of the Pilgrims*, by Clyde Bulla
- *Buffalo Woman*, by Paul Goble
- *Thunderbird and Other Stories*, by Henry Chafetz
- *Down from the Lonely Mountain*, retold by Jane Louise Curry

STEP 5: INTRODUCE THE UNIT

Unit Project

Many Native Peoples travel to powwows all over the United States. The powwow, one of the most colorful and interesting of Native activities, promotes cultural awareness and common interests across tribes. It is also a chance for Indians to gain an appreciation of their ancestry. Booths on the grounds display Indian foods; arts and crafts are for sale; and meals may be served. Many Native Peoples wear ceremonial clothing that they or family members have made; these items can comprise either as little as feathers, beads, leather, or full ceremonial regalia. Entertainment is part of the powwow: Dancers wearing colorful blankets, plumes, and carrying shakers perform traditional dances to the beat of the drum, and singers sit in a circle around the drum and keep time to the music.

For this unit, students will hold their own powwow during Native American Week. In groups students will assume the role of one tribe of Native Peoples, such as the Cherokee, Seminoles, Creek, or Sioux. Each group will be responsible for collecting, displaying, and sharing information about their tribe at the Native American Week powwow. (Alternatively, this activity can be done on one Native group indigenous

Table 8–1: Native Peoples Web Resources	
Web Site URLs	**Description of Websites**
www.nativeweb.org	General information on Native Peoples
www.eagle.ca/~matink/lessons.html	Lesson plans from First Nations
www.magicnet.net/~itms/indian.html	Web quest on Native Peoples
www.magicnet.net/~itms/indianFL.html	History of Florida Native Peoples with additional sites to explore
http://indy4.fdl.cc.mn.us/~isk/ t_webcul.html	Native culture
www.ozemail.com.au:80/~reed/global/ mythstor.html	Myths of Native people
www.seminoletribe.com	Information on the Seminole tribe including history, food, medicine, stories, and crafts
www.doa.state.nc.us/doa/cia/ handout1.htm	Fact sheet on Natives in North Carolina
http://ericir.syr.edu/Virtual/InfoGuides/ Alphabetical_List_of_InfoGuides/ nativeamer12_96.htm1#resources	Lots of Native Peoples sites
http://hanksville.phast.umass.edu/misc/ ojibwe/index.html	Ojibwe culture
www.state.sd.us/state/executive/tourism/ sioux/sioux.html	Information on the Sioux tribe
www.sdcoe.k12.ca.us/score/blue/ bluesgl.html	Unit plan on the *Day of the Blue Dolphin*
www.yahooligans.com/Around_The_ World/Cultures/Native_Cultures	Information *on Native culture*
www.first-nations.com	First Nations' Website
www.lib.uiowa.edu/gw/intl/native.html	Native Peoples resources
www.ed.uiuc.edu/YLP94-95/mini-units/ Altenhoff.Native-American	Mini-unit on Native Peoples
www.pomona.edu/REPRES/NATIVE/ NATIN.HTML	Native Peoples information

to your region. In this scenario, each group is responsible for one aspect about the tribe, such as history, arts and crafts, food, location, and so on). Much of the material needed for these tasks is available through the Internet. For example, a group studying the Seminoles will discover facts about the tribe and examples of their artwork at Website *www.seminoletribe.com.*

Each student group must complete three tasks for the powwow.

1. Create a booth that displays:
   - drawings of Native art
   - a native legend on tape and illustrated in book form
   - a biography of a tribal leader
   - facts about the tribe, including its history, where it lives, and other important information
   - an example of a food (or recipe), a ritual, or a custom
2. Produce a presentation that includes one picture, artifact, legend or additional facts to present to the other tribes at the powwow. Each group member is responsible for one part of the presentation.
3. During Native American Week, all groups rotate through the powwow display area to learn more about the different tribes.

STEP 6: CREATE SAMPLE ACTIVITIES

The elementary, self-contained classroom allows for flexible scheduling, and the absence of rigid timeframes for instruction in specific subjects can make it easier for you to arrange class time to use Web technology effectively as part of this unit. Although this unit focuses on social studies, the activities also incorporate math, language arts, art, and science.

Activities to Introduce the Unit

At the beginning of the unit, it is important to draw upon students' prior knowledge and to provide them with the language necessary to understand concepts that will be discussed throughout the unit. As background on Native Peoples and to assess student information and attitudes, have students complete these four tasks:

1. Identify each tribe on a map of the United States and color each tribal group a different color. Nine major Native cultures that existed in the United States, according to similar modes of living, are listed below:
   - Eastern Woodlands—Iroquois, Mohawk, Algonquin, Delaware
   - Great Lakes Woodlands—Ojibawa, Chippewa, Shawnee, Illinois
   - Southeastern—Cherokee, Creek, Seminole
   - North Central Plains (hunters)—Arapaho, Cheyenne, Crow, Pawnee, Sioux/Dakota
   - South Central Plains—Chickasaw, Choctaw, Comanche, Kansas, Iowa
   - Southwest Area (desert dwellers)—Apache, Hopi, Navajo, Pueblo
   - California—Chumash, Mission, Mohave, Yuma

Figure 8–8: Native Peoples Vocabulary T-Chart	
Vocabulary	**Description**
Trail of Tears	The Cherokee trekked from Georgia to Oklahoma to find a home.
Powwow	Native Peoples tribes come together to celebrate at powwows.
Seminoles	The Seminoles are a Native Peoples tribe whose home is primarily in Florida.

- Northwestern Plateau—Nez Perce, Spokane, Ute, Wallawalla
- Northwest Pacific Coast (fishermen)—Aleuts, Eskimo, Snohomish

2. List new vocabulary words in the social studies section of their notebooks under the topic of Native Peoples. These may be names of Native Peoples, places, or events, such as George Guess, Trail of Tears, Kwakiutl, Tlingit, or Haida. Have them write one sentence of identification. A T-chart, as illustrated in Figure 8-8, works well here.

3. Brainstorm a list of all beliefs they have about Native Peoples. Ask them to complete this sentence at least two times: "An Indian. . . . " As students research their tribe, they should use these beliefs as a baseline for changing any bias they might have and for building their understanding about Natives.

4. Listen to a legend and relate lessons they learned from the oral tradition. Legends tell them of beliefs, values, ceremonies, customs, and games that existed in prior times. Native history has been handed down in large part through these storytellers.

Activities to Be Used During the Unit

Depending on the time allotted for the unit, have each group choose between five and ten tasks from the following list of twenty-one, including at least one language arts and one art activity. A variety of activities is provided because there will not be information available to complete each activity on each tribe. The tasks students choose, however, should be represented as part of their powwow booths or the presentations. Each group member is responsible for Web research for at least one activity. Websites listed in Table 8-1 are good starting points to complete most of the tasks below, but students may also search for their own Websites by selecting keywords as discussed in Chapter 2. (There are also some sample Websites listed with several activities.)

1. Find out how each of the following tribes has contributed to the history of the United States. Sample Websites for each tribe are listed as starting points.

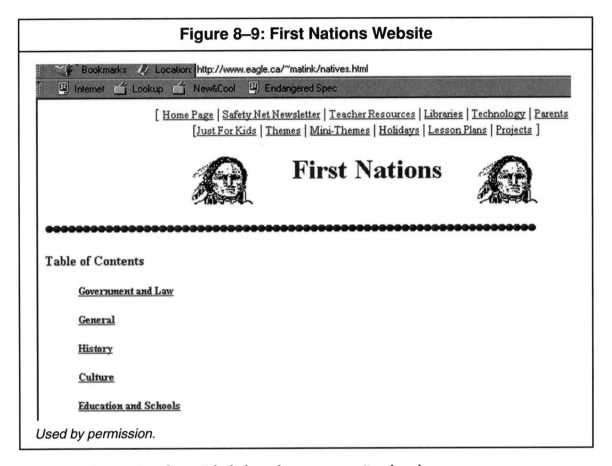

Figure 8–9: First Nations Website

[Home Page | Safety Net Newsletter | Teacher Resources | Libraries | Technology | Parents |
[Just For Kids | Themes | Mini-Themes | Holidays | Lesson Plans | Projects]

First Nations

Table of Contents

Government and Law

General

History

Culture

Education and Schools

Used by permission.

- Iroquois—*http://dickshovel.netgate.net/iro.html*
- Navajo—*http://members.tripod.com/~PHILKON*
- Cree Nation—*http://indy4.fdl.cc.mn.us/~isk/canada/can_cree.html*
- Seminole Nation—*www.seminoletribe.com*
- Sioux Nation—*www.state.sd.us/state/executive/tourism/sioux/sioux.htm*

Figure 8-9 illustrates the contents page for a Website that focuses on the First Nations tribes.

2. Find examples of music and powwow dancing of Native Peoples and explain what it tells us about the time period. Check the Website at *www.powwows.com/dancing/index2.htm*.

3. Write an original narrative poem about an important Native or event occurring between 1492 and 1775. The Website at *http://indy4.fdl.cc.mn.us/~isk/canada/can_gen.html* may provide some stories about the nations.

4. Pick one Native tribe still in existence. To what cultural tribal customs do people of the tribe still adhere? Choose a Website that contains information on that tribe for help; for example, Native myths can be found at *www.ozemail.com.au:80/~reed/global/mythstor.html*.

5. Research what contact the group's tribe had with white people and with what types, such as prospectors, settlers, and trappers. Have each group role-play its Native group and discuss whether they feel threatened by whites and what

they think should be done about the whites. Have each group elect a spokesperson to speak at the powwow to decide what Native policy should be.

6. Write at least five diary entries that would typify a Native Peoples child's day so the reader can form ideas as to the life of the writer.

7. Build a diorama depicting the lifestyle of a specific Native tribe.

8. Research Native recipes and plan a meal featuring Native dishes. List foods we eat today that were introduced by Native Peoples.

9. Prepare to teach two games played by Native Peoples. Cover the equipment, rules, number of players, and any other information needed to take part in the game.

10. Create and illustrate a page to show clothing styles for one tribe of Native Peoples.

11. Create a collage or illustrative chart comparing the work of Native men and women.

12. Find examples of pieces of art depicting Native Peoples. Study and write a report on what each picture shows about their specific lifestyles. Mount the report with an illustration on colored paper. Check the National Museum of the American Indian at Website *www.si.edu/nmai*.

13. Choose a famous Native, such as Squanto, Pocahontas, Pontiac, or Crazy Horse, and write five facts about that person. Website *www.state.sd.us/state/executive/tourism/20reason/crzy_hrs.htm* depicts the image of the famous brave carved in Crazy Horse Mountain.

14. Imagine themselves as men or women Natives of the Great Plains. Buffalo, which is the main source of food and shelter, has disappeared. Write in their journals about how they feel, what they will do, where they will go.

15. Myths and legends are important parts of Native culture. Read one myth and retell it to another member of your group. Myths can be found at *www.ozemail.com.au:80/~reed/global/mythstor.html*.

16. Ceremonies of a people tell about the culture. Describe one ceremony or ritual of the tribe and share it with the class. Act out the ceremony, if possible. Website *www.state.sd.us/state/executive/tourism/sioux/sioux.htm* provides information on the Sioux tribe.

17. Identify animals, such as buffalo or whales, that were important to your tribe. Explain why.

18. Create and illustrate a poem about an animal of the locale where your tribe lived.

19. Read a story about Native Peoples. For example, the *Hiawatha* in picture-book format could serve as an introduction to the poem by Longfellow.

20. Present a legend and write it in a class book.

21. Write a story about a group of Natives on a hunt for food. Create a cluster diagram containing information for the stories—what they should take with them, where they should go, and what animals they will find. Draw the setting for the hunt, cut out pictures of animals, and glue them over the setting to depict the hunt in action.

Activities to Be Used as Follow-up

As an extension activity, have each group of students try one of the following:

- List on butcher paper similarities and differences among the tribes the group has just learned about from its classmates and from viewing their powwow booths.
- Compare customs among tribes. Select one custom, such as a game, art, dance, or death, and show the similarities and differences from one tribe to another.

STEP 7: EVALUATE WHAT WAS LEARNED

Students should enjoy putting on the powwow. However, you need to make sure that evaluation takes place as students are performing this series of activities. It is also important to have students participate in the evaluation process. You will be assessing the content they learned, the way they performed in groups, and their efficiency using multimedia Web resources. Have students:

1. list as many tribes as they can and at least two facts about each one. Have them write down how their ideas about Native Peoples have changed since the beginning of the unit.
2. write five questions based on information about their tribes (for example, climate, animals, homes, vegetation).
3. have students make up one objective question (multiple choice or matching) on what they learned about each of the Native tribes from the powwow displays they visited. These questions can be used as the basis for a unit test on the content.

SUMMARY

By exploring Websites of Native Peoples, students have viewed a wealth of resources created by Native organizations, teachers, and students. The activities have required that students analyze and synthesize the information as part of the research for their powwow booths and presentations. Children have also learned to work together in groups, access technology, and challenge beliefs that they may have held. This unit is only a sample of the ways that you can use the Internet in social studies–based lessons. You should now be able to envision other Web-based units in your own elementary curriculum.

UNIT 2 (SECONDARY LEVEL): IMMIGRANTS: THEN AND NOW

> *"Here is not merely a nation,*
> *but a teeming nation of nations."*
> Walt Whitman

Ever since Alex Haley's mini-series *Roots* was aired on television in 1977, finding our "roots" has become a form of entertainment—even a mania for some. Moreover, tracing our ancestry forms an integral part of social studies, according to the California History–Social Sciences Framework. The United States has, from its beginnings, been a magnet for immigrants from all over the world. Colonized by immigrants from England, Holland, Spain, and France, the United States went on to provide other ethnic groups from around the world with a haven for political, religious, and cultural freedom.

This unit on Immigration is designed to get students involved in activities in which they can work closely with their families, identify their ancestors, appreciate their ethnic backgrounds, and understand the concept of immigration. Through the unit, students should also be able to connect events in history with the movement of their ancestors, become more cognizant of their own unique individual makeup and cultural origins, and develop a better understanding of the United States as a "salad bowl."

There are two major projects in the unit. The first one begins with the broad study of an ethnic group's homeland. It requires students to perform an in-depth study of a single ethnic group to which they belong, such as Chinese, Russian, Irish, or Mexican, and may include those who immigrated of their own free will or those who came here against their will, such as African Americans. Students will research the group's national origins and study what factors caused them to come to America. They also should focus on the problems immigrants encountered and the contributions they have made to the United States. These ethnic groups will be studied in historical context so students understand the economic, social, and political conditions of the times. The unit does not emphasize illegal immigration and all of the issues surrounding this topic.

The second project requires students to look at their own ancestry. Having researched their countries of origin, they can now begin to trace their own roots. Through oral interviews, genealogical sources on the Web, and historical documents, they will formulate pictures of their own heritage. Although this is a social studies unit, it incorporates language arts activities as well.

This unit bases activities and tasks on national standards and state framework goals and objectives. It illustrates some of the resources that are available for projects on the Internet and offers suggestions on how to integrate them into the social studies curriculum. Finally, it provides a model for creative teachers to use as they review their own subject matter for other units and as they tailor the activities to meet the needs of their own students. There are five steps in this unit:.

1. Apply framework standards—what should be taught?
2. Identify general goals and specific objectives.
3. Gather materials.
4. Create sample activities.
5. Provide for evaluation.

STEP 1: APPLY FRAMEWORK STANDARDS—WHAT SHOULD BE TAUGHT?

An important area in courses in American history is the study of major social and cultural changes that have taken place as the United States has developed. One major change has occurred in immigration policies, especially the recent reopening of America's gates to immigrants from Asia and Central America.

Study of ancestors and immigrants can be traced throughout the K–12 curriculum. For example, children in second grade discuss their ancestors—where they came from and what it was like to live there. They listen to stories about men and women from these cultures who have made contributions, and they begin map study identifying homes of their ancestors on the globe. In fifth grade, as part of U.S. history and geography, students read and learn more about immigrants who came to this country—how they settled it, where different ethnic groups located, and the challenges and hardships they faced. In eleventh grade, students delve more deeply into the significance of immigration in producing cultural diversity. Thus, the curriculum provides for an integrated and sequential framework from the elementary grades through high school.

This unit on Immigration accommodates the goals and objectives of Standard 2 of the National Social Studies Standards. Standard 2 states that students should develop an understanding of the major social and economic developments in contemporary America. For example, in grades 9–12, students will draw upon methods of historical research including the use of oral histories, films, local museum exhibits, literature, and the fine arts to evaluate the contributions of diverse peoples and cultures to American society. In addition, as part of Standard 2 students are asked to demonstrate understanding of the new immigration taking place in the United States and how it compares to immigration in earlier times.

STEP 2: IDENTIFY GENERAL GOALS AND SPECIFIC OBJECTIVES

Goals
At the end of this unit, students will be able to:

- explain the factors that prompted the new immigration by analyzing cause-and-effect relationships
- have an awareness of cultural diversity
- brainstorm the reasons that have sparked increased immigration to the United States in recent times
- investigate life stories of recent immigrants to explain the reasons for their decisions to emigrate from their homelands and the challenges they faced in moving to a new land
- see the connections between literature and historical periods
- use technology for research

Objectives
After performing activities in this unit, students will be able to:

- compare current immigration patterns to earlier times by preparing a class chart showing where their ancestors lived before moving to their present residences

- identify from which areas of the world most immigrants to the United States have come
- explain how the immigration acts of 1965, 1986, and 1991 have changed immigration patterns
- conduct an oral interview with a family or community member
- identify contributions of different ethnic groups
- understand the difficulties faced by immigrants
- discuss history, culture, and the current status of different ethnic groups.
- trace their ancestors

STEP 3: GATHER MATERIALS
For this unit, you will have students look at three types of Web resources:

1. information on countries. Students should be able to learn about the country from which their ancestors came—its history and culture. A general site from which to start is *www.yahooligans.com/Around_the_World/Countries*.
2. Websites that provide statistics and facts on immigration in early times and today: laws, such as those of 1965, 1986, and 1991; numbers of immigrants arriving in the United States and their countries of origin; and locations where they settled. The Internet Law Library at *http://law.house.gov/104.htm* provides information on immigration and citizenship law.
3. genealogical Websites to help students trace their "roots." The Internet provides new resources, such as Websites that make it easy to find and share information and chat rooms filled with people seeking advice and sharing leads. Some of the general genealogical sites in Table 8-2 are starting points.

Other sources will include oral interviews with relatives, family documents, records, and pictures. Maps and other printed library resources will also be helpful.

STEP 4: CREATE SAMPLE ACTIVITIES
There are three basic aspects to this unit:

1. researching the countries of origin of ethnic groups
2. understanding the problems, contributions, and conditions existing in the United States when these groups immigrated
3. students tracing their own ancestry

Some of the activities that follow are mandatory; for example, each student must conduct an interview with an immigrant. The mandatory tasks are identified with an asterisk (*).

Activities to Introduce the Unit
These tasks will review some of the concepts about different ethnic groups that students learned in earlier grades and increase their knowledge of immigration to the United States. Students will:

Table 8-2: General Genealogical Websites	
Sample URLs	**Creators of Websites**
www.ngsgenealogy.org	National Genealogical Society (fees)
www.fgs.org	Federation of Genealogical Societies (fees)
www.cyndislist.com	Cyndi's list of genealogical sites
www.ancestry.com	Ancestry.com
www.usgenweb.org	U.S. Genweb Project
www.switchboard.com	Switchboard
www.rootsweb.com	Rootsweb
www.genealogy.com	Broderbund genealogical sites

- *locate on a classroom map areas of the United States where immigrants have settled in large numbers. Explain the reasons that sparked increased immigration to the United States in recent times and from which areas of the world most of these immigrants have come. Note where they entered the country and track the routes to their present locations. Some facts below may help with this exercise:
  — Over 800,000 immigrants enter the United States each year as lawful permanent residents or as refugees fleeing persecution.
  — Immigrants collectively earn $240 billion a year and pay $90 billion a year in taxes, while only receiving $5 billion in welfare.
  — The leading source countries of U.S. immigrants are Mexico, Vietnam, the Philippines, and the republics of the former Soviet Union.
  — Nearly three-fourths of all new immigrants intend to reside in California, New York, Texas, Florida, New Jersey, and Illinois.
- create a cluster diagram containing all of the ideas about immigrants that they can think of. Figure 8-10 provides an example.
- listen to audio clips of immigrants entering the United States via Ellis Island using *www.i-channel.com/ellis*. Then use the following Websites to record the process by which immigrants entered the United States in the 1600–1800s:
  — *www.bergen.org/AAST/Projects/Immigration/ellis_island.html*
  — *www.bergen.org/AAST/Projects/Immigration/process_of_entering.html*
- Construct a historical narrative comparing past immigration history with the reality of present immigration. What were the factors that caused people to move to the United States in the past? How do they compare to the reasons that impel immigrants today? To what extent is the reception afforded immigrants today similar to that of the past? To what extent is it different?

Figure 8–10: Impact of Immigrants

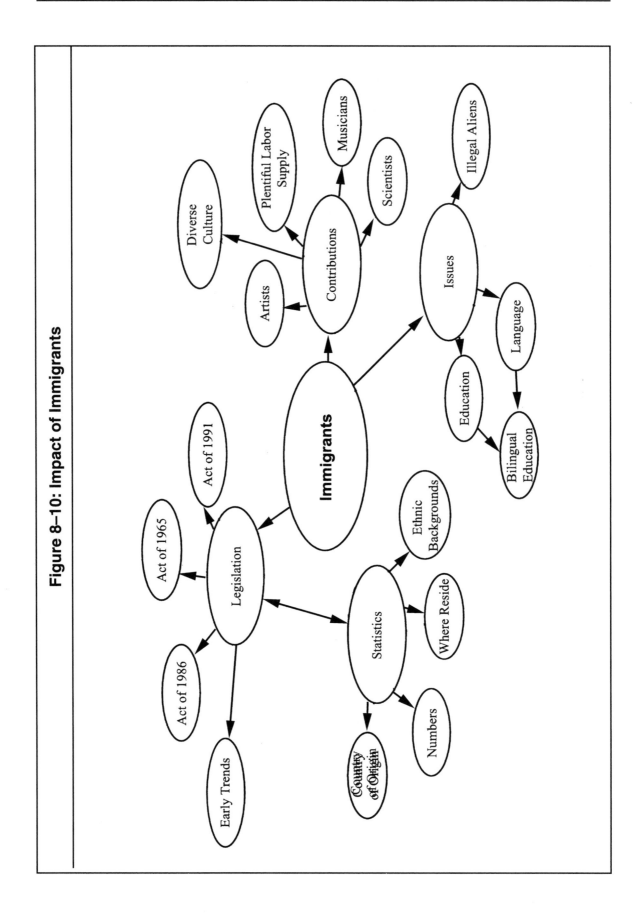

Activities to Be Used During the Unit

These activities will provide new information and reinforce the concepts that students have already attained. The three basic activities comprise:

1. In groups, students will research specific ethnic groups, especially compiling information about the countries of origin of the ethnic groups.
    * Construct historical narratives comparing past immigration history with the reality of present immigration. What were the factors that caused people to move to the United States in the past? How do they compare to the reasons that impel immigrants today? To what extent is the reception afforded immigrants today similar to that of the past? To what extent is it different?
    * *Identify contributions made by specific ethnic groups.
    * Do a collaborative project with another school whose ethnicity is different from their own.
2. *Have students investigate life stories of recent immigrants to explain the reasons for their decisions to emigrate, the challenges they faced in moving to a new land, and the problems that immigrants face in their new homes. Each student will:
    * interview a member of their family, a friend, or neighbor who has immigrated to the United States and remembers his/her experiences. With the interviewee's permission, tape record the conversation, concentrating on the person's thoughts and ideas. This will provide a record for transcription later.
    * record statistics about the interviewee: subject's name, age, occupation, country of origin, and year of arrival in the United States. Check *www.census.gov* (see Figure 8-11) for government census information about the ethnic group from which the interviewee comes. For example, what is the total population of this group? Where does this ethnic group reside in largest numbers?
    * compile a list of ten additional questions to ask the interviewee. By preparing extra questions, the student should be able to add or change questions as the interview requires or to further flesh out the answers the interviewee makes. (For example, if the person says that he came to the United States to escape the war in his country, ask how he felt about leaving his own country, what it felt like coming to the United States, or if he came against his will. Look at *http://vi.uh.edu/pages/mintz/primary.html* to hear some slave narratives for additional anecdotes.
    * write down word-for-word answers given by the interviewee. (The worksheet in Figure 8-4 can assist in preparing for the interview and evaluating the material following it.)
    * write a concluding paragraph that lets the reader know (a) the general impression of the subject (old-fashioned, assimilated, homesick, still adjusting), (b) what the student thought was the most interesting part of the

Figure 8–11: Census Website

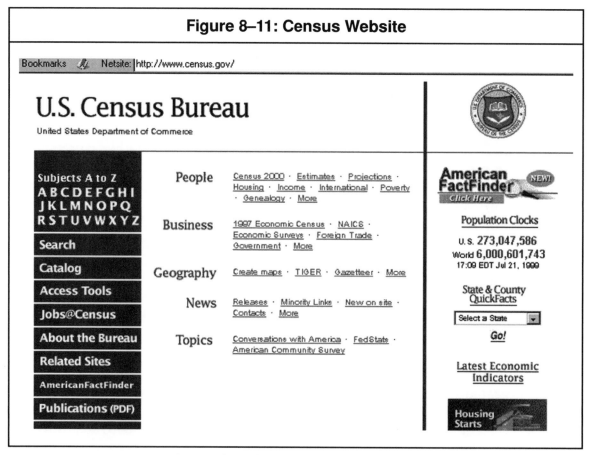

interview, and (c) what the student thinks others can learn (about life, immigration, American society) from reading the interview.

- *find at least three secondary sources on the Internet relating to culture or the historical context of the person being interviewed. Determine some of the customs, religion, art forms, and foods of the nationality of the interviewee. One such site for African American culture might be: *www.scils. rutgers.edu/special/kay/afro.html.*

3. Students will trace their roots.

- Start with their great-grandparents and compile as much of the following information as possible on their parents, grandparents, and great-grandparents: name, relationship, birth date and location, death date and location, marriage date and location, mother's name, father's name, and children's names and birth dates. Record the data on a Family Tree worksheet (see Figure 8-12).

- Draw a family tree identifying their ancestors for three generations (parents, grandparents, great-grandparents) through relatives or other sources. Figure 8-13 has a sample genealogy chart.

- Access some of the genealogical sites on the Internet to see if they can trace ancestors further back in time. For example, if a student's great-great-grandfather came from Italy, see if she can find more information

---

Figure 8–12: Family Tree Worksheet

Fill in the following information:

Name of person _____

Husband _____

Date born _____ in _____

Date died _____ in _____

Wife _____

Date born _____ in _____

Date died _____ in _____

Marriage date _____ in _____

Children	Gender	Birth Date
1. _____	___	_____
2. _____	___	_____
3. _____	___	_____
4. _____	___	_____

---

about him. In addition to general genealogical sites, there are other sites that focus on geographic areas worldwide and on ethnic heritage (see Table 8-3).

- Keep logs of the step-by-step process employed to find information about their ancestors.
- Read books about their ethnic culture. For example, Amy Tan's book *The Joy Luck Club* discusses the experiences of a Chinese mother who immigrated from China and explores her continuing relationship with her daughter. Find accounts of immigrants who entered the United States via Angel Island, the Asian entry point for immigration. Compare and contrast their tales with the stories told by the Asian women in Tan's book. Check the Websites at *www.itp.berkeley.edu/~asam121/angel.html* and *www.fortunecity.com/littleitaly/amalfi/100/angel.htm* for information about Angel Island immigration.

Table 8–3: Specialized Genealogical Websites	
Sample URLs	**Descriptions of Websites**
www.familysearch.org	Church of Jesus Christ of the Latter-Day Saints
www.nara.gov	National Archives and Records Administration
www.archives.ca	Canada
www.archivenet.gov.au/home.html www.naa.gov.au/collect/gen/gene.htm	Australia
www.origins.net/GRO www.open.gov.uk/gros/groshome.html	Scotland
www.nnp.org/dutchlinks.html www.hope.edu/jointarchives/collections	Holland
www.visitbritain.com/activities/wtd%2D9.htm	Great Britain
www.nara.gov/regional/findaids/chirip.html	Chinese heritage
www.genuki.org.uk	United Kingdom and Ireland heritage
www.ccharity.com	African heritage

Activities to Be Used as Follow-up

It is important for students to reflect on what they have learned. A debate or panel presentation on the issue of immigration will provide an opportunity for students to discuss thought-provoking questions related to the research they have just completed. Some follow-up questions might include:

- Do you think the number of immigrants now entering the United States from each of the following areas is too many, too few, or about right—Europe, Latin America, Africa, Asia?
- Do you feel that English only should be used in all public schools, on public signs, in government forms, and for official messages in the United States? Or do you support the use of a second language in some areas to help immigrants participate in education, business, and daily life?
- Should bilingual education be used in the schools? (The CNN Website at *www.cnn.com* provides up-to-the-minute news.)
- Some people say the government should make it more difficult for illegal aliens to get work in the United States by penalizing companies that knowingly hire them. Others oppose such a penalty because it would restrict U.S. businesses too much and limit opportunities for legal immigrants, especially Hispanics. Which view comes closer to your own? Support your viewpoint.

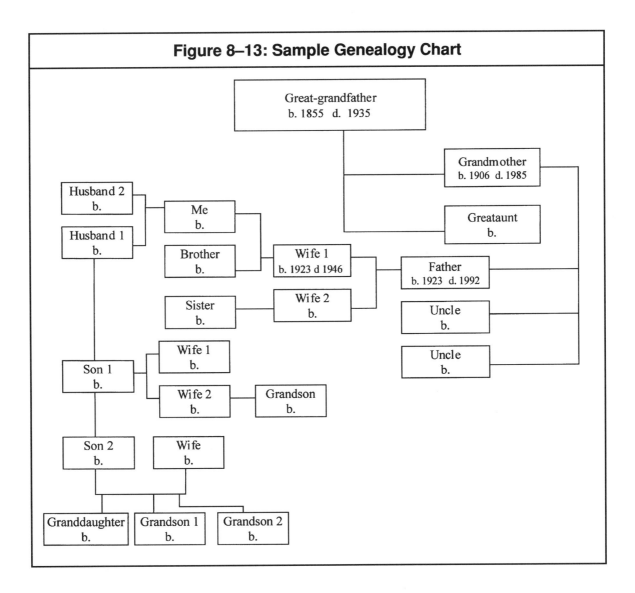

Figure 8–13: Sample Genealogy Chart

- Explain the demographic changes resulting from the Immigration Act of 1965 and consider the following questions: What areas of the world have provided the most immigrants to the United States since passage of the act? What major factors have promoted immigration to the United States from these areas of the world? What effects have the new trends in immigration had on economic opportunity, education, and government services?
- Construct a historical investigation of the factors that led to the Immigration Reform and Control Act of 1986, and examine arguments for and against the legislation and its application. Draw evidence from INS studies, congressional reports, and public opinion polls. How does the increase in immigration in the 1980s compare to that of the early 1900s in terms of the country of origin and size? How did immigration change after the passage of the 1965 and 1991 immigration acts? How did the 1986 act seek to control undocumented immigrants? Does the act offer fair and balanced treatment? To

what extent has the act impacted social services and health care? What is the general perception of the new immigrants toward these laws? To what extent is the "melting pot" analogy applicable today? Is the "salad bowl" metaphor more appropriate? Why?

STEP 5: EVALUATE WHAT WAS LEARNED

Evaluation is an important part of any unit. Some possible evaluation strategies for this unit include:

1. unique presentations. Have students create collages that represent the persons who were interviewed. They should include voice recordings, pictures, and artifacts.
2. panel presentations. Have several students of different ethnic backgrounds form a panel of "immigrants." They will place themselves in the "shoes of the immigrant" based on the information about that person and the culture that they researched.
3. family trees. Students will draw their own family trees and represent them visually with drawings that depict the cultures, such as the homeland locations, typical artifacts from the cultures, and its literature. (Note that there are several family tree software programs, such as Broderbund's *Family Tree Maker,* if students want to delve into this topic in more detail.)

SUMMARY

By combining study of broad ethnic groups with the specific tasks of finding students' roots, this unit has provided an overview of the students' and the United States's ethnic heritage. It is the chance for individual students to appreciate their identity, to take pride in their backgrounds, and to begin to understand each other's similarities and differences. By performing an in-depth study of ethnic groups, including their history, culture, contributions, and current status in the United States, students can develop respect for and acceptance of cultural diversity.

TEACHER EXERCISES: NOW YOU TRY IT...

It is always a good idea to put into practice the ideas that you have just read about. The tasks below will reinforce what you have just learned.

1. Using the unit on Native Peoples or Immigration, try unit activities as a student would: (a) choose one tribe or ethnic group to research; (b) choose at least five activities and try to complete them using the Web; (c) jot down in the social studies part of your notebook any new URLs you discover, bookmark the best ones, and note any special problems, such as slow load time, that might occur (see Figure 1-3). Annotate each URL entry so you can quickly locate it for specific topics.
2. Write journal entries about your experiences exploring these social studies Websites. Answer these questions: How valuable was your Web search in

terms of information gained? What information did the Web provide that was not available at your school?

3. Identify the social studies units you plan to teach in the next six months and explore sites that might provide multimedia resources for each unit. Write all URLs in your Internet notebook with annotations describing the type of information found, grade levels, any URL links, and keywords used to find the sites.

4. With the units on Immigrants or Native Peoples as models, create your own unit:

   - Choose a subject area and write the assignment.
   - Write objectives.
   - Decide what skills you need to teach your students as minilessons.
   - Prepare a timeframe for the unit and structure the time you will spend on the Internet.
   - Decide on sources to be used, including at least two activities on the Web (for example, URLs, collaboration, listservs).
   - Identify and explain the final product for the unit.
   - Determine how you will evaluate students both individually and as part of a group on and off of the Internet.

CONCLUSION

Today, with countries' boundaries changing, new governments being formed, and the balance of power shifting, we need new, up-to-date resources that keep pace with world conditions. There is no set body of knowledge from which to teach; rather, there is a set of ideas and processes that should be taught so that students can make sense of new conditions they will encounter as their community, their state, their nation, and the world change.

The Internet is an effective tool for social studies, but students need certain skills to use it effectively. First, students must have the wisdom to determine whether the Internet is the best tool for the research or whether they should look elsewhere. They must define the search topic and effectively phrase search requests to narrow the search. They must be able to use a variety of search engines, because each will uncover different materials. Students must scan through sources, group them for later analysis, and think of ways to find other resources. Finally, they need to organize and record the material they find.

We have found in our focus on social studies that we, teachers and library media specialists, are no longer isolated in our classrooms or libraries. Teaching students skills about information is as integral to a classroom lesson as the facts we once imparted. "Classrooms without walls" are realities.

In the next chapter, we will focus on active learning in science instruction and how to create units for science topics using the Internet.

REFERENCES

California State Department of Education. 1988. *History–Social Science Framework for California Public Schools, Kindergarten Through Grade Twelve.* Sacramento: California State Department of Education.

National Education Association. 1983. *American Indian/Alaskan Native Education: Quality in the Classroom.* Washington, D.C.: National Education Association.

Piaget, Jean. 1962. *Language and Thought of the Child.* New York: Meridian.

Chapter 9

PROMOTING ACTIVE LEARNING IN THE SCIENCES WITH THE INTERNET

PART 1: IDEAS AND INSIGHTS

OBJECTIVES OF THIS CHAPTER

Many science educators are already using technology in their classes. This chapter will augment their resources and familiarize others with what the Internet can provide in the sciences. At the end of this chapter, educators will be able to:

- state at least five advantages to using the Internet in science education
- explain what is meant by scientific-thinking processes
- identify steps to the research process
- build a science unit that includes the Internet
- identify at least ten science-related Websites

Scientists were among the first to embrace the Internet, using it to share and communicate with each other about their research. They exchanged data over the Internet and collaborated as they analyzed, reviewed, and discussed scientific observations.

As reform takes place in science teaching, teachers, library media specialists, and students have also begun to depend more on computer technology. Goals developed by the National Academy of Sciences include helping students use technology to understand science concepts. For example, they may use probes to gather data, computers to process and manipulate the information, and the Internet to communicate results or ask questions of other scientists.

One of the problems with science education at the K–8 level, however, is that many elementary teachers have limited science education backgrounds themselves. Another problem, especially in low-income areas, is that teachers lack laboratory facilities. Technology can enhance the learning experience by providing cost-effective enrichment that would not be possible using other strategies.

Although the integration of technology into the curriculum in general has been a slow and gradual process, Internet sites for the sciences abound. Organizations such as NASA discuss topics like space exploration or view planets through the Hubble telescope; aquarium Websites allow students to investigate marine biology; and companies like Genentech make exploration of scientific phenomena, such as genetic engineering, available to students. In addition, many universities and school sites offer lesson and unit plans and activities related to the sciences.

Because integrating technology into teaching and learning is now an accepted practice, particularly in science, three general observations should be borne in mind about projects that incorporate technologies:

1. Educational technology that is effectively integrated into the curriculum provides expanded learning opportunities.
2. Research indicates the impact of integrating technology into the curriculum is positive and creates better learning.
3. Integrating computers across the curriculum is allowing teachers to shift from a classroom of lecture/listen to one of hands-on/active learning. This is very important in science, as we will see when we look at science national standards and state framework guidelines.

As a result of new ways of thinking about the teaching of science, goals in science teaching have changed. The chart in Table 9-1 illustrates science teaching of the past and goals for creating science literacy in the future. Part 2 of this chapter contains units of instruction that focus on these future goals for science.

Table 9–1: Comparison of Goals for Science Teaching	
Science Teaching Goals in the 1990s	**Science Teaching Goals in the Year 2000**
Facts	Themes and concepts
Favorite curricula	Balance of life, earth, and physical sciences
Just know it	Learning how we came to know it
Isolated science	Application in technology and implications for society
Textbook, dittos	Inquiry, hands on
Elite	For all students
Individual	Cooperative groups
Text sole source	Many instructional materials: lab equipment, video, software, Internet
Right answer, one way	Flexible solutions
Multiple-choice tests	Authentic assessment

ADVANTAGES OF USING THE INTERNET IN SCIENCE

The Internet fosters an inquiry-based, active approach to teaching science through seven essential features:

1. The Internet's multimedia capabilities, including sound, animation, and visual images, lend themselves to any learning style and stimulate student curiosity and creativity. The quote "A picture is worth a thousand words" is appropriate here, especially for young children who are trying to make sense of scientific phenomena.

2. The diversity of science resources on the Internet to which teachers have access makes it possible for students to connect with scientists, conduct their own research, gather data from Websites, and publish the results online. This hands-on approach not only generates more enthusiasm for studying science than ever before but also diminishes dependence on textbooks. This is important because the body of knowledge in science doubles every six months, and information in texts may be outdated before the books even reach students' hands.

3. The Web offers students the chance to take "virtual field trips" into areas of science that do not come alive through textbooks. For example, at the NASA site *www.jpl.nasa.gov/sl9*, children can view the Shoemaker-Levy Comet and the results of its collision with Jupiter. Exploring the solar system via actual photos of the planets taken by the Hubble telescope, looking at photos of whales crashing into the water, and viewing snapshots of underwater creatures and treasures increases students' interest in the study of science.

4. Using the Internet in the science curriculum helps build critical thinking. It emphasizes quality of understanding rather than quantities of memorized facts, and exposes students to concepts in many contexts. The Internet offers students the ability to experience and explore "what ifs" in situations not normally accessible. The result is a set of learning skills that has applications beyond the classroom. For example, at the WhaleNet site (see Figure 9-1), K–12 classes gather and utilize data by observing the migration patterns and behavior of whales. As a result, they learn how to pose questions, collect and use data, and communicate their results.

5. Students can work together in groups, with teachers assuming the role of collaborative or facilitative scientist. This may be a difficult role for teachers, especially at the elementary-school level where teacher training in, and knowledge of, science is not extensive. The Internet can help here too. Sites such as *www.nasm.edu/ceps* provide teachers with science help such as background information about concepts, and lesson plans to teach them. Indeed, there are sites on the World Wide Web that enable elementary-school students to track weather conditions around the globe, to record temperatures and precipitation for cities at the same latitude to determine weather patterns, or to track tornadoes or earthquakes. Maps and charts help students identify where these weather phenomena take place worldwide.

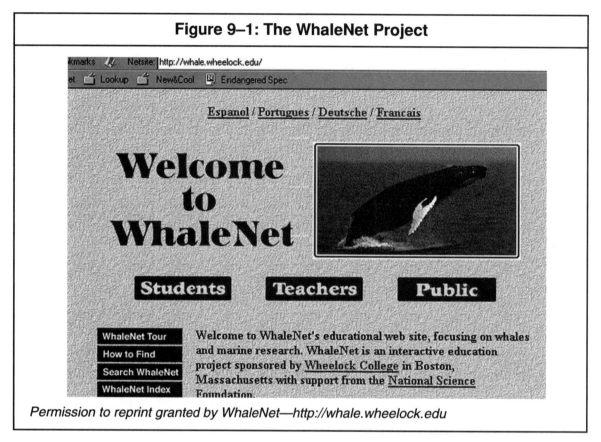

Figure 9–1: The WhaleNet Project

Permission to reprint granted by WhaleNet—http://whale.wheelock.edu

6. Telementoring programs, available via the Internet, enable students (and teachers) to get answers from experts. After all, one of the Internet's first uses was to keep scientists in touch with scientific discoveries. Why not use the Internet to teach "budding" scientists? We want students to pose problems, attempt to solve those problems, and persuade others of their results. The "Ask an Astronomer" site at *http://umbra.nascom.nasa.gov/spartan/ask_ astronomers. html* provides that help.

7. It is easy for classes around the globe to work collaboratively on projects using the Internet. A telecommunications project on measuring shadows, organized by Global School Network (*www.gsn.org*), offered one of the first collaborations among schools worldwide. Students in different time zones looked at and measured their shadows at 12 o'clock noon and used the results to calculate the circumference of the world. This collaborative project was fun, incorporated science and math concepts, and used language arts skills for communicating the results to different school sites.

SCIENTIFIC-THINKING PROCESSES

As educators, we enable our students to become independent learners. The ability to use scientific-thinking processes is a good start in that direction. These processes will be included as part of the activities that students encounter in the units of study in Part 2 of this chapter.

Scientific-thinking processes comprise eight basic areas: observing, communicating, comparing/contrasting, ordering, categorizing, relating, inferring, and applying. The checklist below will help students organize their thoughts and help create inquiry-based classrooms:

1. *Observe the world and construct patterns.* To obtain knowledge, students use all of their senses to understand the characteristics of objects and their interactions. Students might contemplate:
    *   What do we see?
    *   What do we hear?
    *   What does it feel like?
    *   What does it taste or smell like?

    For example, they might compile information about the size and shape of Mars, or they might point out properties of phenomena.

2. *Communicate to convey ideas through social interaction.* Communication may be silent, oral, written, and/or pictorial. Students might:
    *   draw a picture of what they see
    *   plot information they gather on a graph
    *   summarize their findings from an investigation and present them to the class
    *   tell others what they see
    *   write up what they see so someone else can replicate it

3. *Compare and contrast concepts.* Students systematically examine objects and events in terms of similarities and differences. Comparisons might include sensory, weight, capacity, quantity, or linear comparisons. For example, by comparing the known to the unknown, students will gain knowledge about the unknown. Students could look at objects to determine:
    *   How they are alike?
    *   How they are different?
    *   Which is larger/smaller, wetter/drier, heavier/lighter, smoother/rougher?

4. *Order to create patterns of sequence.* Students compile and order observed and compared data to gain knowledge of principles and laws. Students could ask:
    *   Which came first, second, last?
    *   What is the range of information gathered?
    *   Where in the order would they place this/these?

5. *Organize into patterns of groups and classes.* Students classify, group, sequence, and gather data to gain knowledge of principles and laws. Students might create patterns to determine:
    *   On what basis would they group several objects?
    *   What is another way in which these objects can be categorized?
    *   What grouping best reflects the evolutionary history of these items?

6. *Relate principles about interactions.* Students can weave together concrete and abstract ideas to test or explain phenomena, formulate experimental

hypotheses, experiment, and control and manipulate variables. Students might ask:

- What factors caused this event to take place?
- What is the relationship between . . . (for example, the coloration of an animal, environment, and predators)?

An activity might require them to state a hypothesis that can be tested or design a study to compare—for example, the migration habits of the humpback and blue whales.

7. *Infer ideas that are remote in time and space.* Students bring together a variety of information compiled from experimental and observational data. They synthesize, analyze, generalize, recognize and predict patterns, and formulate explanatory models and theories. This process leads to predictive explanations for simple and complex phenomenon. Students might want to know:
   - How can it be explained?
   - What arguments can be given to support predictions?
   - What can be inferred from information that has been gathered?
   - How would . . . be determined?

8. *Apply processes by which knowledge is used.* Students bring together acquired knowledge and experience so that they can invent, create, and solve problems. Students must apply knowledge and principles to their daily lives. They might ask:
   - Who can build a . . . that will . . . ?
   - How did different lines of evidence confirm . . . ?
- What factors must be weighed and addressed in order to . . .

Many of the processes above will be necessary as students follow the steps to undertake their own scientific investigations using the research process.

STEPS TO THE RESEARCH PROCESS

The scientific processes above can be used to solve problems, even those in our daily lives. Often, too, scientific investigations lend themselves well to group work. Here are seven steps students should take as they explore scientific topics:

1. *State the problem.* A problem cannot be solved until researchers know exactly what it is. Identifying the problem involves questioning. Children should ask questions about a problem or issue that they can see needs a solution, starting with: What problem needs solving? What data and insight are required to understand the main question? What are the smaller questions that will help answer the main question? What does the researcher already know? What is missing? Once students have answered these questions, they may want to form a hypothesis, a possible solution to the problem. Figure 9-2 provides a format for stating the problem.

2. *Research the problem.* Researching the problem takes planning. Students begin developing strategies to obtain the information they need to solve the problem. They might ask questions such as: Where might the best informa-

Figure 9–2: Stating the Problem

The Research Process

Answer the following questions to identify the problem to be solved:

1. What problem do you want to solve? _____

    _____

2. What information do you need to understand the problem? _____

    _____

3. What is the main question that needs to be asked? _____

    _____

4. What are some smaller questions that you will need to answer before you can answer the main questions?

    _____

    _____

5. What do you already know about the problem? _____

    _____

6. What information do you still need to gather to come up with a solution to the problem?

    _____

    _____

7. What sources will you use to gather your data? _____

    _____

8. Formulate a hypothesis or solution to the problem based on your evidence.

    _____

tion lie? Which resources are reliable? How can biased sources be identified and a balanced view developed? When should the Internet be used? Can technology be used to organize findings? Students should identify sources of information including books, magazines, and Websites, or ask experts, teachers, and parents to answer questions on the topic. Students must examine the possibilities for solving the problem by eliminating poor choices and considering likely ones.

3. *Gather data.* While students are researching the problem, they should be collecting information that they will consider later. The data they gather should form the basis for testing the hypothesis. Working in groups, students can divide the sources of information they plan to access, with each student being responsible for one source, conducting the research, and reconvening with the group to evaluate the data later in the process.

4. *Organize the collected data.* As their research progresses, students should be writing down their findings. Students should set aside a portion of their science notebooks to organize the collected data so it is readily available. For example, they can label a page with the problem name; or identify columns with the following headings: Sources, Citation (as in URL, book cite), Data, Evaluation of Data. Figure 9-3 provides a sample notebook page.

5. *Synthesize the collected information.* By selecting the best data from the many sources from which it was collected, students must now decide whether they have enough data to support or refute their hypothesis and whether they see patterns emerging. The "evaluation" column of the notebook they have prepared will help here.

6. *Evaluate the information collected.* Students should work together to determine whether the group has enough information and whether it is accurate and unbiased. At this stage they may ask questions such as: Has the problem been solved? Was the hypothesis incorrect? Did the experiment fail? Is more research needed? If students determine that more research is necessary, they should ask: What was wrong with the original hypothesis? Was the experiment flawed? Was poor, inaccurate, or biased information gathered? At this point, they may need to re-evaluate their original hypothesis, gather additional data, and test the new hypothesis.

7. *Report the findings of the investigation.* Students now identify the solution to the problem. For example, they can report to their classmates, publish the results on the Web, communicate results to another class via the Internet, create a visual representation of the solution, or hold a debate outlining the issues. Whatever method is chosen, the product should offer new insights into the problem.

Using the Internet lends itself well to this step-by-step approach, especially during the planning, gathering, and evaluation phases. It may be necessary to repeat the research process to gain the insights necessary. Students will follow all of these steps in the sample science units in Part 2 of the chapter.

Figure 9–3: Sample Data Collection Sheet

Data Collection

Sources	Citation (URL, book cite)	Data Collected	Evaluation of Data

PART 2: PRACTICAL APPLICATIONS

There are many types of information for science classes on the Internet. Several examples are listed. These may serve as models for incorporating the Internet into your own science projects.

SCIENCE PROJECTS USING THE INTERNET

Collaborative activities, research from Websites, answers from experts, and visits to scientific laboratories are ways the Internet can be integrated into your science curriculum.

COLLABORATIONS

Students are usually enthusiastic about communicating with students from other areas. Using the Internet, students can exchange not only written communication but also voice recordings and images. This avenue provides an authentic audience for student communication.

Figure 9–4: Pond Water Project

Water Sample Project

Below are pictures taken at Lincoln Park in Jersey City, New Jersey during a field trip to collect w; samples and looking at them under a microscope, we sent e-mail messages to our project partners Africa to discuss the project and our findings.

We are from Mrs. Roger's class at P.S. 22 in Jersey City.

Click here to see a picture of the lake. We calculated the lake to have a circumference of 284 feet. collected the samples on our map.

Printed with permission of the Trustees of the Stevens Institute of Technology for the Center for Improved Engineering and Science Education (CIESE) at Stevens Institute of Technology, Hoboken, N.J. Copyright 1999.

Activity 1: Study of Pond Water

Website *http://njnie.dl.stevens-tech.edu/curriculum/water.html* gives examples of these types of projects. Once elementary-level students gather data from their own locale, they compare the data via the Internet with a "keypal," a student from another class. The goal of this type of exchange is (1) to add to the body of knowledge of the students, (2) to involve them in active independent study, and (3) to motivate greater interest in and involvement with the experience of learning science. Assets beyond science are the involvement of the students in writing (language arts), and learning about different cultures and daily life of different societies (social studies). It is important, however, to keep in mind when choosing a keypal classroom that the information received should have content that cannot be obtained locally—the physical conditions at the two sites should be different, for example, in altitude, latitude, air quality, or the ecosystem. See Figure 9-4 for an example.

Activity 2: Study of Temperature Around the World

This is another good collaborative project, because students can contact classrooms that have very different climates (see Figure 9-5). In this project, early-elementary-school students look at how average daily temperature is affected by a location's proximity to the equator. Students use measurement, conversion of units, latitude and longitude, and graphing (math skills). They write e-mail to collaborating schools (language arts), locate different school sites on a map (social studies), take temperatures and convert them to Celsius or Fahrenheit (science/math), and graph average

---

Figure 9–5: World Temperature Project

Global Sun / Temperature Project

Hi. Welcome to the Global Temperature Project Page!

The purpose of this project is to see how average daily temperature and hours of sunlight are effected by how close y< the equator. The project will begin on November 17th and run through December 12th. In order to find out about this all over the world are taking the temperature at noon during the week of December 1. Each school will then send their (along with their schools latitude and longitude) to all the other participating schools and we will post this data on our c maps. We will then be able to see if there is a relationship between closeness to the equator and temperature and sunli

 Data

Week 1 (12/1-12/5)

View	To View the entire database from week 1
Print	To Print the data or view in sorted format
tempdat1.exe	To download an Excel file (instructions)
tempproj97b.txt	To view/save the Text file (instructions)

Printed with permission of the Trustees of the Stevens Institute of Technology for the Center for Improved Engineering and Science Education (CIESE) at Stevens Institute of Technology, Hoboken, N.J. Copyright 1999.

Figure 9–6: Stowaway Project

The Stowaway Adventure

General Overview

Teacher Prep

Click here to see the GREAT work done by the students at the Children's Institute.

Printed with permission of the Trustees of the Stevens Institute of Technology for the Center for Improved Engineering and Science Education (CIESE) at Stevens Institute of Technology, Hoboken, N.J. Copyright 1999.

---

weekly temperatures at different latitudes to see if a pattern exists (math). This type of project introduces global understanding and sensitivity—virtually impossible without electronic communication. This project and similar ones are identified at *http://k12science.ati.stevens-tech.edu/curriculum/temp1.*

PROJECTS THAT EXPLORE WEBSITES

Science has been one of the first subject areas to embrace the use of Web technology. As noted in Chapter 1, there are many types of sites available: educational sites maintained by schools and universities; sites hosted by organizations, such as the Monterey Bay Aquarium and the Franklin Museum; sites created by the government, such as the NASA site; and commercial sites, such as the Discovery Channel.

Activity 1: Public Domain Databases on the Web

In this project, students pretend they are stowaways on a ship traveling toward an unknown destination. With the help of Ocean Weather, Inc., which updates the weather and water conditions several times a day, students try to determine the location of the port to which the ship is bound. They use sequential reports of location to calculate the speed and direction of the ship and estimate the time of arrival at the port. Check Website *http://njnie.dl.stevens-tech.edu/curriculum/oceans/stowaway.html* for this and other projects. Figure 9-6 depicts the project page.

Activity 2: Tracking the Sun

This activity uses the wealth of information on the Internet about space, telescopes, and space stations, to name a few. Images of the sun can be studied from the National Oceanographic & Atmospheric Administration's site at *www.globe.gov*. This site shows sunspots as well as reports on positions of the sun's surface. Since sunspots move, students can calculate the rate of the sun's rotation (about 13.3 degrees per Earth day). Figure 9-7 shows a screen from the Globe project.

VISITING SCIENTIFIC LABORATORIES

At the high-school level, visiting scientific laboratories can provide valuable information on rapidly changing fields like molecular biology. Rutgers University has developed tutorials on modern genetics and enables students to explore challenging questions in this field. The Morgan site at *http://morgan.rutgers.edu* will lead students to genome databases and challenge projects.

ASK AN EXPERT

Another way to involve students in science is to have an "expert" associated with the project. Since teachers cannot be expected to have high-level scientific expertise

---

Figure 9–7: Globe Project

GLOBE Schools Login | Learn About GLOBE

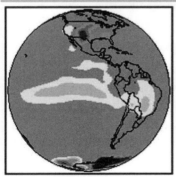

GLOBE Bulletin:
GLOBE Teachers Top 10,000
On June 18, 1999, the Global Learning and Observations to Benefit the Environment (GLOBE) Program reached a major milestone as the number of educators who have completed GLOBE training surpassed 10,000. ...

GLOBE Stars:
GLOBE Stars in the Czech Republic
Nearly 200 students from 20 GLOBE schools throughout the Czech Republic participated in the country's second GLOBE Games April 9-11,

for certain topics, a consultant can provide valuable insight. Look for sites that integrate an Ask-a-Scientist feature as part of the project; many scientists are willing to act as "the expert." Try *www-hpcc.astro.washington.edu/scied/sciask.html* or *http://njnie.dl.stevens-tech.edu/curriculum/aska.html*.

SAMPLE UNIT PLANS

Two unit plans will illustrate using Internet resources in science. These units are designed to transition from a textbook, skill-based classroom to a multisource, active approach to learning. The first unit focuses on Endangered Species, specifically whales. This topic is an important part of study from the third grade forward. For example, in the third grade students study how living things live in habitats and share their environments with other living things to form ecosystems. In the fourth through sixth grade, students learn about animal adaptations that enable them to survive in specific environments and how populations become endangered and even extinct. In grades seven through twelve, students look at ecosystems, specifically the problems posed by the human species due to rapid increase in human population, depletion of resources, pollution, and widespread manipulation of populations of other species. The unit presented here could be taught at a seventh- or eighth-grade level, although many of the activities can be adapted for other grade levels.

The second unit, on Alternative Energy Sources, designed for high-school students, adapts well to state framework competencies in a course of study in the physical sciences. This unit builds upon discussion of energy sources that begins in fourth grade and proceeds through concepts of alternative energy sources in earth science in grades 6–9, and about the development of long-range energy sources for future generations in grades 9–12.

As part of each unit, students will have to use scientific thinking processes for scientific inquiry, as discussed in Part 1 of the chapter. Here are the steps for the units.

1. Apply framework standards—what should be taught?
2. Identify general goals and specific objectives.
3. Gather materials.
4. Plan for individual and small group investigations (elementary unit).
5. Introduce the unit.
6. Create sample activities.
7. Evaluate what was learned.

UNIT 1 (ELEMENTARY LEVEL): ENDANGERED SPECIES: FOCUS ON WHALES

Incorporating environmental education into the curriculum, although typically in the area of science, really has a cross-curricular impact. Instilling civic responsibilities, for example, is a goal promoted in most social studies curricula, and some see the roots of environmental problems as stemming from the basic values upon which society has been built. Since global change is only as good as its smallest players, it is important to instill an environmental ethic into our students.

Scientifically speaking, we want students to identify a real problem, hypothesize, collect data, formulate a step-by-step procedure, and come up with workable results. Thus, this unit is written around the topic of endangered species, specifically species of whales.

STEPS FOR DESIGNING A WEB-BASED SCIENCE UNIT

This unit provides a model to help you construct your own science lessons. Based on state framework goals, its activities allow students to apply skills in scientific problem solving. During the unit, students will become familiar with a variety of Internet resources in environmental science, and they will compile enough information so that they understand different positions on the endangered species issue.

Step 1: Apply Framework Standards—What Should Be Taught?

Many schools have shifted emphasis from teacher- to learner-centered classrooms, resulting in learning that is more active and less authority dependent. Educational strategies that enhance student learning include cooperative learning, debating, peer projects, and actively collaborative endeavors and are alternatives to lectures. Technology itself both mandates active learning and assists it. This unit uses the goals in the California Science Framework (CSDE, 1987a) as its basis and looks to the *Science Model Curriculum Guide* (CSDE, 1987) to define science literacy. This latter document states that science education should strive to:

1. develop positive attitudes about science and encourage students to take an active interest in natural phenomena and technological achievements.
2. teach fundamental concepts of science and how the application of these concepts affects daily lives.
3. help students learn techniques that comprise the scientific method to validate knowledge and to develop thinking skills for lifelong learning.
4. instill attitudes and knowledge about science so students can live as informed citizens in a technologically advanced world.

These points boil down to the concept that a science program should have three sides: knowledge, problem solving, and people (see Figure 9-8).

In the elementary and middle school science curricula, students must:

- be involved in classroom activities that are diverse and exciting
- have multiple opportunities to acquire skills and content through active participation
- work together in collaborative groups searching for solutions to given or selected problems
- use a variety of instructional materials, including lab equipment, reference books, trade books, and relevant educational technology, to facilitate active learning and construction of new knowledge
- employ scientific-thinking processes

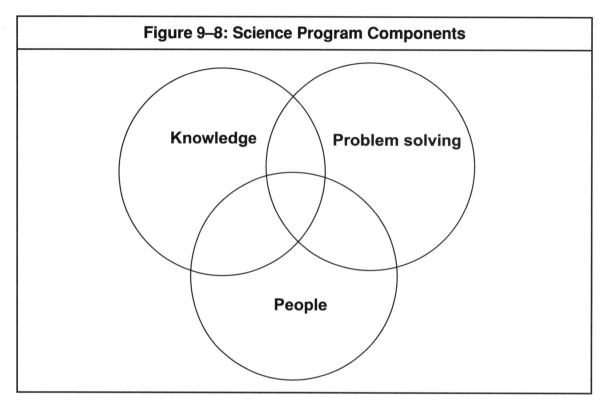

Figure 9–8: Science Program Components

- have opportunities to discuss ethical issues as they arise in the presentation of science

Step 2: Identify General Goals and Specific Objectives

Use the goals and specific objectives that follow as a basis for the content and skills covered in this unit. Goals for learning about endangered species in general and whales specifically should include:

GOALS

By the end of this unit, students will be able to:

- discuss the concept of whales as an endangered species
- perform research via the Internet on whales and other endangered species
- identify issues and articulate a position regarding endangered species
- work cooperatively in teams where each student has a well-defined role within the team

OBJECTIVES

This unit will provide content and strategies that achieve the objectives so that students will be able to:

- identify physical characteristics of several endangered whales
- compare lengths of whales and explore proportional relationships

- give a definition of endangered species
- create a plan of action to protect an endangered species
- identify types of endangered whales
- trace the route of a tagged whale
- write a poem or story about a whale.

The objectives are based on scientific-thinking processes, and the activities on endangered species that follow will practice these processes.

Step 3: Gather Materials

Search engines described in Chapter 2 and Appendix A (such as Yahoo!, AltaVista, Excite) will enable students to search for information on issues about endangered species and whales as mammals on the endangered list. To begin Internet searches, you might have students use the term ENDANGERED SPECIES along with WHALE as keywords to limit their topic. Lessons should not be based on data obtained from only one source; you will want to augment the Internet sources with other materials.

WEB SITES RELATED TO ENDANGERED SPECIES AND WHALES

In this unit students will look at Websites that offer ideas on how species become extinct, what humans can do to fight the problem, as well as facts about specific types of whales. As you check out the Websites in Table 9-2, remember to add useful ones to your Internet science notebook. The Websites in Table 9-2 include some established by educational institutions, ones hosted by commercial enterprises, others maintained by organizations, and some created by students. As students review the sites, make sure that they watch for bias, based on the host group's attitudes toward endangered species. Figure 9-9 provides an example of a Web page highlighting student projects on endangered species.

Step 4: Plan for Individual and Small Group Investigations

As students work on the activities for the unit, they will be working in small groups on one endangered species. Figure 9-10 provides a checklist that students can employ to start their investigations, and below are eight questions students should pose among themselves as they begin their group work.

1. What idea(s) do we plan to investigate? Why?
2. What form(s) will the final product take? Note that the teacher may choose to determine what the final product will be or provide alternatives from which the groups may choose.
3. Who are some possible intended audiences? The audience for the project should be a real-life one (names and addresses of contact persons in organized groups on local, state or national level).
4. How will we get started? What types of information or data will we need to begin the project? Where can we find that information?
5. What materials do we need, and how will we cite our sources? (See Chapter 1 for information on citing Internet sources.)

Table 9-2: Endangered Species and Whale Web Resources	
Sample URLs	**Description of Websites**
http://curry.edschool.Virginia.EDU/go/Whales/Contents.HTML	School site that studied whales using the Internet; thematic unit available
www.discovery.com	TV Discovery Channel on many animal topics
http://physics.helsinki.fi/whale/education/children.html	Whale-watching children's Web page
www.whaletimes.org/whakids.htm	Kids' page on whale information
www.seaworld.org/educational_programs/education.html	Whale and marine life information educational programs
www.webcom.com/~wcwww/iwcwho.html	Whale adoption program
http://whale.wheelock.edu	Extensive information on marine animals, lesson plans, activities, stories, and more
www.fws.gov/r9endspp	U.S. Fish and Wildlife service containing topics on endangered species
www.whaleclub.com/community/penpal_jump.html	Whale penpal site, part of Whale Club

6. In what ways do we plan to get new information:
   * viewing television, videos, films (which?)
   * interviewing people (who?)
   * observing/collecting data (what?)
   * surveying (who?)
   * communicating with others (who?)
   * other (specify)
7. What materials and equipment will we need?
8. What tasks will we need to accomplish? List all tasks in the order necessary to complete the project. Note a date for completion.

STEP 5: INTRODUCE THE UNIT

The unit encompasses two parts: (1) endangered species, and (2) whales. As you introduce students to the project, you will want to focus on the broad concept of endangered species and what the words mean. Once you have explained and discussed this topic, you can then have students conduct a more in-depth study of various types of endangered species. The class can also research one endangered species, such as the whales that are the focus of this unit. Students will participate in a cooperative-learning activity that requires Internet searches and team-oriented classroom

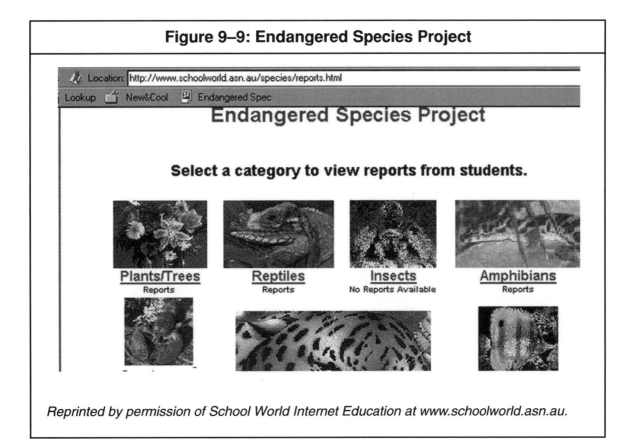

Figure 9–9: Endangered Species Project

Location: http://www.schoolworld.asn.au/species/reports.html

Lookup   New&Cool   Endangered Spec

Endangered Species Project

Select a category to view reports from students.

Plants/Trees
Reports

Reptiles
Reports

Insects
No Reports Available

Amphibians
Reports

Reprinted by permission of School World Internet Education at www.schoolworld.asn.au.

presentations on the research topic. There are two overarching activities:

1. Working in groups, students will present their findings about an endangered species to the class. To prepare for this, students will have to:
   - organize the key ideas on their animals.
   - extract and summarize ideas on key issues about their endangered species, such as why the species became endangered.
   - formulate positions to present to their audience and propose solutions. Students will design several new methods to protect an animal species from endangerment. They will also propose preventative measures to guard against future endangerment of nonthreatened species.
   - plan the presentation, indicating each team member's role.
   - synthesize research and prepare the final product explaining the scientific, regulatory, and public policy issues.
   - communicate the research results orally in an effective way. Students' presentation outlines should contain:
     — characteristics of the animal
     (*Note*: Species of plants are also endangered and can be used as examples.)
     — the main causes of its becoming endangered
     — the effects of its becoming threatened

Figure 9–10: Investigating an Endangered Species

Group Names: _____

Project Completion Date: _____

Directions: Choose a scribe to take notes on the group's investigation of its endangered animal. As a group fill in the information requested below. Include this sheet with your final project.

1. The endangered species we want to investigate is _____

   _____

2. We will gather data on our endangered animal from these sources:

   _____

   _____

3. The action we want to take to protect our endangered species is

   _____

4. The group that we want to take action to protect our endangered species is

   _____

5. The evidence we will use to convince people to take action is

   _____

   _____

6. We will contact _____

to learn more about our endangered animal.

7. We will need to do the following tasks to complete our project:
   A. _____
   B. _____
   C. _____
   D. _____
   E. _____

— regulations currently in effect to protect endangered species
— actions they want their audience to take to protect their species
— criteria the audience should refer to in making its decision

2. Each group should write a letter to the appropriate political body, such as their state legislator, city council, or the Environmental Protection Agency (EPA), requesting a specific action to protect an endangered species. The letter should include:
   • facts stating what the problem is about the endangered species
   • a group position on the issue
   • the action: a hypothesis on how the problem can be corrected
   • information to illustrate that other animals have been protected or saved from extinction by their plan or similar ones

Step 6: Create Sample Activities

The sample activities that follow will enable students to obtain the information they need to create the final presentations and write the follow-up letters.

ACTIVITIES TO INTRODUCE THE UNIT

At the beginning of the unit, it is important to draw upon students' prior knowledge and teach them any new vocabulary necessary to understand concepts discussed throughout the unit. To provide background on endangered species and to assess student information and attitudes, have students:

• answer the following questions: What does endangered species mean? How do humans cause problems for nature? (Discuss how humans take wildlife for granted.) Why is it important to protect endangered species? What can be done to protect endangered species? Have students visit the U.S. Fish and Wildlife Service Website at *www.fws.gov/r9endspp/endspp.html* to garner background for the topic and for answers to these and other questions.
• complete the Anticipation Guide in Figure 9-11 to assess their prior knowledge. At the end of the unit, discuss the same questions to see if students have changed their minds about any of the statements.
• brainstorm a list of interesting questions about whales: Should whales be kept in captivity? Does water pollution hurt whales? What types of whales are on the endangered species list? The Website at *www.scholastic.com/network* provides postings of a marine biologist to help with the list.
• divide into groups of four or five. Have each group compile a list of endangered species and write the list on butcher paper to present to the class. Have students identify endangered species in their own state. The Website sponsored by the U.S. Fish and Wildlife Service at *www.fws.gov/r9endspp/endspp.html* is a starting point (see Figure 9-12).
• from a combined list, each group will choose an animal to research. See Figure 9-13 for an illustration of the endangered Bow whale at *www.schoolworld.asn.au/species/bowhale.html*.

Figure 9–11: Anticipation Guide for Endangered Species

Directions: Before you begin the unit on endangered species, check those statements below that you think are true. Be ready to explain your choices.

True   **False**

1. An endangered species is an animal or plant that might become extinct.

2. Humans are mainly responsible for animals becoming endangered.

3. As a student, I can help protect an endangered species.

4. Protecting endangered species is helpful to humans.

5. Protecting an endangered spotted owl is more important than allowing loggers to cut down forests.

6. All whales are endangered species.

7. The government worries about protecting endangered species.

8. There are more than 100 types of endangered species.

9. Whales are better cared for in Sea World than in the ocean.

10. If an animal becomes extinct, it could affect other animals.

- identify key words and concepts to use in an Internet search about an endangered whale.

ACTIVITIES TO BE USED DURING THE UNIT

Depending on the time allotted for the unit, have each group choose between five and ten tasks from the following list of seventeen activites. The first set of activities focuses on endangered species as a group, including problems, issues, and actions. The second set addresses the whale as one type of endangered species. A number of activities is included because there will not be information to complete each activity

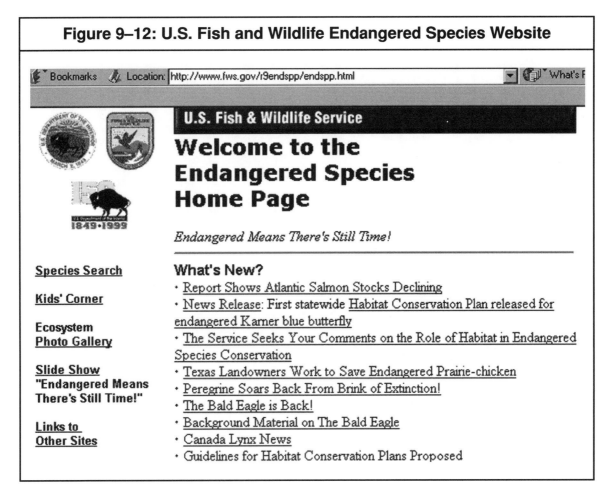

Figure 9–12: U.S. Fish and Wildlife Endangered Species Website

for each animal. Groups must include one language arts and one math activity, and each group member is responsible for Web research for at least one activity. Students should evaluate all information they retrieve for bias, relevance, timeliness, and credibility.

Endangered Species Activities. Students will:

1. create historical timelines of actions taken to protect endangered species. Check Web Site *www.worldbook.com* for information.
2. research the Endangered Species Act at *www.fws.gov/r9endspp/endspp.html* and as a class discuss some of its provisions.
3. survey a variety of sources by looking at governmental, nongovernmental, and commercial Websites to assess varying opinions on the issue of endangered species. They will retrieve information from at least five sources on their whales. (See Table 9-2 for a list of Websites.)
4. list in their resource logs the facts retrieved from five sources, and personal responses to those facts. For example, students will identify specific factors both natural and human that contribute to a species becoming endangered;

Figure 9–13: Example of Endangered Bow Whale

Bowhead Whale
Source Unknown
Photographer Unknown

Description:

The Bowhead Whale grows up to twenty metres in length.

Reprinted by permission of School World Internet Education at www.schoolworld.asn.au.

explain specific actions that have been taken to preserve a species; explain the relationship between habitat destruction and species endangerment; predict the effect on the ecosystem of removing a particular animal from the food web.

Whale Activities. Students will:

1. identify some of the physical characteristics of their whales, then choose one other type of whale and compare and contrast the two. Draw pictures of the whales they are researching. Good information can be obtained at Website *www.seaworld.org.*
2. based on the physical characteristics, write poems from the point of view of someone observing the whale.

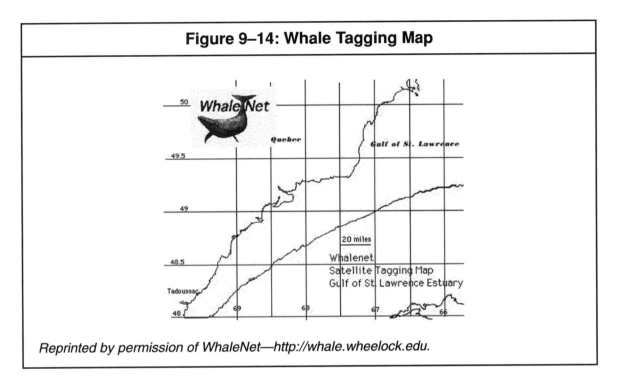

Figure 9–14: Whale Tagging Map

Reprinted by permission of WhaleNet—http://whale.wheelock.edu.

3. choose a few facts about their whales and write coherent paragraphs in their journals that synthesize some of the facts.

4. discuss the importance of a whale's habitat. Design habitats for their whales.

5. create math word problems, such as the following: How long will it take the gray whale that travels 6 mph (9.6 km) to travel the 5,000 miles (8,000 kilometers) from the Arctic to Mexico?

6. participate in or review whale-tagging experiments. At *http://whale.wheelock. edu*, scientists have tagged whales and followed their habitat use, range of movements, and return locations by satellite. Graph the route of tagged whales using the whale-tagging map (see Figure 9-14). What conclusions can be reached about the whales' movements using this data?

7. research the question: Should whales be in captivity? Contrast two Websites for bias, such as the Sea World Web page at *www.seaworld.com* or one created by an environmentalist organization like Greenpeace *www.greenpeace. org.*

8. write to obtain more information on whales at *http://curry.edschool. Virginia. EDU/go/Whales* or contact a marine scientist at *http://whale.wheelock.edu.* For example, how can citizens help protect whale habitats?

9. choose stories about whales and retell the plots in journal paragraphs. The stories should contain the five Ws (who, did what, where, when, why). Some examples include newspaper articles and "A Day on a Whale Watch," an interactive story at *http://whale.wheelock.edu.*

10. create their own "whale tales." See Figure 9-15 for an example.

11. adopt whales to help protect them and their habitats. Contact the Website at

---

Figure 9–15: Whale Stories

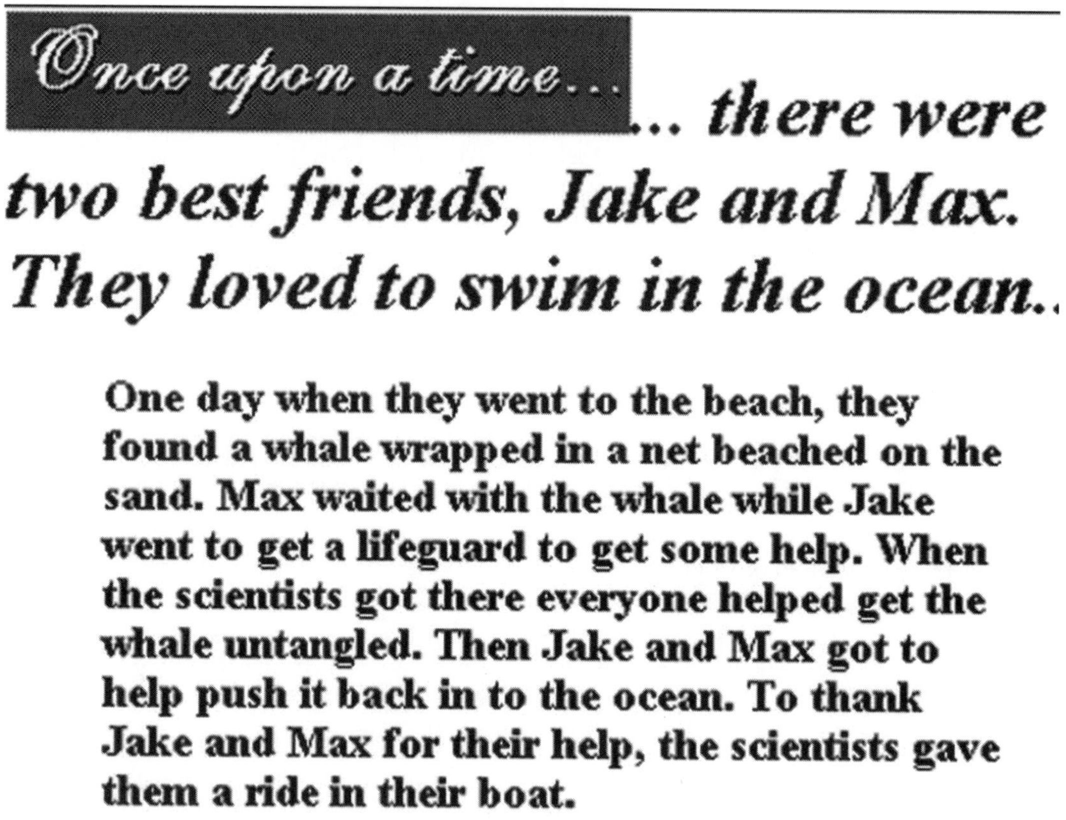

Once upon a time... *... there were two best friends, Jake and Max. They loved to swim in the ocean..*

One day when they went to the beach, they found a whale wrapped in a net beached on the sand. Max waited with the whale while Jake went to get a lifeguard to get some help. When the scientists got there everyone helped get the whale untangled. Then Jake and Max got to help push it back in to the ocean. To thank Jake and Max for their help, the scientists gave them a ride in their boat.

Reprinted by permission of WhaleTimes—www.whaletimes.org

---

www.webcom.com/~iwcwww/whale_adoption/waphome.html for more information.

12. join a listserv so they can collaborate with another class researching whales. Join WhaleNet Pals at *http://whale.wheelock.edu/archives*.

13. write and illustrate stories about the whales they researched to be placed in a class book with other whale tales.

ACTIVITIES TO BE USED AS FOLLOW-UP

As an extension activity resulting from their research, the class will participate in a debate. Groups will:

1. Represent one of the following:
   - environmentalists who are trying to protect endangered species
   - the fishing industry that makes its livelihood from fishing for whales (this group could also be hunters, depending on the species chosen)
   - attendants who work with the fish and mammals at a theme park, such as

Sea World (for other species, this group could also be zookeepers or attendants at wildlife parks)
- the average "Jane Public," who uses and misuses the environment and nature. Some examples of this group could include: (a) concerned citizens who tried to save Humphrey the Whale on the beach in San Francisco, (b) buyers or wearers of fur coats or ivory jewelry, (c) people who recycle, and (d) citizens who clean up the beaches on Earth Day.

2. Defend their group's position in the debate. As part of their presentation, they must:
- create and display a poster or collage that represents their position visually
- explain advantages of their position
- refute challenges to their position from other groups
- cite Web sources using correct procedure (see chapter 1 for more details)

3. Choose activities from the list of sample activities to provide the group with information for the debate on one endangered species, for example, one type of whale. The activities should enable them to understand the issues surrounding endangered species.

Step 6: Evaluate What Was Learned

Students are assessed on their ability to analyze and synthesize information into understandable and scientifically defensible presentations. The final products should include the title, a brief description of the product, and the amount of time students worked on the project. The questions below represent a sampling for evaluating students' final projects in the unit.

PROCESS

The following questions will help evaluate the process students used to create the final product.

1. *focusing on the problem*. Did students clearly define the topic so that they investigated relatively specific problems within a larger area of study—for example, whales within the topic of endangered species?
2. *level of resources*. Did students use resource materials and/or equipment that is more advanced, technical, or complex than materials ordinarily used by students at their own age or grade level?
3. *diversity of resources*. Which of the following sources, in addition to books and encyclopedias, did students use: the Internet, films/videos, letters, phone calls, personal interviews, surveys/polls, and others?
4. *action orientation*. Were investigations clearly directed toward some kinds of actions (Website, scientific expert, video); some types of literary or artistic products (a poem, a picture); scientific devices or research studies (tagged observations of whales); or some types of leadership or managerial endeavors (editing a newspaper, writing a letter, or debating an issue)?
5. *audience*. Did students specify appropriate audiences for their products?

PRODUCT

The following questions will help evaluate the products students created.

1. *knowledge*. Do the products reflect advanced familiarity with the subject matter for students' ages?
2. *quality*. Do the products reflect a level of quality beyond what is normally expected of students at this age and grade?
3. *attitude*. Do the products reflect care, attention to detail, and overall pride in their achievements?
4. *commitment*. Do the products reflect a commitment of time, effort, and energy on the students' parts?
5. *originality*. Are the products original ideas or did students make original contributions for children of their age or grade level?

TECHNOLOGY

Did students identify the process they went through and any problems they encountered in searching the Internet for endangered species and whale information?

Figure 9-16 provides a checklist sheet for you to use in assessing the projects. This checklist can be modified to be a rubric with a five point range, for example 5 = excellent, 4 = good, 3 = average, 2 = fair, 1 = weak or unsatisfactory.

SUMMARY

In this unit, principles of scientific investigation and small- and large-group activities have been used to explore endangered species, specifically whales. Exploring Internet sites and performing various activities have required students to think about ethical issues as part of their study of science. Students have discovered that the Internet can be a tremendous resource for exploring the sciences whether trying telecollaborative projects, looking at Websites, asking an expert, or using the Internet as a laboratory site. Of course, it would be very educational for students to go on a live whale watch; however, not all classes have that opportunity. The Internet, with its photographs, statistics, online experts, and collaborative sites, enables students to experience the adventure almost as if they had been on the whaler themselves.

Information on science on the Internet ranges from the most sophisticated research studies conducted at universities to K–12 projects created by and for teachers and students. There are many more science sites to explore on the Internet. Fill your science notebook with URL addresses and brief synopses of their content. This will be a valuable resource when you write future science units incorporating the Internet.

UNIT 2 (SECONDARY LEVEL): ALTERNATIVE ENERGY SOURCES

Energy is a topic that students study in various forms beginning early in their education. They may examine energy as electricity and magnetism, energy as a source of light, energy as sound, and energy as motion of objects. They may also determine ways to conserve energy. An important aspect of energy is investigating sources of useful energy, from sunlight, wind, nuclear power, water flow, to geothermal energy.

Figure 9–16: Evaluation Checklist

Directions: Fill in the checklist below to assess students' final projects. These can be returned to students.

Process

1. Topic clearly defined? _____

2. Level of resource materials and/or equipment used? _____

_____

3. Resources used? More than 3? Internet? _____

_____

4. Actions resulting from the research? _____

5. Specified audience? _____

Product

1. Shows advanced familiarity with the subject matter for students' ages?

_____

2. Reflects a superior level of quality? _____

3. Reflects care, attention to detail, and overall pride? _____

_____

_____

4. Shows a commitment of time, effort, and energy? _____

_____

5. An original idea or original contribution? _____

_____

Technology

1. Did students identify the process they went through and any problems they encountered in searching the Internet? _____

_____

Other Comments:

_____

_____

_____

Today, we depend on fossil fuels for our current energy needs, especially for power generation, transportation, and heating. We are now using these fuels faster than they can be replenished. Two ways to conserve useful energy are to make choices on how to use energy and to be careful not to waste it (see Chapter 7). We can help to ensure that we have adequate energy supplies in the future by shifting our dependence to alternative energy sources. The focus of this unit is to explore such sources.

STEPS FOR DESIGNING A WEB-BASED SCIENCE UNIT

The unit that follows illustrates how to build your own science lessons incorporating the Internet. It employs active learning, where students apply skills in scientific problem solving. During the unit, students use Internet resources to obtain information about alternative energy resources, build models, and contact scientists to learn from their expertise.

Step 1: Apply Framework Standards—What Should Be Taught?

Scientific instruction should utilize the scientific method, principles, and concepts and maintain a balance within the three major areas of science: physical science, earth science, and biological science. As part of the learning process in science, students should be developing skills necessary to think critically.

Children begin as early as the third grade to develop an understanding of energy so that they can describe some forms of energy and talk about ways energy is produced. They study sources of energy, such as wind, sunlight, nuclear power, water, fossil fuels (coal, oil, natural gas) and wood. By the time students reach the sixth grade, they should be able to compare and contrast all forms of energy and list the advantages and disadvantages of each.

In middle school, students identify pollution problems related to the use of energy sources and investigate such problems as whether a coal-fired generating plant is a better energy choice than a nuclear power plant. At this level, their thinking must become more sophisticated so that they can evaluate problems: for example, the effects of nuclear energy on man and the environment. By high school, students should be thinking about development of long-range energy sources for future generations. They must consider safety and the environmental effects of alternative forms of energy.

Goals students attain through the high-school science curriculum should enable them to:

- have multiple opportunities for active, engaged learning while they are investigating the world around them: for instance, making models based on research from books, contacting experts to answer questions, and re-evaluating the construction of those models
- work together in collaborative groups, searching for solutions to selected problems
- use a variety of instructional materials, including lab equipment, reference books, trade books, and relevant educational technology to facilitate active learning and construction of new knowledge

- employ scientific thinking processes
- have opportunities for open-ended discussion of ethical issues as they arise in the presentation of science
- use technology as an integral part of science investigation

Step 2: Identify General Goals and Specific Objectives

Use the goals and specific objectives that follow as a basis for the content and skills covered in this unit.

GOALS

Students will achieve the following goals related to alternative energy sources by being able to:

- discuss the need for shifting to other energy sources
- teach others about different types of energy sources
- demonstrate teamwork
- articulate defensible positions orally and in writing on alternative energy
- use the Internet for their research

OBJECTIVES

This unit will provide content and strategies for students to achieve the following objectives:

- identify and discuss wind, solar, nuclear, and geothermal energy sources
- describe advantages and disadvantages of alternative energy sources
- demonstrate one type of energy using a model
- compare and contrast different energy sources
- evaluate the effectiveness of alternative energy sources

Step 3: Gather Materials

A number of Internet sites provide material on alternative energy sources. You should have students explore several sites that engage students in active participation. For example, at a Website on nuclear energy, students can take a "virtual tour" of a nuclear power plant. At another site, they can view photographs depicting the destructive effects of the Chernobyl disaster. Other sites provide instructions for building models, such as a solar cooking device. In addition, scientists offer their time and expertise to answer student questions. You will want to make sure that students investigate a range of sites, accumulating enough information so that they become the "experts" on a specific energy source and can teach the class about it. The Energy Quest Website (depicted in Figure 9-17) is a good starting point.

The Websites listed in Table 9-3 offer facts, expertise, and ideas on solar, wind, nuclear, and geothermal energy. They include sites maintained by organizations such as the Franklin Institute, businesses, and university experts. They are grouped according to energy type.

Figure 9–17: Energy Quest

Reprinted by permission of the California Energy Commission at www.energy.ca.gov.

Step 4: Introduce the Unit

In order to understand the concept of alternative energy sources, students will do an in-depth study of one energy source, such as wind energy, solar power, nuclear power, or geothermal power. Throughout this project, students will work in groups to:

- compile facts and gain additional knowledge from researching frequently asked questions about their specific types of energy; they will be able to state what the energy sources are, describe how they work, provide examples of their use, and articulate advantages and disadvantages of using them.
- build models that will use the alternative sources. Models may include a windmill, a solar cooker, a solar car, or a solar house, to name a few. Write journal entries discussing problems encountered in constructing the models.
- conduct experiments in which their forms of energy are involved.
- include a language component, for example, read and discuss poems or stories that relate to their energy sources.
- contact an "energy expert" to answer questions about their energy sources.
- give demonstrations that teach the class about each group's alternative sources.

Table 9-3: Alternative Energy Web Resources	
Sample URLs	**Description of Websites**
www.oneworld.org/energy/whatis.html	Defines energy sources—what, why, and how of alternative energy
	Wind Energy
http://sln.fi.edu/tfi/units/energy/windguide.html	The Franklin Institute site provides characteristics of wind, forces that cause wind, building a windmill, and the effects of wind.
www.windpower.dk/tour/wres/index.htm	Shows how a wind turbine works
	Expert Sites
www.eren.doe.gov	Ask an expert about energy-related questions.
www.sciam.com/askexpert/physics/physics.html	Ask an expert about energy-related questions
	Nuclear Power
www.cochems.com/chornobyl http://tqd.advanced.org/3426	Information about the Chernobyl nuclear plant and the aftermath of the disaster
www.insc.anl.gov	Locate nuclear power plants on a map
www.pbs.org/wgbh/pages/frontline/shows/reaction/etc/terms.html	Facts and vocabulary about nuclear energy
www.formal.stanford.edu/jmc/progress/nuclear-faq.html	Frequently asked questions about nuclear energy
www.canlink.com/profbeaker/all_themes.html	
www.cannon.net/~gonyeau/nuclear/tour-a.html	Tour of a nuclear power plant provided
www.ida.liu.se/~her/npp/demo.html	An experiment using nuclear energy
	Solar Energy
http://ericir.syr.edu/Virtual/Lessons/Science/Physical/PHY0045.html	Build a solar hotbox, complete with directions
www.accessone.com/~sbcn/index.htm	Build a solar cooker, complete with directions and cook marshmallows using it
http://explorer.scrtec.org/explorer/explorer-db /rsrc/783750991-447DED81.1.htm	
www.leeric.lsu.edu/educat/lesson3.htm	
www.winstonscience.org/wsci/index.html	Build a solar car
www.sunrayce.com/sea/education/education.html	
www.its.canada.com/reed/index.html	Build a solar house, plans included
www.nrel.gov/research/pv/docs/pvpaper.html	Facts about solar energy
	Geothermal Energy
http://solstice.crest.org/renewables/geothermal/grc/index.html	Definition and facts about geothermal energy
	Fusion Energy
http://FusionEd.gat.com	Facts about fusion energy

Step 5: Create Sample Activities

The sample activities that follow will enable students to obtain the information they need to create the final presentations.

ACTIVITIES TO INTRODUCE THE UNIT

You should have students draw upon any prior knowledge that they have gained about alternative energy sources. Remember they will be building upon their knowledge of types of energy learned about in elementary and middle school. To assess students' prior knowledge, have them:

- brainstorm a list of alternative energy sources on the blackboard, including any information they remember about these sources.
- review characteristics of wind, forces that cause wind, the effects of wind, and wind as a viable source of alternative energy for the twenty-first century. The Franklin Institute Website at *http://sln.fi.edu/tfi/units/energy/windguide.html* will provide help.
- identify vocabulary words related to nuclear energy at *www.pbs.org/wgbh/pages/frontline/shows/reaction* and write definitions in their energy notebooks. Explain how solar energy is captured and turned into electricity, using Website *www.nrel.gov/research/pv/docs/pvpaper.html* as a guide.
- define geothermal energy and how it will benefit the environment. Check Website *http://solstice.crest.org/renewables/geothermal/grc/index.html* for advice.
- define fusion energy. Website *http://FusionEd.gat.com* gives some answers. Present brief facts on solar, wind, kinetic, and nuclear energy. Sites to try are *www.solardome.com/SolarDome60.html* and *http://solstice.crest.org/renewables/index.html*.

These activities present information on various types of alternative energy sources. Exploring the above Websites will answer questions students have about alternative energy sources and refresh concepts they learned in previous grades.

ACTIVITIES TO BE USED DURING THE UNIT

Each group should choose activities based on its energy source. Tasks must encompass those necessary to complete the requirements for the final project. For instance, group members must select one language activity, such as reading a poem about energy, and each group member is responsible for Internet research on at least one activity. All students should be involved in the group construction projects. As students review Websites, they should evaluate all information they have retrieved for bias, credibility, and relevance. Students will:

- read the poem "The Wind" by Robert Louis Stevenson or "Ode to the West Wind" by Shelley and discuss the images related to "wind" in the poem.

- build a windmill in the classroom. Directions are given at *http://sln.fi.edu/tfi/units/energy/windguide.html*.
- visit the Website Solar Energy at *http://flash.lakeheadu.ca/~dlkosowi/enmain.html* for an activity in which an everyday piece of glass is transformed into a solar cell.
- brainstorm a list of questions to ask an energy expert. Contact experts at one of the following sites: *www.eren.doe.gov* or *www.sciam.com/askexpert/physics/physics.html*.
- find out facts about the two power plant disasters (Three-Mile Island in Pennsylvania and Chernobyl in Russia). How are they similar? Different? What caused the accidents? How are the people coping with the aftermath? More information exists on the Web for the Chernobyl disaster than for Three-Mile Island.
- investigate the complete picture of the nuclear disaster at Chernobyl. Locate the site, see why and what happened, understand its consequences. The following two Websites should prove helpful: *www.cochems.com/chornobyl* and *http://tqd.advanced.org/3426*.
- at *http://solstice.crest.org/renewables/wlord/index.html*, see how a family in Maine created its own solar home. Review Figure 9-18 to compare the Maine family's energy costs to those at their own homes.
- build their own solar hotboxes with information found at Website *http://ericir.syr.edu/Virtual/Lessons/Science/Physical/PHY0045.html*, or build solar cookers with directions at *www.accessone.com/~sbcn/index.htm* and *http://*

Figure 9–18: Solar House in Maine

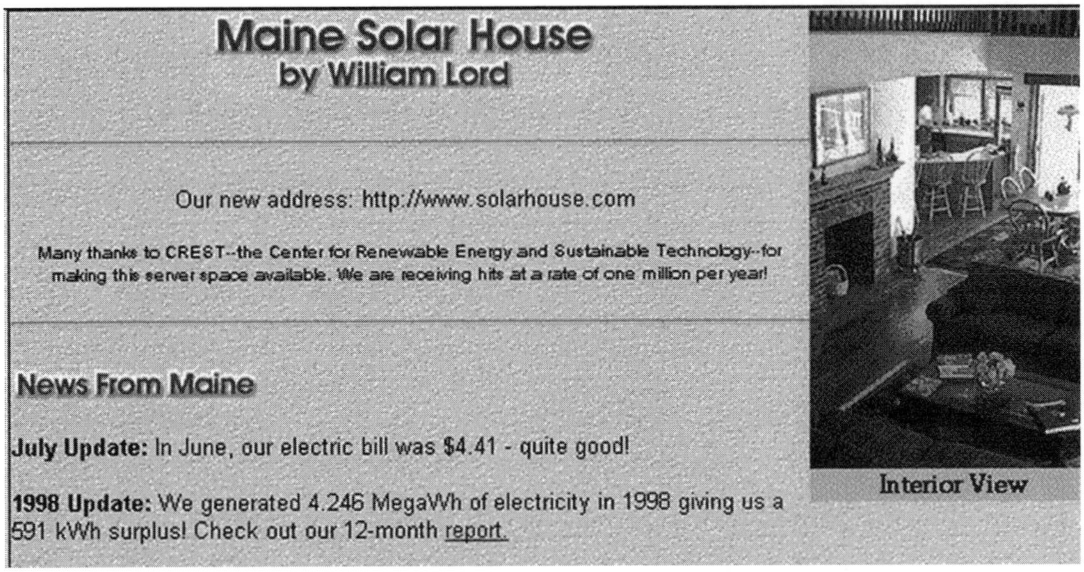

Reprinted by permission—www.solarhouse.com.

explorer.scrtec.org/explorer/explorer-db/rsrc/783750991-447DED81.1.htm. Use Website *www.leeric.lsu.edu/educat/lesson3.htm* for information about cooking marshmallows in the solar cooker.

- conduct experiments at site *www.ida.liu.se/~her/npp/demo.html*, where students are in their own nuclear reactor and can control the processes.
- draw maps identifying the location of power plants. Identify what safety precautions people living near these plants should be aware of. Use *www.insc. anl.gov* for advice.
- build solar cars with help from *www.winstonscience.org/wsci/index.html* or *www.sunrayce.com/sea/education/education.html.*
- determine what the most frequently asked questions about nuclear energy are. Check the following Websites for help: *www-formal.stanford.edu/jmc/ progress/nuclear-faq.html* or *www.canlink.com/profbeaker/all_themes.html.*
- take "virtual" tours of a nuclear power plant at *www.cannon.net/~gonyeau/ nuclear/tour-a.html* (see Figure 9-19).
- explain the nuclear fuel cycle; Website *www.uic.com.au/graphics/nfc1-3.gif* can help.
- build model solar houses in the classroom using the information, designs,

---

Figure 9–19: Virtual Nuclear Power Plant Tour

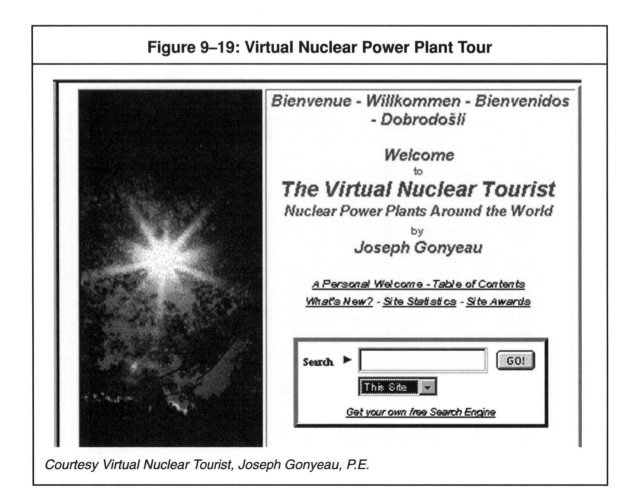

Courtesy Virtual Nuclear Tourist, Joseph Gonyeau, P.E.

and numbers from *www.its.canada.coom/reed/index.html*. Floor plans and drawings are available for different styles of homes.

- create their own projects on solar power, wind energy, hydroelectric power, nuclear power and geothermal power. Check Website *www.rmplc.co.uk/eduweb/sites/dcastle/renew.html*.
- identify and explain why atomic energy should be used and what uses there are for it.
- learn all about solar energy and how it works at *http://ourworld.compuserve.com/homepages/bhuebner/why.htm*. Find out some of the myths about solar energy. Understand the workings of solar panels.
- take a guided tour about energy at *www.windpower.dk/tour/wres/index.htm*, compute wind turbine energy output, or find out how a wind turbine works.

ACTIVITIES TO BE USED AS FOLLOW-UP

As an extension activity resulting from the research students compiled on alternative energy sources, the class might create its own alternative energy Website. Each group will be responsible for:

- determining what information the site should contain about its energy source
- designing how the data will appear on its Web pages
- including images and/or sound where possible

STEP 6: EVALUATE WHAT WAS LEARNED

Students are evaluated to determine how well they are progressing and what they have achieved. Evaluation will also help you adjust aspects of this unit to meet student needs better. At the beginning of the unit, you addressed two main questions through the introductory activities:

1. What are students' current levels of understanding in the subject area? For example, what learning have they already accomplished? What do they already know about alternative energy sources?
2. What are the students' learning needs?

As students participate in various activities, you can also do some evaluation by determining:

1. Are students interested and involved in the instructional activities?
2. Do students demonstrate an understanding of the basic concepts that are being presented?
3. Are the Internet activities and processes employed effectively and according to plan?

When students have completed the unit, you will be judging them on their ability to analyze and synthesize information into an understandable and scientifically defensible demonstration so that they can teach the class about their energy sources.

You will also be evaluating the strengths and weaknesses of your teaching unit. Some of the questions cited in the evaluation section of the unit on Endangered Species will be useful for evaluating this unit. You will also want to assess the process students used in their Internet research. Have them write journal entries indicating the steps they used to obtain information from the Internet, including problems they encountered, URLs of sites they visited, and usefulness of each site. This will help you to make any revisions necessary for future Internet-based units.

Summary

This unit on Alternative Energy Sources has provided diverse activities to help students learn about energy. Students have conducted hands-on experiments, learned facts, retrieved data about energy sources, and contacted experts to answer their questions. As a result of the information they have compiled, they are able to teach their classmates about alternative energy sources. Information viewed on the Internet has enabled students to experience "virtual tours" and build models, causing science to come alive.

Through the Internet, people can access science topics ranging from the most sophisticated research studies conducted at universities to projects created by and for teachers and students K–12. Students at the high-school level should have the intellectual capabilities to gain expertise from the many different Websites on the Internet. In this unit, you only looked at Internet sites on alternative energy sources. You will want to fill your science notebook with URL addresses pertinent to other science units and annotate them with brief synopses about the information they contain. The science information available on the Internet can also help you increase your knowledge of science.

TEACHER EXERCISES: NOW YOU TRY IT...

It is always a good idea to put into practice the ideas that you have just read about. The tasks below will reinforce what you have just learned:

1. Using the units on Endangered Species and Alternative Energy Sources as models, try some of the activities as students would.
   - If you choose activities from the Endangered Species Unit, you will (a) find a list of endangered species on the Web, (b) choose one species, (c) list specific characteristics of the animal and its habitat, and (d) determine what action you would take to protect this animal.
   - If you choose activities from the Alternative Energy Sources Unit, you will (a) select one energy source, (b) find out the advantages and disadvantages of that type of energy, (c) look at directions for a model, and (d) ask questions of an expert.
   - Write journal entries in which you reflect on your experiences exploring these science sites. Which sites do you think will be most useful for upcoming units? Which search engines were easiest to use? Which of your next three units will allow you to incorporate the Internet? Based on your experiences, in which part of the search process will you need minilessons

to instruct students about search techniques—choosing keywords, using a search engine, evaluating data?

2. Explore at least ten additional science Websites included within this chapter. Bookmark and annotate the ones you find most useful, especially those for upcoming units you plan to teach (see Figure 1-3). Make sure to visit the following sites to start your exploration:
   - *www.energy.ca.gov/education*
   - *www.fws.gov/r9endspp*
   - *www.EnchantedLearning.com*

3. Select your own science topic to use with students in your classroom.
   - Create a lesson plan incorporating the Internet as a resource.
   - Have students explore at least five Internet sources in completing activities for the lesson.
   - Keep track of the material and the URLs in your science notebook, labeled by topic.
   - Test the lesson with your class and/or share it on an Internet Website.

CONCLUSION

We have spent a great deal of time in this chapter exploring different types of projects, activities, lessons, and information sites on science that are available on the Internet. In Part 2 we focused on using the Internet in science unit plans. Of course, this is just one of the sources that students will be using in the classroom; however, we have placed most emphasis on it in these units so that teachers will gain familiarity in using the Internet as a tool for research and communication about science.

In the last three chapters you have seen that the Internet can be used in almost any subject area; however, students need certain skills to use it effectively. First, they must have the skill to determine whether the Internet is the best tool for the research, or whether they should look elsewhere. Depending on the grade level of the students, teachers may make that choice for them by supplying the direction and, in many cases, the URLs to guide them to the correct spot on the Internet. It is important that young children do not "surf" the Web unattended! Next, students must gain skill in accessing information using keywords and search engines. Finally, they must evaluate the material they retrieve for usefulness and bias. It is also important for students and teachers to reflect on the process of using the Web.

The Internet has opened vistas to educators and their students. The resources cross all subjects and take many forms. As teachers or library media specialists, we are no longer dependent on resources only at schools and in the community. Teaching students skills to find information on the Internet will be as integral to classroom lessons as the straight facts that used to be our main job. Our challenge is to teach students these skills and take advantage of the benefits to integrating the Internet into science-based lessons, while addressing the problems students may encounter. With information-literacy skills and the ability to access and employ the resources of the Internet, students will be ready to enter the world of work and meet the challenges of the twenty-first century. In the final chapter, we will look at how we can use Internet-based activities in elective subject areas, such as the arts, foreign languages, health education, and government courses.

REFERENCES

California State Department of Education. 1987. *Science Framework for California Public Schools, Kindergarten Through Grade Twelve*. Sacramento: California State Department of Education.

California State Department of Education. 1987. *Science Model Curriculum Guide, Kindergarten Through Grade Twelve*. Sacramento: California State Department of Education.

Chapter 10

BRINGING THE INTERNET INTO OTHER SUBJECT AREAS

PART 1: IDEAS AND INSIGHTS

OBJECTIVES OF THIS CHAPTER
At the end of this chapter educators will be able to:

- identify Internet sites that are available for elective subjects
- integrate the Internet into courses in the arts, foreign languages, health education, and government
- create lessons with an Internet-based component in elective courses

Throughout this book, we have examined ways to use Internet technology as part of the core curriculum—science, social studies, and language arts. We've even focused on cross-curricular learning to illustrate the connections among different subjects. The Internet has much to offer in elective courses as well, and this chapter looks at resources currently available on the Internet for the visual arts, foreign languages, health education, and government. The lesson plans in Part 2 illustrate how to create Web-based lessons in these elective subjects.

THE VISUAL ARTS
The visual arts are constructed around four components of arts education: aesthetic perception, creative expression, arts heritage, and aesthetic value. Investigating the contributions of great creators in the arts, studying the basic styles, and becoming receptive to artistic productions from different cultures all foster understanding about the role of the arts in communicating the values and hopes of specific groups of people.

Figure 10–1: Student Drawings about Energy

Bookmarks Location: http://www.energy.ca.gov/education/artcontest/99contest/index.htm

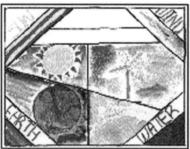
Cover

"ENERGY"
Allison Phillips
Grade 6
Thurston Middle School
Laguna Beach

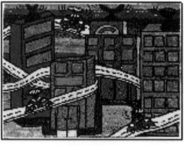
January

"Solar Power City"
Christopher Abkarians
Grade 3
Pomelo Elementary School
West Hills

"A Healthy Future"
Stephanie Vitales
Grade 6
Curtner Elementary School

Reprinted by permission of California Department of Energy at www.energy.ca.gov.

There are strong, natural connections among core courses and the arts. For example, students studying World Cultures in social studies may compare and contrast major themes in art throughout the world to understand better the effects of the arts on today's societies. At the elementary level, one class of California fourth graders as part of a unit on Mexico compared and contrasted art and folk music from Mayan, Aztec, and Mexican cultures. In an elementary science class, students drew pictures of ways to conserve energy for an art contest sponsored by the California Department of Energy (see Figure 10-1 for some of their drawings illustrating solar energy).

The Internet has a plethora of resources for the arts educator. Examples of art from the National Gallery of Art at Website *www.nga.gov* can instill in students a

Table 10–1: Arts Web Resources	
Sample URLs	**Descriptions of Websites**
http://wwar.com/museums.html	Art museums listed by country
www.guggenheim.org	Resources from the Guggenheim Museum with different exhibits changing over time
www-oi.uchicago.edu/OI/MUS	Virtual tour of the Oriental Institute Museum
www.moma.org	The Museum of Modern Art in New York City
www.artsednet.getty.edu/ ArtsEdNet/Resources/index.html	Lessons and resources from the Getty Institute
www.artsednet.getty.edu/ArtsEdNet/ Images/index.html	Art images and student artwork from the Getty
www.nga.gov/copyright/onlinetr.htm	Virtual tour of the National Gallery with over 110,000 works
http://nmaa.si.edu/collections/index.html	National Museum of American Art contains over 3,000 images by subject
www.allexperts.com/edu/arthistory.shtml	Art experts who will answer questions
www.artswire.org/kenroar/lessons/ lessons.html	Art lessons for all age groups

feeling for the vivid colors and distinct patterns of Native Peoples. Websites given in Chapter 8 can help students obtain a complete picture of Native Peoples' culture, which encompassed art, music, and dance as important components of their social and ceremonial gatherings. Art museums offer examples of different periods in art history, such as the Renaissance period. Websites exhibit different types of art like cubism, romanticism, and surrealism or art from different countries. There is even pop art represented at the Andy Warhol Museum Website and graffitists at *www.graffiti.org*. In addition, art organizations like the Getty Institute for the Arts have created numerous lesson plans complete with Internet resources to enable the art teacher or a teacher of core subjects to incorporate art ideas from the Internet.

Table 10-1 provides a sampling of Websites for the arts educator.

FOREIGN LANGUAGES

Websites contain resources for students studying foreign languages. For example, an important aspect of studying a language is to understand the culture of the country. What better way to explore the Mayan culture of Mexico than through an interactive Mayan journey? Students can learn more about France and practice their language skills by discussing culture with keypals in Paris. Communicating online with other students can make a foreign country come alive. Websites abound that enable students studying a foreign language to keep abreast of world news in France or Spain, hear broadcasts by native speakers of German, and see images of the Louvre in Paris or a castle in Spain. In addition, documents in other languages, such as the writing of Walt Whitman as he reflected on the war with Mexico in 1846, enable students to practice reading the language they are studying.

Language resources specifically for teachers also exist on the Web. Foreign language associations, such as the American Council on the Teaching of Foreign Languages, the American Association of Teachers of French, and the American Association of Teachers of Spanish and Portuguese, include instructional resources and links to educational materials on their Websites. For instance, teachers now have access to a collection of electronic newspapers and magazines in French, Chinese, German, Russian, and Spanish. The Library of Congress provides country studies of ninety-one countries that include history, geography, and economic information about each.

Activities like "virtual field trips" can be enhanced with information from tourist bureaus in different countries. Website *www.w3i.com/eng/home.htm* gives students ideas on what to expect when visiting France, and Website *www.ibmpcug.co.uk/~owls/european_cuisines.html* contains recipes for food on the European continent. To appeal to different learning styles, students can read *Le Monde*, France's daily newspaper, at *www.lemonde.fr* to learn about current events in Paris, or visit the Website *www.cnnespanol.com* to hear news stories in Spanish. Students can even brush up on their Spanish language skills through tutorials at Website *www.umr.edu/~amigos/Virtual*.

The Websites in Table 10-2 are a starting point to explore the Internet for foreign language resources.

HEALTH EDUCATION

One of the most popular offerings available on the Internet is health information. Health educators can keep up-to-date on the latest health-related topics, such as nutrition and drug and alcohol education. Not only are these issues of interest to health educators, but they can also entice students to use technology to find out about an ailment of a family member, a treatment for acne, or information on the effects of drug abuse on an unborn child. Health education also has connections to the science curriculum. Research on DNA, gene therapy, and genetic engineering, available on the Internet, dovetail with the topics studied in science classes.

Health information on the Internet ranges from data for the medical professional—such as results from clinical trials of a new drug, new medications sold over-the-counter, and diseases that the layperson probably cannot even pronounce—to material that is written for the consumer. A search engine at *www.healthatoz.com* leads the novice to hundreds of health information resources available on the Internet. This is a good starting point whether the student is looking for information on dialysis and kidney transplants, a new laser cane for the blind, or pacemakers.

When researching health-related issues, it is important to determine the level of

Table 10–2: Foreign Language Web Resources	
Sample URLs	**Descriptions of Websites**
http://lcweb2.loc.gov/frd/cs/cshome.html	Contains info on the history, geography and economy of 91 countries
www.oanda.com/converter/travel	Provides currency conversion rates worldwide
www.travlang.com/index.html	Includes links to weather, currency rates, travel and cultural information
www.xs4all.nl/~pwessel/country.html	Compiles annotated links to the literature of many countries in native languages
www.cortland.edu/www/flteach	Includes information about resources for foreign language teachers
http://actfl.org	American Council on the Teaching of Foreign Languages includes learning standards and instructional resources
www.red2000.com/spain	Photo tour of cities of Spain, including information on food and fiestas
www.teachspanish.com/teacher.html	Contains Spanish teacher resources
www.awesomelibrary.org/Classroom/ English/Languages/Spanish.html	Includes K–12 lesson plans for Spanish classes

the information at a Website. It is also vital to check the sources of information. Some information may be suspect because the articles do not come from reputable medical journals. Nonetheless, determining which are the best articles can also be instructional, because students must analyze and evaluate the information, thus building critical-thinking skills. A Website at *http://mel.lib.mi.us/health/health-evaluating.html* will help students verify sites with appropriate health data. In addition, the Federal Drug Administration (FDA) maintains its own Website on health issues (see Figure 10-2).

The Websites in Table 10-3 contain medical information that students can understand on diverse topics.

GOVERNMENT

In the fourth grade students start learning about government. They learn how bills become laws and identify the different branches of state governments. In ninth grade students take a course in civics and explore the legislative, executive, and judicial branches of Congress in more depth. By twelfth grade, students have specifically learned about the government of the United States in a course that usually has a unit focused on the U.S. Constitution and the Bill of Rights. As students examine the

Figure 10–2: FDA Website

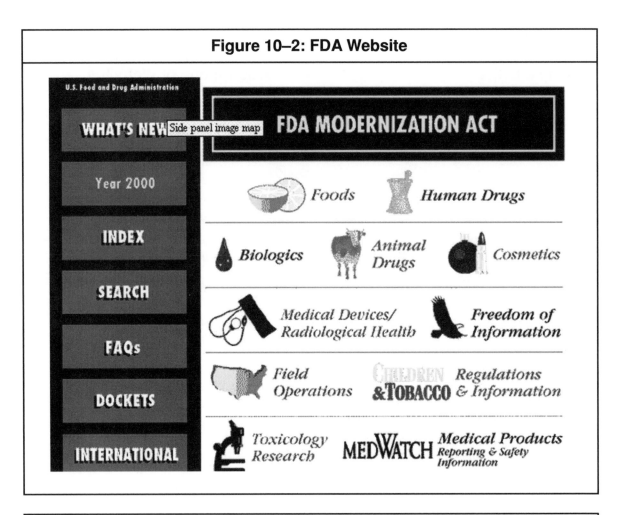

Table 10-3: Health Education Web Resources

Sample URLs	Descriptions of Websites
www.healthatox.com	Access to hundreds of health information resources
www.fda.gov	Includes topics about health
www.nal.usda.gov/fnic/etext/fnic.html	Links to resources on health topics, especially food and nutrition
www.medicinenet.com	Medical information for the public, including diseases, drugs, and more
www.cspinet.org/kids/index.html	Just for Kids page with top 10 best and worst foods, eating tips, and more
www.graylab.ac.uk/omd	Medical dictionary
www.itds.sbcss.k12.ca.us/curriculum/tobacco.html	Activities to promote learning about the dangers of tobacco on the body

---

Figure 10–3: Congressional Documents

THE BILL OF RIGHTS
Amendments 1-10 of the Constitution

| Search the Constitution | Browse Constitution + Other Amendments | About the Constitution |

The Conventions of a number of the States having, at the time of adopting the Constitution, expressed a desire, in order to prevent misconstruction or abuse of its powers, that further declaratory and restrictive clauses should be added, and as extending the ground of public confidence in the Government will best insure the beneficent ends of its institution;

Resolved, by the Senate and House of Representatives of the United States of America, in Congress assembled, two-thirds of both Houses concurring, that the following articles be proposed to the Legislatures of the several States, as amendments to the Constitution of the United States; all or any of which articles, when ratified by three-fourths of the said Legislatures, to be valid to all intents and purposes as part of the said Constitution, namely:

Preamble to the Constitution, legislative actions, court decisions, and our rights as citizens, they learn the fundamentals of what it means to live in a democratic society.

There are many Internet resources that contain information on government—its organization, the laws it makes, and the issues discussed among members of Congress. For example, the Library of Congress site at *http://thomas.loc.gov* provides a searchable index to the *Congressional Record* containing all House and Senate bills; the Bureau of the Census presents data about the people and economy of the United States; Supreme Court opinions are available; and facts about any state in the union are also online. Figure 10-3 demonstrates just one aspect of this range of information, and the sample URLs in Table 10-4 can help in locating Internet resources about government.

Part 2 of this chapter contains sample lessons that include a Web component. These lessons provide educators with models for integrating their own Web-based activities into elective courses.

Table 10–4: Government Web Resources	
Sample URLs	**Descriptions of Websites**
www.census.gov	Information about people and the economy of the U.S.
www.access.gpo.gov/su_docs	Data such as the Congressional Record, Supreme Court decisions, U.S. budget, and more
http://supct.law.cornell.edu/supct	Supreme Court opinions
www.library.Yale.edu/govdocs/gdchome.html	Links to many government documents and other resources
www.house.gov www.senate.gov	U.S. House of Representatives and Senate sites including a listing of representatives and senators and how they voted
www.loc.gov/global/state/stategov.html	Links to state and local government resources
http://ipl.org/ref/POTUS	Biographies, historical documents, speeches of U.S. presidents

PART 2: PRACTICAL APPLICATIONS

The four lesson plans in Part 2 complement the discussion of the elective areas of the arts, foreign languages, health education, and government in Part 1. Each Web-based lesson plan, designed as part of a larger unit, contains the following components:

1. a context and purpose for the lesson
2. objectives
3. materials
4. procedures
5. evaluation
6. extensions for further study

Grade levels are suggested for each lesson, although most plans can be adapted by creative teachers for students at any level. Each lesson plan explores one major concept, unlike the units in preceding chapters, which investigated larger themes through the use of many activities.

LESSON 1 (SECONDARY LEVEL): ART SCAVENGER HUNT

At the elementary level, children sing, dance, paint, and draw pictures. They are exposed to art in books, and they learn to tell stories through pictures. At the secondary level, art is integral to core subjects. Students draw symbols representing themes in literature, and in social studies they learn about different cultures by studying their artwork. In many schools, art is also taught as an elective subject. This lesson plan asks students to conduct a treasure hunt to find art resources on the Internet to help them visualize different styles of painting. It is focused at the secondary level, but can be adapted for elementary-level students by choosing other Websites.

PURPOSE

The purpose of this lesson is twofold: (1) to familiarize students with the art resources available on the Internet; and (2) to use those resources to learn about artists who paint in different styles. Let's say that students have been studying industrial changes that occurred in Europe in the late-nineteenth and early-twentieth centuries in history class. Study of this period in art dovetails nicely with their history lessons.

In the nineteenth century, reforms led to revolutionary movements in art. Realism focused on direct observation of society. In the 1860s and continuing into the twentieth century, the Impressionist style began in Paris. Impressionism was concerned with direct observation of nature rather than with social conditions. Post-Impressionism denotes late-nineteenth-century artists who were influenced by Impressionism.

Students will examine artwork on the Internet from these three schools of art— Realism, Impressionism, and Post-Impressionism. They should discover similarities and differences among them. As a summative experience, students will have opportunities to practice their own art making in the styles of these periods in art.

OBJECTIVES

Upon completion of the activities for this lesson, students will:

- gain a historical perspective on different artists of the Realist, Impressionist, and Post-Impressionist periods
- compare and contrast the works of artists using these styles
- identify characteristics of these artists' works
- understand how earlier artists influence later artists

MATERIAL

While there are many arts Websites available on the Internet, the sites in Table 10-5 will enable students to view paintings of artists who emerged in the late-nineteenth and early-twentieth centuries. These sites offer thousands of images of famous artwork often not available in school libraries.

Figure 10–4: Art Timeline

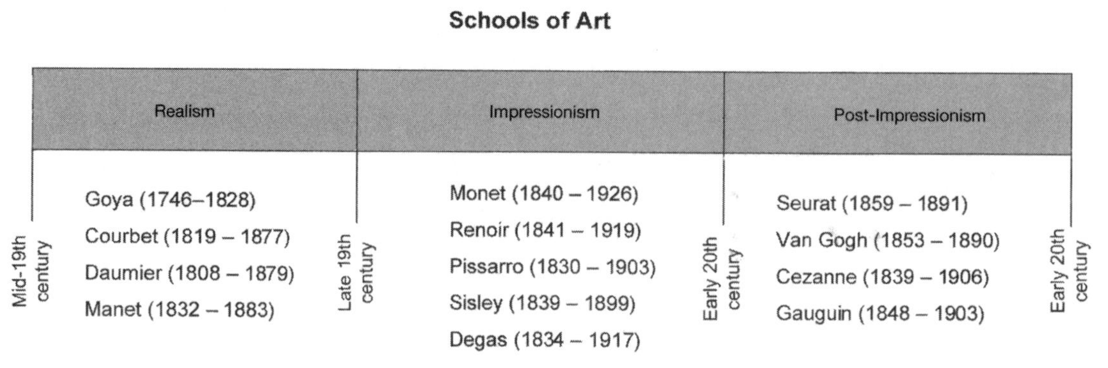

Schools of Art

Realism	Impressionism	Post-Impressionism

Mid-19th century		Late 19th century		Early 20th century		Early 20th century
	Goya (1746–1828)		Monet (1840 – 1926)		Seurat (1859 – 1891)	
	Courbet (1819 – 1877)		Renoir (1841 – 1919)		Van Gogh (1853 – 1890)	
	Daumier (1808 – 1879)		Pissarro (1830 – 1903)		Cezanne (1839 – 1906)	
	Manet (1832 – 1883)		Sisley (1839 – 1899)		Gauguin (1848 – 1903)	
			Degas (1834 – 1917)			

PROCEDURES

Using the URLs in Table 10-5, students will view in groups of four different artists' works whose paintings represent styles from Realism through Post-Impressionism. Groups will:

- create timelines (see Figure 10-4) identifying the styles of painting in Europe in the late-nineteenth and early-twentieth centuries and the artists whose work represented those styles. They will then search the National Gallery of Art Website, shown in Figure 10-5, to identify artists and their works.
- choose one of the following artists from the timeline and find paintings by these artists. The National Gallery at *www.nga.gov/copyright/onlinetr.htm* with its 100,000 images will be invaluable to this task. See Figure 10-6 to view an example of Cezanne.
- create T-charts in their journals that include their chosen artists and charac-

---

Table 10–5: Art Lesson Web Resources

Sample URLs	Description of Websites
www.nga.gov/copyright/onlinetr.htm	National Gallery of Art has a virtual tour that can be taken by artist, title, subject, collection, and more. It gives a history of the artwork as well
www.allexperts.com/edu/arthistory.shtml	E-mail an art expert to answer questions about art
www.artsednet.getty.edu/ArtsEdNet/ Images/index.html	The Getty Institute of Art contains an image collection and has educational activities for the arts
www.oir.ucf.edu/wm/paint/auth/cezanne	Information on Cezanne and Impressionism

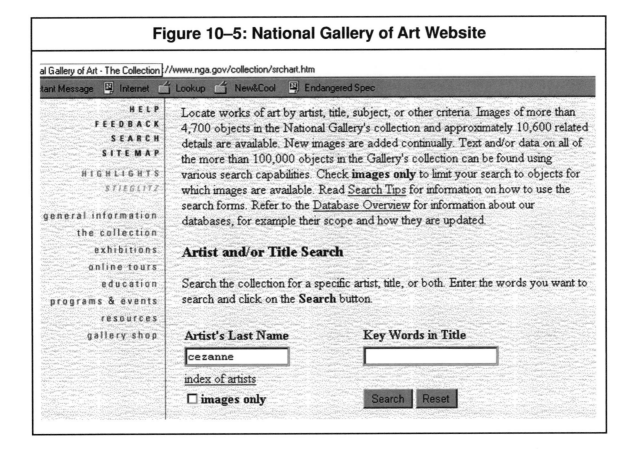

Figure 10–5: National Gallery of Art Website

teristics of their works (see Figure 10-7). Answer the following questions: What is the subject matter of each of these works? What styles did the artists use? What are characteristics of the paintings? This chart will be completed as student groups report on their artists.

- choose two works by the same artist painted at different times during his or her career. Compare and contrast the two works based on the characteristics in the T-chart below.

- choose paintings that have given them ideas for their own art making. Name the artists in their journals and tell what they especially like about those artworks.

- individually, write essays describing the artwork that appeals to them the most. Some possible points to discuss include: How are the shapes or elements in the picture arranged? How is the eye led around the painting? How does each part relate to the other parts? Do lines define the edges of objects, or do they create abstract patterns? What are the subjects, and why were they chosen? How is color used? How does use of color compare to color in another period? What period does the picture represent? How does the painting differ from art in another period?

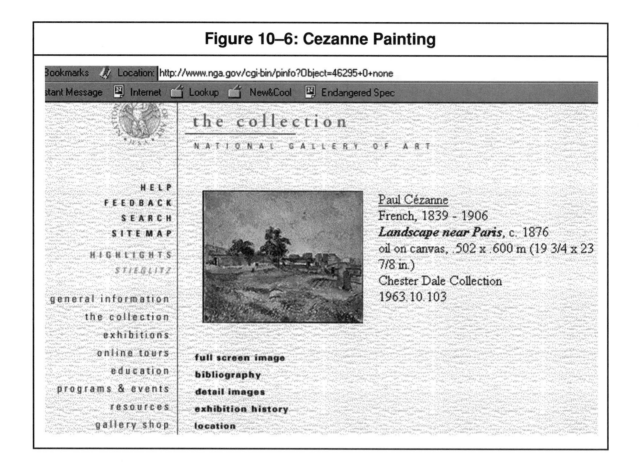

Figure 10–6: Cezanne Painting

EVALUATION

Each group will report to the rest of the class on the artists chosen. Each member of the group will contribute to the presentation. Teachers will also review students' timelines and T-charts in their journals. The essays will be graded based on standard English grammar and how well students represent the artwork to enable readers to visualize the pieces of art through their use of language.

EXTENSIONS

When students are exploring other periods of art history during the school year, have them:

- identify influences that artists have on one another by comparing two artists from different styles
- discuss the similarities and differences between two styles—for example, Impressionism and Realism
- use paint, crayons, or pastels to create pictures of themselves that resemble the style of the artists that they have chosen to research, and display their pictures on bulletin boards in the classroom

Figure 10–7: Characteristics of Artists	
Artists	**Characteristics**
Monet	Light tones, brightness, pastels Impressionistic Painted nature, especially water garden at Giverny
Renoir	Feathery soft touch Impressionistic Figure painter

SUMMARY

Through the multimedia capabilities of the Internet, students now have access to lifelike images that would have been otherwise difficult to view. Whether students are learning to appreciate art for its own sake or to understand different cultures through their art, music, and dance in other subjects they are studying, the Internet can bring resources into the classroom that make art appreciation easier.

LESSON 2 (SECONDARY LEVEL): UNDERSTANDING MEXICAN HISTORY

When students study languages, it is important that they understand the countries where the languages are spoken, including the people, customs, geography, and culture. Many Internet sites make such information readily available. For a French class, students must know key historical events in French history and be able to identify France, its major cities, and topography on a map of Europe. In a Spanish class, students may study facts about Spain; or they might want to learn about other Spanish-speaking countries such as Mexico, Panama, or other Latin American countries.

PURPOSE

This lesson is appropriate for students who have begun their study of the language, in this case Spanish. They must now become familiar with historical events in the lives of people who speak Spanish. One Mexican holiday, Cinco de Mayo, is celebrated on May 5 by Mexican Americans in the United States. It marks the victory of the Mexican Army over the French at the Battle of Puebla. Although it is not a big holiday for Mexico, understanding the significance of Cinco de Mayo will help students studying Spanish learn about historical events in Mexico and identify with Mexican American students.

OBJECTIVES

As a result of participating in this lesson, students will be able to:

- discuss the significance of Cinco de Mayo

- state five facts about Cinco de Mayo
- represent Mexican history by creating a mural of events

MATERIAL

The Internet contains several excellent sites (see Table 10-6) to provide groups with data they need to identify events in Mexican history.

PROCEDURES

Students will:

1. draw a map of Mexico, identifying cities, rivers, and regions of the country. The map will become part of the students' artistic representation of the events celebrated by Cinco de Mayo and help them visualize where the battle of Puebla took place. The Websites at *www.odci.gov/cia/publications/factbook* and *www.lib.texas.edu/PCL/Map_collection/americas/Mexico.GIF* have sample maps.
2. divide into groups, with each team responsible for one aspect about the Cinco de Mayo holiday. For example, one group will study the causes and effects of the war between Mexico and France; another will determine the significance of the holiday. Websites at *http://latino.sscnet.ucla.edu/demo/cinco.html* and *www.kqed.org/fromKQED/cell/calhist/cinco.html* will support their re-

Table 10–6: Mexican Web Resources	
Sample URLs	**Descriptions of Websites**
http://latino.sscnet.ucla.edu/demo/cinco.html	History of the Mexican holiday
www.legrand.k12.ca.us/edm	Web site of elementary school students celebrating Cinco de Mayo
www.avocado.org/recipes/recil59.shtml	Recipes for Cinco de Mayo
www.kqed.org/fromKQED/cell/calhist/cinco.html	Background information on the holiday
http://128.123.31.49/vista/esl/m5_hstry.html	ESL students' Website on the origin of Cinco de Mayo
www.mexonline.com/history.htm	Mexican history, including heroes and historical documents
http://northcoast.com/~spdtom/revl.html	Timeline of Mexican history
www.geocities.com/Athens/Forum/9061/mexico/mexico.html	Historical text archives

search.
3. write summaries of the information in their journals.
4. with each group contributing its part, create a mural to represent the history and celebration of the holiday.
5. on May 5th present orally to the class. The presentations must include information about the historical events surrounding the holiday and the way it is celebrated, including costumes and food. They will use the mural to represent the holiday visually.

EVALUATION

Students will demonstrate their knowledge of the history of the holiday in their oral reports and their contributions to the class mural (see Figure 10-8 for a sample rubric for assessing an oral report). If they want to bring traditional food to the celebration (for extra credit!), check Website *www.avocado.org/recipes/reci159.shtml* for suggestions.

EXTENSIONS

Students should create a context for the Cinco de Mayo holiday by identifying and discussing other events important to the history of Mexico.

* Have students create a timeline of other historical events in Mexico. Website *http://northcoast.com/~spdtom/revl.html* will help.
* Students should identify other important holidays such as Mexican Independence Day on September 16 and November 20, the celebration of the Mexican Revolution.

SUMMARY

Understanding the culture of a people is just as important as learning their language. By familiarizing themselves with national holidays in Mexico, students will develop better understanding of those classmates and community members who are Mexican Americans.

LESSON 3 (SECONDARY/ELEMENTARY LEVELS): STAYING HEALTHY

Many sites on the World Wide Web discuss different aspects of health and healthy living. Some focus on treatments for illnesses; others emphasize maintaining a healthy body and mind. For this lesson, students will apply what they learn about nutrition in order to maintain their own health. This lesson can easily be adapted for any age level.

PURPOSE

Students in health classes or home economics will have already studied food groups and what constitutes a healthy diet and lifestyle. This lesson requires students to apply these concepts to their own health.

Figure 10–8: Rubric for Oral Reports

Name_____   Date_____

Directions: Evaluate students on a scale of 1 to 5, with 5 being the highest score (5 = Excellent, 4 = Good, 3 = Average, 2 = Fair, 1 = Poor).

Clarity: The class could hear and understand the words and content.

Enunciation	5	4	3	2	1
Rate of speed	5	4	3	2	1
Volume	5	4	3	2	1
Pitch	5	4	3	2	1

Delivery: The student presented the material effectively.

Posture	5	4	3	2	1
Eye contact	5	4	3	2	1
Gestures	5	4	3	2	1
Facial expression	5	4	3	2	1

Content: The information was understandable.

Organized material clearly	5	4	3	2	1
Concluding information present	5	4	3	2	1
Used supporting evidence	5	4	3	2	1
Captured audience's interest	5	4	3	2	1

Response to questions:

Clarity of answers	5	4	3	2	1

Other Comments:

OBJECTIVES

Students will:

- identify calories in food
- create one-week diets that suit their height, weight, age, and gender
- plan their own exercise programs

MATERIAL

Information on the Web for health and nutrition is voluminous. The sample Websites in Table 10-7 offer medical data for consumers and health and nutrition sites for children and teen-agers.

PROCEDURES

Students will:

1. use the Food Guide Pyramid at *www.nal.usda.gov:8001/py/pmap.htm* to review the different food groups to determine what USDA Dietary Guidelines say they should eat each day.
2. find out their Basal and Active Metabolic Rates at *http://library.advanced.org/10991* or *www.shapeup.org/bmi/start.htm*.
3. analyze their current eating habits at the Nutrition Cafe at *www.exhibits.pacsci.org/nutrition*. Check charts based on their genders and ages and choose

Table 10–7: Health and Nutrition Web Resources	
Sample URLs	**Descriptions of Websites**
http://library.advanced.org/10991	Nutrition on the Web for teens, including information about exercise, world nutrition, and recipes
www.itdc.sbcss.k12.ca.us/curriculum/ personaltrainer.html	A simulation for students to develop customized diet and exercise plans
www.nal.usda.gov:8001/py/pmap.htm	Explains what to eat each day based on USDA Dietary Guidelines
www.shapeup.org	Info on weight management and physical fitness
http://Fscn.che.umn.edu/NutrExp/ default.html	Resources for school nutrition education
www.fda.gov/oc/opacom/kids/default.htm	FDA Kids Home Page on all aspects of health issues
www.healthatoz.com	Search engine for health information resources

the foods they would currently eat for each meal of the day. Determine how they can change their diets to eat more healthily.

4. learn recommended daily allowances of each food group and plan three-meal-a-day diets for one week for themselves. Use the Calorie Database and Diet Planner at *http://library.advanced.org/10991* to determine the number of calories in common foods. Keep track of their calories for one week.

5. write journal entries for each day justifying their choices of food and the advantages of their chosen menus.

EVALUATION

Students will be evaluated on the completeness of their one-week diets and review of their journal entries that support the choices they made for the diets. Upon completing the extension activities below, students can also be assessed on the letters to their peers promoting their diet and exercise programs. The writing assessment rubric in Figure 5-9 can guide you.

EXTENSIONS

Students will:

1. plan exercise programs to go along with the diet. Use Personal Trainer at Website *www.itdc.sbcss.k12.ca.us/curriculum/personaltrainer.html* or *http://library.advanced.org/10991/exercises.html* for help with types of exercises and advantages of each.

2. write letters to other teens promoting their physical fitness programs of diet and exercise.

3. check the food they eat at fast-food restaurants for its nutritional content. Compare and contrast hamburgers at different restaurants for calories, number of fat grams, sodium, and cholesterol. Use Website *www.olen.com/food*.

4. create a list of tips for food safety. The FDA Food Safety tips at *http://vm.cfsan.fda.gov/~dms/educate.html* (see Figure 10-9) will get them going.

SUMMARY

When students check their diets, exercise habits, and places where they eat frequently—like McDonald's or Taco Bell—they are actively involved in staying healthy. The Internet provides tools to help students personalize their own dietary habits. The activities in this lesson re-emphasize to students the importance of nutrition and maintaining good health to their daily lives.

LESSON 4 (SECONDARY LEVEL): THE PROTECTION OF PEOPLE'S RIGHTS

Students study the U.S. Constitution and the Bill of Rights in their civics classes. This lesson is a culminating activity that requires students become expert witnesses before a congressional committee tasked with examining how people's rights are being protected. Each group will be asked to testify as "expert witnesses" on some of the following questions:

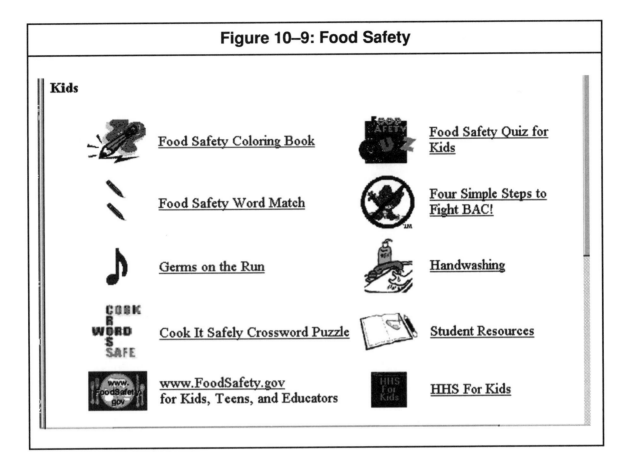

Figure 10–9: Food Safety

Kids

Food Safety Coloring Book

Food Safety Quiz for Kids

Food Safety Word Match

Four Simple Steps to Fight BAC!

Germs on the Run

Handwashing

Cook It Safely Crossword Puzzle

Student Resources

www.FoodSafety.gov for Kids, Teens, and Educators

HHS For Kids

- What freedoms do we currently enjoy? How are these freedoms protected?
- Which of the basic rights guaranteed by the Constitution seem the most important to people today? Do teenagers think their opinions will change when they are adults?
- Are there times when freedoms should be limited? Why or why not? Give examples.

PURPOSE

To prepare for the testimony before the committee, students combine reading, researching on the Internet, writing, speaking, and thinking critically—integrating language skills with social studies content. Moreover, they will have to make decisions about their own ideas on different freedoms and assess others' opinions. This will require teamwork, cooperation, and shared responsibilities.

Finally, this lesson will require that students apply their ideas about the Bill of Rights to controversial issues today, such as gun control, abortion, freedom on the Internet, and others of their choosing.

OBJECTIVES

Students will:

- describe the content of the first ten amendments to the U.S. Constitution
- research the Internet for information on the Bill of Rights and different points of view on individual freedoms
- practice speaking skills
- relate their understanding of individual "freedoms" guaranteed by the Bill of Rights to everyday situations

MATERIALS

Students will use the Internet to research the Bill of Rights. The Websites in Table 10-8 provide definitions, the content of the first ten amendments, and differing viewpoints on the meanings of the amendments and what they guarantee.

PROCEDURES

Students will:

1. write journal entries on "What is freedom?" and as a class discuss the meaning of "freedom." For discussion, assume the roles of different audiences, such as students, family members, television late-night talk-show hosts, doctors at abortion clinics, and news reporters. Information at Website *www.excite.com/reference/almanac/?id=A0341699* will get things moving.
2. brainstorm a list of the freedoms stated in the Bill of Rights and situations or issues that are affected by the freedoms listed.

| Table 10–8: Bill of Rights Web Resources ||
Sample URLs	**Descriptions of Websites**
www.excite/com/reference/almanac/?id=A0341699	Dictionary definition of the Bill of Rights
www.excite.com/reference/almanac/?id=CEO12456	Encyclopedia-like explanations of each amendment of the Bill of Rights
www.lsu.edu/guests/poli/public_html/bor.htm	Bill of Rights page as it relates to law and court decisions
www.bill-of-rights.org/bill-of-rights.html	Current interpretations of the Bill of Rights
www.libertywon.com	Libertarian/Christian interpretations of the Bill of Rights and links to news sites
http://webleyweb.com/lneil/bor_enforcement.html	Discussion of online freedom

3. in groups, choose one amendment, describe its contents, and compare how the protection of rights matches grievances in the Declaration of Independence. Website *www.excite.com/reference/almanac/?id=CEO12456* may help with the research.

4. in pairs, select several different views on the concept of guaranteed freedoms and research their viewpoints, including examples they use to support them. Websites *www.bill-of-rights.org/bill-of-rights.html* and *www.libertywon.com* illuminate differing views.

5. within their groups, determine roles for each member at the congressional hearing. They should write out the testimony they plan to give before the committee and read it aloud within the groups.

6. discuss the testimony based on completeness, nonbiased representation, and examples that illustrate freedoms today that are being threatened.

7. present testimony in a "mock" congressional hearing to a panel of congress members.

EVALUATION

The testimony students provide in the mock hearing will demonstrate whether they have an integrated knowledge of the meaning of the Bill of Rights and its applications to diverse situations in today's world. Students will be evaluated on the content and persuasiveness of their testimony as well as by teacher observations of how well they work together in their groups.

EXTENSIONS

To continue exploring this topic, students will:

1. apply research and discussion of the Bill of Rights to a current issue: for example, whether there should be censorship on the Internet (see Website *http://webleyweb.com/lneil/bor_enforcement.html*.

2. send their opinions on an issue related to "freedoms" to a local news station, such as NBC, CBS, or a television program like *Meet the Press*. Website *www.libertywon.com/actionlinks.htm* has links to the news sites.

SUMMARY

This lesson plan provides a series of activities for students at a middle- or high-school level who are studying government. Because of its versatility, the Internet can provide historic information on the Bill of Rights, as well as information that reflects situations and issues affecting students today. Different Websites also present varying opinions for students to analyze. Because the Bill of Rights guarantees "freedom of speech," students have opportunities to judge information and accept or reject viewpoints of others. It is important for students to gain critical-thinking skills to face problems outside the school environment.

TEACHER EXERCISES: NOW YOU TRY IT...

Now is a good time to reflect on what you have learned throughout this book. Self-evaluation is always helpful. In your journals:

1. List five new ideas that you gained from information in this book that you can employ in your lesson plans. Review Part 1 of each chapter to jog your memory.
2. Check the list of Websites you have bookmarked after each chapter. Identify at least five that you will incorporate into a new lesson.
3. If you teach courses in language arts, social studies, or science, reflect on ways to use elements of the arts, health, or other elective subjects as part of your lessons.
4. Include Web-based components in at least five lessons for this school year.
5. Incorporate at least one cooperative learning activity into your next unit. Make sure that you have provided for interdependence and individual accountability. Check Chapter 5 for advice.

CONCLUSION

Throughout this book, we have examined how the Internet can be used in the core subjects—language arts, science, social studies—and elective courses. As the Internet becomes a standard reference tool for students, it will create patterns of usage that will carry over into higher education and the workplace.

Samuel Johnson said, "We know a subject or we know where we can find information on it," but in the eighteenth century he could not envision an information superhighway such as the Internet. However, his statement reinforces the reason for writing this book: The Internet is a place for educators and students to find information. It is a tool for educators to use to enhance their teaching. It gives learners the opportunity to do authentic tasks—to be astronomers viewing comets and meteorites, or geologists digging up fossils. It allows students around the world to know each other better by enabling them to communicate with peers through conversations, discussions, and the sharing of ideas. It also connects experts—scientists, writers—to the classroom.

The Internet is a powerful, multifaceted resource that teachers can use to stimulate students with rich content and to reinforce skills they will need to be successful contributors to the work force in the twenty-first century. Now is the time for educators to take that first leap to integrating the Internet into the classroom. This book is the jumping-off point.

Appendices

Appendix A

HOW TO USE SEARCH ENGINES

A search engine is a tool to help the user navigate the Internet. Without one, it is almost impossible to wade through the myriad of sites available to get the results desired. The search engine performs queries of the Internet based on the input of the user—keywords, phrases, or other criteria. By conducting searches of sites, the search engines can locate information and point the user to sites with the data requested.

There are many search engines available on the Internet—AltaVista, Yahoo!, Excite, Northern Lights, to name some of the most popular. The most common type scans huge databases of words, phrases, and topics and matches the user's input against its database and displays the resulting matches on the screen. We will be looking at two examples of this type of search engine—AltaVista (*www.altavista.com*) and Yahoo! (*www.yahoo.com*). A directory, on the other hand, is a listing that is divided into categories. Searches are conducted by clicking a category and seeing what it contains.

 TIP 1 Log on to Yahoo! at *www.yahoo.com* to see the directory listing. Note the main headings.

FEATURES OF SEARCH ENGINES

Although many search engines exist, most have the same basic features. The most basic component is the search form, a box where keywords or phrases can be entered. There are three steps to follow when using the search-entry form:

 TIP 2 Log on to AltaVista at *www.altavista.com* to take a look at the AltaVista Search Form.

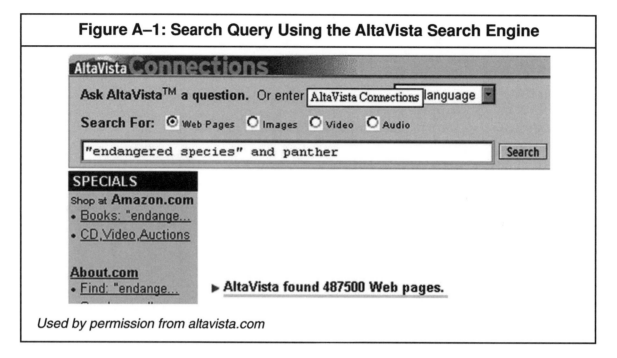

Figure A–1: Search Query Using the AltaVista Search Engine

AltaVista **Connections**

Ask AltaVista™ a question. Or enter [AltaVista Connections] language ▾

Search For: ⦿ Web Pages ○ Images ○ Video ○ Audio

`"endangered species" and panther`   [Search]

SPECIALS
Shop at **Amazon.com**
• Books: "endange...
• CD,Video,Auctions

About.com
• Find: "endange...

▶ **AltaVista found 487500 Web pages.**

Used by permission from altavista.com

1. Type the terms—words, phrases, or both in the entry form. For example, to perform a topic search (the most likely kind for students to do) let's say to find information on ENDANGERED SPECIES, a student would enter these words in the search-form box. (Chapter 2 details how to determine search terms for topic-based search queries.) Figure A-1 provides a sample search. This search retrieved over 400,000 Web pages with our search terms.

2. Click the SEARCH or SUBMIT button to send the query to the search engine. It will display a list of results, ten at a time. If users do not find any relevant sites on the first page, they simply click the NEXT PAGE button to see the next ten entries. The results are shown in Figure A-2.

 TIP 3 Try a search by typing El Niño in the search box using the Yahoo! search engine and view the results.

Note that the list of results displays the number of sites that match the search criteria. For example, a search that retrieves 975,046 entries is too broadly defined, and users might want to refine the search by adding more search terms.

3. Click the URL (Uniform Resource Locator), which usually appears in blue, to see an entry. Choose the one that most closely matches the search criteria.

Figure A–2: Search Results on AltaVista

1. <u>Florida panther, Links, Endangered Species: U.S. Fish & Wildlife Service</u>
   U.S. FISH AND WILDLIFE SERVICE DIVISION OF ENDANGERED SPECIES
   ============================== = [[Return to the Endangered Species Home Page.]...
   URL: www.fws.gov/r9endspp/i/a05.html
   Last modified 26-Jan-99 - page size 2K - in English [<u>Translate</u>]

2. <u>THE COUGAR</u>
   The Cougar. (Felis concolor) Also known as Puma, Mountain Lion or Panther. This large, graceful,
   New World Cat is often compared in size and strength to...
   URL: www.simmons.edu/~hickey/cougar.html
   Last modified 22-Mar-98 - page size 4K - in English [<u>Translate</u>]

3. <u>FPS poster</u>
   PROTECTED. FLORIDA PANTHER AN ENDANGERED SPECIES--COUGAR A PROTECTED
   SPECIES. WARNING: Under State/Federal, code and regulation it is unlawful to harass,..
   URL: www.atlantic.net/~oldfla/panther/post.html
   Last modified 7-Sep-97 - page size 2K - in English [<u>Translate</u>]

4. <u>Feedback from Participants Incorporated into Lease</u>
   Havens for Threatened & Endangered Species. Building Consensus on the Lease. Please scroll
   down or click on your choice below: FEEDBACK ON THE DRAFT...
   URL: www.fl-panther.com/598lease.htm

Used by permission from altavista.com

ADVANCED FEATURES

Search engines have additional features to help users narrow their search results. For example on AltaVista, using quotation marks around words like "global warming" will search the words as a phrase, not as single words. By searching for the exact phrase, the user narrows the search. Another feature—the plus (+) and minus (–) signs—requires or prohibits words from a search. Note that the Boolean AND functions the same as the plus sign. For instance, the search strategy PANTHER + "ENDANGERED SPECIES" – FLORIDA will search for the panther as an endangered species but not in Florida. Both terms—panther and endangered species—must appear in each resulting entry. Finally, the asterisk (*) is a wildcard for finding instances of a root word. The word ENDANGER* will retrieve endanger, endangered, endangering, endangers.

YAHOO! SEARCH ENGINE OPTIONS

The Yahoo! search engine uses the search-entry form, but it also has a directory with a list of topics located below the form on the screen (see Figure A-3). Searches on Yahoo! can be conducted by entering keywords in the search-entry form or by browsing the Internet using the topics in the directory. A search can be restricted—for example, by time—by using options located on the Yahoo! main screen. Advanced features discussed for the AltaVista search engine above are similar on Yahoo!.

Yahoo! through its directory lists a number of major topics and subtopics on its main page. By clicking topics, users can see lists of related subtopics until they reach their subjects of choice. Often, sites will be found that otherwise would not seem to be associated with specific topics. For example, by clicking "Education," the user

Figure A–3: Yahoo! Directory Screen

Reproduced with permission of Yahoo! Inc. © 1999 by Yahoo! Inc. Yahoo! and the Yahoo! logo are trademarks of Yahoo! Inc.

sees a list of relevant educational topics like K–12, Libraries, Math and Science, Online Teaching and Learning, and more.

SUMMARY

We have briefly discussed two of the popular search engines on the Internet—AltaVista and Yahoo!. Using entry forms on these two search engines or the directory of topics approach on Yahoo! will permit students to navigate the Web. Each search engine offers advantages, and it is a good idea to use both because the results will often be quite different. For more details, check the online course on search engines at the American Association of School Librarians' Website at *www.ala.org/ICONN*. The minilesson that follows describes a procedure teachers can use to familiarize their students with the Internet before they begin to incorporate resources from the Web into their curriculum.

MINI-LESSON (ALL LEVELS): USING SEARCH ENGINES

PURPOSE
The purpose of this minilesson is to familiarize students with how to use Yahoo! and AltaVista. This lesson should occur prior to students' logging on to the Internet so that they will make the best use of their time online and so that they do not become frustrated as they try to locate information from the voluminous amounts of data available.

OBJECTIVES
Once students have completed the exercises in this lesson, they will be able to:

- understand general principles about search engines
- use a search form on Yahoo! and AltaVista search engines to find information
- navigate search engine directories

PROCEDURES
First, model the use of search engines on the Internet. Next, have students, working in pairs, practice logging on and searching with a selected set of questions. Finally, ask each pair to choose a topic and find its own information. Throughout, request that students reflect in their journals on the procedure they use to search the Internet and the results they obtain.

Students will:

1. review basic concepts that you provide about search engines: types, uses, typical features, search techniques. This information appears in the Introduction to this lesson.
2. watch you demonstrate the search process—logging on to the Internet and using the search engine at *www.altavista.com*. They should watch as you type in the URL for Yahoo!'s kid's site at *www.yahooligans.com* to illustrate the use of a directory search engine. Figure A-4 shows the Yahooligans' search directory.
3. log on to the Internet and practice using search forms to find the information listed below. First have them use the AltaVista search engine at *www.altavista. com*, then the directory at Yahoo! using the URL *www.yahooligans.com*. Here are some sample topics:
   - Find information on Gandhi and his achievements that helped India.
   - Locate facts on Harriet Tubman and how she was connected to the Underground Railroad.
   - Find out about the Hubble telescope. Locate pictures taken by this telescope.

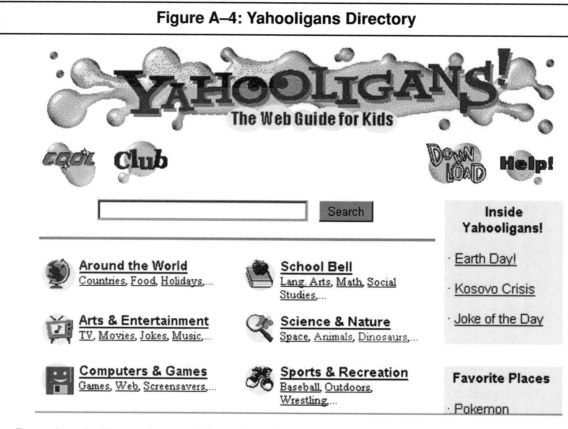

Figure A–4: Yahooligans Directory

Reproduced with permission of Yahoo! Inc. © 1999 by Yahoo! Inc. Yahoo! and the Yahoo! logo are trademarks of Yahoo! Inc.

- Search for information about Michael Jordan and the date he retired from basketball.
- Find a recent news story.

4. practice using the Yahoo! directory at *www.yahoo.com*. They should find the following information:
   - five endangered species
   - a map of Brazil
   - information on Chief Joseph
   - a site that provides references to the author John Steinbeck
   - the phenomenon called El Niño

5. write two journal entries describing the processes they used to search using:
   - search forms
   - directories

   Included in the entries should be a description of the screens they saw, the search terms they used, and the value of the information they retrieved.

6. choose topics of their own:
   - Using either a directory or search-form search engine, select subjects to retrieve.

- In their journals, write their step-by-step procedures to locate the material, identifying each screen and search terms used.
7. Discuss as a class their successes, failures, the search engine they liked best and least, and the type of search—search form or directories—they felt most comfortable using.

EVALUATION

Monitor students at the computers, noting the processes they use to answer the questions and making suggestions as they work. Review their journal entries to determine whether they are able to use search engines and which type is easier for their grade level.

SUMMARY

This is just a brief overview illustrating how to use search engines. Educators and students will need to become familiar with search techniques so they can look for information on the Internet. Once students have practiced using search engines, they will be able to navigate the Web easily and quickly and will be ready to begin Web-based lessons.

Appendix B

COMPLETE LISTING OF WEBSITES MENTIONED IN THIS BOOK

All Websites in this Appendix were verified as of September 1999; however the Web is a dynamic entity. Websites are modified; URLs change; sites are deleted; and some no longer update their information. It is important to visit any site you plan to use in a lesson to make sure that it is current and suitable.

The list of URLs is categorized alphabetically by subject. Subjects usually refer to one of the units, for example, Animal Rights or Heroes, discussed in chapters of this book. However, some categories, such as "Ask an Expert," may have URLs referenced in several chapters for different subject areas. Also bear in mind that there are many more sites on the Internet appropriate to use in teaching subject content, and that these are just to get you launched.

ANIMAL RIGHTS

www.api4animals.org/LegislativeUpdates.htm—state and federal laws on animal rights
www.api4animals.org/StateLegMA.htm—legislation on animal rights
http://animalrights.tqn.com/msublaw.htm—legislation on animal rights
www.justiceforanimals.org—help in writing legislation for animal rights
http://arrs.envirolink.org/ar-voices/poem.html—poems by famous poets discussing animal rights
http://arrs.envirolink.org/bill_of_rights.html—an animal bill of rights
http://arrs.envirolink.org/arrs/gallery/gallery.html—photos on animal-rights issues

http://arrs.envirolink.org/Faqs+Ref—frequently asked questions about animal rights

ARTS

www.nga.gov—examples of art from the National Gallery of Art
www.graffiti.org—graffiti art
http://wwar.com/museums.html—art museums listed by country
www.guggenheim.org—resources from the Guggenheim Museum
www-oi.uchicago.edu/OI/MUS/QTVR96/QTVR96_Tours.html—virtual tour of the Oriental Institute Museum
www.moma.org—Museum of Modern Art in New York City
www.artsednet.getty.edu/ArtsEdNet/Resources/index.html—lesson plans and resources from the Getty Institute
www.artsednet.getty.edu/ArtsEdNet/Images/index.html—art images and student artwork from the Getty
www.nga.gov/copyright/onlinetr.htm—virtual tour of the National Gallery with over 110,000 works
www.nmaa.si.edu/collections/index.html—National Museum of American Art with over 3,000 images by subject
www.alexperts.com/edu/arthistory.shtml—art experts who will answer questions
www.artswire.org/kenroar/lessons/lessons.html—art lessons for all age groups
www.oir.ucf.edu/win/paint/auth/cezanne—information on Cezanne and Impressionism

ASK AN EXPERT

http://whale.wheelock.edu—ask a marine biologist
www-hpcc.astro.washington.edu/scied/sciask.html—ask a scientist
http://njnie.dl.stevens-tech.edu/curriculum/aska.html—ask an expert on different topics
http://image.gsfc.nasa.gov/poetry/astro/qanda.html—ask an astronomer
www.eren.doe.gov—ask an expert about energy-related questions
www.sciam.com/askexpert/physics/physics.html—ask an expert about energy-related questions
http://umbra.nascom.nasa.gov/spartan/ask_astronomers.html—ask an astronomer

EDUCATIONAL ORGANIZATIONS

www.ncte.org—National Association of Teachers of English
www.nsta.org—National Science Teachers Association
www.ncss.org—National Council of Social Studies
www.ala.org/ICONN—American Association of School Librarians Website

ENGLISH–LANGUAGE ARTS

www.tech-mit.edu/Shakespeare/works.html—all-inclusive site on Shakespeare from MIT
http://falcon.jmu.edu/~ramseyil/shakless.htm—lesson plans for Shakespeare
www.promo/net/pg—Project Gutenberg, with many novels online
www.sdcoe.k12.ca.us/score/cyberguide.html—units of instruction for core works of literature
http://salwen.com/mtrace.html—discussion of *Huck Finn* as a racist book
www.ala.org/ICONN/lan_art.html—Association of School Librarians' language arts Website
http://phnet.esuhsd.org/legend/features/huck.finn.html—school site with positions pro and con on reading *Huck Finn*

CENSORSHIP

www.clairescorner.com/censorship—site with different aspects of censorship such as First Amendment and varying opinions
www.humanities-interactive.org—informational site on censorship and works of literature that have been censored
www.booksatoz.com/censorship/banned.htm—information on banned books and censorship
www.neffzone.com/huckfinn—*Huck Finn* as a banned book, as well as most challenged book list
www.excite.com/guide/entertainment/books_and_literature/ book_banning?search=censorship+books—links to sites on censorship, including a chat room
www.libertywon.com/actionlinks.htm—libertarian Christian site with links to ABC, CBS, *Meet the Press*, *Washington Post*, etc.; write and send opinions on censorship
http://webleyweb.com/lneil/bor_enforcement.html—talks about online freedom
www.lib.wmc.edu/lib/staff/suttle/censorship/censors.html—information on U.S. law and links to government sites with court decisions
http://marktwain.miningco.com—list of Mark Twain sites including one with arguments for and against banning *Huck Finn*

www.cs.cmu.edu/People/spok/banned-books.html—list of books frequently banned

www.banned.books.com—links to freedom of speech, censorship, and the First Amendment

www.vtw.org/speech/#appeal—freedom of speech on the Internet

www.seattletimes.com/extra/browse/html/huck_092596.html—newspaper stories on challenges to reading *Huck Finn*

www.kentuckyconnect.com/hearldleader/news/022798/op3lit.shtml—Kentucky newspaper stories on book censorship

www.sfgate.com/cgi-bin/chronicle/article.cgi?file=mn42343.DTL&director=chronicle/archive/1995/10/17—stories from the San Francisco *Chronicle* on censorship

www.mcall.com/cgi-bin/slivebsto.cgi?DBLIST=mc85&DOBNUM=7357—newspaper story on censorship

www.inkspot.com—publishing site for student work

CITING INTERNET RESOURCES

www.mla.org—citing format for Internet sources by the Modern Language Association (MLA)

www.apa.org/journals/webref.html—citing format for Internet sources by the American Psychological Association (APA)

www.quinion.com/words/articles/citation.htm—models of cites for Internet sources

www.utexas.edu/depts/uwc/html/citation.html—citing format for Internet sources

HEROES

http://myhero.com/home.asp—interactive writing project on heroes

www.biography.com—over 15,000 names from A&E TV's Homework Central

www.ites.k12.mn.us/ugrr/lessons/week7—heroes and heroines of the Underground Railroad

http://isd.ingham.k12.mi.us/~99mich/bios.html—student-written biographies on historical figures, athletes, etc.

http://106.183.164.3/cmslmc/Grade6/heroes.htm—heroes of the Civil Rights Movement

http://marin.k12.ca.us/~parkweb/african_american/Hero-Contents.html—a Website of biographies on African American heroes written by third graders

www.smsu.edu/contrib/library/gandhi.html—the legacy of Gandhi

www.bangalornet.com/system1/pooch/index.html—Gandhi facts and accomplishments

www.gale.com/gale/cwh/teresa.html—biography of Mother Teresa, including early years

www.ewtn.com/motherteresa—quotes and accomplishments about Mother Teresa

www.kn.pacbell.com/wired/fil/pages/huntharriettu.html—information on Harriet Tubman created by middle school students

www.camalott.com/~rssmith/Moses.html—Tubman as Moses of her time

http://lcweb2.loc.gov/ammem/jrhtml—information on Jackie Robinson, baseball, and breaking the color line.

www.seattletimes.com/mlk/classroom/index.html—about Martin Luther King, created as a school resource

TO KILL A MOCKINGBIRD

www.chebucto.ns.ca/Culture/HarperLee/quizzes.html—quizzes on content of *To Kill a Mockingbird*

www.chebucto.ns.ca/Culture/HarperLee/index.html—background on the author Harper Lee

www.chebucto.ns.ca/Culture/HarperLee/discussion.html—discussion groups on Harper Lee and the novel

www.lausd.k12.ca.us/Belmont_HS/tkm/index.html—annotations, pictures, vocabulary explanations given chapter by chapter for the novel

http://educeth.ethz.ch/english/readinglist/lee,harper.html—lesson plans, chapter summaries, lists of student activities on the novel

http://library.advanced.org/12111/novel.html—background on life and times when the novel was written

www.tokillamockingbird.com—picture of the Monroe County Courthouse where the trial of Tom Robinson took place

www.sdcoe.k12.ca.us/score/tokil/mocktg.htm—pictures and facts about mockingbirds

www.bell.k12.ca.us/BellHS/Fac.Staf/Free/tkamqs.html—chapter-by-chapter discussion of the novel

ENGLISH AS A SECOND LANGUAGE

www.ai.tech.ac.jp/ ~iteslj—online TESOL (Teachers of English to Speakers of Other Languages) journal

www.eduplace.com/ss/index.html—commercial company that produces ESL materials

www.teachnet.com/index.html—company that maintains ESL lesson plans and a teacher forum

www.csun.edu/~hcedu013/eslindex.html—ESL teaching material and links to ESL sites

www.stolaf.edu/network/iecc/index.html—ESL penpal projects

www.pacificnet.net/~sperling/student.html—ESL penpal communications

www.pacificnet.net/~sperling/guestbook.html—teacher forum on questions relating to ESL instruction

www.teachnet.com/ttforum.html—chat site for ESL teachers

http://eslcafe.com/chat/chatpro.cgi—chat site for ESL teachers

http://eslgames.com—ESL games

www.links2go.com/topic/English_As_a_Second_Language—ESL lesson ideas and projects *www.ncte.org/notesplus/Owen-March1994.html*—ESL lesson plan on Shakespeare

www.shakespeare.uiuc.edu—Shakespeare for LEP students

FOREIGN LANGUAGES

www.w3i.com/eng/home.htm—information about France

www.ibumpcug.co.uk/~owls/european_cuisines.html—recipes on food for the European continent

www.lemonde.fr—France's daily newspaper

www.cnnespanol.com—news stories in Spanish from CNN

www.umr.edu/~amigos/Virtual—Spanish tutorials

http://lcweb2.loc.gov/frd/cs/cshome.html—history, geography, and economy of ninety-one countries

www.oanda.com/converter.travel—currency conversion rates worldwide

www.travlang.com/index.html—currency conversion rates, travel and cultural information

www.xs4all.nl/~pwessel/country.html—annotated links to the literature of many countries in their native languages

www.cortland.edu/www/flteach—information about resources for foreign language teachers

http://actfl.org—includes learning standards and instructional resources by the American Council on the Teaching of Foreign Languages

www.teachspanish.com/teacher.html—Spanish teacher resources

www.awesomelibrary.org/Classroom/English/Languages/Spanish.html—K–12 lesson plans for Spanish classes

www.red2000.com/spain—photo tour of cities in Spain, including information on food and fiestas

CULTURE

www.afroam.org/children/discover/discover.html—information on African nations and their people

www.afroam.org/children/myths/myths.html—myths from different countries

www.sas.upenn.edu/African_Studies/Home_page/AFR_GIDE.html—a K–12 guide for African resources

http://pharos.bu.edu/Egypt/Cairo—information on Egyptian culture

JAPAN

www.jinjapan.org/kidsweb/japan/q-a.html—questions and answers about Japanese culture and the country

http://lcweb2.loc.gov/frd/cs/jptoc.html—information about Japan

www.jinjapan.org/kidsdweb/japan/map/I_regi.html—map of Japan *www.cc.matsuyama-u.ac.jp/~shiki/English-Haiku.html*—lessons on creating Haiku poetry

MEXICO

http://latino.sscnet.ucla.edu/demo/cinco.html—history of the Cinco de Mayo holiday
www.legrand.k12.ca.us/edm—elementary school Website celebrating Cinco de Mayo
www.avocado.org/recipes/recil59.shtml—recipes for Cinco de Mayo
www.kqed.org/fromKQED/cell/calhist/cinco.html—background information for Cinco de Mayo holiday
http://128.123.31.49/vista/esl/m4_hstry.html—ESL students' Website on the origins of Cinco de Mayo
www.mexonline.com/history.htm—Mexican history, including heroes and historical documents
www.geocities.com/Athens/Forum/9061/mexico/mexico.html—historical text archives
http://northcoast.com/~spdtom/revl.html—historical events in Mexico

GENERAL

www.ustc.org—Tech Corp. chapters available for funding for Internet connections
www.bham.wednet.edu/policies.htm—school site policies for Internet usage
www.ala.org/ICONN/rating.html—criteria for rating Websites
www.scholastic.com/EL—*Scholastic Magazine* offers lesson plans in various subject areas
www.cnn.com—news website good for social studies
www.discovery.com—Discovery Channel, especially for science
www.microsoft.com/education/k12—Microsoft educational Website
http://ericir.syr.edu—the ERIC Website for educational research
http://edweb.sdsu.edu—San Diego State University educational Website
www.kn.pacbell.com/wired/bluewebn/apptypes.html—directory to lots of educational examples, including lesson plans
www.digital.com—commercial Website that features Eudora, a free e-mail program
www.eduplace.com/techcent/staff/glossary.html—glossary of Internet terminology
www.applecomputer.com—Apple Computer's education site
www.cs.rice.edu/~sboone/Lessons/Titles/hunt/homebse.html—information on creating a Scavenger Hunt
www.realaudio.com/products/player/index.html#download—download the Real Audio player for hearing sound at Websites
www.vdonet.com—player for viewing video clips

www.ualberta.ca/~schard/projects.htm—understanding the Project Approach

www.amazon.com—site for finding books, book reviews, adult and children, and videos

www.barnesandnoble.com—Barnes and Noble book site for ordering books

HEALTH

www.healthatoz.com—search engine to consumer health sites

http://mel.lib.mi.us/health/health-evaluating.html—site to help students verify sites with appropriate health data

www.nal.usda.gov/fnic/etext/fnic.html—links to resources on health topics

www.nal.usda.gov:8001/py/pmap.htm—menus illustrating daily diets based on USDA Dietary Guidelines

www.shapeup.org—information on weight management and physical fitness

http://Fscn.che.umn.edu/NutrExp/default.html—resources for school nutrition education

www.fda.gov/oc/opacom/kids/default.htm—resources for school nutrition education

www.medicinenet.com—medical information for the public, including diseases and drugs

www.graylab.ac.uk/omd—medical dictionary

www.itdc.sbcss.k12.ca.us/curriculum/tobacco.html—activities to teach about the dangers of tobacco to the body

www.itds.sbcss.k12.ca.us/curriculum/personaltrainer.html—simulation for students to help develop customized diets and exercise plans

www.scpinet.org/kids/index.html—for kids, the ten best and worst foods and eating tips

http://library.advanced.org/10991—nutrition on the Web for teens, including exercise, world nutrition, and recipes

www.exhibits.pacsci.org/nutrition—charts to analyze eating habits at the Nutrition Cafe

www.olen.com/food—calorie counting at fast-food restaurants

LISTSERVS

TAWL@listserv.Arizona.edu—forum on whole language

Listserv@psuvm.psu.edu—listserv for fiction writers

Listserv@vmd.cso.uiuc.edu—critical issues in education

Listserv@nic.umass.edu—issues in education and projects for teachers

PUPPETS

www.puppet.org/teachers.html—instructions and drawings for making puppets, along with curriculum ideas

www.puppet.org/links.html—puppetry sites around the world

www.muppets.com—the Muppet home page, including games

www.henson.com/creatures/creatures_stage_how.htm—step-by-step procedure on how to create a creature and bring it to life

www.sagecraft.com/puppetry—answers to questions about puppetry by e-mail

www.sp.uconn.edu/~wwwsfa/bimp—how to construct different types of puppets, including puppets in other countries

http://family.go.com/Categories/Activities/Features/family_1998_04/famf/fam/ 48puppetstage/famf48puppetstage.html—ideas on making a a puppet play-house, including instructions from Disney

www3.ns.sympatico.ca/onstage/puppets/activity—definitions of director, play-wright, and set designer for creating puppet shows; includes puppet patterns

SCHOOL WEBSITES

www.zbths.k12.il.us/projects.proj.html—sample school Website

SCIENCE

www.seaworld.org/animal%5Fbytes/tigerab.html—Sea World site with information on marine animals

www.discovery.com—the Discovery Channel on many animal topics

http://curry.edschool.virginia.edu/go/frog—dissecting a frog

http://george.lbl.gov/ITG.hm.pg.docs/Whole.Frog/Whole.Frog.html—dissecting a frog

www.birminghamzoo.com—animal facts and a chat room with the zookeeper

ALTERNATIVE ENERGY SOURCES

http://sln.fi.edu/units/energy/windguide.html—building a windmill, all about wind energy

www.cochems/com/chornobyl—information about the Chernobyl nuclear plant and the aftermath of the disaster

http://tqd.advanced.org/3426—nuclear power plants located on a map

www.pbs.org/wgbh.pages/frontline/shows/reaction/etc/terms.html—facts and vocabulary about nuclear energy *www.leeric.lsu.edu/educat/lesson3.htm*—instructions on using a solar cooker to cook marshmallows

www.nrel.gov/research/pv/docs/pvpaper.html—facts about solar energy

http://solstice.crest.org/renewables/geothermal/grc.index.html—definitions and facts about geothermal energy

http://FusionEd.gat.com—facts about fusion energy

www.oneworld.org/energy/whatis.html—what, why, and how of alternative energy sources

http://hillside.coled.umn.edu/Wind/Wind.html—hands-on science studying wind energy

DINOSAURS

www.sedl.org/scimath/pasopartners/dinosaurs/focus.html—lesson plans and activities about dinosaurs

www.nationalgeographic.com/dinorama/frame.html—information about dinosaurs

www.EnchantedLearning.com/subjects/dinosaurs—dinosaur facts, myths, and activities

www.yahooligans.com/Science_and_Nature/Living_Things/Paleontology/Dinosaurs/Dinosaur_Extinction—theories on how dinosaurs became extinct

www.mov.vic.gov.air/dinosaurs/dinosintro.htm—global classroom on dinosaurs

www.ZoomDinosaurs.com/allabout—facts on dinosaurs of every kind

www.dinodon.com/dinosaurs/kidsart.html—place to publish kids' art about dinosaurs

www.isgs.uiuc.edu/dinos—questions about dinosaurs answered

www.dinodon.com/gallery—pictures of dinosaurs

ENDANGERED SPECIES

www.fws.gov/r9endspp/endspp.html—questions about endangered species

www.scholastic.com/network—comments of a marine biologist to create endangered species list

ENERGY CONSERVATION

www.energyed.ecw.org—Energy Education online site

www.energy.ca.gov/education—Energy Quest with activities, projects, and games

www.energynet.net—energy conservation project for students

www.leeric.lsu.edu/educat/what's_a_watt.htm—definitions of energy-related concepts

www.spring.com/epatrol/ep-energy.html—model for doing energy audits

http://k12.cnidr.org/gsh/schools/ny/che.html—how to conserve energy at home

http://solardome.com/SolarDome72.html—determines how much energy home appliances use

SOLAR SYSTEM

www.jpl.nasa.gov/s19—Shoemaker-Levy Comet and the results of its collision with Jupiter

www.nasm.edu/ceps—Center for Earth and Planetary Studies that includes background on solar system, including images

www.nasa.org—extensive information from NASA

www.sciam.com/exhibit/033197halebopp/033197.html—information on the Hale-Bopp Comet

http://seds.lpl.arizona.edu/nineplanets/nineplanets/nineplanets.html—the Solar System

http://AtoZTeacherStuff.com/themes/space.html—annotated links to space sites

http://tommy.jsc.nasa.gov/~woodfill/SPACEED/SEHHTML/earlysf.html—views of a spaceship, walk on the moon, and the first golf shot on the moon

http://quest.arc.nasa.gov/interactive/index.html—NASA's Website and space contest sponsored by NASA

www.seti-inst.edu/sci-det.html—measurement of the orbits of the planets

http://tqjunior.advanced.org/3521—graphing space routes

http://liftoff.msfc.nasa.gov/kids/adventure/jigsaw/puzzle.html—puzzles about space

www.seds.org/pub/images/planets—images of all planets

www.nasm.edu/ceps/SII/SII.html—facts about Saturn

www.aspsky.org/html/tnl/25/25.html—faces visible in pictures of the planet Mars

http://starchild.gsfc.nasa.gov/docs/StarChild/StarChild.html—map skills to get home from space

www-k12.atmos.washington.edu/k12—instructions to construct Mars Pathfinder Landing models

www.soest.hawaii.edu/SPACEGRANT/class_acts/EdibleRocksTe.html—recipe for edible meteorites

www.seds.org/pub/images/planets—facts about each planet in the solar system

http://spaceplace.jpl.nasa.gov/spacepl.htm—share pictures with other students studying space

www.yahooligans.com/Science_and_Oddities/Space/Comets/Shoemaker_Levy-9—Information about the Shoemaker-Levy Comet

WEATHER

http://itds.sbscc.k12.ca.us/curriculum/weather.html—facts on weather, especially clouds

www.pmal.noaa.gov/toga-tao/el-nino/1997.html—facts about El Niño

www.weather.com/education—up-to-date weather information

www.millersv.edu/~edfound/intered/elemplan.html—lesson plans on weather for elementary students

www.cmi.k12.il.us/~fosterbr/WeatherHome.html—lesson plans on weather for grades 4–6

www.athena.ivv.nasa.gov/curric/weather—projects on predicting weather, clouds, hurricanes

www.fema.gov/kids/dizarea.htm—kids' site on weather and natural disasters

WHALES

www.whale.wheelock.edu—WhaleNet site containing migration patterns and
  behavior of whales
http://curry.edschool.Virginia.EDU/go/Whales/Contents.HTML—school site that
  studied whales using the Internet, contains a thematic unit
www.physics.helsinki.fi/whale/education/children.html—whale-watching children's
  Website
www.whaletimes.org/whakids.htm—kids' page on whale information
www.iwc.org/WorldWideWeb/marine.html—links for marine mammals
www.webcom.com/~iwcwww/whale_adoption/waphome.html—whale adoption
  project
www.whaletour.edu—good general site for exploring whales
www.whaleclub.com/community/penpal_jump.html—whale penpal site

SEARCH ENGINES

www.yahoo.com—Yahoo! search engine
www.yahooligans.com—children's search engine from Yahoo!
www.altavista.com—AltaVista search engine
www.excite.com—Excite search engine
www.hotbot.com—HotBot search engine

SOCIAL STUDIES

www.cia.com—CIA fact book, including facts on over ninety-one countries
www.audionet.com/speeches—speeches such as Martin Luther King's "I Have a
  Dream"
www.nationalgeographic.com—*National Geographic Magazine* Website
http://tourismthailand.org—information for tourists on Thailand
www.chicagohs.org/fire—facts about the great fire in Chicago
www.jinjapan.org/kidsweb/japan/q-a.html—answers to common questions about
  Japan
http://memory.loc.gov/ammem/cwphome.html—Library of Congress American
  Memory collection
www.i-channel.com/ellis—Ellis Island site good for immigrant information
www.nara.gov—view posters from World War II
www.cnn.com—CNN news information

BEN FRANKLIN

http://earlyamerica.com/lives/franklin/index.html—information about Ben Franklin's life

http://library.advanced.org/22254/home.htm—the life and times of Ben Franklin

www.english.udel.edu/lemay/franklin—historical events in the life of Ben Franklin

http://sln.si.edu/franklin/rotten.html—the Franklin Institute site

BILL OF RIGHTS

www.excite.com/reference/almanac/?id=CEO12456—an encyclopedia-like information on the Constitution, Bill of Rights and amendments

www.excite.com/reference/almanac/?id=A0341699—dictionary definition of Bill of Rights

http://lth3.k12.il.us/PET/washington-giftpet/kbrproj.htm—Kids' Bill of Rights project

www.luc.edu/libraries/banned—addresses First Amendment, banned books, intellectual freedom

www.lsu.edu/guests/poli/public_html/bor.htm—Bill of Rights page and links to other sources on censorship

www.bill-of-rights.org/bill-of-rights.html—current interpretations of the Bill of Rights

GENEALOGY

www.ngsgenealogy.org—National Genealogical Society (fees)

www.fgs.org—Federation of Genealogical Societies (fees)

www.cyndislist.com—Cyndi's list of genealogical sites

www.ancestry.com—ancestry site

www.usgenweb.org—U.S. Genweb Project

www.rootsweb.com—general genealogical site

www.genealogy.com—Broderbund site for checking ancestry

www.familysearch.org—Church of Jesus Christ of the Latter Day Saints' extensive site on genealogy

www.archives.ca—Archives of Canadian genealogical information

www.archivenet.gov.au/home.html—Australian genealogical information

www.origins.net/GRO—Scotland genealogical information

www.open.gov.uk/gros/groshome.htm—Scotland genealogical information

www.visitbritain.com/activities/wtd%2D9.htm—Great Britain genealogical information

www.nara.gov/regional/findaids/chirip.html—Chinese heritage

www.ccharity.com—African heritage

www.genuki.org.uk—United Kingdom and Ireland heritage

GOVERNMENT

www.census.gov—government census data

www.access.gpo.gov/su_docs—data such as the *Congressional Record*, Supreme Court decisions, and the U.S. budget

http://supct.law.cornell.edu/supct—Supreme Court opinions

www.library.Yale.edu/govdocs/gdchome.html—links to government documents and other resources

www.house.gov—U.S. House of Representatives site

www.loc.gov/global/state/stategov.html—links to state and local government resources

www.ipl.org/ref/POTUS—presidential speeches and biographies

HISTORY

http://library.advanced.org—collaborative study of American History site

http://thomas.loc.gov— Library of Congress and how laws are made

www.cnn.com—CNN news site

IMMIGRANTS

www.bergen.org/AAST/Projects/Immigration/ellis_island.html—Ellis Island Website

http://vi.uh.edu/pages/mintz/rpimary.html—slave narratives

www.scils.rutgers.edu/special/kay/afro.html—African American culture

www.itp.berkeley.edu/~asam121/angel.html—information about Asian immigrants at Angel Island

www.fortunecity.com/littleitaly/amalfi/100/angel.htm—information about Angel Island immigration

http://law.house.gov/104.htm—immigration and citizenship law at the Internet Law Library

MAPS

www.yahooligans.com/Around_the_World/Countries—maps of different countries

www.nationalgeographic.com/xpeditions/main.html?main=atlas—maps of different countries

www.lib.utexas.edu/Libs/PCL/Map_collection/Map_collection.html—maps of locales

www.city.net/countries—maps of city areas

www.sas.upenn.edu/African_Studies/CIA_Maps/Africa_19850.gif—map of Africa

www.odci.gov/cia/publications/factbook/figures/802641.jpg—map of Africa

NATIVE AMERICANS

www.nativeweb.org—general information on Native Peoples

www.magicnet.net/~itms/indian.html—Web quest on Native Peoples

www.magicnet.net.~itms/indianFL.html—history of Florida Native Peoples

http://indy4fdl.cc.mn.us/~isk/t_webcul.html—Indian culture *www.ozemail.com.au:80/~reed/global/mythstor.html*—myths of Indian people

www.seminoletribe.com—information on the Seminole tribe, including history, food, medicine

www.doa.state.nc.us/doa/cia/handout1.htm—fact sheet on Indians in North Carolina

http://ericir.syr.edu/Virtual/InfoGuides/Alphabetical_List_of_InfoGuides/nativeamer12_96.htm#resources—List of Native American sites

http://hanksville.phast.umass.edu/misc/ojibwe/index.html—Ojibwe culture

www.state.sd.us/state/executive/tourism/sioux/sioux.html—information on the Sioux tribe

www.sdcoe.k12.ca.us/score/blue/blulesgl.html—unit plan on the Day of the Blue Dolphin

www.yahooligans.com/Around_The_World/Cultures/Native_Cultures—information on Native culture

www.pomona.edu/REPRES/NATIVE/NATIN.HTML—Native American information

www.eagle.ca/~matink/lessons.html—lesson plans from First Nations

www.first-nations.com—First Nations Website

www.lib.uiowa.edu/gw/intl/native.html—Native American resources

www.ed.uiuc.edu/YLP94-95/mini-units/Altenholl.Native-American—miniunit on Native Americans

www.powwows.com/dancing/index2.html—Native American powwow dancing

http://members.tripod.com/~PHILKON—Navajo information

www.si.edu/nmai—National Museum of the American Indian

STAFF DEVELOPMENT

www.videojournal.com—staff development aids

www.ties.k12.mn.us—staff development projects in Minnesota

STOCK MARKET

http://quote.yahoo.com—basic stock quotes, free stock portfolio setup

http://dailystocks.com—stock resources using a stock symbol

www.internetstocks.com/launch.html—news about Internet stocks

www.stocksheet.com—company profiles on stocks

http://askmerrill.com/mlol/main/index.asp—research reports from Merrill Lynch

www.freeedgar.com—company financial statement

www.crews.org/media_tech/compsci/8thgrade/stkmkt/glossary.htm—basic terminology on the stock market *www.youngmoney.com*—articles on finances and stock market for teens

http://ecedweb.unomaha.edu/teachsug.htm—teaching suggestions to review economic concepts

www.excite.com/reference/almanac/?id=A0672446—facts on the stock market and terminology

www.investorguide.com/Kids.htm—understanding how to manage money

www.iionline.com/investor_university—different aspects of investing and basic money management for beginners

http://secapl.com/secapl/quoteserver/search.html—lists of ticker symbols

http://cbs.marketwatch.com—CBS news related to the financial world

www.cnnfs.com—CNN news related to the financial world

www.virtualstockexchange.com—student stock tournaments

www.agedwards.com/bma/index.shtml—student stock tournaments

www.quicken.com—setting up a stock portfolio

TELECOLLABORATION PROJECTS

www.gsn.org—telecollaboration projects in different subject areas

www.learner.org/jnorth—global study of wildlife migration

www.tme.nl/dln/mayaquest.html—MayaQuest to Mayan ruins

http://ics.soe.umich.edu/ed712/IAPProfile.html—projects from the University of Michigan

http://njnie.dl.stevens-tech.edu/curriculum/water.html—study of pond water

http://k12science.ati.stevens-tech.edu/curriculum/temp1—study of temperature around the world

http://njnie.dl.stevens-tech.edu/curriculum/oceans/stowaway.html—the stowaway project

www.globe.gov—study reporting on positions of the sun's surface

http://morgan.rutgers.edu—study of genome databases and challenge projects

www.gsn.org/project/newsday/index.html—newspaper-based project

www.worldtrek.org—understand nonwestern cultures project

www.adventureonline.com—exploration of different geographic areas like the North Pole and Africa

www.chariho.k12.ri.us/curriculum/MISmart/ocean/sands.htm—view and understand sand samples from all over the world

www.onesky.umich.edu/index.html—project based on information about hurricanes and weather

www.mars2030.net—setting up a space village on Mars

INDEX

ABOUT THE AUTHOR

BEVERLEY E. CRANE received her B.S. in Spanish and English and her M.Ed. in Bilingual Education and English as a Second Language from Penn State University. She has also received an Ed.D. in Curriculum and Instruction, with emphases in Language Arts and Educational Technology, from Oklahoma State University. She has taught English-language arts at the middle-, high-school, and college levels.

While working on a grant for a five-state multi-cultural resource center, she conducted workshops for K-12 teachers on topics such as literacy, writing and the writing process, ESL, and integrating technology into the curriculum. In addition, for the last eleven years at the Dialog Corporation she has created materials and conducted workshops for K-12 library media specialists and teachers on using online searching in the curriculum. She has presented yearly at conferences throughout the U.S., including the American Association of School Librarians (AASL), the National Educational Computing Conference (NECC), Computer-Using Educators (CUE), American Educational Research Association (AERA), National Council for the Social Studies Conference (NCSS), and the California Media and Library Educators Association (CMLEA), to name a few, on topics ranging from using online searching in the elementary curriculum to computers and writing to integrating online searching into social studies to online research across the curriculum.

As Director of the English Education Program at San Jose State University for five years, she worked closely with classroom teachers and administrators to provide guidelines for mentor teachers supervising English student teachers at SJSU.

Currently, she continues to write a guest column on using the Internet in the curriculum for the *Information Searcher*, edited by Pam Berger. She is the English-language arts specialist for C.E.R.F.—Curriculum Education Resource Finder—a K-12 project to make finding excellent Internet sites easier for educators and students. She also creates training materials, including distance education online courses in searching techniques for Dialog.

An American citizen, she lives with her husband on the Baja Peninsula in Mexico.